Geometry to Go

Teacher's Resource Book

GREAT SOURCE
EDUCATION GROUP
A Houghton Mifflin Company
New Ways to Know

Credits:

Editorial and Development: Laurie Boswell, Carol DeBold, Jo Anne Gerules, Gloria Robinson, Sam Robinson
Design and Production: Taurins Design Associates

Illustration Credits:

Robot Characters: Bill SMITH STUDIO with Jon Conrad
Creative Art: Joe Spooner *page 9*, Rob Dunleavy *pages 33, 116, 117.*
Technical Art: Taurins Design Associates

Printed in the United States of America

Great Source® and *New Ways to Know®* are registered trademarks of Houghton Mifflin Company.

International Standard Book Number: 0-669-48807-0

1 2 3 4 5 6 7 8 9 10 MZ 05 04 03 02 01

Visit our website: http://www.greatsource.com/

Geometry to Go is a reference handbook for students, teachers, and parents. It provides concise explanations and examples that are written on the student level. *Geometry to Go*, with instructional support from teachers, is a tool that can empower students to become more responsible for their own learning, relearning, research, and extended thinking.

TEACHER USES

Geometry to Go is organized by topics, not by chapters. Some students may need only a review of Similarity before tackling Congruence. Others may need to revisit the concepts of ratio and proportion in order to understand Similarity. *Geometry to Go* brings all those skills together in one section.

Geometry to Go is also a handy resource for teachers in other disciplines. Non-math teachers can refer to topics in *Geometry to Go* as they connect other subject areas with mathematics.

Vocabulary is an area of mathematics that is often overlooked. *Geometry to Go* contains definitions and examples with each topic and in a complete Glossary of Mathematical Terms in the Yellow Pages Section. Students are encouraged to look up related topics through the More Help feature, which lists item numbers for topics that students might find helpful as they review a particular concept.

STUDENT USES

Geometry to Go provides a ready reference for students whose notes are unavailable, incomplete, or indecipherable when they are doing homework. There are times when textbook presentations need further clarification or simply a different perspective. *Geometry to Go* gives clear explanations that allow students to understand a difficult topic more fully. The illustrations, charts, and simple explanations fill gaps in learning that a student may experience, but may not voice in class. Students can get into *Geometry to Go* in several ways:

- They can look up a term in the glossary, found in the Yellow Pages section. The terms are cross-referenced to items in the other parts of the handbook.
- They can look up Postulates, Theorems, Formulas, or symbols in their own separate glossaries.
- They can thumb through the sections related to their topics. Each section is color coded with a key on the back cover.
- They can look for subtopics in the Table of Contents.
- They can use the index to find specific skills and concepts.

PARENT USES

Geometry to Go is a concise handbook of geometry topics that parents can readily use. Geometry textbooks are usually organized to build an axiomatic system step by step. This means that related topics are often widely separated in the textbook. It also means that different texts are organized differently and present different theorems and postulates. *Geometry to Go* ties concepts together and presents a variety of theorems and proofs related to each topic all in the same place. Many parents may find this a useful tool for recalling geometric ideas that have grown rusty over time.

The wide number of illustrations and clear explanations in *Geometry to Go* give parents a great resource to help with homework assignments.

The organization of this resource book parallels the sections of *Geometry to Go*. You may first want to correlate the chapters of your textbook to the sections of *Geometry to Go*. This will provide a ready reference to the practice and applications in this resource book. Each section may include topics from more than one chapter of your textbook.

Geometry to Go Teacher's Resource Book provides practice and test preparation pages for each subsection of *Geometry to Go*. At the end of each subsection is an answer page containing answers to both the practice and test prep questions. Each section concludes with an application activity, designed to connect topics that relate to more than one area of mathematics.

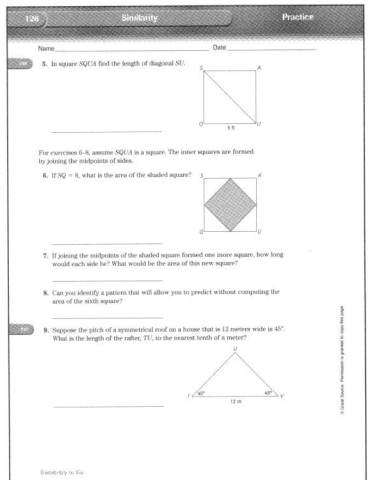

The practice pages are copymasters that follow the organization of each subsection of *Geometry to Go*. Each problem is cross-referenced to show students which item number(s) in *Geometry to Go* will provide additional help. This feature also allows you to identify specific concepts that students may need help with. Students should be encouraged, where appropriate, to use the Handy Tables section of the Yellow Pages to find values they need and to use a calculator. The practice pages can be assigned by subsection in their entirety or by question number to accompany material recently covered in the textbook.

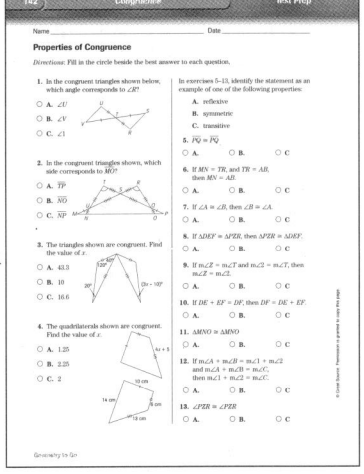

The test prep pages present the concepts of each subsection of *Geometry to Go* in a variety of standardized formats. This enables students to become familiar with question formats they may encounter when taking standardized tests. Students who have had experience with these formats often achieve higher test scores than students who have had no prior encounters with the types of question formats used in standardized tests.

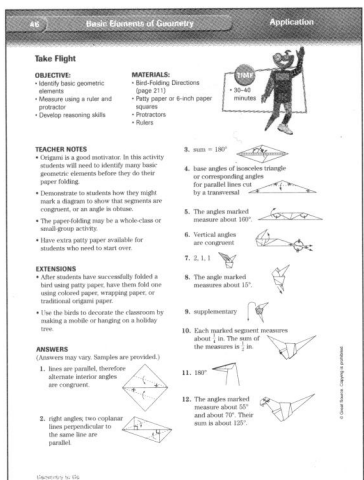

The application activities at the end of each section are designed to provide examples of Geometry as it relates to real-world or just-plain-fun situations. Each application includes extension activities on the teacher page to continue to explore interesting aspects of the topic. Also in this book is a rubric, related to the rubric in the Almanac section of the handbook, that you may use for evaluating student work and performance.

At Your Fingertips

OBJECTIVE
* Explore the *Geometry to Go* handbook to determine the format of the book

MATERIALS
* *Geometry to Go* handbook

TIME
* 10 minutes

TEACHER NOTES
* This activity leads students on a tour through the *Geometry to Go* handbook and helps them to become more familiar with the organization and features of the book. It also introduces them to the structure of the twelve application activities in this resource book.

EXTENSIONS
* Provide students with four mathematical terms that are new to them. Direct students to the Glossary at the back of *Geometry to Go*. Have them write an explanation for each term in their own words.

* Have students select a topic and create a web of information.

ANSWERS

1. 15 including the Almanac, Yellow Pages, and Index

2. Each section has its own color.

3. Definitions, procedures, explanations, and rules are given as examples of things that might be looked up in *Geometry to Go.*

4. Index: 004, 019, 432–433 and specific references for postulate-related entries

   Glossary: 019

   Table of Contents: 432

5. The Glossary of Mathematical Terms

6. The *Math Alert* feature calls attention to special cases or alerts you to common errors.

7. ★ calls attention to the answer at the end of a worked-out example.

   ! calls attention to *Math Alert* boxes, showing possible errors or misunderstandings.

8.

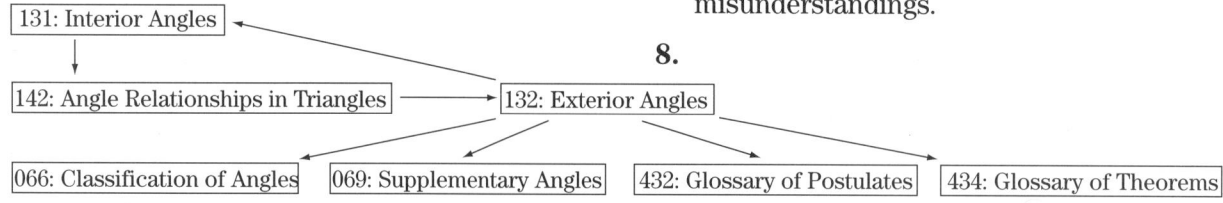

Name _____ Date _____

This spot will list references to Geometry to Go to help you find information you can use to solve the problems on the activity pages. This activity will help you discover how the Geometry to Go handbook is organized.

At Your Fingertips

1. How many sections are there in *Geometry to Go*? _____

2. How can you tell one section from another section?

_____

3. Find item number vi, *How This Book Is Organized*. What four things might you want to look up in this book?

_____

4. Item number ix, *How to Use This Book*, shows three ways to find information about math topics. Look up *Postulates* in each of the three sections and write the item number(s) you find.

Index: _____

Glossary of Mathematical terms: _____

Table of Contents: _____

5. Suppose you want to find definitions for the terms *median* and *midsegment*. What is the quickest place to look in *Geometry to Go* to find the definitions?

_____

6. Take a look at the *Math Alert* box in item numbers 171 and 264. What is the purpose of the *Math Alert* feature?

_____

7. *Geometry to Go* uses several symbols to call things to your attention. Write the meaning of each of these symbols.

★ _____

❗ _____

8. For many topics in *Geometry to Go* there are More Help messages. These messages refer you to related topics, creating a web of information you can use. On a separate sheet of paper, start with item number 131, *Interior Angles*, and follow the path through the web for each item number until you have found all the related topics. Draw arrows connecting the items.

Name _____ Date _____

	Excellent	Well Done	Adequate	Weak	Inadequate
Comprehension	All facts and relationships identified and well defined; arguments are logical and complete.	Most facts and relationships identified and well defined; arguments are logical but may not be complete.	Most facts are identified but arguments and relationships may have minor faults in logic or completeness.	Some facts are identified but arguments and relationships may have faults in logic or completeness.	Facts are incorrect or inappropriate; relationships and logic are not established.
Application and Analysis	A strong plan is developed and executed correctly.	A strong plan is developed and implemented with minor errors in computation or notation.	A logical plan is developed but implementation may be inefficient with minor errors in computation or notation.	The plan is apparent but flawed; implementation is flawed.	The plan is not logical and/or is inappropriate to the task at hand; implementation is seriously flawed.
Mechanics	Computation, mathematical representation, and diagrams are appropriate and correct.	Computation, representation, and diagrams are appropriate but may have minor flaws.	Computation and representation, are appropriate but may have flaws; diagrams are appropriate and correct.	Computation, representation, and diagrams are appropriate but flawed.	Computation, representation, and/or diagrams are inappropriate.
Presentation	Argument and results are strong and succinct.	Argument and results are strong but may not be efficient.	Argument may have flaws in flow or efficiency; results make sense.	Argument shows signs of being on the right track but has flaws and/or digressions; results are not appropriate.	Argument is not on the right track; results are not appropriate.
Aesthetics	Diagrams are clear and complete; text is neat, easy to follow, and relates well to diagram.	Diagrams are neat and complete; text is neat.	Diagrams are complete but may not be neat or easily related to text.	Diagrams and text are not well related or easy to follow.	Diagrams are missing or inappropriate with no relation to text.

Name _____ Date _____

	Excellent	Well Done	Adequate	Weak	Inadequate
Do I know what to do?	I used the correct geometric reasoning and the most appropriate plan.	I used the correct geometric reasoning and plan but there are holes in my logic.	I used some correct geometric reasoning but my plan and my logic have some holes.	I identified most of the geometric facts and arguments but I didn't carry out my plan.	I haven't got a clue.
Can I do it?	I got it all done and I know I can defend my strategies and my answers.	I got it all done and I know most of it is on target.	I got some of it done and I think it's right.	I could show my plan but I didn't carry it out very well.	I tried to work from what I know to a logical solution but I didn't have all of my facts straight.
Is it right?	There are no mistakes. I think my calculations and diagrams are mathematically correct.	I made a few careless mistakes.	I made mistakes that caused errors in other parts of the answer.	I wasn't sure of my calculations or my logic.	I can't tell where I went wrong.
Is my work clear?	Everyone easily understands my work.	People understand my work but may have to reread parts to make sense of them.	My diagrams make sense, but I definitely need to clarify my work.	My diagrams and arguments start out OK, but people have a hard time making sense of them.	I hope no one asks me to explain my work.
How does it look?	Terrific! I am really pleased with the results.	I could have put more effort into the presentation.	My diagrams aren't neat or they don't help people understand what I wrote.	My diagrams don't work and they don't relate to what I wrote.	I need help.

Name _____ Date _____

Reasoning

003

1. A student is asked to prove that if a line segment bisects any angle of a triangle and also bisects the opposite side, then the other two sides of the triangle are congruent.

   Decide whether the following argument is valid. Explain your answer. • **MORE HELP** See 145, 263

   The given information is: $\overline{AD}$ bisects $\angle BAC$ and $\overline{BC}$ in $\triangle ABC$. Then $\angle BAD \cong \angle DAC$ and $\overline{BD} \cong \overline{DC}$ by the definition of bisect. By the Converse of the Base Angles Theorem, $\angle B \cong \angle C$. By the AAS Congruence Theorem, $\triangle BAD \cong \triangle CAD$. Therefore, $\overline{AB} \cong \overline{AC}$ because corresponding parts of congruent triangles are congruent.

   _____

   _____

   _____

   _____

005-007

For exercises 2–4, decide whether the argument is an example of deductive or inductive reasoning.

2. All isosceles triangles have two congruent angles; $\triangle MNO$ is an isosceles triangle. Two angles of $\triangle MNO$ are congruent.

   _____

3. John used a computer software program to draw a variety of pentagons, to measure each angle, and finally to compute the sum of the measures of the interior angles in each pentagon. John observed his data and decided that the sum of the measures of the angles of any pentagon is always 540 degrees.

   _____

4. The radii in a circle are equal; $\overline{OP}$ and $\overline{OR}$ are radii in $\odot O$. $OP = OR$

   _____

008-014

For exercises 5–6, true statements are given. Write the converse, inverse, and contrapositive and decide whether each is true or false.

5. Statement: *If two angles are right angles, then they are supplementary.*

   Converse: _____

   Inverse: _____

   Contrapositive: _____

Name _____ Date _____

6. Statement: *If two polygons are similar, then all pairs of corresponding angles are congruent.*

Converse: _____

Inverse: _____

Contrapositive: _____

For exercises 7–8, give the hypothesis and the conclusion for each of the statements. `009`

7. Statement: *Supplements of the same angle are congruent.*

Hypothesis: _____

Conclusion: _____

8. Statement: *The perpendicular bisector of a segment is a line of symmetry of the segment.*

Hypothesis: _____

Conclusion: _____

9. Write the following as a biconditional statement: `011`

An equilateral triangle is an equiangular triangle.

_____

_____

The truth values of p and q are given. Construct the truth tables for each statement. `015`

		10.	**11.**	**12.**
p	q	$\sim p$	$\sim q$	$p \leftrightarrow \sim q$
T	T			
T	F			
F	T			
F	F			

Name_____ Date_____

In exercises 13–16, draw a valid conclusion from the information given and decide whether the reasoning uses the Law of Syllogism or the Law of Detachment.

13. If a triangle is obtuse, then one angle has a measure greater than 90 degrees.
    $\triangle ABC$ is obtuse.

    Conclusion: _____

    _____

    Law:_____

14. If two angles form a linear pair, then they are supplementary.
    If two angles are supplementary, then the sum of their measures is 180°.

    Conclusion: _____

    _____

    Law:_____

15. If a quadrilateral is a parallelogram, then both pairs of opposite sides are congruent.
    $ABCD$ is a parallelogram.

    Conclusion: _____

    _____

    Law:_____

16. If two circles are congruent, then their diameters are equal.
    If the diameters of two circles are equal, then the areas of the circles are equal.

    Conclusion: _____

    _____

    Law:_____

Name _____ Date _____

Reasoning

Directions: Write the letter for the best possible answer.

For exercises 1–4, use A–C to describe the relationship of the hypothesis to the conclusion.

A. sufficient but not necessary
B. necessary but not sufficient
C. necessary and sufficient

_____ **1.** If two angles are vertical angles, then they are congruent.

_____ **2.** If a quadrilateral is a kite, then the diagonals are perpendicular.

_____ **3.** If two parallel lines are cut by a transversal, then the corresponding angles are congruent.

_____ **4.** If both pairs of opposite angles are congruent, then the quadrilateral is a rectangle.

For exercises 5–7, use D–F to describe how the second statement is related to the first.

D. converse
E. inverse
F. contrapositive

5. Statement 1: *If a point lies on the bisector of an angle, then it is equidistant from the sides.*

_____ Statement 2: *If a point does not lie on the bisector of an angle, then it is not equidistant from the sides.*

6. Statement 1: *If a quadrilateral is a trapezoid, then one pair of opposite sides is parallel.*

_____ Statement 2: *If one pair of opposite sides is not parallel, then the quadrilateral is not a trapezoid.*

7. Statement 1: *If two angles form a linear pair, then the angles are supplementary.*

_____ Statement 2: *If two angles are supplementary, then they form a linear pair.*

For exercises 8–9, use G–I to tell what form of reasoning is demonstrated.

G. Law of Detachment
H. Law of Syllogism
I. Circular Reasoning

8. Statement 1: *If a quadrilateral is a square, then the diagonals are perpendicular.*

Statement 2: *ABCD has perpendicular diagonals.*

_____ Conclusion: *ABCD is a square.*

9. Statement 1: *If all angles of a triangle are congruent, then the triangle is equilateral.*

Statement 2: *If a triangle is equilateral, its area equals $\frac{(s^2\sqrt{3})}{4}$, where s is the length of one side.*

_____ Conclusion: *If all angles of a triangle are congruent, then the area is $\frac{(s^2\sqrt{3})}{4}$, where s is the length of one side.*

PRACTICE ANSWERS
Page 10

1. The student used the converse of the Base Angles Theorem to state that $\angle B \cong \angle C$.

   This theorem requires that a triangle be isosceles. This is what must be proved, so the argument is an example of circular reasoning.

2. deductive

3. inductive

4. deductive

5. Converse: If two angles are supplementary then they are right angles; false

   Inverse: If two angles are not right angles then they are not supplementary; false

   Contrapositive: If two angles are not supplementary then they are not right angles; true

Page 11

6. Converse: If all pairs of corresponding angles of two polygons are congruent then the polygons are similar; false

   Inverse: If two polygons are not similar then all pairs of their corresponding angles are not congruent; false

   Contrapositive: If all pairs of corresponding angles of two polygons are not congruent then the polygons are not similar; true

7. Hypothesis: angles are supplements of the same angle
   Conclusion: the supplement angles are congruent

8. Hypothesis: a line is a perpendicular bisector of a segment
   Conclusion: the line is a line of symmetry for the segment

9. A triangle is equilateral if and only if the triangle is equiangular.

Page 12

13. $\triangle ABC$ has one angle with a measure greater than $90°$; Law of Detachment

14. If two angles form a linear pair, then their sum is $180°$; Law of Syllogism

15. Both pairs of opposite sides of $ABCD$ are congruent; Law of Detachment

16. If two circles are congruent, then their areas are equal; Law of Syllogism

TEST PREP ANSWERS
Page 13

1. A
2. A
3. C
4. B
5. E
6. F
7. D
8. I
9. H

		10.	11.	12.
p	q	$\sim p$	$\sim q$	$p \leftrightarrow \sim q$
T	T	F	F	F
T	F	F	T	T
F	T	T	F	T
F	F	T	T	F

Name _____ Date _____

Properties of Algebra

Write the property of real numbers that justifies each statement.

023-027

1. $a + (b + c) = a + (c + b)$ _____

2. $a + (b + c) = (a + b) + c$ _____

3. If $x + 5 = 12$, then $x = 7$ _____

4. $a + (b + c) = (c + b) + a$ _____

5. If $\frac{t}{3} = 15$, then $t = 45$ _____

6. $a(b + c) = ab + ac$ _____

7. $\frac{1}{2}(13xy)(8x^2y) = \frac{1}{2}(8x^2y)(13xy)$ _____

8. If $a + b = c$, then $b = c - a$ _____

9. $2x + 6y = 2(x + 3y)$ _____

10. $\frac{1}{2}(8x^2y) = \left[\frac{1}{2}(8)\right](x^2y)$ _____

11. If $x + y = 6$ and $6 = z$, then $x + y = z$ _____

12. $6x^2 - 2 - 5x^2 + 14 = 6x^2 - 5x^2 - 2 + 14$ _____

13. If $2m + 14 = v$, then $v = 2m + 14$ _____

14. $(a + b)(c + d) = (a + b)c + (a + b)d$ _____

15. $^-2abc + 7bca = {}^-2abc + 7abc$ _____

16. $a(b + c) = a(b + c)$ _____

17. If $m\angle A + m\angle B = 180°$ and $180° = \pi$ radians, then $m\angle A + m\angle B = \pi$ radians _____

18. If $SE + RT = 63$ in., then 63 in. $= SE + RT$ _____

Name _____ Date _____

Exercises 19–25 represent the steps in a proof. Justify each step with a property of real numbers.

Statements	**Reasons**
$4x - 2(4 - 6x) + 6 = 22 + 8x$	Given

19. $4x - 8 + 12x + 6 = 22 + 8x$ _____

20. $4x + 12x - 8 + 6 = 22 + 8x$ _____

21. $(4 + 12)x - 8 + 6 = 22 + 8x$ _____

22. $16x - 2 = 22 + 8x$ _____

23. $8x - 2 = 22$ _____

24. $8x = 24$ _____

25. $x = 3$ _____

26. **Given:** $AF = 101$ cm; $BC = EF$; $DE = 15$ cm; EF is 10 cm longer than AB; CD is three times as long as AB

Find: the length of each segment shown.

$AB =$ _____

$BC =$ _____

$CD =$ _____

$DE =$ _____

$EF =$ _____

27. **Given:** $m\angle 2 = m\angle 6$; $m\angle 3 = m\angle 5$; $m\angle COG = 150°$

Find: another angle that has a measure of $150°$ _____

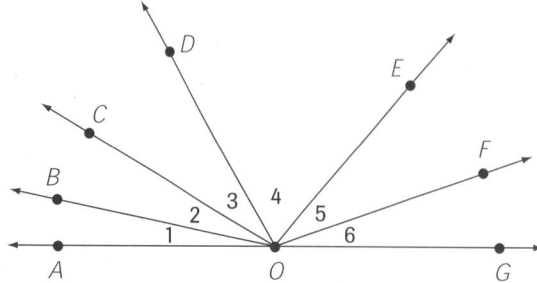

Name _____ Date _____

28. **Given:** $m\angle A + m\angle B + m\angle C + m\angle D = 360°$;
$m\angle B + m\angle D = 210°$; $m\angle B$ is 40° more than $m\angle A$;
$m\angle C$ is twice the measure of $\angle A$

Find: the measures of all four angles of $ABCD$

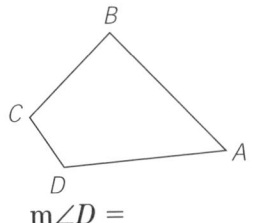

$m\angle A =$ _____ $m\angle B =$ _____ $m\angle C =$ _____ $m\angle D =$ _____

In exercises 29–44, justify each step of the proof.

Given: $AP = QB$; $PB = BC$
Prove: $AQ = BC$ • **MORE HELP** See 057

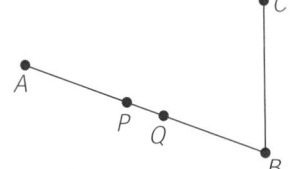

Proof

Statements	Reasons
29. $AP = QB$	_____
30. $PB = BC$	_____
31. $PQ = PQ$	_____
32. $AP + PQ = QB + PQ$	_____
33. $AQ = AP + PQ$	_____
34. $PB = PQ + QB$	_____
35. $AQ = PB$	_____
36. $AQ = BC$	_____

Given: $\angle BAD \cong \angle EAC$
Prove: $\angle 1 \cong \angle 3$ • **MORE HELP** See 256

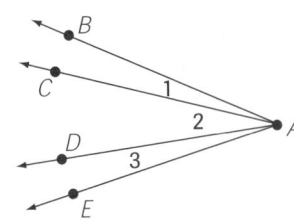

Proof

Statements	Reasons
37. $\angle BAD \cong \angle EAC$	_____
38. $m\angle BAD = m\angle EAC$	_____
39. $m\angle 2 = m\angle 2$	_____
40. $m\angle BAD = m\angle 1 + m\angle 2$	_____
41. $m\angle EAC = m\angle 3 + m\angle 2$	_____
42. $m\angle 1 + m\angle 2 = m\angle 3 + m\angle 2$	_____
43. $m\angle 1 = m\angle 3$	_____
44. $\angle 1 \cong \angle 3$	_____

Name_____ Date_____

Properties of Algebra

Directions: Use A–K to name the property demonstrated by the exercises.

A. Associative Property
B. Commutative Property
C. Distributive Property
D. Reflexive Property
E. Symmetric Property
F. Transitive Property
G. Substitution Property
H. Addition Property of Equality
I. Subtraction Property of Equality
J. Multiplication Property of Equality
K. Division Property of Equality

1. $6x^2 + x = x(6x + 1)$

   _____

2. $(m\angle 1 + m\angle 2) + m\angle 3 = m\angle 1 + (m\angle 2 + m\angle 3)$

   _____

3. $(m\angle 1 + m\angle 2) + m\angle 3 = (m\angle 2 + m\angle 1) + m\angle 3$

   _____

4. If $AB + BC = AC$, then $BC + AB = AC$

   _____

5. $2(AB)(MN) = (AB)(2)(MN)$

   _____

6. If $m\angle A = m\angle B$ and $m\angle B = 35°$, then $m\angle A = 35°$

   _____

7. If $AB + BC = AC$, then $AC = AB + BC$

   _____

8. If $m\angle P - m\angle T = 75°$ and $m\angle P = 115°$, then $115° - m\angle T = 75°$

   _____

9. $BD = BD$

   _____

10. If $PQ + QR = MN$ and $MN = ST + UV$, then $PQ + QR = ST + UV$

    _____

11. If $AB + BC = AC$ and $BC = 15$ cm, then $AB + 15 = AC$

    _____

12. $m\angle ABC = m\angle ABC$

    _____

13. $AB + BC = PQ$, therefore $AB = PQ - BC$

    _____

14. $m\angle A = m\angle B$, therefore $m\angle A + 90° = m\angle B + 90°$

    _____

15. $2(PQ) = 16$ m, therefore $PQ = 8$ m

    _____

16. $m\angle P = \frac{1}{2}m\angle Q$, therefore $2m\angle P = m\angle Q$

    _____

17. If $m\angle 1 + m\angle 2 + m\angle 3 + m\angle 4 = 360°$, and $m\angle 2 + m\angle 3 = 180°$, then $m\angle 1 + m\angle 4 = 180°$

    _____

18. If $m\angle P - 86° = 150°$, then $m\angle P = 236°$.

    _____

PRACTICE ANSWERS
Page 15

1. Commutative Property of Addition
2. Associative Property of Addition
3. Subtraction Property of Equality
4. Commutative Property of Addition
5. Multiplication Property of Equality
6. Distributive Property
7. Commutative Property of Multiplication
8. Subtraction Property of Equality
9. Distributive Property
10. Associative Property of Multiplication
11. Transitive Property of Equality
12. Commutative Property of Addition
13. Symmetric Property of Equality
14. Distributive Property
15. Commutative Property of Multiplication
16. Reflexive Property of Equality
17. Transitive Property of Equality
18. Symmetric Property of Equality

Page 16

19. Distributive Property
20. Commutative Property of Addition
21. Distributive Property
22. Substitution Property of Equality
23. Subtraction property of Equality
24. Addition Property of Equality
25. Division Property of Equality
26. $AB = 11$ cm, $BC = 21$ cm, $CD = 33$ cm, $DE = 15$ cm, $EF = 21$ cm
27. $\angle BOF$

Page 17

28. $m\angle A = 50^\circ$, $m\angle B = 90^\circ$, $m\angle C = 100^\circ$, $m\angle D = 120^\circ$
29. Given
30. Given
31. Reflexive Property of Equality
32. Addition Property of Equality
33. Segment + Postulate (P09)
34. Segment + Postulate (P09)
35. Substitution Property of Equality
36. Transitive Property of Equality
37. Given

38. Definition of $\cong$
39. Reflexive Property of Equality
40. $\angle$ + Postulate (P13)
41. $\angle$ + Postulate (P13)
42. Substitution Property Equality
43. Subtraction Property of Equality
44. Definition of $\cong$

TEST PREP ANSWERS
Page 18

1. C
2. A
3. B
4. B
5. B
6. accept F or G
7. E
8. G
9. D
10. F
11. G
12. D
13. I
14. H
15. K
16. J
17. I
18. H

Name_____ Date_____

Styles of Proof

1. Choose the diagram that best represents the description. Explain why you rejected the other two diagrams.

   $\triangle PQR$ with perpendicular segment from P to $\overline{QR}$.

   A. 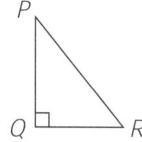   **B.** 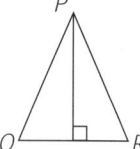   **C.**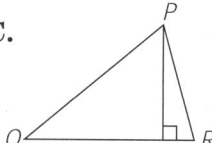

   _____

2. Draw and label a diagram that represents the description. • **MORE HELP** See 056, 480

   $\overleftrightarrow{AB}$ is the perpendicular bisector of $\overline{PQ}$.

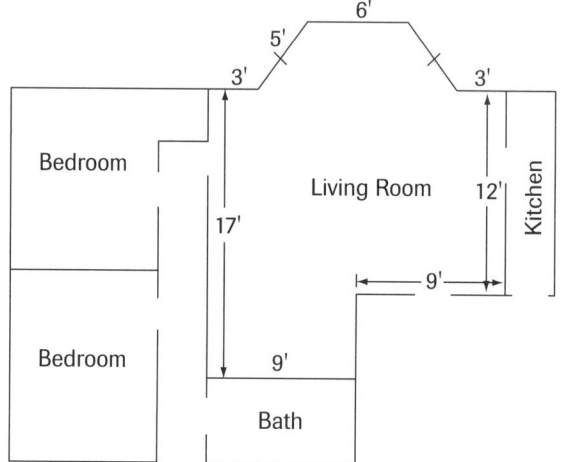

3. Given the information shown in this floor plan, you are asked to find the area of the living room. Draw auxiliary lines and write in missing measures and labels that will help. • **MORE HELP** See 152-153

4. Complete the proof. • **MORE HELP** See 022-037

   Given: $n + (n + 1) + (n + 2) = 24$

   Prove: $n = 7$

Statements	**Reasons**
❶ $n + (n + 1) + (n + 2) = 24$	Given
❷ $n + n + n + 1 + 2 = 24$	Commutative Prop. of $=$
❸ $3n + 3 = 24$	Addition of like terms
❹ $3n = 21$	_____
❺ _____	_____

5. Mark the diagram with what you know, then write a two-column proof. • **MORE HELP** See 141

   Given: P, Q, and R are midpoints

   Prove: $PBQR$ is a parallelogram

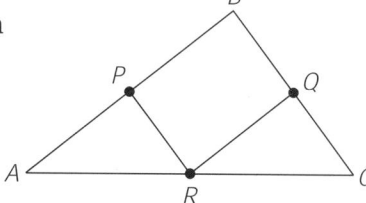

   _____

   _____

   _____

Name _____ Date _____

6. Label the coordinates of each vertex of this parallelogram.

• **MORE HELP** See 157

043

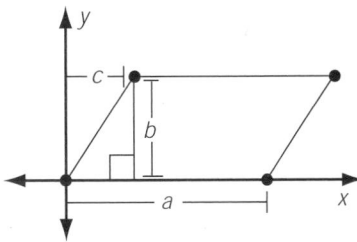

7. **Given:** $\triangle ABC$ has coordinates $A(0,8)$, $B(0,0)$, and $C(10,0)$

Prove: $\triangle ABC$ is a right triangle

_____

_____

_____

_____

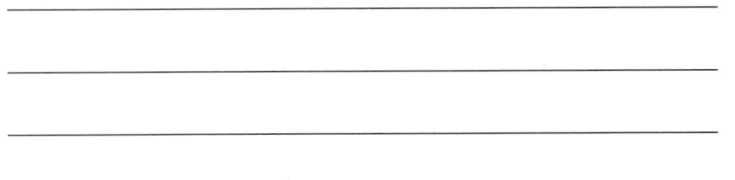

For exercises 8–10, find and correct the factual or logical error in the proof. Underline the error, then write your correction on the line provided.

044

8. **Given:** square $ABCD$

Prove: diagonal $\overline{BD}$ is longer than side $\overline{AB}$ • **MORE HELP** See 143, 148

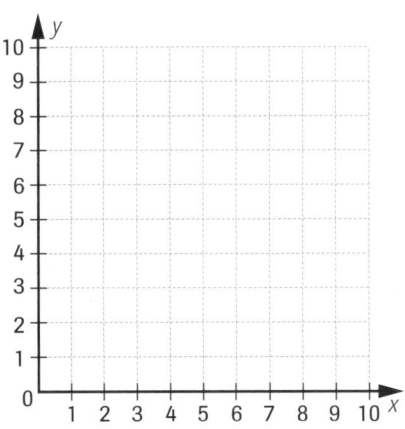

Proof: Since $ABCD$ is a square, $\angle A$ is a right angle so $\triangle ABD$ is isosceles. In a right triangle, the right angle is the largest angle, so the hypotenuse is always the longest side. Since BD is the hypotenuse of right $\triangle ABC$, $\overline{BD}$ is longer than $\overline{AB}$.

_____

_____

9. **Given:** figure $MNOP$

Prove: the sum of the lengths of adjacent sides is greater than the length of diagonal $\overline{NP}$ • **MORE HELP** See 148

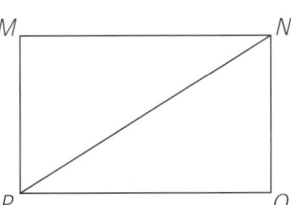

Proof: Since $MNOP$ is a rectangle, $\triangle MNP$ is a right triangle. Since, in any triangle, the sum of the lengths of any two sides must be greater than the length of the third side, $MN + MP > PN$ and $PO + NO > PN$.

_____

_____

Name _____ Date _____

10. **Given:** $a \cdot a = x$; $a \neq 0$; a is a real number

Prove: $x > 0$

Proof: $a \cdot a = a^2$. If $a < 0$, then $a^2 < 0$. If $a > 0$, then $a^2 > 0$. Since $a^2 = x$, x must be greater than zero.

_____

11. Write a paragraph proof.

Given: A snowboard rental costs $25 for insurance plus $10 per day.

Show: The cost of renting a snowboard for five days is $75.

_____

_____

_____

_____

045

For exercises 12–15, fill in the blanks.

12. **Given:** $m\angle1 = 50°$

Prove: $m\angle2 = 130°$

• **MORE HELP** See 070

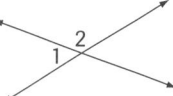

| $m\angle1 = 50°$ | → | $50° + m\angle2 = 180°$ |

Given

a.

| $\angle1$ and $\angle2$ are a linear pair |

Def. of linear pair

| $m\angle2 = 130°$ |

b.

| $m\angle1 + m\angle2 = 180°$ |

Linear Pair Postulate (P14)

13. **Given:** Triangle Park as shown

Prove: It's farther from A to C through B than from A to C through D.

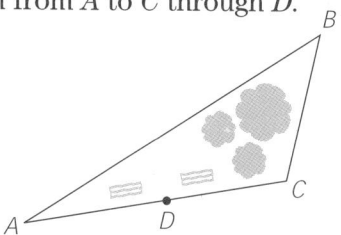

| $\triangle ABC$ |

Given

| $AD + DC = AC$ | → | **a.** |

Seg. + Postulate (P09)

b. _____

| $AB + BC > AC$ |

$\triangle$ Inequality Theorem (T055)

14. **Definition:** A creature is a zingorn if it has at least three horns.

Given: Rover has four horns.

Prove: Rover is a zingorn.

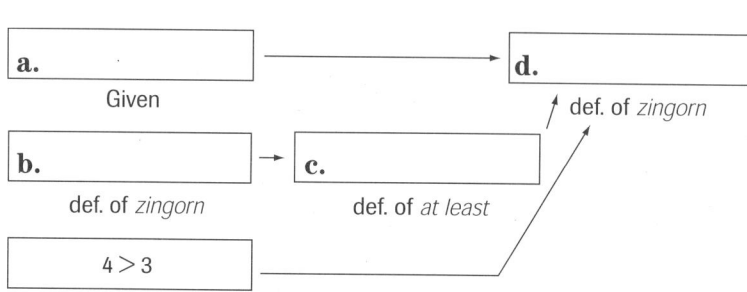

| **a.** | → | **d.** |

Given

def. of *zingorn*

| **b.** | → | **c.** |

def. of *zingorn*

def. of *at least*

| $4 > 3$ |

def. of $>$

Name _____ Date _____

15. **Given:** $n + (n + 1) + (n + 2) = 24$
Prove: $n = 7$

$n + (n + 1) + (n + 2) = 24$	→	$n + n + n + 1 + 2 = 24$	→	$3n + 3 = 24$
Given		Commutative prop. of =		+ prop. of =

a. _____

b. _____

16. Write a flow proof.
Given: About 73% of cats in your town have been neutered. There are about 65,000 neutered cats in your town.
Prove: About 89,000 cats live in your town.

c. _____

d. _____

For exercises 17–18, choose a useful assumption (A, B, or C) that will lead to a contradiction. Then explain how that contradiction will help prove your point.

17. **Given:** $xy = 1$ **A.** $x = 1$ **B.** $x \neq 1$ **C.** $x = 0$
Prove: $x \neq 0$

_____

_____

18. **Given:** square $MNOP$ **A.** $m\angle 1 = m\angle 2$ **B.** $m\angle 1 > m\angle 2$ **C.** $m\angle 1 \neq m\angle 2$
Prove: $m\angle 1 = m\angle 2$
• **MORE HELP** See 075

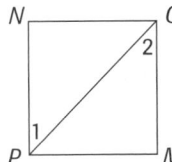

_____

_____

19. Write an indirect proof.
Given: $\triangle ABC$; $\angle A \not\cong \angle C$
Prove: $\overline{AB} \not\cong \overline{BC}$ • **MORE HELP** See 145

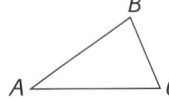

_____

_____

_____

_____

Name_____ Date_____

Styles of Proof

Directions: Mark the best answer.

1. Which diagram best shows quadrilateral *MNOP* with $\overline{MO} \perp \overline{NP}$.
   A. 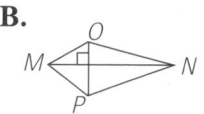   **B.** 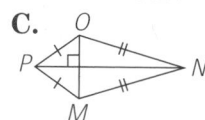   **C.** 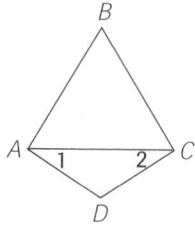   **D.** None of these

For exercises 2–3, find the missing statement and reason for this proof.
Given: $\overline{AB} \perp \overline{AD}$; $\overline{BC} \perp \overline{CD}$; $AB = BC$
Prove: $\angle 1 \cong \angle 2$
Proof

Statements	Reasons
❶ $\overline{AB} \perp \overline{AD}$; $\overline{BC} \perp \overline{CD}$; $AB = BC$	Given
❷ $\angle BAD$ and $\angle BCD$ are rt. $\angle$s	Def. of $\perp$
❸ (Choose A, B, or C, from exercise 2.)	Base $\angle$s Theorem (T050)
❹ $\angle BAC$ is the complement of $\angle 1$	Def. of comp. angles
❺ $\angle BCA$ is the complement of $\angle 2$	Def. of comp. angles
❻ $\angle 1 \cong \angle 2$	(Choose A, B, or C, from exercise 3.)

2. **A.** $\angle BAD \cong \angle BCD$ **B.** $\angle BAC \cong \angle BCA$ **C.** $\angle DAC \cong \angle DCA$

3. **A.** Complements of $\cong$ $\angle$s are $\cong$ **B.** Base $\angle$s Theorem (T050)   **C.** $\angle DAC \cong \angle DCA$

4. Find the missing statement and reason.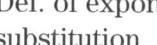
   Given: $\odot$s *O* and *Q*; $AB = 2CD$
   Prove: The area of $\odot O$ is four times the area of $\odot Q$
   A. Area of $\odot Q = 4$(Area of $\odot O$) $\div$ prop. of $=$
   B. Area of $\odot O = 4$(Area of $\odot Q$) $\div$ prop. of $=$
   C. Area of $\odot Q = 4$(Area of $\odot O$) Def. of exponent; substitution
   D. None of these

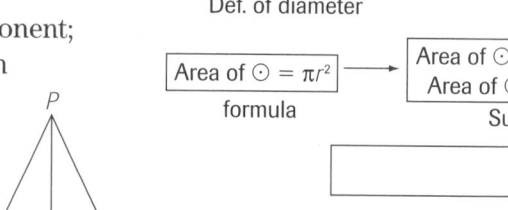

5. Choose the indirect proof that shows that $\triangle OPQ$ is isosceles.
   Given: $\triangle OPQ$; $\overline{PR}$ is $\perp$ bisector of $\overline{OQ}$
   Prove: $\triangle OPQ$ is isosceles
   A. Assume that $\triangle OPQ$ is obtuse. Then m$\angle O$ would be greater than m$\angle Q$, but we know that m$\angle O$ = m$\angle Q$ so $\triangle OPQ$ is not obtuse.
   B. Assume that $\triangle OPQ$ is not isosceles. Then OP would not equal QP, but we know that $OP = QP$, so $\triangle OPQ$ is isosceles.
   C. Assume that $\triangle OPQ$ is not isosceles. then m$\angle O$ would not equal m$\angle Q$, but we know that m$\angle O$ = m$\angle Q$, *so* $\triangle OPQ$ is isosceles.
   D. None of these

PRACTICE ANSWERS
Page 20

1. *C* is the best diagram. *A* and *B* are both special cases not justified by the description.

2.
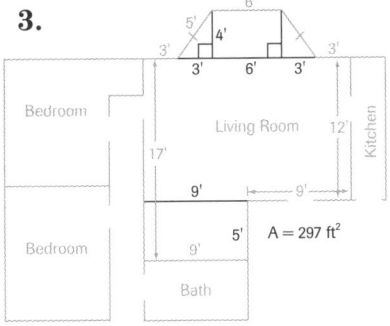

3.
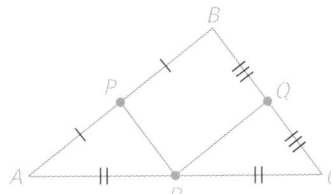

4. ❹ Subtraction Prop. of =;
   ❺ *n* = 7; ÷ Prop. of =

5. **Sample proof:**

Statements	Reasons
❶ *P*, *Q* and *R* are midpoints	Given
❷ $\overline{QR} \parallel \overline{PB}$; $\overline{PR} \parallel \overline{BQ}$	Midsegment Theorem (T045)
❸ *PBQR* is a parallelogram	Def. of parallelogram

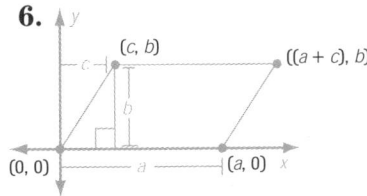

Page 21

6.
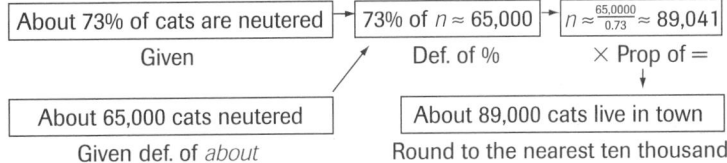

7. Sample proof: The *x*-coordinate for *A* and *B* is zero, so they are on the *y*-axis. The *y*-coordinate for *B* and *C* is zero, so they are on the *x*-axis. Since the *x*- and *y*-axes are perpendicular, then $\overline{AB}$ and $\overline{BC}$ must also be

perpendicular. Perpendicular lines meet to form right angles, so *ABC* is a right triangle.

8. so △*ABD* is isosceles should read so △*ABD* is a right triangle

9. Since *MNOP* is a rectangle, △*MNP* is a right triangle is not justified by the given; Since *MNOP* is a quadrilateral, diagonal *NP* forms two triangles, △*PMN* and △*PON*.

Page 22

10. $\underline{a^2 < 0}$ should read $\underline{a^2 > 0}$

11. Proofs will vary but should justify multiplying cost per day by number of days, then adding the one-time insurance fee.

12. **a.** Substitution;
    b. Subtraction Prop. of =

13. **a.** $AB + BC > AD + DC$;
    b. Substitution

14. **a.** Rover has 4 horns;
    b. Zingorns have at least 3 horns;
    c. The number of a zingorn's horns is greater than or equal to 3;
    d. Rover is a zingorn

Page 23

15. **a.** $3n = 21$;
    b. Subtraction Prop. of =
    c. $n = 7$;
    d. ÷ Prop. of =

16. **Sample proof:**

About 73% of cats are neutered	→	73% of $n \approx 65{,}000$	→	$n \approx \frac{65{,}0000}{0.73} \approx 89{,}041$
Given		Def. of %		× Prop of =

About 65,000 cats neutered		About 89,000 cats live in town
Given def. of *about*		Round to the nearest ten thousand

17. The useful assumption is *C*. If $x = 0$, then xy must also equal zero. Since $xy \neq 0$, then $x \neq 0$.

18. The most useful assumption is *C*. If m∠1 ≠ m∠2, then because alternate interior angles of parallel lines cut by a transversal are congruent, $\overline{OP}$ would not be parallel to $\overline{MN}$. However, since *MNOP* is a square, $\overline{OP}$ is parallel to $\overline{MN}$ and m∠1 = m∠2.

19. Sample Proof: Assume that $\overline{AB} \cong \overline{BC}$. In that case, the Base Angles Theorem says that ∠*A* ≅ ∠*C*. But, since ∠*A* ≇ ∠*C*, you know that $\overline{AB} \ncong \overline{BC}$.

TEST PREP ANSWERS
Page 24

1. C　　2. B　　3. A
4. C　　5. D

Prove It!

OBJECTIVES
- Develop reasoning skills
- Understand and apply rules of logic
- Prove statements

MATERIALS
none

TIME
- 30 minutes

TEACHER NOTES

- Review each property, along with the example given. It is necessary for students to understand how each property is applied.

- You may wish to have students work with a partner or in groups as they prove each theorem.

- There is more than one way to prove each theorem. Encourage students to think about efficient ways to prove the theorems.

EXTENSIONS

- Have students present their proofs to the class.

- Encourage students to write their own theorems for classmates to prove.

- Students who enjoy these problems should investigate Lewis Carroll's problems where one word is transformed into another word, one letter at a time. (CAT – COT – COG – DOG)

ANSWERS
Answers may vary.

1. C B D C B → ?   Given
   C B D C B → C B D B C   Property 1
   C B D B C → C B C   Property 2
   C B C → C C B   Property 1
   C C B → A B   Property 3

2. A B C D C B A → ?   Given
   A B C D C B A → A B A   Property 2
   A B A → A A B   Property 1
   A A B → A B   Property 3

3. D C B A A B → ?   Given
   D C B A A B → D B C A A B   Property 1
   D B C A A B → B D C A A B   Property 1
   B D C A A B → B B B   Property 2
   B B B → A B   Property 3

4. C A D C A D C A D → ?   Given
   C A D C A D C A D →
   A C D C A D C A D   Prop. 1
   A C D C A D C A D →
   A C D C A D C D A   Prop. 1
   A C D C A D C D A → A B A   Prop. 2
   A B A → A A B   Prop. 1
   A A B → A B   Prop. 3

5. A B B A C C A D D → ?   Given
   A B B A C C A D D →
   A B B A C C D A D   Prop. 1
   A B B A C C D A D →
   A B B A C C D D A   Prop. 1
   A B B A C C D D A → A B A   Prop. 2
   A B A → A A B   Prop. 1
   A A B → A B   Prop. 3

Name_____ Date_____

Deductive Reasoning:
 007

Logical Statements:
 008

Commutative Property:
 024

Substitution Property
 of Equality: 037

Prove It!

You have used properties of algebra to prove and solve algebraic statements. To do so, you applied the rules of algebra that you knew and followed a logical sequence in solving the problem.

Directions: You will be given three properties that are applied to the letters A, B, C, and D. You will be asked to prove a theorem that consists of a string of letters that are to be transformed (→) to a new string of letters. You will prove the theorem by applying the three properties.

Property 1: Any two adjacent letters can change place with one another. This is similar to the Commutative Property.
Example: $\boxed{C\ A}\ D \rightarrow \boxed{A\ C}\ D$

Property 2: If a string of letters begins and ends with the same letter, all of the letters between them may be replaced with the letter B. This is similar to the Substitution Property.
Example: $\text{C}\ \boxed{C\ A\ A\ B}\ \text{C} \rightarrow \text{C}\ \boxed{B}\ \text{C}$

Property 3: If the first two letters of a string are the same, they may be replaced with the letter A. This is similar to the Substitution Property.
Example: $\boxed{C\ C}\ A\ D \rightarrow \boxed{A}\ A\ D$

Sample Proof:

Prove that D C C A D A → A B

D C C A D A → ?	Given
D C C A <u>D A</u> → D C C A <u>A D</u>	Property 1
D <u>C C A A</u> D → D <u>B</u> D	Property 2
D <u>B D</u> → D <u>D B</u>	Property 1
<u>D D</u> B → <u>A</u> B	Property 3

Use the properties to prove the following theorems.

1. C B D C B → A B

2. A B C D C B A → A B

3. D C B A A B → A B

4. C A D C A D C A D → A B

5. A B B A C C A D D → A B

Name _____ Date _____

Planes and Points

048   Draw a sketch for each of the following.

1. three collinear points

2. three noncollinear points

3. a point and a line that are coplanar

4. four coplanar points

5. four noncoplanar points

For exercises 6–10, use the diagram to determine whether the statements are true or false.

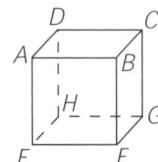

6. Points *A*, *B*, and *C* are collinear. _____

7. Points *A*, *B*, and *C* are coplanar. _____   **8.** Points *A*, *B*, *G* and *H* are coplanar. _____

9. $\overleftrightarrow{AE}$ and $\overleftrightarrow{BF}$ are coplanar. _____   **10.** $\overleftrightarrow{DC}$ and $\overleftrightarrow{FG}$ and are coplanar. _____

Explain why the following are not good definitions. • **MORE HELP** See 156

11. A rectangle is a quadrilateral. _____

12. A pencil is a six-inch writing tool with graphite.

_____

For exercises 13–15, refer to the diagram. Describe the intersection of the planes.

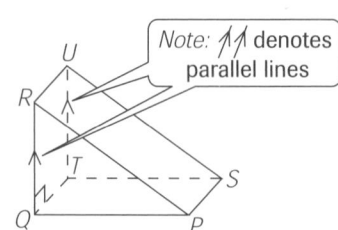

13. Plane *PQR* and plane *QRUT* _____

14. Plane *PQR* and plane *STU* • **MORE HELP** See 060, 162 _____

15. Plane *PQTS* and plane *QRUT* _____

State the postulate that shows that the statement is false.

16. Three points, *X*, *Y*, and *Z*, are noncollinear, and two planes *A* and *B*, each contain points *X*,

    Y, and *Z*. _____

17. Two planes intersect in exactly one point. _____

Name _____ Date _____

Planes and Points

Directions: Select the best answer to each question.

1. Two quantities are described below. Choose the letter of the statement that is true.

   Column A
   The number of lines that can be drawn through two points.

   Column B
   The number of planes that can be drawn through three noncollinear points.

   A. The quantity in column A is greater.
   B. The quantity in column B is greater.
   C. The two quantities are equal.
   D. The relationship cannot be determined from the given information.

Use the given diagram to answer exercises 2–4.

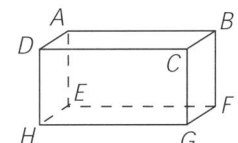

2. Points *A*, *B*, and *C* are

   A. collinear

   B. coplanar

   C. collinear and coplanar

   D. none of the above

3. $\overleftrightarrow{AB}$ and $\overleftrightarrow{HG}$ are

   A. collinear

   B. coplanar

   C. collinear and coplanar

   D. none of the above

4. Points *E*, *F* and *C* are coplanar with

   A. point *G*

   B. point *H*

   C. point *A*

   D. none of the above

5. Which of the following statements is *not* true?

   A. A line has no thickness and cannot be measured.

   B. A plane has no boundaries.

   C. A segment has no thickness and is one half of a line.

   D. A point has no length, width or height.

6. Which of the following statements is *not* true.

   A. If two planes intersect then their intersection is a point.

   B. If two points lie in a plane then the line containing them lies in the plane.

   C. If a line and a plane intersect, then their intersection is a point.

   D. A plane contains at least three noncollinear points.

Decide whether the following statements are Always, Sometimes, or Never True. Write the letter of the correct answer.

   A. Always True

   B. Sometimes True

   C. Never True

7. Through three noncollinear points there exists exactly one line. _____

8. Four noncollinear points are coplanar. _____

9. If two distinct planes intersect, then their intersection is a line. _____

10. The intersection of a plane and a line could be two points. _____

11. A half-plane is the part of a plane that is on one side of a line in that plane. _____

12. Two parallel lines do not lie in the same plane. _____

PRACTICE ANSWERS
Page 28

Diagrams vary for exercises 1–5; samples are given

1.

2.

3.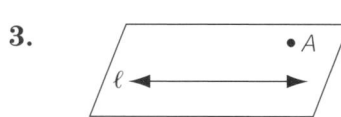

4.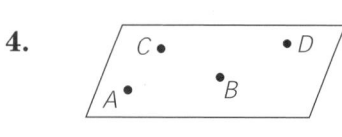

5.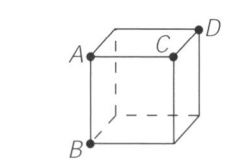

6. false

7. true

8. true

9. true

10. false

11. not enough information; there are many quadrilaterals that are not rectangles

12. too much information; pencils may be other lengths

13. $\overleftrightarrow{QR}$

14. none, the planes are parallel

15. $\overleftrightarrow{QT}$

16. (P04) Three noncollinear points determine a plane.

17. (P03) If two distinct planes intersect, then their intersection is a line.

TEST PREP ANSWERS
Page 29

1. C

2. B

3. B

4. D

5. C

6. A

7. C

8. B

9. A

10. C

11. A

12. C

Name _____ Date _____

Lines and Planes and Their Relationships

Use the diagram of a cube to answer each question.
(Note: A cube has six square faces; all of its angles are right angles.)

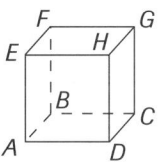

1. Name two segments parallel to $\overline{AB}$. _____

2. Name two segments perpendicular to $\overline{AB}$. _____

3. Name two segments skew to $\overline{AB}$. _____

4. Name three concurrent segments. _____

5. $\overline{EB}$ is parallel to what segment? _____

6. Name the intersection of $\overline{EB}$ and $\overline{DB}$. _____

Write the name for each diagram in as many ways as possible.

7.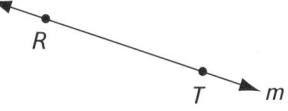

8.

9.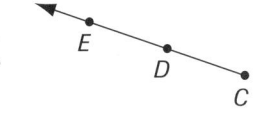

_____   _____   _____

Circle true or false.

10. A line segment is a part of a line.   true   false

11. A ray is part of a line segment.   true   false

12. KM represents the length of a segment.   true   false

13. Two lines are parallel if they don't intersect.   true   false

14. Skew lines are not in the same plane.   true   false

15. $\overrightarrow{KM}$ and $\overrightarrow{MK}$ name the same set of points.   true   false

For exercises 16–18, use the diagram to help you write an example of the postulate stated.

16. Through any two distinct points there exists exactly one line.

_____

17. A line contains at least two points.

_____

18. If two distinct lines intersect, then their intersection is exactly one point.

_____

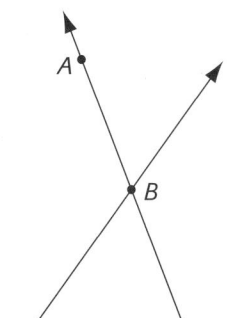

Name_____ Date_____

055 Use the ruler to determine the length of each segment.

19. $AB =$ _____

20. $CD =$ _____

21. $EF =$ _____

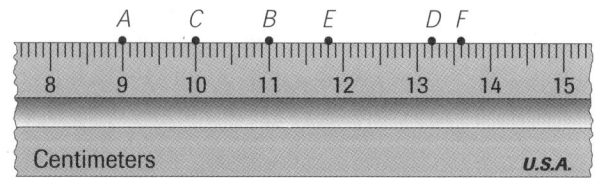

056 Draw a segment or segments to bisect each figure into congruent halves. • **MORE HELP** See 129

22.

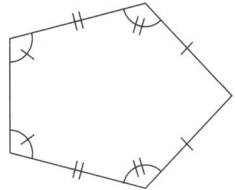

_____

23.

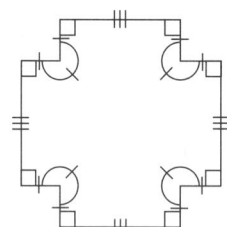

_____

24.

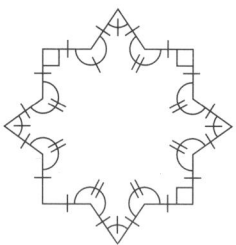

_____

Points A and B are the ruler coordinates of the endpoints of a segment. M is the ruler coordinate for its midpoint. Determine the missing ruler coordinate.

25. $A(3$ in.$)$, $B(4$ in.$)$, M (_____)

26. $A(6$ in.$)$, $B(2\frac{1}{2}$ in.$)$, M (_____)

27. $A(4\frac{1}{4}$ in.$)$, $B($_____$)$, $M(2\frac{1}{8}$ in.$)$

28. $A($_____$)$, $B(6\frac{1}{4}$ in.$)$, $M(4\frac{3}{8}$ in.$)$

Use the diagram to answer the following. • **MORE HELP** See 152

29. $BE =$ _____

30. $AC =$ _____

31. $CE =$ _____

32. $AD =$ _____

33. $BD =$ _____

34. $AB =$ _____

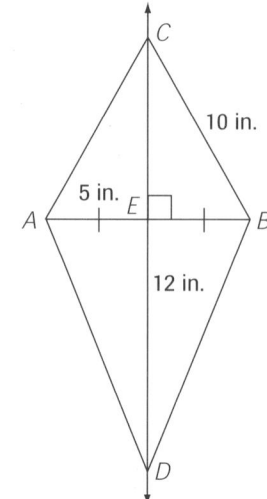

Name _____ Date _____

In the diagram points L, M, N, P, and T are collinear. $LT = 24$ cm, $MP = 8$ cm, and $LM = MN = NP$. Find the lengths for exercises 35–40.

35. $MN =$ _____

36. $LP =$ _____

37. $MT =$ _____

38. $TP =$ _____

39. $NT =$ _____

40. $PN =$ _____

Refer to the diagram of a perfect staircase to answer exercises 41–43.

41. Describe the parallel lines shown in the diagram.

_____

42. Describe the parallel planes shown in the diagram.

_____

43. What should be true about the distance between the steps?

_____

Write True or False.

_____ **44.** If two parallel planes are cut by a third plane, then the lines of intersection are perpendicular.

_____ **45.** In Euclidean Geometry, if there is a line and a point not on the line, then there is exactly one line through the point and parallel to the given line.

_____ **46.** If two lines are parallel to the same line then they are parallel to each other.

_____ **47.** If two lines are perpendicular to the same line then they are perpendicular to each other.

_____ **48.** If two or more lines are perpendicular to the same plane, then they are perpendicular.

Name_____ Date_____

Sketch the following.

49. Parallel lines ℓ and m that are both parallel to line n.

50. Lines ℓ and m that are both perpendicular to plane N.

51. Two planes N and P that are both perpendicular to line ℓ.

52. Two parallel planes, N and P, that are cut by a third plane Q.

For exercises 53–56, refer to the diagram.

Given: $\ell \parallel m \parallel n$. Solve for the length of the missing segment.

53. $DE = 8$ units, $EF = 12$ units, $AC = 25$ units, $BC =$ _____

54. $DE = 8$ units, $EF = 6$ units, $BC = 10$ units, $AB =$ _____

55. $DE = 3$ units, $EF = 6$ units, $BC = 8$ units, $AC =$ _____

56. $EF = 5x$ units, $AB = 60$, $BC = 8x$ units, $DE =$ _____

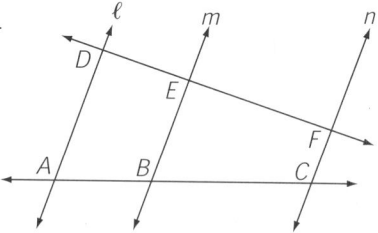

State a valid conclusion for each statement.

57. $\ell \perp m$ _____

_____

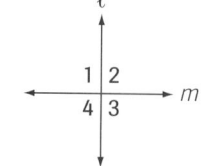

58. $\ell \perp m$ and $n \perp m$ _____

_____

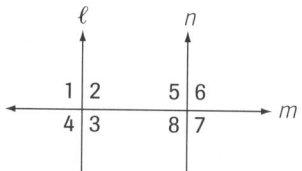

061

Name _____ Date _____

Lines and Planes and Their Relationships

Directions: Select the best answer to each question.

1. If two lines intersect, then they must be
   A. parallel
   B. skew
   C. coplanar
   D. perpendicular

2. R, S, and T are collinear. S is between R and T. $RS = 2w + 1$, $ST = w - 1$, and $RT = 18$. Determine RS.
   A. 16   C. 5
   B. 13   D. 6

3. In which diagram are the following statements all true? A, B, C, and D are collinear with opposite rays $\overrightarrow{AC}$ and $\overrightarrow{AB}$; $\overrightarrow{AC}$ and $\overrightarrow{AD}$ are the same ray.

   A.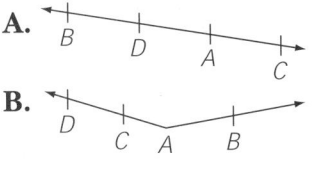
   B.
   C.
   D.

4. Given points X, at 6 on a number line, and Y, at 3.5 on the same number line, determine the midpoint of $\overline{XY}$.
   A. 4.5   C. 9.5
   B. 2.5   D. 4.75

5. In the diagram $\overline{AB}$ is the perpendicular bisector of $\overline{CD}$. Determine x and y.
   A. $x = 2$, $y = 8$
   B. $x = 8$, $y = 2$
   C. $x = 8$, $y = 11$
   D. $x = 2$, $y = 11$

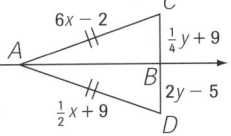

6. Which is a pair of parallel planes? (Naming three points will identify a plane.)
   A. *EKJ* and *GAF*
   B. *BCE* and *KLF*
   C. *BCE* and *KJL*
   D. *FAB* and *GAF*

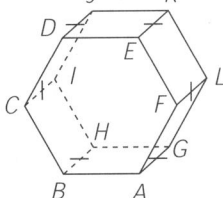

7. Given line ℓ and point P not on line ℓ. Let x = the number of lines through P parallel to ℓ and let y = the number of lines through P perpendicular to ℓ. Find $x + y$.
   A. 1   C. infinite
   B. 2   D. cannot be determined

8. Given: $\ell \parallel m \parallel n$; $DE = 2x$, $EF = 4x - 3$, $AB = 8$, $BC = 15$
   $DE =$ _____
   A. 24
   B. 12
   C. 3
   D. 8

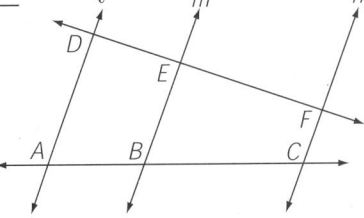

Use the diagram for exercises 9 and 10. Think of each segment in the diagram as part of a line.

9. $\overleftrightarrow{DC}$ and $\overleftrightarrow{EH}$ are
   A. parallel
   B. perpendicular
   C. skew
   D. none of these

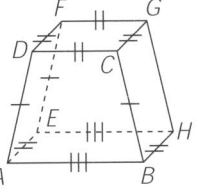

10. plane *ADF* and plane *BHG* are
    A. parallel
    B. perpendicular
    C. skew
    D. none of these

PRACTICE ANSWERS
Page 31

1. any two: $\overline{EF}$, $\overline{HG}$, or $\overline{DC}$
2. any two: $\overline{AD}$, $\overline{AE}$, $\overline{BF}$, or $\overline{BC}$
3. any two: $\overline{HD}$, $\overline{CG}$, $\overline{HE}$, or $\overline{FG}$
4. Answers may vary. Sample answer: $\overline{AB}$, $\overline{BF}$, $\overline{BC}$
5. $\overline{HC}$
6. point B
7. $\overrightarrow{RT}$, $\overrightarrow{TR}$, m
8. $\overrightarrow{PQ}$, $\overrightarrow{QP}$
9. $\overrightarrow{CD}$, $\overrightarrow{CE}$
10. true
11. false
12. true
13. false
14. true
15. false
16. Line m is the only line through points A and B.
17. Line m contains at least two points, A and B.
18. Lines m and l intersect at point B.

Page 32

19. 2 cm
20. 3.2 cm
21. 1.8 cm

For exercises 22–24, any one of the segments shown counts as a correct answer.

22.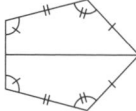

23.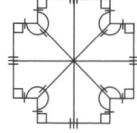

24.

25. $M(3\frac{1}{2}$ in.)
26. $M(4\frac{1}{4}$ in.)
27. $B(0$ in.)
28. $A(2\frac{1}{2}$ in.)
29. $BE = 5$ in.
30. $AC = 10$ in.
31. $CE = \sqrt{75}$ or $5\sqrt{3}$ in.
32. $AD = 13$ in.
33. $BD = 13$ in.
34. $AB = 10$ in.

Page 33

35. $MN = 4$ cm
36. $LP = 12$ cm
37. $MT = 20$ cm
38. $TP = 12$ cm
39. $NT = 16$ cm
40. $PN = 4$ cm
41. the rails
42. the posts or balusters, edges of steps, edges of risers, treads
43. the steps are the same distance apart
44. false
45. true
46. true
47. false
48. false

Page 34

For exercises 49–52, diagrams may vary. Samples are given.

49.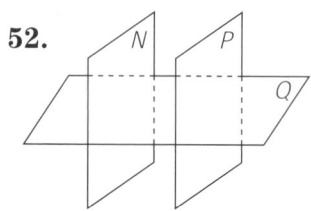

50.

51.

52.

53. 15 units
54. $13\frac{1}{3}$ units
55. 12 units
56. 37.5 units
57. all angles formed are right angles
58. all angles are right angles; $l \parallel n$

TEST PREP ANSWERS
Page 35

1. C
2. B
3. C
4. D
5. A
6. C
7. B
8. A
9. C
10. D

Name _____ Date _____

Angles and Their Relationships

Name the vertex and sides of the angle.

1.

2.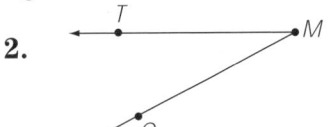

3.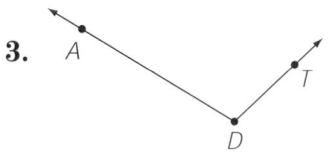

_____ _____ _____

Write two names for the angle.

4.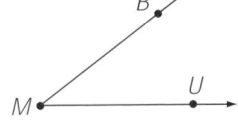

5.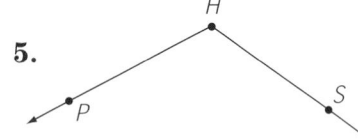

6.

_____ _____ _____

Write True or False. Use the diagram to answer exercises 10–12.

_____ **7.** If two angles are congruent, then their measures are equal.

_____ **8.** If two angles are congruent, then they are adjacent.

_____ **9.** If m∠A = m∠B then ∠A ≅ ∠B.

_____ **10.** ∠M ≅ ∠R.

_____ **11.** ∠1 is adjacent to ∠3.

_____ **12.** ∠RAM is adjacent to ∠RAT.

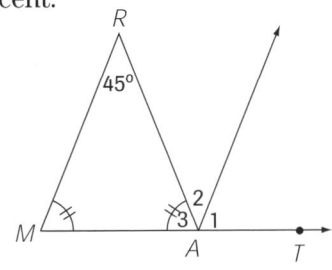

For exercises 13–18, refer to the protractor diagram.

13. m∠AOC = _____

14. m∠BOC = _____

15. m∠DOB = _____

16. m∠EOF = _____

17. m∠FOC = _____

18. m∠BOE = _____

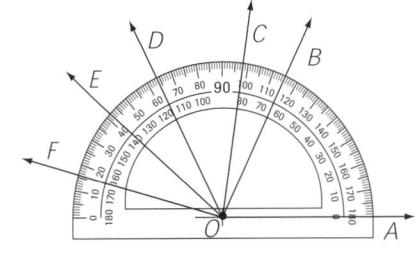

For exercises 19–22, refer to the diagram.

19. m∠CDA = 27°, m∠ADF = 38°; find m∠CDF _____

20. m∠CDA = 82°, m∠CDF = 130°; find m∠ADF _____

21. m∠CDA = 3x + 7°, m∠ADF = 5x − 2°, m∠CDF = 61°; find m∠ADF _____

22. m∠CDA = x + 4°, m∠ADF = 2x − 2°, m∠CDF = 26°; m∠CDA _____

Name _____ Date _____

066
Draw five points *A*, *B*, *C*, *D*, and *E* so that all three statements are true.

23. ∠*ADE* is a straight angle,
∠*ADC* is a right angle,
∠*BDE* is an acute angle.

24. *E* is in the interior of obtuse ∠*ABC*,
∠*DBE* is a right angle,
∠*ABD* is a straight angle.

068-069
Assume that ∠*A* and ∠*B* are complementary and ∠*B* and ∠*C* are supplementary.

25. If m∠*A* = 37°, then m∠*B* = _____ and m∠*C* = _____

26. If m∠*B* = 85°, then m∠*A* = _____ and m∠*C* = _____

27. If m∠*C* = 124°, then m∠*B* = _____ and m∠*A* = _____

Decide whether the statement is *Always*, *Sometimes*, or *Never True*.

28. If two angles are supplementary then they are adjacent. _____

29. If two angles are supplementary then one angle is acute and the other is obtuse.

_____

30. If two angles are complements of the same angle then they are congruent.

_____

31. If two angles are congruent and adjacent, then the two angles are supplementary.

_____

32. If two angles are right angles then they are complementary. _____

Solve.

33. Two angles are complementary and one angle has five times
the measure of the other. What are the measures of the angles? _____

34. Two angles are supplementary. One angle measures 30° less
than twice the other. What are the measures of the angles? _____

Name _____ Date _____

Find the values of the variables. You may wish to use a calculator.

070-072

35.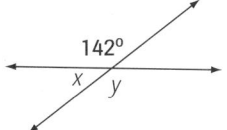

36.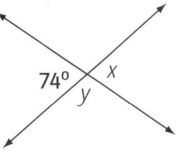

37.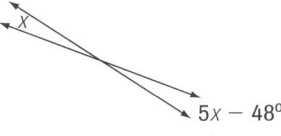

_____   _____   _____

38.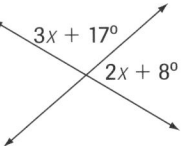

39.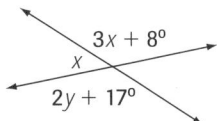

40.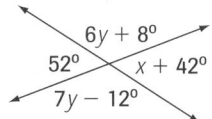

_____   _____   _____

Sketch the following if possible. If not possible, explain why.

41. A pair of vertical angles that are right angles.

42. A pair of non-adjacent supplementary angles that are both acute.

43. A pair of congruent angles that are a linear pair.

44. A pair of vertical angles that are complementary.

073

$\overrightarrow{AC}$ bisects $\angle BAD$. You may wish to use a calculator.

45. $m\angle CAD = 24°$; $m\angle BAC =$ _____, $m\angle BAD =$ _____

46. $m\angle BAD = 105°$; $m\angle BAC =$ _____, $m\angle CAD =$ _____

47. $m\angle CAD = 2x + 35°$; $m\angle BAC = 5x - 22°$, $x =$ _____, $m\angle BAD =$ _____

48. $m\angle CAD = 2x + 7°$; $m\angle BAC = 4x - 9°$, $x =$ _____, $m\angle BAD =$ _____

Name_____ Date _____

Use the diagram to solve for the segment length.

49. *AF* _____   **50.** *BF* _____

51. *BD* _____   **52.** *BE* _____

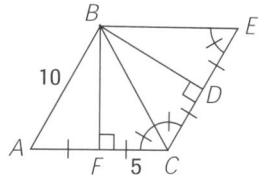

074

Complete the statement with *corresponding, alternate interior, alternate exterior, same side interior.*

53. $\angle 1$ and $\angle 10$ are ___?___ angles. _____

54. $\angle 7$ and $\angle 11$ are ___?___ angles. _____

55. $\angle 8$ and $\angle 2$ are ___?___ angles. _____

56. $\angle 10$ and $\angle 5$ are ___?___ angles. _____

57. $\angle 4$ and $\angle 9$ are ___?___ angles. _____

58. $\angle 12$ and $\angle 1$ are ___?___ angles. _____

075–080

59.

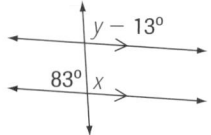

_____

60.

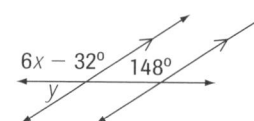

_____

61.

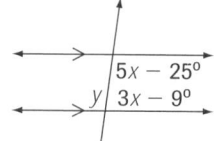

_____

62. **Given:** $\ell \parallel m$,; $\angle 1$ and $\angle 2$ are supplementary

     Prove: $p \parallel q$

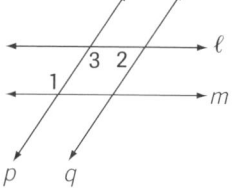

Statements   **Reasons**

_____

_____

_____

_____

_____

_____

_____

Name _____ Date _____

Angles and Their Relationships

Directions: Select the best answer to each question.

1. If two lines do not intersect and are not in the same plane, then they must be

    A. parallel

    B. skew

    C. coplanar

    D. perpendicular

2. Which of the following is not necessarily true if $\ell \perp m$.

    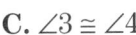

    A. $\angle 1 \cong \angle 2$

    B. $m\angle 2 = 90°$

    C. $\angle 3 \cong \angle 4$

    D. $m\angle 3 + m\angle 4 = 90°$

3. In the diagram find the value of x.

    A. 12

    B. 14

    C. 15

    D. cannot be determined

4. In the diagram, what are the values of x and y?

    A. $x = 47$, $y = 75$

    B. $x = 47$, $y = 74$

    C. $x = 75$, $y = 47$

    D. $x = 71$, $y = 51$

    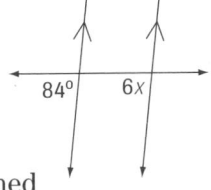

5. Given $\angle BAD$, and point C in the exterior of $\angle BAD$, if $m\angle BAC = 129°$ and $m\angle CAD = 51°$, then $\angle BAC$ and $\angle CAD$ are

    A. supplementary

    B. a linear pair

    C. supplementary and a linear pair

    D. cannot be determined

For exercises 6–8, choose the statement that is true about the diagram. In the diagram, $\angle 9$ is obtuse and $m\angle 5 = 37°$. • **MORE HELP** See 143

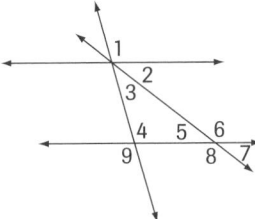

A. The quantity in column A is greater.

B. The quantity in column B is greater.

C. The two quantities are equal.

D. The relationship can't be determined from the given information.

	Column A	Column B
6.	$m\angle 3$	$m\angle 7$
7.	$m\angle 3 + m\angle 4 + m\angle 5$	$m\angle 6 + m\angle 8$
8.	$m\angle 6 + m\angle 5$	$m\angle 1 + m\angle 2$

9. C is in the interior of $\angle BOD$. B is in the interior of $\angle AOC$. Then, B is also in the interior of which angle?

    A. $\angle DOB$

    B. $\angle AOB$

    C. $\angle DOC$

    D. $\angle AOD$

PRACTICE ANSWERS
Page 37
1. B, $\overrightarrow{BR}$, $\overrightarrow{BJ}$
2. M, $\overrightarrow{MT}$, $\overrightarrow{MQ}$
3. D, $\overrightarrow{DA}$, $\overrightarrow{DT}$
4. any two: $\angle M$, $\angle BMU$, $\angle UMB$
5. any two: $\angle H$, $\angle PHS$, $\angle SHP$
6. any two: $\angle T$, $\angle MTA$, $\angle ATM$
7. true
8. false
9. true
10. false
11. false
12. true
13. $82°$
14. $17°$
15. $51°$
16. $26°$
17. $82°$
18. $73°$
19. $65°$
20. $48°$
21. $33°$
22. $12°$

Page 38
23. sample diagram:

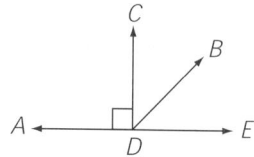

24. sample diagram:

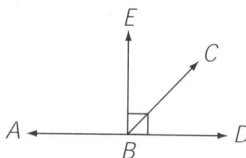

25. $53°$, $127°$
26. $5°$, $95°$
27. $56°$, $34°$
28. sometimes true
29. sometimes true
30. always true
31. sometimes true
32. never true
33. $15°$ and $75°$
34. $70°$ and $110°$

Page 39
35. $x = 38°$, $y = 142°$
36. $x = 74°$, $y = 106°$
37. $x = 12°$
38. $x = 31°$
39. $x = 43°$, $y = 60°$
40. $x = 10°$, $y = 20°$
41.

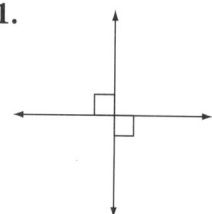

42. Not possible. If one $\angle$ is acute, then the other must be obtuse.
43.

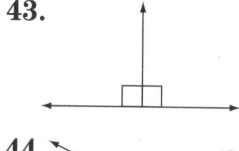

44.
45. $24°$, $48°$
46. $52.5°$, $52.5°$
47. $x = 19°$, $146°$
48. $x = 8°$, $46°$

Page 40
49. 5 units
50. $\sqrt{75}$ or $5\sqrt{3}$ units
51. $\sqrt{75}$ or $5\sqrt{3}$ units
52. 10 units
53. alternate interior
54. corresponding
55. alternate exterior
56. same side interior
57. alternate interior
58. corresponding
59. $x = 97°$, $y = 110°$
60. $x = 30°$, $y = 32°$
61. $x = 26.75°$, $y = 108.75°$
62.

	Statements	Reasons
❶	$l \parallel m$	Given
❷	$\angle 1$ and $\angle 2$ are supplementary	Given
❸	m$\angle 1$ + m$\angle 2$ = 180°	Def. of supp. $\angle$s
❹	$\angle 1 \cong \angle 3$	Alt. Int. $\angle$s Theorem (T027)
❺	m$\angle 1$ = m$\angle 3$	Def. of $\cong$ $\angle$s
❻	m$\angle 3$ + m$\angle 2$ = 180°	Substitution
❼	$\angle 3$ and $\angle 2$ are supplementary	Def. of supp. $\angle$s
❽	$p \parallel q$	Same Side Int. $\angle$s Theorem (T031)

TEST PREP ANSWERS
Page 41
1. B
2. C
3. B
4. A
5. A
6. D
7. B
8. A
9. D

Name _____ Date _____

Graph Theory

Which two-dimensional figure is not topologically equivalent to the others? Circle the answer.

1. **A.** 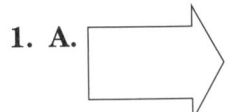   **B.**    **C.** 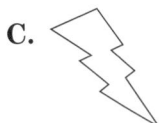   **D.**

Which three-dimensional figure is not topologically equivalent to the others? Circle the answer.

2. **A.**    **B.** 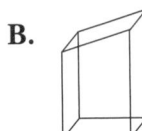   **C.** 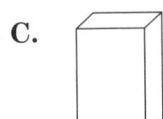   **D.**

State the number of nodes and edges for each network. State whether the network is connected (or closed).

3. 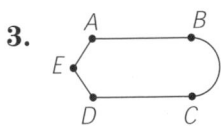   4. 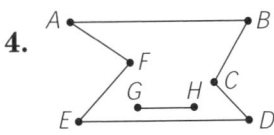   5.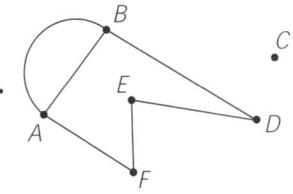

_____   _____   _____

Determine the degree of each node.

6. 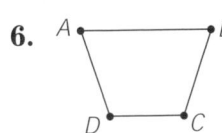   7. 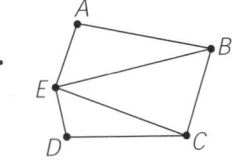   8.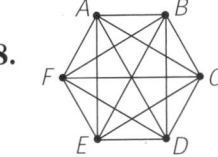

_____   _____   _____

Decide whether each network is traceable. If it is, list a sequence of segments that demonstrates traceability. If it is not, explain why.

9. 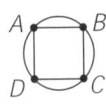   10. 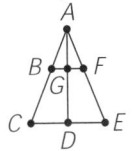   11.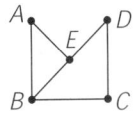

_____   _____   _____

12. 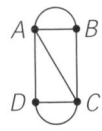   13. 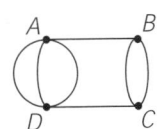   14.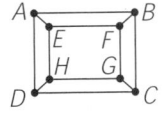

_____   _____   _____

If it is possible, draw a network that satisfies the following conditions.

15. The network is both connected and traceable.

16. The network is connected, but not traceable.

17. The network is not connected and not traceable.

Name_____ Date_____

Graph Theory

Directions: Select the best answer to each question.

1. Which two-dimensional figure is not topologically equivalent to the others?

   A.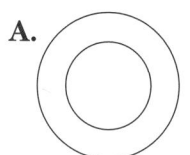

   C.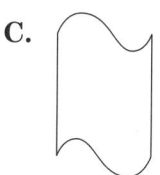

   B.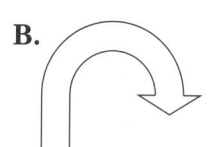

   D.

2. Which three-dimensional figure is not topologically equivalent to the others?

   A.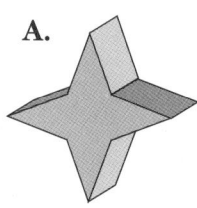

   C.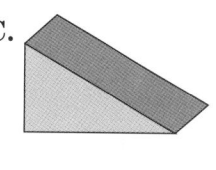

   B.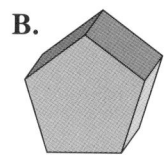

   D.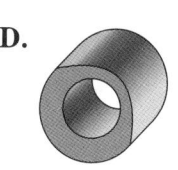

3. Identify the numbers of nodes and edges for the network shown.

   A. 5 nodes, 6 edges

   B. 4 nodes, 7 edges

   C. 4 nodes, 5 edges

   D. 7 nodes, 4 edges

For exercises 4 and 5, refer to the diagram.

4. In the network, node *D* has degree

   A. 1

   B. 2

   C. 3

   D. 4

   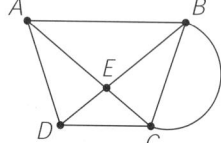

5. The network is

   A. not connected but traceable.

   B. not connected and not traceable.

   C. connected and not traceable.

   D. connected and traceable.

6. Which network is *not* traceable?

   A.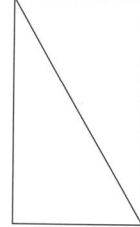

   C.

   B.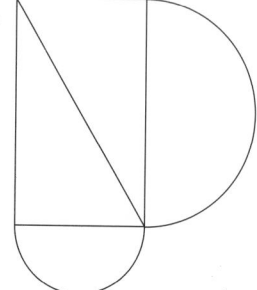

   D.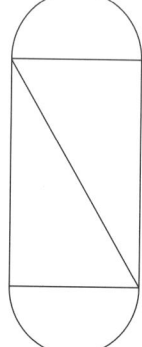

PRACTICE ANSWERS
Page 43

1. B

2. D

3. 5 nodes, 5 edges, connected

4. 8 nodes, 7 edges, not connected

5. 6 nodes, 7 edges, not connected

6. each node is degree 2

7. A: 2, B: 3, C: 3, D: 2, E: 4

8. each node is degree 5

9. traceable; possible answer: A → B → C → D → A → D → C → B → A

10. not traceable; it has 4 odd nodes

11. traceable; possible answer: E → A → B → C → D → E → B

12. traceable; possible answer: B → C → D → A → B → A → C → D

13. traceable; possible answer: B → A → D → A → D → C → B → C

14. not traceable; all nodes are odd

15. possible answer

16. possible answer

17. possible answer

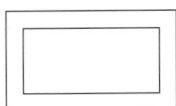

TEST PREP ANSWERS
Page 44

1. A

2. D

3. B

4. C

5. D

6. B

Take Flight

OBJECTIVES
- Identify basic geometric elements
- Measure using a ruler and protractor
- Develop reasoning skills

MATERIALS
- Bird-Folding Directions (page 211)
- Patty paper or 6-inch paper squares
- Protractors
- Rulers

TIME
- 30–40 minutes

TEACHER NOTES
- Origami is a good motivator. In this activity students will need to identify many basic geometric elements before they do their paper folding.

- Demonstrate to students how they might mark a diagram to show that segments are congruent, or an angle is obtuse.

- The paper-folding may be a whole-class or small-group activity.

- Have extra patty paper available for students who need to start over.

EXTENSIONS
- After students have successfully folded a bird using patty paper, have them fold one using colored paper, wrapping paper, or traditional origami paper.

- Use the birds to decorate the classroom by making a mobile or hanging on a holiday tree.

ANSWERS
(Answers may vary. Samples are provided.)

1. lines are parallel, therefore alternate interior angles are congruent.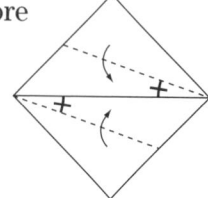

2. right angles; two coplanar lines perpendicular to the same line are parallel.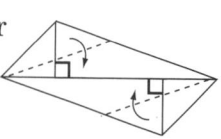

3. sum = 180°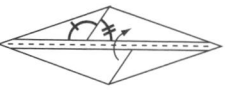

4. base angles of isosceles triangle or corresponding angles for parallel lines cut by a transversal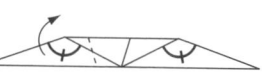

5. The angles marked measure about 160°.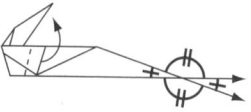

6. Vertical angles are congruent.

7. 2, 1, 1

8. The angle marked measures about 15°.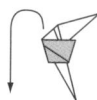

9. supplementary

10. Each marked segment measures about $\frac{1}{4}$ in. The sum of the measures is $\frac{1}{2}$ in.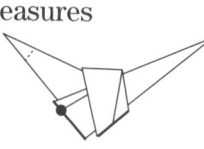

11. 180°

12. The angles marked measure about 55° and about 70°. Their sum is about 125°.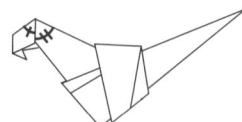

Name _____　　Date _____

Lines and Segments:
  054-056

Perpendicular Lines
  and Planes: 061

Angle Addition
  Postulate: 065

Classification of
  Angles: 066

Special Pairs of
  Angles: 067-080

Take Flight

Origami is the process of folding paper into shapes representing, for example, flowers and birds. Origami originated in Japan and has become a popular hobby for people around the world. It's fun, very visual, and with each fold, more geometry reveals itself!

Directions: You have been given a sheet that gives the visual directions for folding a bird. Before you fold, identify the following geometric concepts, shapes, or figures on the diagrams. Use labels or standard symbols to mark the diagrams.

1. In figure 1 mark a pair of alternate interior angles for the dotted lines. Are the angles congruent? Explain.

2. In figure 2 mark the segments perpendicular to the horizontal line segment. What type of angles are made by the perpendiculars? How do you know that the two perpendicular segments are parallel to one another?

3. In figure 3 mark a linear pair of angles. What is the sum of these angles?

4. In figure 4 mark a pair of acute angles. Explain why they are congruent.

5. In figure 5 mark two obtuse angles that appear to be congruent. Use a protractor to measure each.

6. In figure 6 extend a pair of segments to form two pairs of vertical angles. What is true about the measure of each pair?

7. In figure 7 shade the figure that appears to be a right trapezoid. How many right angles are in the figure? Obtuse angles? Acute angles?

8. In figure 8 mark the angle that appears to be most acute. Use a protractor to measure this angle.

9. In figure 9 shade the figure that appears to be an isosceles trapezoid. What is the relationship between one of the acute and one of the obtuse angles of this figure?

10. In figure 10 mark two collinear segments that share a common endpoint. Use a ruler to measure their lengths. What would the Segment Addition Postulate allow you to conclude?

11. In figure 11 mark a straight angle. What is the measure of this angle?

12. In figure 12 mark two adjacent angles that are not supplementary. Use a protractor to measure each angle. What would the Angle Addition Postulate allow you to conclude?

Now that you've answered the questions, get folding, and have a good flight!

Name _____ Date _____

Using the Coordinate Plane

087-088   Write *True* or *False*.

_____ **1.** The intersection of the x- and y-axes is called the origin.

_____ **2.** The coordinate plane is also called the Cartesian Plane.

_____ **3.** The x-coordinate of a point is called the ordinate.

_____ **4.** If a point lies in the second quadrant, then the x-coordinate is positive and the y-coordinate is negative.

_____ **5.** The Cartesian Plane is named after Jacques Cartier.

_____ **6.** The point ($^-2$, $^-6$) is located in the third quadrant.

_____ **7.** Any point on the y-axis has a y-coordinate of zero.

_____ **8.** The x-coordinate of the midpoint of a line segment is the mean of the x-coordinates of the endpoints.

_____ **9.** If a point has a negative x-coordinate and a positive y-coordinate, then it lies in the fourth quadrant.

089   For exercises 10–15, find the midpoint of $\overline{PQ}$.

10. $P(1, 2)$, $Q(1, 6)$ _____   **11.** $P(^-2, 3)$, $Q(6, 3)$ _____

12. $P(^-1, 6)$, $Q(0, ^-5)$ _____   **13.** $P(3, ^-2)$, $Q(8, 10)$ _____

14. $P(^-5, ^-6)$, $Q(^-3, 4)$ _____   **15.** $P(2a, 2b)$, $Q(^-4a, 6b)$ _____

The coordinates of one endpoint of $\overline{AB}$ and the coordinates of the midpoint, M, are given. For exercises 16–19, find the coordinates of the missing endpoint.

16. $A(^-3, 6)$, $M(^-3, 2)$ _____   **17.** $B(0, 5)$, $M(^-2, 5)$ _____

18. $A(5, ^-1)$, $M(^-3, 7)$ _____   **19.** $B(^-4, ^-3)$, $M(1, ^-7)$ _____

For exercises 20–21, the endpoints of the diameter, $\overline{AB}$, of a circle are given. Find the coordinates of the center of the circle. • **MORE HELP** See 298

20. $A(^-4, 2)$, $B(6, ^-4)$ _____   **21.** $A(5, 5)$, $B(^-1, 7)$ _____

Name _____ Date _____

090

For exercises 22–27, find the length of $\overline{RS}$. You may wish to use a calculator.

22. $R(0, 0)$, $S(6, 0)$ _____

23. $R(5, 5)$, $S(5, 0)$ _____

24. $R(^-4, 2)$, $S(^-5, 4)$ _____

25. $R(^-1, 7)$, $S(^-2, 4)$ _____

26. $R(2, {}^-3)$, $S(^-1, {}^-1)$ _____

27. $R(a, b)$, $S(3a, b)$ _____

092

For exercises 28–29, find the distance from point P to line ℓ.

_____ **28.** $P(2, 4)$, ℓ: $x + y + 3 = 0$

_____ **29.** $P(5, {}^-1)$, ℓ: $2x - 3y - 2 = 0$

093

For exercises 30–31, the equations of two parallel lines are given. Find the distance between the lines.

_____ **30.** ℓ_1: $x - y + 5 = 0$, ℓ_2: $x - y - 3 = 0$

_____ **31.** ℓ_1: $3x + y - 1 = 0$, ℓ_2: $3x + y + 6 = 0$

087-093

_____ **32.** Find the radius of a circle that passes through $(^-6, {}^-8)$ and has its center at the origin.

_____ **33.** A circle whose center is $(5, 4)$ is tangent to the x-axis. Find the coordinates of the point of tangency. • **MORE HELP** See 305

_____ **34.** Find the perimeter of the triangle with vertices $A(0, 0)$, $B(0, 5)$, and $C(12, 0)$. • **MORE HELP** See 170

_____ **35.** $\triangle PQR$ has coordinates $P(^-2, 0)$, $Q(4, 0)$, $R(1, 3)$. Find the length of the altitude from R to $\overline{PQ}$. • **MORE HELP** See 135

For exercises 36 and 37, the triangle has coordinates $A(4, 0)$, $B(12, 0)$ and $C(8, 6)$. • **MORE HELP** See 141

_____ **36.** Find the coordinates of the endpoints of the midsegment parallel to $\overline{BC}$.

_____ **37.** Find the length of the midsegment found in exercise 36.

_____ **38.** The vertices of $\triangle OMN$ are $O(0, 0)$, $M(4, 0)$, and $N(4, 6)$. Find the area of $\triangle OMN$. • **MORE HELP** See 181

Name_____ Date_____

Exercises 39–42 use the same diagram.

39. Find the length of each diagonal. _____

40. Find the midpoint of each diagonal. _____

41. What conclusion can you draw about the diagonals?

_____

42. Review your answers to exercises 39–41. What conclusion can you draw about the quadrilateral? • **MORE HELP** See 161, 162

_____

43. Find the coordinates of the fourth vertex of a rectangle that has three vertices located at ($^-$5, $^-$1), (4, $^-$1), and (4, 2). _____

Diagram for exercise 44.

44. Refer to the diagram. Find the length of the median from A to $\overline{BC}$. • **MORE HELP** See 136 _____

45. The vertices of $\overline{OP}$ are $O(0, 0)$ and $P(6, 2)$. Show that $Q(2, 4)$ lies on the perpendicular bisector of $\overline{OP}$. • **MORE HELP** See 056

_____

46. **Given:** $A(2, 1)$, $B(5, 5)$ and $C(5, 1)$ are the coordinates of the vertices of $\triangle ABC$

Prove: $\triangle ABC$ is a right triangle • **MORE HELP** See 152

_____

_____

_____

_____

_____

47. **Given:** Quadrilateral $OABC$ has vertices $O(0, 0)$, $A(2, 6)$, $B(9, 9)$, and $C(7, 3)$

Prove: $OABC$ is a parallelogram • **MORE HELP** See 158

_____

_____

_____

_____

_____

Name _____ Date _____

Using the Coordinate Plane

Directions: Write T or F, or circle the appropriate letter. You may wish to use a calculator for some exercises.

For exercises 1–9, decide whether the statement is true or false.

_____ 1. If $x > 0$ and $y < 0$, then the point (x, y) lies in the second quadrant.

_____ 2. The x-coordinate of a point is also called the abscissa.

_____ 3. In the third quadrant both coordinates are negative.

_____ 4. Rene Descartes helped to develop coordinate geometry.

_____ 5. The distance between two points on a horizontal line equals the absolute value of the difference between the y-coordinates.

_____ 6. All points on the x-axis have an ordinate of zero.

_____ 7. $a^2 - b^2$ is the distance of the point (a, b) from the origin.

_____ 8. $\left(\frac{a}{2}, \frac{b}{2}\right)$ are the coordinates of the midpoint of the segment joining the point (a, b) to the origin.

9. The distance between $(6, 2)$ and $(^-3, 4)$ is about
   A. 9.2 units   B. 3.6 units   C. 10.8 units

10. The midpoint of $\overline{PQ}$ with endpoints $P(^-1, ^-3)$ and $Q(5, 7)$ is
    A. $(^-3, ^-2)$ B. $(3, 2)$ C. $(2, 2)$

11. The perimeter of $\triangle MNO$ with vertices $M(^-6, 0)$, $N(^-6, 8)$, and $O(0, 0)$ is
    A. $\sqrt{24}$ units
    B. 24 units
    C. $24\sqrt{2}$ units

12. The diameter of a circle has endpoints $A(5, 5)$ and $B(^-3, ^-2)$. The coordinates of the center are
    A. $(4, 3.5)$ B. $(1, 1.5)$ C. $(3.5, 3.5)$

13. $ABCD$ is a parallelogram. The vertices are $A(7, ^-2)$, $B(3, 1)$, $C(6, 3)$, and $D(10, 0)$. The point of intersection of the diagonals is
    A. $(6.5, 0.5)$ B. $(4.5, 2)$ C. $(8, 1.5)$

14. A circle with center at the origin passes through the point $(^-5, 12)$. Which of the following points does NOT lie on the circle?
    A. $(^-12, ^-5)$ B. $(13, 0)$ C. $(5, 13)$

15. $\triangle ABC$ is isosceles with vertices $A(^-1, 2)$, $B(5, 2)$, and $C(2, 6)$. The length of the congruent sides is
    A. 4 units   B. 5 units   C. 6 units

16. If a circle has center $(^-4, 5)$ and is tangent to the y-axis, the point of tangency is
    A. $(0, 5)$ B. $(5, 0)$ C. $(^-4, 0)$

For exercises 17–22, use this diagram of an isosceles trapezoid.

17. The length of the congruent sides is
    A. $2\sqrt{6}$ units   B. 5 units   C. $\sqrt{26}$ units

18. The midpoint of $\overline{DC}$ is
    A. $(2.5, 4.5)$ B. $(2, 4)$ C. $(2.5, 4.75)$

19. The midpoint of $\overline{AB}$ is
    A. $(2.5, ^-0.5)$ B. $(2 , ^-4)$ C. $(2.5, ^-4.75)$

20. The length of the longer base is
    A. 4 units   B. 6 units   C. 8 units

21. The length of the midsegment is
    A. 3 units   B. 4 units   C. 5 units

22. The length of a diagonal is
    A. 5 units   B. $5\sqrt{3}$ units   C. $5\sqrt{2}$ units

PRACTICE ANSWERS
Page 48
1. true
2. true
3. false
4. false
5. false
6. true
7. false
8. true
9. false
10. (1, 4)
11. (2, 3)
12. $(\frac{-1}{2}, \frac{1}{2})$
13. (5.5, 4)
14. ($^-$4, $^-$1)
15. ($^-$a, 4b)
16. ($^-$3, $^-$2)
17. ($^-$4, 5)
18. ($^-$11, 15)
19. (6, $^-$11)
20. (1, $^-$1)
21. (2, 6)

Page 49
22. 6
23. 5 units
24. $\sqrt{5}$ or about 2.24 units
25. $\sqrt{10}$ or about 3.16 units
26. $\sqrt{13}$ or about 3.61 units
27. |2a| or about 2 |a| units
28. $\frac{9\sqrt{2}}{2}$ or about 6.36 units
29. $\frac{11\sqrt{13}}{13}$ or about 3.05 units
30. $4\sqrt{2}$ or about 5.66 units
31. $\frac{7\sqrt{10}}{10}$ or about 2.21 units
32. 10 units
33. (5, 0)
34. 30 units
35. 3 units

36. (6, 3); (8, 0)
37. $\sqrt{13}$ or about 3.61 units
38. 12 units^2

Page 50
39. $AC = 2\sqrt{17}$ units,
$BD = 2\sqrt{17}$ units
40. ($^-$1, 6); ($^-$1, 6)
41. The diagonals are congruent and bisect each other.
42. *ABCD* is a square.
43. ($^-$5, 2)
44. $3\sqrt{10}$ units
45. $OQ = \sqrt{4 + 16} = \sqrt{20}$;
$OP = \sqrt{16 + 4} = \sqrt{20}$;
$OQ = OP$;
Therefore, *Q* lies on the perpendicular bisector of $\overline{OP}$.
46. Given that the coordinates of the vertices of $\triangle ABC$ are $A(2, 1)$, $B(5, 5)$ and $C(5, 1)$. Use the distance formula:
$AB = \sqrt{3^2 + 4^2} = 5$;
$AC = \sqrt{3^2 + 0} = 3$
and $BC = \sqrt{0 + 4^2} = 4$.
Since $5^2 = 3^2 + 4^2$, the converse of the Pythagorean theorem says that $\triangle ABC$ is a right $\triangle$.
47. Given that the coordinates of the vertices of quadrilateral *OABC* are $O(0, 0)$, $A(2, 6)$, $B(9, 9)$ and $C(7, 3)$. From the midpoint formula, the coordinates of the midpoint of OB are $(\frac{0 + 9}{2}, \frac{0 + 9}{2})$ or (4.5, 4.5) and the

coordinates of the midpoint of *AC* are $(\frac{2 + 7}{2}, \frac{6 + 3}{2})$ or (4.5, 4.5). Since the midpoints are the same, the diagonals of *OABC* bisect each other. If the diagonals of a quadrilateral bisect each other, then the quadrilateral is a parallelogram (T071). So *OABC* is a parallelogram. *Note*: This can also be proved by showing that opposite sides are congruent.

TEST PREP ANSWERS
Page 51
1. F
2. T
3. T
4. T
5. F
6. T
7. F
8. T
9. A
10. C
11. B
12. B
13. A
14. C
15. B
16. A
17. C
18. A
19. A
20. B
21. C
22. C

Name _____ Date _____

Straight Lines in the Coordinate Plane

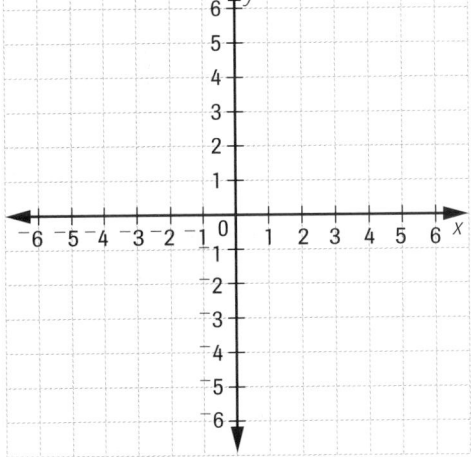

For exercises 1–4, find three solutions,
then graph the equation.

1. $3x - y + 6 = 0$ _____

2. $y = \frac{1}{2}x - 3$ _____

3. $y = 4$ _____

4. $2x + y = 0$ _____

For exercises 5–10, find the slope of the line
determined by the given pair of points.

5. $(0, 0), (5, {}^-6)$ _____

6. $(2, 2), (2, 5)$ _____

7. $(1, {}^-1), (3, 4)$ _____

8. $(3, {}^-1), (5, {}^-1)$ _____

9. $(10, {}^-4), (5, {}^-5)$ _____

10. $(a, b), ({}^-2a, 3b)$ _____

For exercises 11–16, write the letter of the proper description of the slope of the line.

A positive **B** negative **C** zero **D** undefined

11.

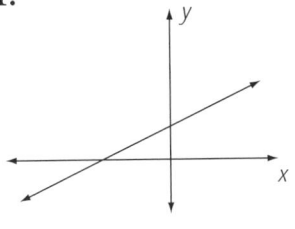

_____

12.

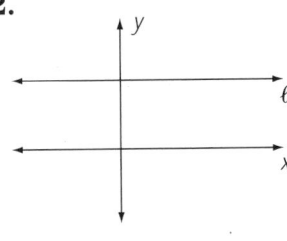

_____

13.

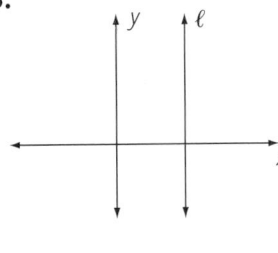

_____

14.

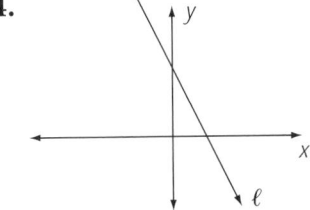

_____

15.

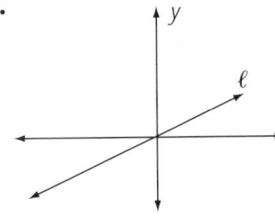

_____

16.

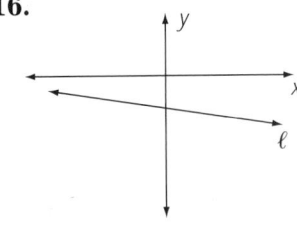

_____

096

099

101

Name_____ Date_____

102, 106

For exercises 17–22, find the slope and write the equation of the line.

17.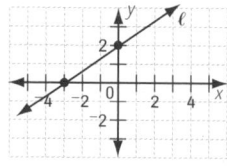

18.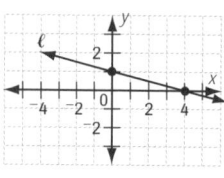

19.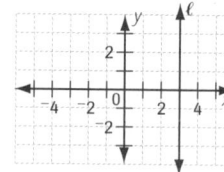

_____

_____

_____

29.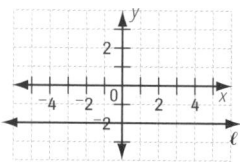

21.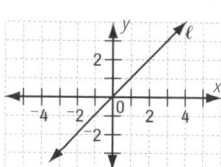

22.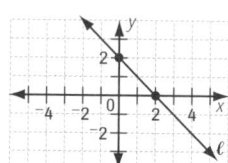

_____

_____

_____

106

For exercises 23–26, find the slope and y-intercept, then graph the equation.

23. $y = x - 2$ _____

24. $y = \frac{-3}{2}x + 4$ _____

25. $x = {}^-2$ _____

26. $x - 4y = 0$ _____

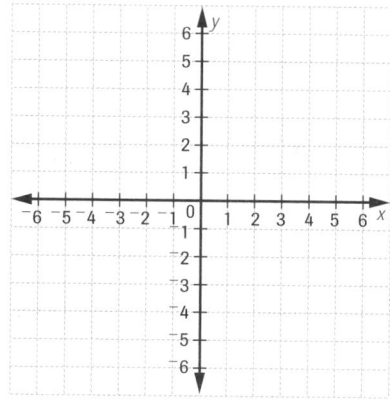

For exercises 27–28, find the x- and y-intercepts. Write your answers as ordered pairs. Graph.

27. $5x + 3y - 15 = 0$ _____

28. $2x - 5y = 10$ _____

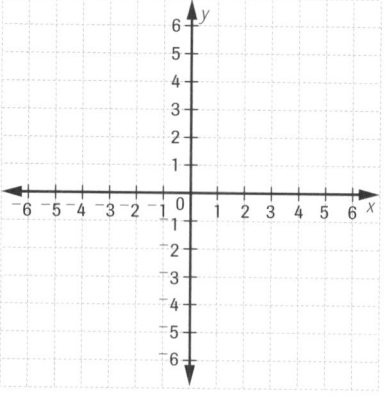

097, 107

For each system of equations in exercises 29–31:
A. State whether the graphs of the lines are *parallel*, *intersecting*, or *collinear*.
B. State whether the systems have *one solution*, *no solution*, or *infinitely many solutions*.

29. $y = x + 4$
$y = x - 5$ _____

30. $2x + y = 6$
$x - y = 6$ _____

31. $x + 2y = 2$
$3x + 6y = 6$ _____

Name _____ Date _____

For exercises 32–39, use this diagram.

32. Find the slope of the perpendicular bisector of $\overline{PQ}$._____

33. Find the midpoint of $\overline{PQ}$. _____

34. Find the equation of the perpendicular bisector of $\overline{PQ}$. _____

35. Find the equation of the altitude from R to $\overline{PQ}$. • **MORE HELP** See 135.

_____

36. Find the equation of the median from R to $\overline{PQ}$. • **MORE HELP** See 136. _____

37. Find the slope of the altitude from Q to $\overline{PR}$. _____

38. Find the equation of the line through R and parallel to the x-axis. _____

39. Find the equation of the line through Q and parallel to the y-axis. _____

40. A circle has center at the origin. Find the equation of the line tangent to the circle at $(3, 4)$.

   • **MORE HELP** See 306 _____

41. A car rental company charges a flat rate of $150 plus $0.15 per mile. If x is the number of miles driven by a customer and y is the total cost to rent the car, write the linear equation relating the total cost to the number of miles driven.

   _____

42. A manufacturer of t-shirts has fixed costs (such as rent, insurance, salaries) of $2500 per month. The cost for producing each t-shirt is $5.50. If x is the cost of producing one shirt, then write a function relating total cost to number of shirts produced in one month. If the company produced 1000 t-shirts this month, what is their total cost for the month?

   _____

43. **Given:** Quadrilateral with vertices $A(0, 2)$, $B(4,4)$, $C(9, 0)$, and $D(5, {}^{-}2)$
   Prove: $ABCD$ is a parallelogram

   _____

   _____

   _____

   _____

   _____

   _____

   _____

Name _____ Date _____

105-108

For exercises 44–50, graph the line determined by the given information. You will need graph paper.

44. The point $(2, {}^-1)$ lies on the line and the slope is $\frac{1}{3}$.

45. The point $(4, 5)$ lies on the line and the slope is $^-2$.

46. The x-intercept is 5 and the slope is 1.

47. The line passes through the point $({}^-2, 3)$ and is parallel to the x-axis.

48. The line contains the point $(3, 5)$ and has an undefined slope.

49. The y-intercept is $^-1$ and the line is parallel to $y = {}^-3x + 6$.

50. The line passes through the origin and is perpendicular to $y = 3x - 1$.

For exercises 51–59, write the equation of the line determined by the given information.

51. The line has y-intercept of $^-2$ and the slope is 3. _____

52. The line has a slope of $\frac{-1}{2}$ and a y-intercept of 3. _____

53. The line contains the points $(0, 1)$ and $({}^-5, 6)$. _____

54. The line contains the origin and the point $(3, {}^-4)$. _____

55. The line contains the origin and is parallel to $y = \frac{1}{2}x - 6$. _____

56. The line contains the point $(1, 2)$ and is parallel to the y-axis. _____

57. The line has a y-intercept of 8 and is perpendicular to $y = \frac{1}{2}x - 1$. _____

58. The line has an x-intercept of 2 and a y-intercept of 3. _____

59. The line contains the point $(2, 6)$ and is perpendicular to the y-axis. _____

For exercises 60–61, find k.

60. Find k so that the slope of $\overline{AB}$ will be 2. $A({}^-1, 2)$, $B(4, k)$. _____

61. Find k so that these points are collinear: $A(0, 0)$, $B(-8, {}^-2)$, $C(4, k)$ _____

108

62. **Given:** $\triangle ABC$ has vertices $A(0, 0)$, $B({}^-6, {}^-2)$, $C({}^-5, {}^-5)$

Prove: $\triangle ABC$ is a right triangle

_____

_____

_____

_____

_____

_____

_____

Name _____ Date _____

Straight Lines in the Coordinate Plane

Directions: Write T or F, or circle the letter of the correct answer.

For exercises 1–10, decide whether the statement is true or false.

_____ 1. The slope of $ax + by + c = 0$ is a.

_____ 2. The y-intercept of $ax + by + c = 0$ is $\frac{-c}{a}$.

_____ 3. If two lines are perpendicular, then the product of their slopes is one.

_____ 4. The line $ax + by = 0$ passes through the origin.

_____ 5. A vertical line has a slope of zero.

_____ 6. If two linear equations are multiples of each other, then the graphs are collinear.

_____ 7. If a system of linear equations has more than one solution then their graphs are collinear.

_____ 8. If two equations are given in $y = mx + b$ form, $m_1 = m_2$, and $b_1 \neq b_2$, then the lines are parallel.

_____ 9. The angle of inclination is the angle the line makes with the positive y-axis.

_____ 10. Any equation of the form $y = $ constant is the equation of a vertical line.

For exercises 11–21, choose the best answer.

11. If one line has a positive slope and a second line has a negative slope, then the graphs of the lines are
  A. parallel
  B. perpendicular
  C. intersecting

12. If a system of equations has no solution, then the lines are
  A. parallel   B. intersecting
  C. collinear

13. How many solutions does the following system have?
  $\frac{2}{3}x + y = 5$
  $2x + 3y = 15$
  A. None   B. one
  C. infinitely many

14. Which of the following is NOT a solution of $2x - 7y = 9$?
  A. $(0, \frac{-9}{7})$ B. $(\frac{9}{2}, 0)$ C. $(1, 1)$

15. The slope of the line $3x - 5y = 8$ is
  A. $\frac{3}{5}$ B. $\frac{-5}{3}$ C. 3

16. The equation of the line through $(^-7, 2)$ with slope $^-2$ is
  A. $y + 2 = {}^-2(x + 2)$
  B. $y - 2 = {}^-2(x + 7)$
  C. $x + 7 = {}^-2(y - 2)$

17. The slope of a line perpendicular to $6x - 5y = 1$ is
  A. $\frac{-5}{6}$ B. $\frac{-6}{5}$ C. $\frac{6}{5}$

18. **Given:** $R(4, {}^-2)$ and $S(k, 3)$
  Find: k so that the slope of $\overline{RS} = 5$
  A. 4 B. 5 C. $^-5$

19. If a line has an x-intercept of 2 and a y-intercept of 4, then the equation of the line is
  A. $y = {}^-2x + 2$ B. $y = 2x + 4$
  C. $y = {}^-2x + 4$

20. If a line contains $(^-2, 3)$ and is parallel to the x-axis, then its equation is
  A. $y = 3$ B. $x = 3$ C. $y = {}^-2$

21. An equation whose graph is a line parallel to $x - 2y = 4$ is
  A. $2x - 4y = 8$ B. $y = \frac{1}{2}x - 2$
  C. $y - 1 = \frac{1}{2}(x + 6)$

PRACTICE ANSWERS
Page 53

1. sample solutions (0, 6), ($^-$2, 0), (1, 9)

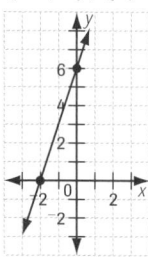

2. sample solutions (0, $^-$3), (6, 0), (1, $^-$2.5)

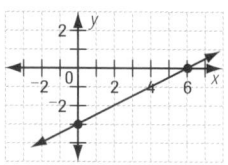

3. sample solutions (0, 4), (1, 4), (2, 4)

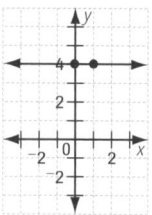

4. sample solutions (0, 0), (1, $^-$2), (2, $^-$4)

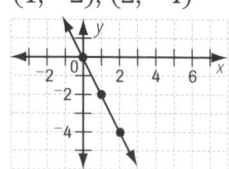

5. $m = \frac{-6}{5}$
6. $m =$ undefined
7. $m = \frac{5}{2}$
8. $m = 0$
9. $m = \frac{1}{5}$
10. $m = \frac{2b}{-3a}$
11. A
12. C
13. D
14. B
15. A
16. B

Page 54

17. $m = \frac{2}{3}, y = \frac{2}{3}x + 2$
18. $m = \frac{-1}{4}, y = \frac{-1}{4}x + 1$
19. $m =$ undefined, $x = 3$
20. $m = 0, y = {}^-2$
21. $m = 1, y = x$
22. $m = {}^-1, y = {}^-x + 2$
23. $m = 1, b = {}^-2$

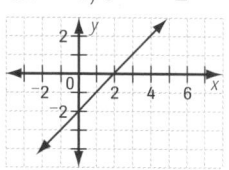

24. $m = \frac{-3}{2}, b = 4$

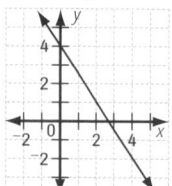

25. $m =$ undefined, $b =$ none

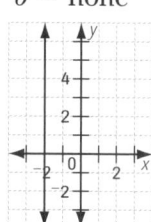

26. $m = \frac{1}{4}, b = 0$

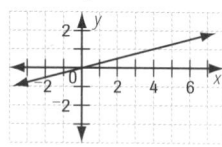

27. (3, 0), (0, 5)

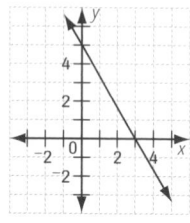

28. (5, 0), (0, $^-$2)

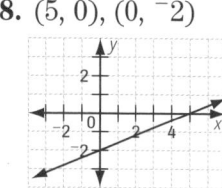

29. A: parallel, B: no solution
30. A: intersecting, B: one solution
31. A: collinear, B: infinitely many solutions

Page 55

32. undefined
33. (3, 0)
34. $x = 3$
35. $x = 2$
36. $y = {}^-5x + 15$
37. $\frac{-2}{5}$
38. $y = 5$
39. $x = 6$
40. $y = \frac{-3}{4}x + \frac{25}{4}$
41. $y = 0.15x + 150$
42. $y = 5.50x + 2500$; cost = \$8000.00
43. Given that the vertices of quadrilateral $ABCD$ are $A(0, 2)$, $B(4, 4)$, $C(9, 0)$ and $D(5, {}^-2)$. By the slope formula, $m_{AB} = \frac{1}{2}$, $m_{CD} = \frac{1}{2}$ and $m_{BC} = \frac{4}{-5}$, $m_{AD} = \frac{4}{-5}$. So $\overline{AB} \parallel \overline{CD}$ and $\overline{BC} \parallel \overline{AD}$, because if slopes are equal, lines are $\parallel$. Therefore by the definition of parallelogram, quadrilateral $ABCD$ is a parallelogram.

Page 56
(see page 213 for answers)

TEST PREP ANSWERS
Page 57
(see page 213 for answers)

Name _____ Date _____

Curves in the Coordinate Plane

For exercises 1–6, $y = ax^2 + bx + c$. Write the letter of the appropriate graph next to each statement.

110-111

A.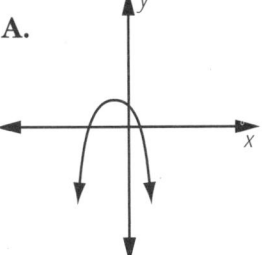

B.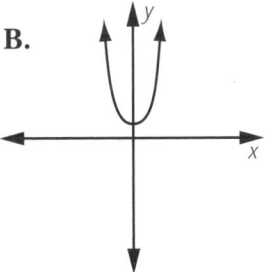

C.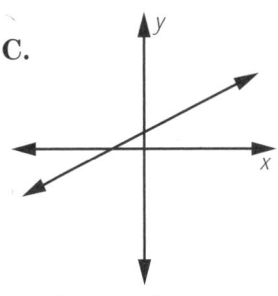

1. $a > 0$ ____

2. $a < 0$ ____

3. $a = 0$ ____

4. No upper or lower bound ____

5. An upper bound ____

6. A lower bound ____

For exercises 7–12, use $y = {}^-x^2 - 2x + 3$. You will need graph paper.

112

7. Find the equation of the line of symmetry. _____

8. Give the coordinates of the vertex. _____

9. Find the y-intercept. _____

10. Find the reflection of the point $(0, 3)$ across the line of symmetry. _____

11. Find the two x-intercepts. _____

12. Sketch the graph of the parabola.

For exercises 13–16, use the equation of the circle: $(x - 1)^2 + (y + 2)^2 = 4$.

13. Find the coordinates of the center. _____

14. Find the coordinates of four points on the circle. _____

15. Find the length of the radius. _____

16. Sketch the graph of the circle.

17. Write the equation of a circle with its center at the origin and a radius of 4 units.

_____

18. Write the equation of a circle with its center at $(2, 3)$ and a radius of 5 units.

_____

19. Write the equation of a circle tangent to the y-axis with its center at $({}^-3, {}^-2)$.

• **MORE HELP** See 305 _____

Name _____ Date _____

116

For exercises 20–22, choose the mapping diagram that matches the statement.

A. 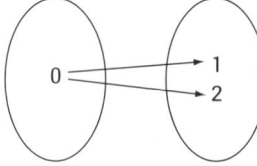 **B.** 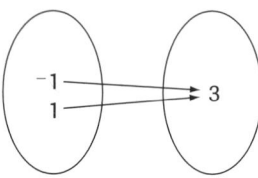 **C.**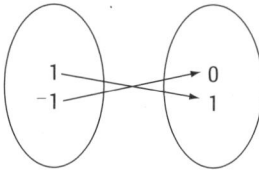

20. A one-to-one function _____

21. Not a function _____

22. A many-to-one function _____

For exercises 23–25, write the letter for the equation that matches the statement.

  A. $x^2 = y^2$ **B.** $x = y$ **C.** $x^2 = y$

23. Not a function _____

24. A many-to-one function _____

25. A one-to-one function _____

26. The weekly salary of a worker who earns $9.00 per hour at the Burger Palace depends upon the number of hours worked. Write an equation describing this relationship. Is this relation a function? Why or why not?

_____

_____

_____

For exercises 27–30, $h(t) = {}^-16t^2 + 48t$ describes the motion of a ball that is kicked from the ground into the air. The height (in feet) of the ball above the ground at time t (in seconds) is $h(t)$.

27. After how many seconds will the ball reach its maximum height? _____

28. What is the maximum height of the ball? _____

29. How many seconds after it's been kicked will the ball reach the ground again? _____

30. Sketch the graph of the parabola.

Name _____ Date _____

Curves in the Coordinate Plane

Directions: Write T or F, or circle the letter of the correct answer.

For exercises 1–11, decide whether the statement is true or false.

_____ 1. If $y = ax^2 + bx + c$ and a > 0, then the parabola opens upward.

_____ 2. The line of symmetry for $y = ax^2 + bx + c$ is $x = \frac{-b}{a}$.

_____ 3. The y-coordinate of the vertex of $y = {}^-2x^2 + 3x + 6$ is a lower bound of the parabola.

_____ 4. The graph of $y = x^2 + 6x + 3$ will never cross the x-axis.

_____ 5. The reflection of every point on a parabola across the line of symmetry is also a point on the parabola.

_____ 6. The circle with center (h, k) and radius r has equation $(x - h)^2 - (y - k)^2 = r^2$.

_____ 7. A unit circle is any circle with a radius of one unit and center at the origin.

_____ 8. In any function, the first coordinate is paired with exactly one second coordinate and the second coordinate is paired with exactly one first coordinate.

_____ 9. $y = ax^2 + bx + c$ is a one-to-one function.

_____ 10. $y = mx + b$ is a one-to-one function.

_____ 11. The vertical line test can be used to show that any circle is not a function.

For exercises 12–14, use $y = {}^-x^2 + 2x + 3$.

12. Find the equation of the line of symmetry.
    A. $x = {}^-1$ **B.** $y = 1$ **C.** $x = 1$

13. Find the coordinates of the vertex.
    A. $(1, 4)$ **B.** $({}^-1, 4)$ **C.** $(1, 6)$

14. Find the reflection of $(0,3)$ across the line of symmetry.
    A. $(0, {}^-2)$ **B.** $(2, 3)$ **C.** $({}^-2, 3)$

15. A parabola has a vertex at $({}^-2, 1)$. Find the equation of the line of symmetry.
    A. $x = {}^-2$ **B.** $x = 1$ **C.** $y = 0$

16. The point $({}^-4, 5)$ lies on the parabola defined in exercise 15. Find the point's reflection across the line of symmetry.
    A. $({}^-2, 5)$ **B.** $(0, 5)$ **C.** $(1, 5)$

For exercises 17–18, use this equation for a circle: $(x + 5)^2 + (y - 1)^2 = 25$.

17. The center is
    A. $(5, {}^-1)$ **B.** $({}^-5, 1)$ **C.** $({}^-5, {}^-1)$

18. The radius is
    A. 5 units   **B.** $\sqrt{5}$ units   **C.** 25 units

19. The equation of a circle with center $(2, {}^-2)$ and a radius of $2\sqrt{2}$ units is
    A. $(x - 2)^2 + (y - 2)^2 = 2\sqrt{2}$
    B. $(x - 2)^2 + (y + 2)^2 = 16$
    C. $(x - 2)^2 + (y + 2)^2 = 8$

20. If a circle has center $(3, {}^-3)$ and radius of 4 units, which of the following is NOT a point on the circle?
    A. $(7, {}^-3)$ **B.** $({}^-1, {}^-3)$ **C.** $(3, 0)$

21. The perimeter of a regular hexagon depends on the length of a side. This relationship is
    A. not a function
    B. a one-to-one function
    C. a many-to-one function

22. When a ball is thrown into the air, its height above the ground depends on the time in the air. This relationship is
    A. not a function
    B. a one-to-one function
    C. a many-to-one function

PRACTICE ANSWERS
Page 59

1. B
2. A
3. C
4. C
5. A
6. B
7. $x = {}^-1$
8. $({}^-1, 4)$
9. $y = 3$
10. $({}^-2, 3)$
11. $x = 1; x = {}^-3$
12.

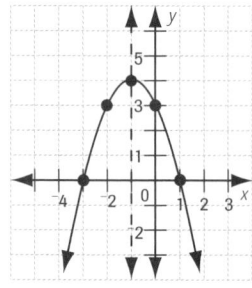

13. $(1, {}^-2)$
14. Sample answers: $(1, 0)$, $({}^-1, {}^-2), (1, {}^-4), (3, {}^-2)$
15. 2 units
16.

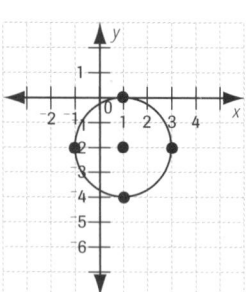

17. $x^2 + y^2 = 16$
18. $(x - 2)^2 + (y - 3)^2 = 25$
19. $(x + 3)^2 + (y + 2)^2 = 9$

Page 60

20. C
21. A
22. B
23. A
24. C
25. B
26. $S(h) = 9h$

    Yes, For each hour h, there is exactly one salary, S.

27. 1.5 sec
28. 36 ft
29. 3 sec
30.

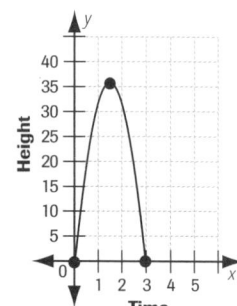

TEST PREP ANSWERS
Page 61

1. T
2. F
3. F
4. F
5. T
6. F
7. T
8. T
9. T
10. T
11. T
12. C
13. A
14. B
15. A
16. B
17. B
18. A
19. C
20. C
21. B
22. C

Name _____ Date _____

Polar Coordinates

For exercises 1–6, plot the points on the polar coordinate system. Label each point with the corresponding letter.

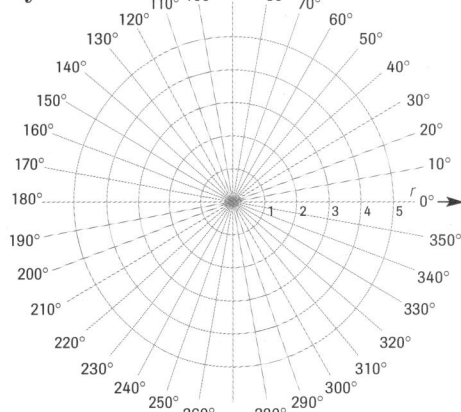

1. $A(4, 45°)$

2. $B(2, 120°)$

3. $C(1, 270°)$

4. $D(2, {}^{-}30°)$

5. $E(4, {}^{-}270°)$

6. $F({}^{-}3, 60°)$

For exercises 7–9, convert degree measure to radian measure.

7. $135°$ _____

8. $330°$ _____

9. $270°$ _____

For exercises 10–12, convert radian measure to degree measure.

10. $\frac{\pi}{6}$ _____

11. $\frac{2\pi}{3}$ _____

12. $\frac{{}^{-}5\pi}{4}$ _____

For exercises 13–15, convert polar coordinates to rectangular coordinates.

13. $(5, 90°)$ _____

14. $(3, 225°)$ _____

15. $(4, {}^{-}120°)$ _____

For exercises 16–18, convert rectangular coordinates to polar coordinates.

16. $(6, 6)$ _____

17. $({}^{-}2\sqrt{3}, 2)$ _____

18. $(4, {}^{-}4\sqrt{3})$ _____

For exercises 19–22, write the rectangular coordinates expressed as decimals. Then plot the coordinates. Label each point with the corresponding letter.

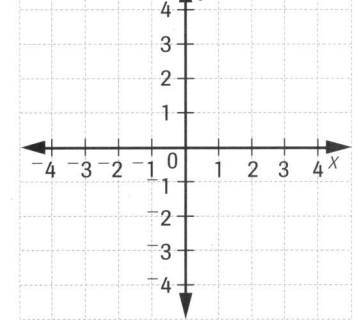

19. $A(3, 90°)$ _____

20. $B(2, 30°)$ _____

21. $C(4, {}^{-}45°)$ _____

22. $D(2, {}^{-}120°)$ _____

23. Which of the following coordinates do NOT plot the same point as $(3, 120°)$?

   A $(3, \frac{2\pi}{3})$ **C** $(3, {}^{-}240°)$ **E** $(3, \frac{\pi}{3})$ **G** $({}^{-}3, \frac{{}^{-}\pi}{3})$

   B $({}^{-}3, 60°)$ **D** $(3, {}^{-}60°)$ **F** $(3, \frac{{}^{-}\pi}{3})$ **H** $(3, \frac{4\pi}{3})$

_____

Name_____ Date_____

Polar Coordinates

Directions: Write T or F, or circle the appropriate letter.

For exercises 1–6, decide whether the statement is true or false.

_____ 1. The pole is a fixed ray in the polar coordinate plane.

_____ 2. If q is positive in the ordered pair (r, q), then the angle is generated by a clockwise rotation of a ray from the polar axis.

_____ 3. A radian is approximately 57°.

_____ 4. Polar coordinates are not unique.

_____ 5. To convert a measurement in degrees to one in radians, multiply by the conversion factor $\frac{180}{\pi}$.

_____ 6. A radian is a real number.

For exercises 7–10, use this polar coordinate graph.

7. The coordinates of P are
   A. $(60°, 2)$ **B.** $(2, 60°)$ **C.** $(2\sqrt{3}, 60°)$

8. The coordinates of Q are
   A. $(3, 300°)$ **B.** $(315°, 3)$ **C.** $(3, {}^-45°)$

9. The coordinates of R are
   A. $({}^-3, 150°)$ **B.** $(3, 510°)$ **C.** $(3, {}^-150°)$

10. The coordinates of S are
   A. $(90°, 1)$ **B.** $(1, {}^-90°)$**C.** $(1, 450°)$

11. 60° in radian measure is
   A. $\frac{\pi}{6}$ **B.** $\frac{\pi}{3}$ **C.** $\frac{1}{3}$

12. 315° in radian measure is
   A. $\frac{5\pi}{4}$ **B.** $\frac{\pi}{4}$ **C.** $\frac{7\pi}{4}$

13. 90° in radian measure is
   A. $\frac{3\pi}{2}$ **B.** $\frac{\pi}{2}$ **C.** π

14. ${}^-150°$ in radian measure is
   A. $\frac{5\pi}{6}$ **B.** $\frac{{}^-5\pi}{6}$ **C.** $\frac{{}^-7\pi}{6}$

15. $\frac{5\pi}{4}$ radians in degree measure is
   A. 225°   **B.** 315°   **C.** 135°

16. $\frac{4\pi}{3}$ radians in degree measure is
   A. 120°   **B.** 300°   **C.** 240°

17. $\frac{{}^-5\pi}{6}$ radians in degree measure is
   A. 150°   **B.** 210°   **C.** ${}^-210°$

18. π radians in degree measure is
   A. 180°   **B.** 90°   **C.** 360°

19. If (6, 30°) is converted to rectangular coordinates, the coordinates are
   A. $(3\sqrt{3}, 3)$ **B.** $(3, 3\sqrt{3})$ **C.** $(3\sqrt{2}, 3)$

20. The polar coordinates for $({}^-5, 5)$ are
   A. $({}^-5, 225°)$
   B. $(5\sqrt{2}, 135°)$
   C. $(5, 225°)$

21. The rectangular coordinates for (7, 180°) are
   A. $(0, {}^-7)$ **B.** $({}^-7, 0)$ **C.** $(0, 7)$

22. The polar coordinates of $({}^-4, 4\sqrt{3})$ are
   A. $(4\sqrt{2}, 135°)$
   B. $(8, 135°)$
   C. $(8, 120°)$

23. The point which does NOT have the same graph as (6, 120°) is
   A. $(6, {}^-240°)$ **B.** $(6, \frac{2\pi}{3})$ **C.** $(6, \frac{{}^-2\pi}{3})$

24. The point which does NOT have the same graph as $(4, \frac{{}^-\pi}{4})$ is
   A. $(4, {}^-405°)$ **B.** $(4, 315°)$ **C.** $(4, \frac{3\pi}{4})$

PRACTICE ANSWERS
Page 63

1–6.

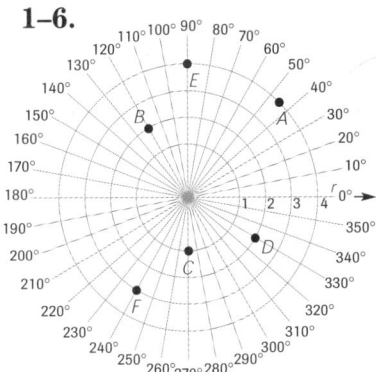

7. $\dfrac{3\pi}{4}$

8. $\dfrac{11\pi}{6}$

9. $\dfrac{3\pi}{2}$

10. $30°$

11. $120°$

12. $^-225°$

13. $(0, 5)$

14. $(\dfrac{^-3\sqrt{2}}{2}, \dfrac{^-3\sqrt{2}}{2})$

15. $(^-2, ^-2\sqrt{3})$

16. $(6\sqrt{2}, 45°)$

17. $(4, 150°)$

18. $(8, 300°)$

19. $A(0, 3)$

20. B(about 1.7, 1)

21. C(about 2.8, about $^-2.8$)

22. $D(^-1,$ about $^-1.7)$

23. B, D, E, F, H

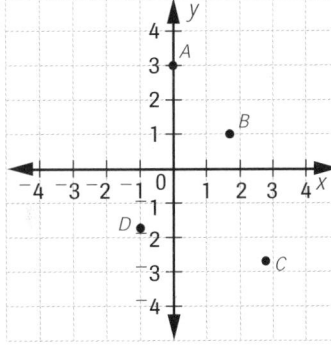

TEST PREP ANSWERS
Page 64

1. F

2. F

3. T

4. T

5. F

6. T

7. B

8. C

9. C

10. B

11. B

12. C

13. B

14. B

15. A

16. C

17. B

18. A

19. A

20. B

21. B

22. C

23. C

24. C

Name _____ Date _____

Graphing in Three Dimensions

121 For exercises 1–8, name the coordinates of the point.

1. the origin. _____

2. a point in the first octant. _____

3. a point on the *x*-axis. _____

4. a point on the *y*-axis. _____

5. a point on the *z*-axis. _____

6. a point in the *xy*-plane. _____

7. a point in the *xz*-plane. _____

8. a point in the *yz*-plane. _____

122 **9.** Using this three-dimensional grid, draw the coordinate box determined by the point $P(5, 2, 3)$ and write the coordinates of all eight vertices.

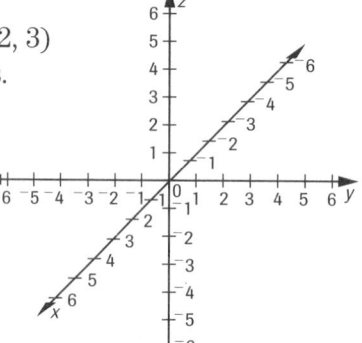

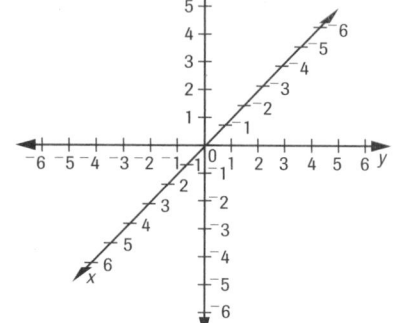

10. Using this three-dimensional grid, draw the coordinate box determined by the point $P(^-5, 4, ^-6)$ and write the coordinates of all eight vertices.

123 **11.** An airplane and a submarine are located on a grid in a three-dimensional coordinate system. The airplane has coordinates $(^-3, ^-5, 2)$ and the submarine has coordinates $(5, ^-6, ^-1)$. These coordinates are expressed in miles. At this instant in time, approximately how far apart are the airplane and the submarine? _____

For exercises 12–13, use $P(3, ^-2, 8)$ and $Q(^-5, 4, ^-6)$.

12. Find PQ. _____

124 **13.** Find the midpoint of $\overline{PQ}$. _____

125 **14.** Write the equation of the sphere with center $(1, ^-2, 3)$ and radius 5.

For exercises 15–16, use the equation of the sphere: $(x - 4)^2 + (y + 5)^2 + (z + 2)^2 = 64$.

15. Find the coordinates of the center. _____

16. Find the radius. _____

Name _____ Date _____

Graphing in Three Dimensions

Directions: Circle the appropriate letter.

For exercises 1–6, decide whether the statement is true or false.

1. P lies in the first octant if all coordinates are positive.

T   F

2. $P(x, y, z)$ lies on the x-axis if $y = z = 0$.

T   F

3. $P(x, y, z)$ lies on the yz-plane if $y = z = 0$.

T   F

4. The intersection of the xy- and yz-planes is the z-axis.

T   F

5. The intersection of the xy-, yz-, and xz-planes is the origin.

T   F

6. The only points which the yz- and xz-planes have in common lie on the z-axis.

T   F

For exercises 7–17, use this three-dimensional graph.

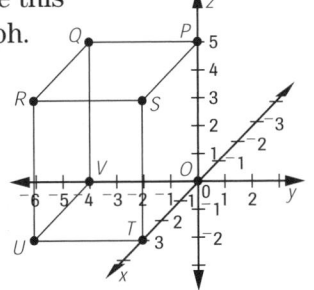

7. Find the coordinates of point O.
   A. $(4, 0, 0)$ **B.** $(0, 0, 4)$ **C.** $(0, 0, 0)$

8. Find the coordinates of point P.
   A. $(5, 0, 0)$ **B.** $(0, 0, 5)$ **C.** $(0, 5, 0)$

9. Find the coordinates of point Q.
   A. $(^-4, 0, 5)$ **B.** $(0, ^-4, 5)$ **C.** $(^-4, 5, 0)$

10. Find the coordinates of point R.
   A. $(3, ^-4, 5)$ **B.** $(^-4, 5, 3)$ **C.** $(^-4, 3, 5)$

11. Find the coordinates of point S.
   A. $(5, 3, 0)$ **B.** $(0, 3, 5)$ **C.** $(3, 0, 5)$

12. Find the coordinates of point T.
   A. $(3, 0, 0)$ **B.** $(0, 3, 0)$ **C.** $(0, 0, 3)$

13. Find the coordinates of point U.
   A. $(^-4, 3, 0)$ **B.** $(3, ^-4, 0)$ **C.** $(^-4, 0, 3)$

14. Find the coordinates of point V.
   A. $(0, ^-4, 0)$ **B.** $(^-4, 0, 0)$ **C.** $(0, 0, ^-4)$

15. The length of $\overline{RO}$ is
   A. 5 units
   B. $5\sqrt{2}$ units
   C. $\sqrt{51}$ units

16. The coordinates of the midpoint of $\overline{QT}$ are
   A. $(^-0.5, 0, 2.5)$
   B. $(0, ^-0.5, 2.5)$
   C. $(1.5, ^-2, 2.5)$

17. The coordinates of the midpoint of $\overline{UP}$ are
   A. $(^-0.5, 0, 2.5)$
   B. $(0, ^-0.5, 2.5)$
   C. $(1.5, ^-2, 2.5)$

18. The equation of the sphere with center $(1, ^-3, ^-4)$ and radius 4 is
   A. $(x - 1)^2 + (y + 3)^2 + (z + 4)^2 = 16$
   B. $(x - 1)^2 + (y + 3)^2 + (z + 4)^2 = 4$
   C. $(x + 1)^2 + (y - 3)^2 + (z - 4)^2 = 16$

For exercises 19–20, the equation of the sphere is: $(x + 3)^2 + (y + 6)^2 + (z - 2)^2 = 9$.

19. The center of the sphere is
   A. $(3, 6, ^-2)$
   B. $(^-3, ^-6, 2)$
   C. $(3, 6, 2)$

20. The radius of the sphere is
   A. 3 units   **B.** 9 units   **C.** $\sqrt{3}$ units

21. Which of the following is NOT the equation of a sphere?
   A. $x^2 + y^2 + (z - 1)^2 = 8$
   B. $(x - 35.2)^2 + (y - 26)^2 + (z + 7)^2 = 100$
   C. $(x + 1)^2 + (y + 6)^2 + (z - 5)^2 = ^-9$

PRACTICE ANSWERS
Page 66

1. $(0, 0, 0)$

For exercises 2–8, answers may vary. Samples are given.

2. $(1, 2, 3)$

3. $(1, 0, 0)$

4. $(0, 1, 0)$

5. $(0, 0, 1)$

6. $(1, 1, 0)$

7. $(1, 0, 1)$

8. $(0, 1, 1)$

9. Letter names for points will vary:
$A\ (0, 0, 0)$
$B\ (0, 2, 0)$
$C\ (0, 2, 3)$
$D\ (0, 0, 3)$
$E\ (5, 0, 3)$
$F\ (5, 0, 0)$
$G\ (5, 2, 0)$
$P\ (5, 2, 3)$

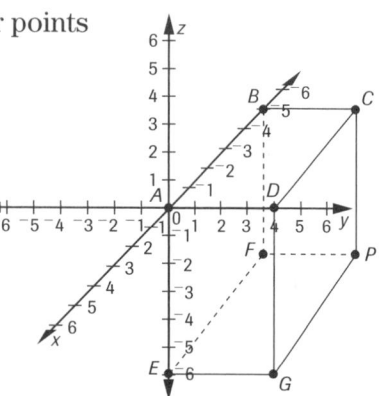

10. Letter names for points will vary:
$A\ (0, 0, 0)$
$B\ (^-5, 0, 0)$
$C\ (^-5, 4, 0)$
$D\ (0, 4, 0)$
$E\ (0, 0, ^-6)$
$F\ (^-5, 0, ^-6)$
$P\ (^-5, 4, ^-6)$
$G\ (0, 4, ^-6)$

11. $\sqrt{74}$ or about 8.6 mi

12. $\sqrt{296}$ or about 17.2 units

13. $(^-1, 1, 1)$

14. $(x - 1)^2 + (y + 2)^2 + (z - 3)^2 = 25$

15. $(4, ^-5, ^-2)$

16. 8 units

TEST PREP ANSWERS
Page 67

1. T
2. T
3. F
4. F
5. T
6. T
7. C
8. B
9. B
10. A
11. C
12. A
13. B
14. A
15. B
16. C
17. C
18. A
19. B
20. A
21. C

Name _____ Date _____

Locus of Points

126

For exercises 1–8, draw a diagram and write a description of the locus.

1. What is the locus of all points equidistant from the rays of ∠*ABC*?

   _____

2. As a bicycle with 26-inch wheels is pedaled down the street, what is
   the locus of the centers of the wheels?

   _____

3. What is the locus of all the points in space exactly two inches
   from a given line?

   _____

4. Describe the locus of all points equidistant from two concentric
   circles with radii four and six inches respectively?

   _____

5. Describe the locus of all points in a plane equidistant from two
   parallel lines eight inches apart.

   _____

6. A quarter is placed flat on a table and a nickel, also flat on the table and
   tangent to the quarter, is rolled around the circumference of the quarter,
   which remains stationary. What is the locus of the center of the nickel?

   _____

7. A state plans to build an airport equidistant from two major cities,
   A and *B*. What is the locus of points at which the airport can be built?
   • **MORE HELP** See 056

   _____

8. Two rangers are 10 miles apart. They are both receiving signals
   from a transmitter collar worn by a tiger. Each ranger can receive
   signals at distances up to six miles away. Describe the
   locus of the position of the tiger.

   _____

9. The Andersons are planning a trip to Stowe, Vermont.
   It will be possible for them to drive to any destination
   within 100 miles of Stowe. Describe the locus of the area
   they can visit.

   _____

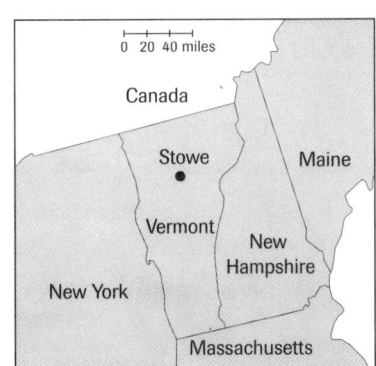

Name_____ Date_____

Locus of Points

Directions: Circle the letter of the best completion for the sentence.

1. The locus of points in a plane equidistant from two intersecting lines is
   A all points on a circle centered at the point of intersection of the lines.
   B all points on one line, the angle bisector of a pair of vertical angles.
   C all points on either of two lines which bisect the pairs of vertical angles.

2. In a plane, circles with five-centimeter diameters are tangent to a line. The locus of points of the centers of all such circles is
   A a line parallel to the given line, a distance of 2.5 cm away from the given line.
   B two lines parallel to the given line, each a distance of 2.5 cm away from the given line.
   C a circle, center on the given line, with diameter five cm.

3. The locus of the midpoints of all radii of a sphere, center O, with diameter 10 inches is
   A a circle, center O, with radius 5 inches.
   B a sphere, center O, with radius 5 inches.
   C a sphere, center O, with radius 2.5 inches.

4. In rhombus $ABCD$, the locus of points equidistant from $\overline{AB}$ and $\overline{BC}$ is
   A all the points on diagonal $\overline{BD}$.
   B all the points on a segment parallel to $\overline{AB}$ and intersecting the midpoints of $\overline{AD}$ and $\overline{BC}$.
   C all the points on diagonal $\overline{AC}$.

5. The locus of all the midpoints of all chords parallel to a given chord in a circle is
   A all the points on the diameter which is perpendicular to the given chord.
   B all the points on the diameter which is parallel to the given chord.
   C all the points on the radius which is perpendicular to the given chord.

6. In the plane of $\triangle ABC$, consider all of the circles containing both A and B. The locus of points of the centers of these circles is
   A all the points on the angle bisector of angle C.
   B all the points on the perpendicular bisector of $\overline{AB}$.
   C all the points on the median from C to $\overline{AB}$.

7. The locus of all points in space equidistant from two points, A and B, is
   A all the points on a plane which is the perpendicular bisector of $\overline{AB}$.
   B all the points on a line, the perpendicular bisector of $\overline{AB}$.
   C all of the points on a sphere centered at the midpoint of $\overline{AB}$.

8. Given kite $ABCD$, $AB = BC$. The locus of points within the kite and equidistant from A and C is
   A all points on diagonal $\overline{AC}$.
   B all points on the angle bisector of $\angle A$.
   C all points on diagonal $\overline{BD}$.

PRACTICE ANSWERS
Page 69

1. Locus is all points on the angle bisector of ∠*ABC*.

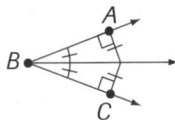

2. Locus is all points on a line ‖ to road, 13 inches above the road.

3. Locus is all points on a cylinder, radius 2 inches, with the line as its axis.

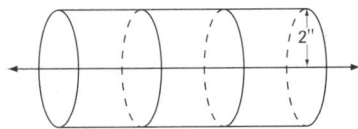

4. Locus is all points on a circle, center same as given circles, radius 5 inches.

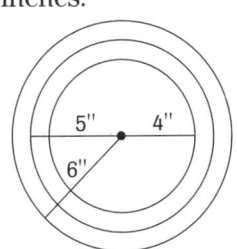

5. Locus is all points on a line parallel to given lines, 4 inches from each line.

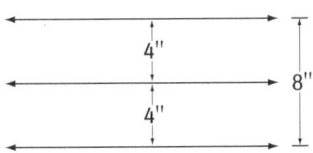

6. Locus is all points on a circle, center at quarter's center, radius = radius of quarter + radius of nickel.

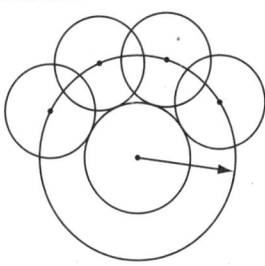

7. Locus is all points on perpendicular bisector of $\overline{AB}$.

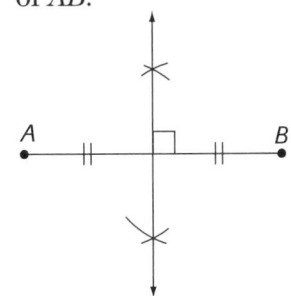

8. Locus is all points in or on the intersection of arcs shown.

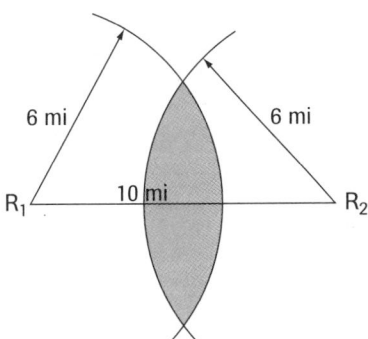

9. They can visit points in New York, Vermont, New Hampshire, Maine, Canada that are in or on a circle with radius 100 miles, centered at Stowe.

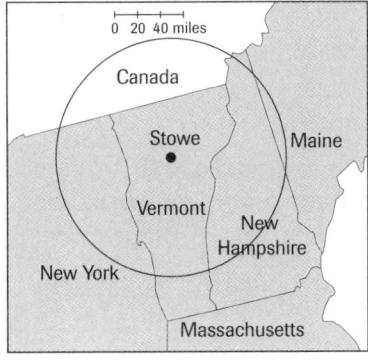

TEST PREP ANSWERS
Page 70

1. C
2. B
3. C
4. A
5. A
6. B
7. A
8. C

Symmetry in Motion

OBJECTIVES
- Plot ordered pairs
- Compute slope
- Compute distance between two points
- Compute midpoint

MATERIALS
- straightedge
- graph paper (p. 212)

TIME
- 30–40 minutes

TEACHER NOTES
- In this activity students will plot ordered pairs and connect them in order. The design is a model airplane drawn in perspective.

- Students may find it helpful to label the points using the capital letter as they are plotting.

- Since the plane is not drawn from a top view, the sides appear parallel but they are not. The wing and body appear perpendicular but they are not.

EXTENSIONS
- Students could determine the equations of any of the lines drawn in the diagram.

- Draw a template for an airplane that is symmetric about one of the axes.

- Have students design a template for an airplane or any other object. Make a list of the ordered pairs to be plotted and give them to classmates to plot.

ANSWERS

1.

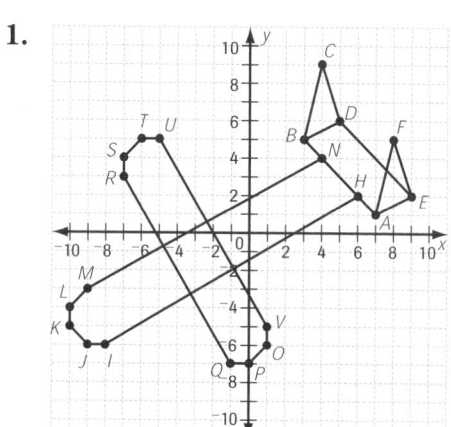

2. slope $\overline{HI} = \frac{4}{7}$ and slope $\overline{MN} = \frac{7}{13}$; sides are not parallel since their slopes are not equal

3. $AB = 4\sqrt{2}$, $CF = 4\sqrt{2}$, and $GD = 4\sqrt{2}$; lengths are the same

4. slope $\overline{UV} = \frac{^-5}{3}$ and slope $\overline{MN} = \frac{7}{13}$; they are not perpendicular since their products $\neq {^-}1$

5. midpoint $\overline{IM} = ({^-}8.5, {^-}4.5)$

Name _____ Date _____

Symmetry in Motion

Sarah owns a company that manufactures templates for building model airplanes. Her design specialists submit draft templates for new models on a coordinate grid. To see if the model airplane will actually have a chance to fly, answer the questions below.

Ordered Pairs and
  Locating Points:
  088

Midpoint: 089

Distance Between Two
  Points: 090

Finding Slope Given
  Two Points: 099

Slopes of Parallel
  Lines: 107

Slopes of
  Perpendicular Lines:
  108

1. Plot the ordered pairs and connect them in order.

Tailplane: $A(7, 1)$, $B(3, 5)$, $C(4, 9)$, $D(5, 6)$, $B(3, 5)$, $D(5, 6)$, $E(9, 2)$, $A(7, 1)$, $F(8, 5)$, $E(9, 2)$

Main Body: $H(6, 2)$, $I(^-8, ^-6)$, $J(^-9, ^-6)$, $K(^-10, ^-5)$, $L(^-10, ^-4)$, $M(^-9, ^-3)$, $N(4, 4)$

Main Wing: $O(1$ $^-6)$, $P(0, ^-7)$, $Q(^-1, ^-7)$, $R(^-7, 3)$, $S(^-7, 4)$, $T(^-6, 5)$, $U(^-5, 5)$, $V(1, ^-5)$, $O(1$ $^-6)$

2. Are the two sides, $\overline{HI}$ and $\overline{MN}$, of the main body parallel? Show your work.

_____

3. Is the length of the tailplane from side to side the same? Check A to B, C to F, and E to D. Show your work.

_____

4. Is the main wing perpendicular to the main body? Check $\overline{UV}$ and $\overline{MN}$. Show your work.

_____

5. A decal will be placed at the midpoint of $\overline{IM}$. Find its midpoint. Show your work.

_____

Name _____ Date _____

Attributes of Polygons

129

For exercises 1–3, label the polygon as concave or convex.

1.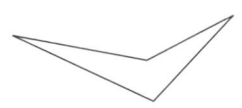

2.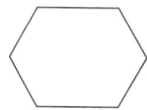

3.

_____   _____   _____

131

For exercises 4–6, find the sum of the measures of the interior angles of these polygons.

4. octagon _____

5. decagon _____

6. 13-gon _____

For exercises 7–8, find the value of x.

7.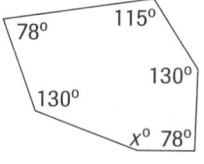

8.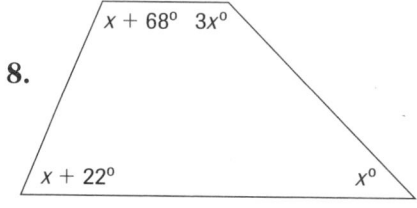

_____   _____

9. Each interior angle of a regular polygon is 157.5°. Find the number of sides. _____

10. The interior angles of a quadrilateral are in the ratio of 2:3:4:6. Find the measure of the largest angle. _____

132

For exercises 11–13, find the measure of one exterior angle of each regular polygon.

11. pentagon _____

12. nonagon _____

13. 30-gon _____

14. If each exterior angle of a regular convex polygon measures 72°, find the number of sides.

_____

15. Is there a regular polygon such that each exterior angle measures 75°? Explain.

_____

_____

_____

Name _____ Date _____

Attributes of Polygons

Directions: Fill in the letter of the best answer.

(1) Which polygon is concave (non-convex)?

  A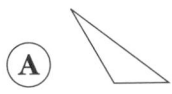

  B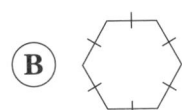

  C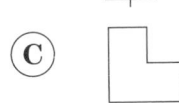

(2) Which of the following is not a polygon?

  A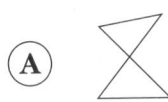

  B

  C

For exercises 3–5, determine the sum of the measures of the interior angles of the polygon.

(3) hexagon

  A 540°   **B** 720°   **C** 900°

(4) dodecagon

  A 1440°   **B** 1670°   **C** 1800°

(5) 15-gon

  A 2340°   **B** 2520°   **C** 2700°

For exercises 6–8, find the measure of one exterior angle of the regular convex polygon.

(6) quadrilateral

  A 60°   **B** 90°   **C** 120°

(7) heptagon

  A 60°

  B 45°

  C about 51.4°

(8) triangle

  A 60°   **B** 90°   **C** 120°

For exercises 9–10, find the value of x.

(9)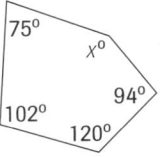

  A 139°

  B 159°

  C 149°

(10)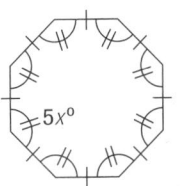

  A 27°

  B 135°

  C 216°

(11) One exterior angle of a regular convex polygon is 40°. Find the number of sides.

  A 9   **B** 10   **C** 11

(12) Two interior angles of a quadrilateral measure 52° and 118°. If the two remaining angles have the same measure, what is the measure of each?

  A 90°   **B** 95°   **C** 100°

(13) In which of the following regular convex polygons is each exterior angle congruent to each interior angle?

  A triangle

  B quadrilateral

  C pentagon

PRACTICE ANSWERS
Page 74

1. concave
2. convex
3. concave
4. 1080°
5. 1440°
6. 1980°
7. 189°
8. 45°
9. 16
10. 144°
11. 72°
12. 40°
13. 12°
14. 5
15. No, because $\frac{360}{75} = 4.8$, and a polygon can not have 4.8 sides

TEST PREP ANSWERS
Page 75

1. C
2. A
3. B
4. C
5. A
6. B
7. C
8. C
9. C
10. A
11. A
12. B
13. B

Name _____ Date _____

Triangles

For exercises 1–19, decide whether each statement is always, sometimes, or never true. Write the appropriate letter in the blank.

A   always

B   sometimes

C   never

_____ 1. An isosceles triangle has two congruent angles.

_____ 2. An obtuse triangle is scalene.

_____ 3. The vertex angle of an isosceles triangle is acute.

_____ 4. If one angle of an isosceles triangle measures 60 degrees, then the triangle is equilateral.

_____ 5. An altitude drawn to a side of a triangle passes through the midpoint of that side.

_____ 6. A perpendicular bisector of a side of a triangle passes through the midpoint of that side.

_____ 7. The circumcenter of a triangle is used to circumscribe a triangle about a circle.

_____ 8. In a scalene triangle, the altitude and the angle bisector from a given vertex are different line segments.

_____ 9. In an equilateral triangle, the altitude, median, angle bisector, and perpendicular bisector from any vertex to the opposite side are congruent.

_____ 10. An angle bisector in a triangle also bisects the opposite side.

_____ 11. The angle bisector of the vertex angle of an isosceles triangle divides the triangle into two congruent triangles.

_____ 12. The two acute angles in a right triangle are supplementary.

_____ 13. The measure of an exterior angle of a triangle is greater than the sum of the measures of the two opposite interior angles.

_____ 14. In a scalene triangle, the exterior angles are all obtuse angles.

134

137

139-140

144

Name _____ Date _____

148

_____ **15.** The sum of the lengths of any two sides of a
triangle is greater than the length of the third side.

_____ **16.** The longest side of a triangle is opposite the smallest angle.

154

_____ **17.** If a, b, and c are the lengths of sides of a triangle with
c the longest and $a^2 + b^2 < c^2$, then the triangle is acute.

136, 155

_____ **18.** A median is a line of symmetry in a scalene triangle.

155

_____ **19.** A triangle has three lines of symmetry.

136-138

In exercises 20–22, choose the letter of the correct answer to complete each statement.

A   altitudes

B   medians

C   angle bisectors

D   perpendicular bisectors

_____ **20.** The centroid of a triangle is formed by the intersection of the _____.

_____ **21.** The orthocenter in a triangle is the intersection of the _____.

_____ **22.** The point of concurrency in a triangle formed by the intersection of the _____
is the center of a circle in which this triangle is inscribed.

23. The coordinates of $\triangle ABC$
are $A(^-3, 0)$, $B(1, 4)$ and $C(3, ^-2)$.
Find the length of the median
from A to $\overline{BC}$. • **MORE HELP** See 090

_____

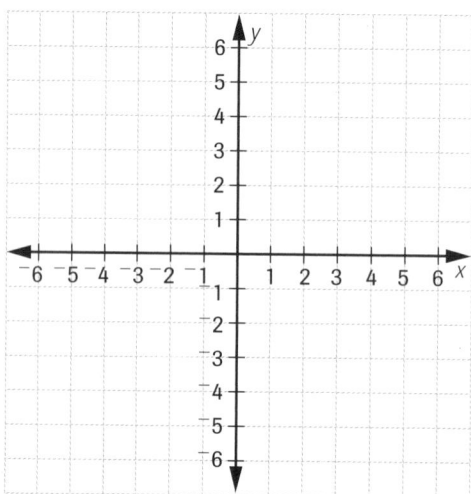

Name _____ Date _____

For exercises 24–26, in △ABC, m∠A = 9x°, m∠B = 3x – 6°, and m∠C = 11x + 2°.

24. Is the triangle acute, right or obtuse? _____

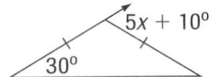

25. Find the measures of all three angles. _____

26. Which side of the triangle is the longest? _____

27. Find x. _____

28. List the sides in order from shortest to longest.

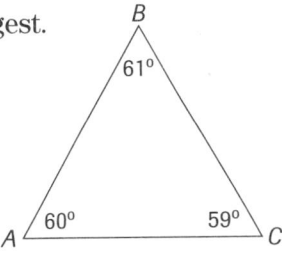

_____

29. Which side is longer, $\overline{AC}$ or $\overline{RQ}$?

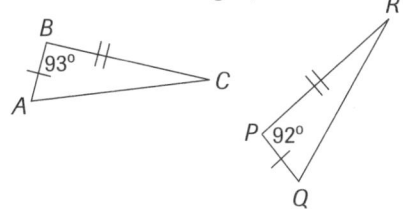

_____

30. Which angle is larger, ∠1 or ∠2?

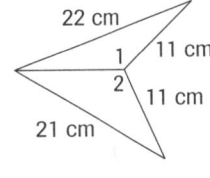

_____

31. Is it possible to draw a triangle with sides 9 inches, 5 inches, and 15 inches long? Explain.

_____

_____

_____

_____

_____

For exercises 32–35, find x.

32.

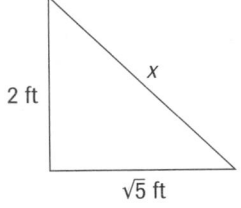

_____

33.

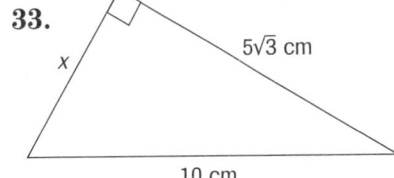

_____

Name _____ Date _____

34.

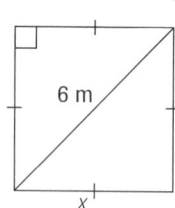

_____

35.

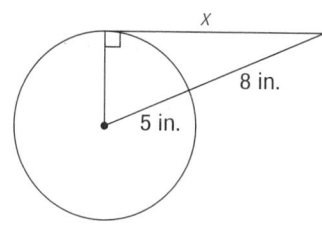

_____

36. Which of the following are Pythagorean triples?

    A. 5, 12, 13

    B. 9, 12, 15

    C. 7, 24, 25

    D. 8, 15, 17

_____

37. In obtuse $\triangle ABC$, the shorter two sides are 3 inches and 4 inches long. Give a possible length for the longest side.

_____

In exercises 38–41, the lengths of the sides of triangles are given. Write the letter of the best description of the triangle.

    A. acute

    B. right

    C. obtuse

38. 6 cm, 8 cm, 9 cm   _____

39. 10 m, 15 m, 21 m   _____

40. 4 ft, $4\sqrt{3}$ ft, 8 ft   _____

41. 11 mi, 60 mi, 61 mi   _____

Name _____ Date _____

Triangles

Directions: Choose the best answer and circle the appropriate letter.

For exercises 1–3, the lengths of the sides of triangles are given. Choose the letter for the best description of the triangle.

A. right

B. acute

C. obtuse

D. none of these

1. 16 cm   30 cm   34 cm   _____

2. 8 m   12 m   14 m   _____

3. 17 in.   32 in.   34 in.   _____

4. For the given diagram, choose the letter of the true statement.

A. $AB = BC$

B. $AB > BC$

C. $AB < BC$

D. $AB = BD$

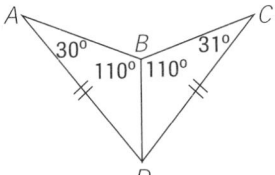

5. In $\triangle ABC$, the measure of $\angle A$ is $x°$, the measure of $\angle B$ is $(x + 35)°$, and the measure of $\angle C$ is $(x - 5)°$. Which side of $\triangle ABC$ is the longest?

A. $\overline{AB}$ **C.** $\overline{AC}$

B. $\overline{BC}$ **D.** none of these

For exercises 6–12, decide whether the statement is always, sometimes, or never true. Circle the appropriate letter.

6. The angle bisector of the vertex angle of an isosceles triangle divides the triangle into two congruent triangles.

     A. always   **B.** sometimes   **C.** never

7. If a median, an altitude, and an angle bisector are the same segment in a triangle, the triangle is scalene.

     A. always   **B.** sometimes   **C.** never

8. A scalene triangle is an acute triangle.

     A. always   **B.** sometimes   **C.** never

9. The sum of the lengths of any two sides of a triangle equals the length of the third side.

     A. always   **B.** sometimes   **C.** never

10. Two of the angles of a right triangle are complementary.

     A. always   **B.** sometimes   **C.** never

11. A median is a line of symmetry in a triangle.

     A. always   **B.** sometimes   **C.** never

12. The shortest side of a triangle is opposite the smallest angle.

     A. always   **B.** sometimes   **C.** never

For exercises 13–15, complete the sentence by circling the appropriate letter.

13. The intersection of the perpendicular bisectors in a triangle is called the _____.

     A. orthocenter   **C.** circumcenter

     B. centroid   **D.** incenter

14. The point of concurrency in a triangle used as the center of the inscribed circle is called the _____.

     A. orthocenter   **C.** circumcenter

     B. centroid   **D.** incenter

15. The intersection of the altitudes of a triangle is called the _____.

     A. orthocenter   **C.** circumcenter

     B. centroid   **D.** incenter

PRACTICE ANSWERS
Page 77
1. A
2. B
3. B
4. A
5. B
6. A
7. C
8. A
9. A
10. B
11. A
12. C
13. C
14. B

Page 78
15. A
16. C
17. C
18. C
19. B
20. B
21. A
22. D
23. $\sqrt{26}$ or about 5.10 units

Page 79
24. right
25. $m\angle A = 72°$,
    $m\angle B = 18°$, $m\angle C = 90°$

26. $\overline{AB}$
27. $10°$
28. $AB < BC < AC$
29. $\overline{AC}$
30. $\angle 1$
31. No, $9 + 5 < 15$. By the Triangle Inequality Theorem the sum of any two sides must be greater than the length of the third side.
32. 3 ft
33. 5 cm

Page 80
34. $3\sqrt{2}$ or about 4.24 m
35. 12
36. all are Pythagorean triples
37. Answers will vary; any value between 5 and 7 is correct.
38. A
39. C
40. B
41. B

TEST PREP ANSWERS
Page 81
1. A
2. C
3. B
4. B
5. C
6. A
7. C
8. B
9. C
10. A
11. B
12. A
13. C
14. D
15. A

Name _____ Date _____

Quadrilaterals

For exercises 1–20, decide whether the statement is always, sometimes, or never true. Write the appropriate letter.

A. always   **B.** sometimes   **C.** never

_____ 1. A rectangle is a square.

_____ 2. A kite is a parallelogram.

_____ 3. A trapezoid is isosceles.

_____ 4. A rhombus is a square.

_____ 5. The adjacent angles of a rhombus are supplementary.

_____ 6. A quadrilateral is a parallelogram if one pair of opposite sides is both congruent and parallel.

_____ 7. The adjacent angles of a rectangle are congruent and supplementary.

_____ 8. The diagonals of a parallelogram are congruent.

_____ 9. If the diagonals of a quadrilateral are both perpendicular and congruent, then the quadrilateral is a square.

_____ 10. The diagonals of a parallelogram bisect both pairs of opposite angles.

_____ 11. The diagonals of a parallelogram divide it into four congruent triangles.

_____ 12. A square is a parallelogram, a rhombus, and a rectangle.

_____ 13. An equilateral quadrilateral is a square.

_____ 14. The diagonals of a trapezoid are congruent.

_____ 15. The base angles of an isosceles trapezoid are supplementary. • **MORE HELP** See 069

_____ 16. The midsegment of an isosceles trapezoid is a line of symmetry.

_____ 17. Both pairs of opposite angles of a kite are congruent.

_____ 18. A kite has two lines of symmetry.

_____ 19. A rectangle has rotational symmetry.

_____ 20. The diagonals of a parallelogram are lines of symmetry.

156

156, 160

160, 162

162

162-164

163

164

165

165, 167

166

167

Name _____ Date _____

For exercises 21–26, choose the statement that is NOT a conclusion you can make from the given information.

157-160 **21.** **Given:** *ABCD* is a parallelogram.

    A. Opposite angles are congruent.   **C.** Adjacent angles are supplementary.

    B. Opposite sides are congruent.   **D.** Adjacent sides are congruent.

162 **22.** **Given:** *ABCD* is a rectangle.

    A. Opposite angles are congruent.   **C.** Diagonals are perpendicular.

    B. Opposite sides are parallel.   **D.** Diagonals are congruent.

163 **23.** **Given:** *ABCD* is a rhombus.

    A. Diagonals are congruent.   **C.** Diagonals bisect both pairs of opposite angles.

    B. Adjacent sides are congruent.   **D.** Diagonals are perpendicular.

164 **24.** **Given:** *ABCD* is a square.

    A. All angles are right angles.   **C.** Diagonals are perpendicular.

    B. Adjacent angles are complementary.   **D.** Diagonals are congruent.

165 **25.** **Given:** *ABCD* is an isosceles trapezoid.

    A. Base angles are congruent.   **C.** One pair of opposite sides is parallel.

    B. Diagonals are congruent.   **D.** Diagonals are perpendicular.

166 **26.** **Given:** *ABCD* is kite.

    A. Diagonals are perpendicular.   **C.** One pair of adjacent sides is congruent.

    B. One pair of opposite angles is congruent.   **D.** Diagonals are not congruent.

Name _____ Date _____

For exercises 27–38, write the letter of the quadrilateral that is best determined by the given information. Remember, the vertices of a polygon are listed in order.

A. parallelogram

157–161

B. rectangle

162

C. rhombus

163

D. square

164

E. trapezoid

165

F. isosceles trapezoid

165

G. kite

166

27. **Given:** $ABCD$ is a quadrilateral; $AB = BC = CD = AD$; $\angle B$ is a right angle _____

28. **Given:** $ABCD$ is a quadrilateral; $AB = BC = CD = AD$ _____

29. **Given:** $ABCD$ is a quadrilateral; $AB = DC$, $BC = AD$; $\angle D$ is a right angle _____

30. **Given:** $ABCD$ is a quadrilateral; E is the midpoint of $\overline{AC}$; $D, E,$

and B are collinear; $DE = EB$ _____

31. **Given:** $ABCD$ is a quadrilateral; $\overline{AB} \parallel \overline{DC}$ _____

32. **Given:** $ABCD$ is a quadrilateral; $\overline{AB} \parallel \overline{DC}$, $AB = DC$ _____

33. **Given:** $ABCD$ is a quadrilateral; $\angle A \cong \angle B \cong \angle C \cong \angle D$ _____

34. **Given:** $ABCD$ is a quadrilateral; $\overline{AC} \perp \overline{DB}$; $AB = AD$; $AB \neq BC$ _____

35. **Given:** $ABCD$ is a quadrilateral; $\overline{DC} \parallel \overline{AB}$; $AC = DB$ _____

36. **Given:** $ABCD$ is a quadrilateral; $AB = BC = CD = AD$; $AC = BD$ _____

37. **Given:** $ABCD$ is a quadrilateral; $AB = BC = CD$; $\overline{AB} \parallel \overline{DC}$ _____

38. **Given:** $ABCD$ is a quadrilateral; $AC = BD$; $\overline{AC} \perp \overline{BD}$ _____

Name _____ Date _____

Quadrilaterals

Directions: Write the letter of the best possible answer.

For exercises 1–10, decide whether the statement is always, sometimes, or never true. Write the appropriate letter.

A. always

B. sometimes

C. never

1. The diagonals of a kite are perpendicular. _____

2. Adjacent sides of a parallelogram are congruent. _____

3. The diagonals of an isosceles trapezoid are congruent. _____

4. Adjacent angles of a rectangle are congruent. _____

5. The non-parallel sides of a trapezoid are congruent. _____

6. A rhombus has rotational and line symmetry. _____

7. A square is a kite. _____

8. The diagonals of a square are both perpendicular and congruent. _____

9. Consecutive (adjacent) angles of a parallelogram are supplementary. _____

10. A rectangle has at least two lines of symmetry. _____

For exercises 11–13, choose the statement that is NOT a conclusion you can make from the given information.

11. **Given:** *ABCD* is a rhombus.

   A. The diagonals bisect each other.

   B. All sides are congruent.

   C. The diagonals are perpendicular.

   D. Opposite angles are supplementary.

12. **Given:** *ABCD* is a rectangle.

   A. Opposite angles are bisected by the diagonals.

   B. The diagonals are congruent.

   C. Opposite sides are congruent.

   D. Opposite angles are congruent.

13. **Given:** *ABCD* is an isosceles trapezoid.

   A. One pair of sides is parallel and congruent.

   B. The diagonals are congruent.

   C. The base angles are congruent.

   D. One pair of sides is parallel.

For exercises 14–16, choose the letter for the quadrilateral that is guaranteed by the given information.

   A. parallelogram

   B. rhombus

   C. rectangle

   D. square

   E. kite

   F. isosceles trapezoid

14. **Given:** *ABCD* is a quadrilateral; $AB = AD$; $BC = CD$; $AD \neq CD$ _____

15. **Given:** *ABCD* is a quadrilateral; $\overline{AC}$ and $\overline{BD}$ bisect other. _____

16. **Given:** *ABCD* is a quadrilateral; $\angle D$ is a right angle; the diagonals bisect opposite angles. _____

PRACTICE ANSWERS
Page 83

1. B
2. C
3. B
4. B
5. A
6. A
7. A
8. B
9. A
10. B
11. B
12. A
13. B
14. B
15. C
16. C
17. C
18. C
19. A
20. B

Page 84

21. D
22. C
23. A
24. B
25. D
26. B

Page 85

27. D
28. C
29. B
30. A
31. E
32. A
33. B
34. G
35. F
36. D
37. C
38. D

TEST PREP ANSWERS
Page 86

1. A
2. B
3. A
4. A
5. B
6. B
7. C
8. A
9. A
10. A
11. D
12. A
13. A
14. E
15. A
16. D

Make the Connection

OBJECTIVES
- Investigate angle relationships in polygons
- Make connections among geometric relationships and algebraic representations

MATERIALS
- Graph paper (page 212)
- Graphing Calculator (optional)

TIME
- 40 minutes

TEACHER NOTES
- This is an activity that helps students to make connections between a common geometric investigation and algebraic functions.

- Even if students are familiar with the various formulas for angles in a polygon, they tend not to think about the formulas as they are graphing the ordered pairs.

- Ask students whether it is appropriate to connect the ordered pairs for each graph. They are discrete functions. The number of sides must be a counting (natural) number ≥ 3.

EXTENSIONS
- Have students write each formula using function notation.

  A. $f(n) = (n - 2)180$ **B.** $f(n) = 360$
  C. $f(n) = \dfrac{(n - 2)180}{n}$ **D.** $f(n) = \dfrac{360}{n}$

- Have students overlay graphs C and D and describe any patterns they observe. For instance, the two graphs are symmetric with respect to $y = 90$. As the measure of an interior angle increases, the exterior angle measure is decreasing. The angles are supplementary.

ANSWERS
1. See page 214

2. *Note*: If a graphing calculator is used, be sure students set x-min and y-min at zero.

   See page 214

3. $y = (n - 2)180$; slope $= 180$; geometrically, every time the number of sides increases by one, the number of degrees increases by 180°.

4. $y = 360$; slope $= 0$; geometrically, the sum of the exterior angles always equals 360 regardless of the number of sides.

5. possible answer: the graph is increasing, but is not linear; 140°

6. possible answer: the graph is decreasing, but is not linear; 40°

APPLICATION ANSWERS
(continued on page 214)

Name _____ Date _____

Make the Connection

HANDBOOK
HELP

Ordered Pairs and
  Locating Points: 88

Linear Equations: 95

Positive, Negative,
  Zero, and Undefined
  Slope: 101

Definitions and
  Hierarchy: 129

You have probably filled in a table similar to the one below when you studied the relationships among angles and sides in a polygon. From the patterns in the table you were able to develop a formula for the angles of an n-gon. Have you ever considered what you might observe if you graphed two columns of data in a scatter plot? Time to make some connections between geometry and algebra!

1. Use methods developed in class, or suggested by your teacher, to complete the table below. It has been started for you.

Polygon Name	Number of Sides	Number of ∠s	A. Sum of Interior ∠s	B. Sum of Exterior ∠s	C. One Interior ∠ of Regular Polygon	D. One Exterior ∠ of Regular Polygon
	3	3	180°			
	4	4		360°		
	5				108°	
Hexagon	6					60°
	7					
	8					
	10					
	n					

2. Use graph paper, or a graphing calculator to make four scatter plots. For each plot the coordinates will be the following:
   Graph A: (x = Number of Sides, y = Sum of Interior ∠s)
   Graph B: (x = Number of Sides, y = Sum of Exterior ∠s)
   Graph C: (x = Number of Sides, y = One Interior ∠ of a Regular Polygon)
   Graph D: (x = Number of Sides, y = One Exterior ∠ of a Regular Polygon)

Once you have completed the scatter plots, answer the following.

3. Graph A should look like a linear function. Write the equation of this graph. What is the slope of this line? Explain why the slope makes sense geometrically.

4. Graph B should look like a constant function. Write the equation of this graph. What is the slope of this line? Explain why the slope makes sense geometrically.

5. Describe any features of Graph C that you observe. Use your graph to predict the measure of an interior angle of a regular nonagon (nine sides).

6. Describe any features of Graph D that you observe. Use your graph to predict the measure of an exterior angle of a regular nonagon (nine sides).

Name _____ Date _____

Linear Measurement

170-171

Find the perimeter. Write your answer in the space provided.

1.

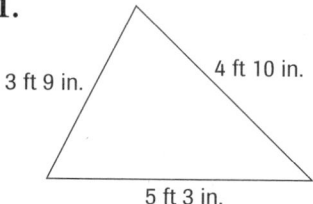

3 ft 9 in. 4 ft 10 in. 5 ft 3 in.

_____

2.

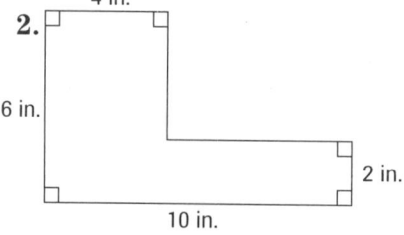

4 in. 6 in. 10 in. 2 in.

_____

3. MORE HELP See 152

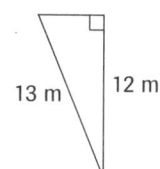

13 m 12 m

_____

4. MORE HELP See 238–239

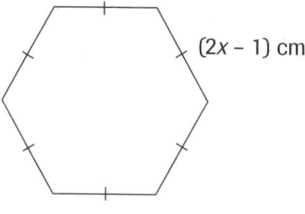

(2x – 1) cm

_____

5.

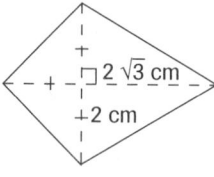

2 √3 cm 2 cm

_____

6. MORE HELP See 169

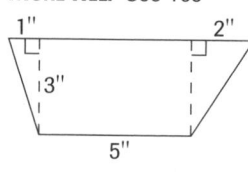

1" 2" 3" 5"

_____

Solve each problem. You may want to draw a diagram and/or use a calculator for some exercises.

170

7. Give the dimensions of a square with the same perimeter as the rectangle shown.

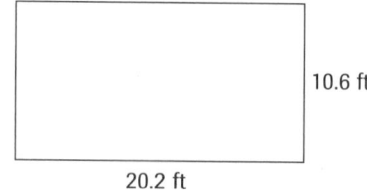

10.6 ft

20.2 ft

_____

8. Find the perimeter of square *ABCD*. • MORE HELP See 153

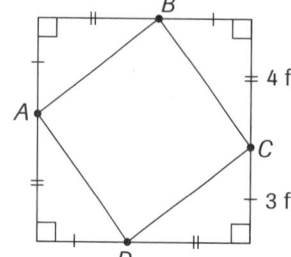

B 4 ft A C 3 ft D

_____

Name _____ Date _____

9. The width of a rectangle is 7 inches and its perimeter is 32 inches. Find the length.

_____

10. A regular hexagon has a perimeter of 33 cm. Find the length of one side.

_____

11. A quadrilateral has sides with measures $6x - 1, 5 - x, 3x + 4$, and $7 - 4x$ centimeters. The perimeter is 23 cm. Find the value of x.

_____

12. A wooden frame is made for an 8×10 inch picture. If the wood for the frame is 1.5 inches wide, find the perimeter of the frame.

_____

13. The length of a side of an equilateral triangle equals the length of a side of a square. Find the ratio of their perimeters. • **MORE HELP** See 214

_____

14. The circumference of a circle is 24π units. Find the perimeter of the inscribed regular hexagon.

172

_____

15. $\triangle ABC \sim \triangle PQR$, $AB = 12$ m and $PQ = 15$ m. Find the ratio of their perimeters.

173

_____

16. The ratio of the perimeters of two similar figures is 3:2. If one side of the smaller figure has a measure of 8 yards, find the measure of the corresponding side of the larger figure.

_____

17. Find the exact circumference of a circle with radius 2.5 cm.

_____

Name _____ Date _____

18. The circumference of the inside of a sewer pipe is 14.74 feet. Find the diameter of the pipe to the nearest hundredth of a foot.

_____

19. At the equator, Earth has a radius of about 3960 miles. Find the earth's circumference at the equator. Use 3.14 for π and/or use your calculator.

_____

20. A bicycle has wheels with 11 inch radii. About how far, in miles, will the bike have traveled in one hour if the rider is pedaling at a rate of 250 revolutions per minute? Use 3.14 for π. • **MORE HELP** See 420

_____

21. A circle is inscribed in a square with sides 12 yards long. Find the exact circumference of the circle. • **MORE HELP** See 174

_____

22. A square with sides 12 yards long is inscribed in a circle. Find the exact circumference of the circle. • **MORE HELP** See 174, 238

_____

23. The minute hand of a small clock is 3 inches long. How far does the tip of the minute hand travel in one day? Use 3.14 for π.

_____

24. The perimeter of a regular octagon equals the circumference of a circle. Using $\frac{22}{7}$ for π, find the ratio of the length of a side of the octagon to the radius of the circle.

_____

Name _____   Date _____

Linear Measurement

Directions for exercises 1–5: Solve each problem. Write your answer in the space provided.

1. The circumference of a circle is 10π units. Find the perimeter of the regular hexagon inscribed in the circle.

_____

2. Find the perimeter.

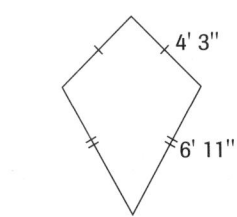

4' 3"

6' 11"

_____

3. Find the perimeter

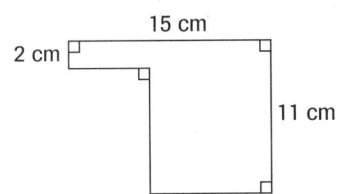

15 cm

2 cm

11 cm

_____

4. In the following diagram, the perimeter of *ABCD* is 173 yards. Find the value of *x*.

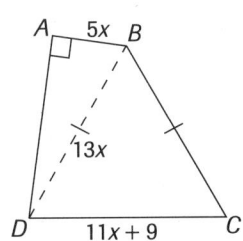

A   5x   B

13x

D   11x + 9   C

_____

5. The circumference of a circle is equal to the perimeter of a square whose side is 3 inches. Find the exact radius of the circle.

_____

Directions for exercises 6–10: Write

A   if the quantity in Column A is greater;
B   if the quantity in Column B is greater;
C   if the two quantities are equal;
D   if the relationship cannot be determined from the information given.

Column A	Column B
___**6.** The circumference of a unit circle	The perimeter of a square with side 0.75 units
___**7.** The perimeter of *ABCD*	62 inches

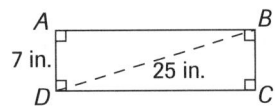

A   B

7 in.   25 in.

D   C

___**8.** x in a regular hexagon: P = 80 in., $s = (3x - 1)$ in.	5
___**9.** The ratio of corresponding sides of *ABCD* to *A'B'C'D'*	3:2

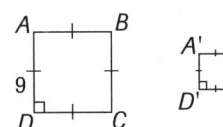

A   B

9

D   C

A'   B'

4

D'   C'

___**10.** Perimeter of *ABCD*	$4\sqrt{2}$ units

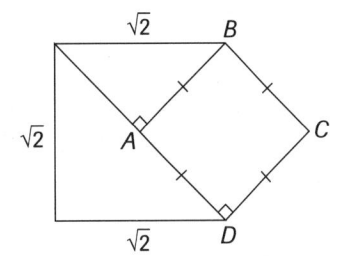

$\sqrt{2}$ B

$\sqrt{2}$ C

A

$\sqrt{2}$ D

PRACTICE ANSWERS
Page 90

1. 13' 10"
2. 32 in.
3. 30 m
4. $(12x - 6)$ cm
5. $8 + 4\sqrt{2}$ or about 13.66 cm.
6. $13 + \sqrt{10} + \sqrt{13}$ or about 19.77 in.
7. $s = 15.4$ ft
8. 20 ft

Page 91

9. 9 in.
10. 5.5 cm
11. 2 cm
12. 48 in.
13. 3:4
14. 72 units
15. 4:5
16. 12 yds
17. 5π cm

Page 92

18. about 4.69 ft
19. about 24,869 mi
20. about 16.35 mi
21. 12π yds
22. $12\sqrt{2}\,\pi$ yds
23. about 452 in.
24. 11:14

TEST PREP ANSWERS
Page 93

1. 30 units
2. 22' 4"
3. 52 cm
4. 4 yds
5. $\frac{6}{\pi}$ in.
6. A
7. C
8. B
9. A
10. B

Name _____ Date _____

Square Measurement in Polygons

181

For exercises 1–3, find the perimeter and the area. You may wish to draw or add auxiliary lines to diagrams and/or use a calculator.

1.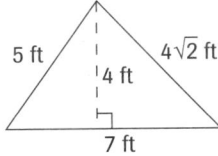

2.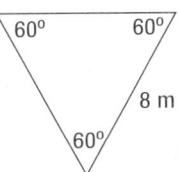

3. • **MORE HELP** See 152

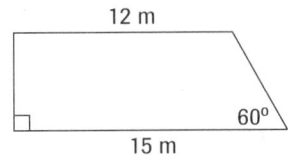

_____ _____ _____

4. Find the area of an isosceles right triangle whose hypotenuse is 18 cm. • **MORE HELP** See 238

_____

5. The vertices of a triangle are $A(0, 4)$, $B(0, {}^{-}2)$, and $C(5, 1)$. Find the area of the triangle.
• **MORE HELP** See 087-088

_____

6. Find the area of $\triangle ABC$, if $AB = 6$ cm, $AC = 12$ cm, and the measure of $\angle A$ is 20°. Express your answer to the nearest tenth of a square centimeter.
• **MORE HELP** See 240, 422

_____

182-183

7.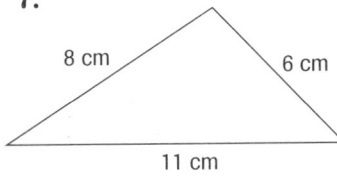

8.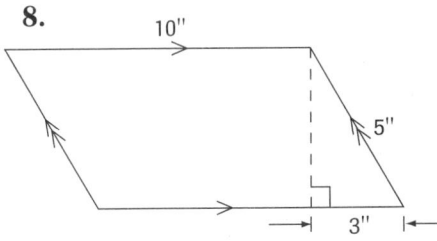

_____ _____

Name_____ Date_____

9. Each side of a baseball diamond is 90 feet. Find the perimeter of the baseline and the area of the infield.

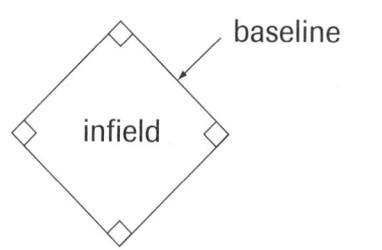

_____

10. Find the area of a square circumscribed about a circle whose radius is 22 inches.
• **MORE HELP** See 302

_____

11. One angle of a rhombus is 60° and the length of a side is 8 inches. Find the area.
• **MORE HELP** See 239 or 241

_____

12. A parallelogram is equal in area to a square whose side is 4 centimeters. If one of the sides of the parallelogram exceeds the altitude to that side by 6, find the length of the base and the height of the parallelogram.

_____

13. In the diagram, *ABCD* is a parallelogram. Is the area of △*ABP* equal to, greater than, or less than the area of △*BPD*? Explain your answer. • **MORE HELP** See 137

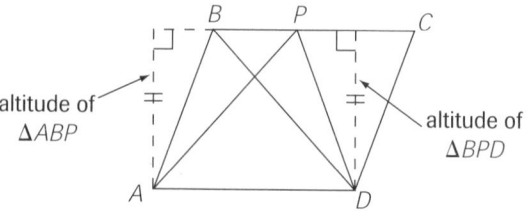

_____

_____

_____

_____

Name _____ Date _____

14. A regular dodecagon has a side with length 10 cm and
an apothem 12 cm long. Find the area. • **MORE HELP** See 370

184

_____

15. A circle with radius 4 in. is inscribed in an
equilateral triangle. Find the area of the triangle.
   • **MORE HELP** See 073, 239, 302

185

_____

16. The ratio of a pair of corresponding sides in two similar
polygons is 5:3. The area of the smaller polygon is 108 cm².
Find the area of the larger polygon. • **MORE HELP** See 220

186

_____

For exercises 17–18, find both perimeter and area.

187-188

17. 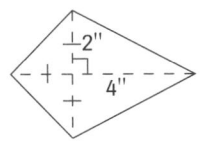   **18.**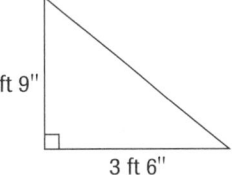

_____   _____

19. The area of a trapezoid is 60 in.² If the longer base
is three times the shorter base, and the altitude is 5 in.,
find the length of both bases.

_____

20. Find the perimeter and area of this figure.
   • **MORE HELP** See 153

193

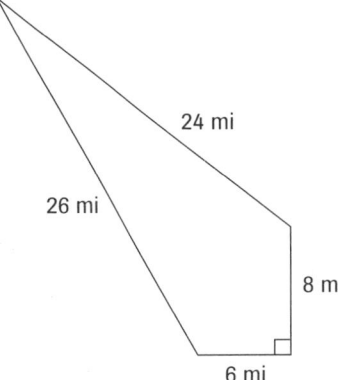

_____

Name _____ Date _____

Square Measurement in Polygons

Directions: Mark the letter beside the correct answer to each question.

1. A regular hexagon has a side x and apothem a. The area is

   A. $6xa$ C. $3xa$

   B. $\frac{1}{2}xa$ D. $12xa$

2. The ratio of the areas of two similar polygons is 4:25 and one side of the smaller polygon is 3 centimeters. The corresponding length of the larger polygon is

   A. 7.5 cm   C. 25 cm

   B. 15 cm   D. 75 cm

3. The vertices of a rectangle are $(^-2, 3)$, $(3, 3)$, $(3, 0)$, and $(^-2, 0)$. The area of the rectangle is

   A. 8 units^2 C. 12 units^2

   B. 10 units^2 D. 15 units^2

4. What is the area of an equilateral triangle whose side-length is 4 inches?

   A. 8 in.^{2} C. 4 in.^{2}

   B. $8\sqrt{3}$ in.^{2} D. $4\sqrt{3}$ in.^{2}

5. The area of the polygon shown is

   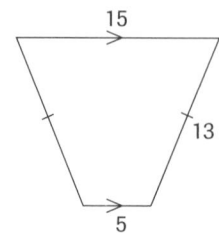

   A. 120 units^2 C. 60 units^2

   B. 46 units^2 D. 240 units^2

6. The area of a parallelogram is 50 square feet and the length of the base is 20 feet. The height is

   A. 2.5 feet   C. 7.5 feet

   B. 5 feet   D. 10 feet

7. What is the area of a right triangle whose perimeter is 12 units and whose sides have measure x, $x + 1$, and $x + 2$ units?

   A. 6 units^2 C. 12 units^2

   B. 10 units^2 D. 18 units^2

8. How many square yards of carpet are needed to cover a rectangular floor that is 15 feet by 18 feet?

   A. 30 yd^2 C. 135 yd^2

   B. 36 yd^2 D. 270 yd^2

9. A side and an angle of a rhombus measure 8 m and 60° respectively. The area of the rhombus is

   A. $32\sqrt{2}$ m^2 C. $32\sqrt{3}$ m^2

   B. 32 m^2 D. 64 m^2

10. The shorter diagonal of a kite is 10 in. and a pair of noncongruent sides are 10 in. and 13 in. The area in square inches is

    A. 65   C. $120 + 50\sqrt{3}$

    B. $60 + 25\sqrt{3}$ D. 130

PRACTICE ANSWERS
Page 95

1. $(12 + 4\sqrt{2})$ ft., 14 ft^2
2. 24 m; $16\sqrt{3}$ m^2
3. $33 + 3\sqrt{3}$ m; $36\sqrt{3} + \frac{9\sqrt{3}}{2}$ m^2
4. 81 cm^2
5. 15 units^2
6. 12.3 cm^2
7. 25 cm; 23.42 cm^2
8. 30 in.; 40 in.^{2}

Page 96

9. 360 ft; 8100 ft^2
10. 1936 in.^{2}
11. $32\sqrt{3}$ in.^{2} or about 55.4 in.^{2}
12. $b = 8$ cm; $h = 2$ cm
13. Areas are equal. The triangles have the same base and equal heights since $\overline{BC} \parallel \overline{AD}$.

Page 97

14. 720 cm^2
15. $48\sqrt{3}$ in.^{2}
16. 300 cm^2
17. about 14.6 in.; 12 in.^{2}
18. 10 ft 8 in. or 10.7 ft; 4.81 in.^{2}
19. 6 in.; 18 in.
20. 64 mi; 144 mi^2

TEST PREP ANSWERS
Page 98

1. C
2. A
3. D
4. D
5. A
6. A
7. A
8. A
9. C
10. B

Name _____ Date _____

Square Measurement in Circles

190

Find the area to the nearest tenth of a square inch.

1.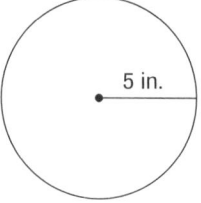

5 in.

_____

2.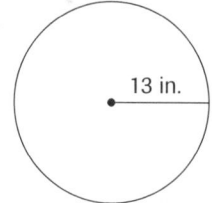

13 in.

_____

3. The area of a circle is $36\pi x^2$, find the diameter of the circle.

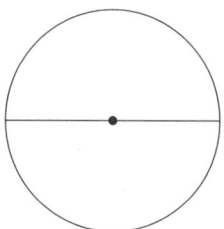

_____

4. Find the area of the shaded region.

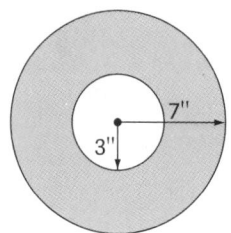

7″

3″

_____

5. A circle with 10-inch diameter is cut from a square piece of tin with 10-inch sides. To the nearest tenth of a square inch, find the amount of tin that is wasted.

_____

6. Find the radius of a circle whose area is equal to the sum of the areas of two circles whose radii are 4 inches and 3 inches.

_____

191

7. The area of the shaded sector is 9π in². Find the radius of the circle.

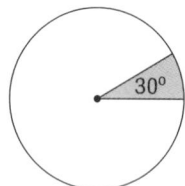

30°

_____

Exercises 8 and 9 use the same diagram. Round your answer to the nearest hundredth.

8. Find the area of the sector._____

192

9. Find the area of the segment. • **MORE HELP** See 139, 239

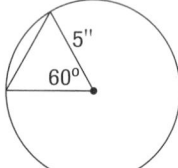

5″

60°

_____

Name _____ Date _____

Square Measurement in Circles

Directions: Fill in the circle beside the best answer to each question.

1 Find the area of the shaded region.

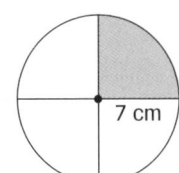

7 cm

A 7π cm^2

B 49π cm^2

C 1.75π cm^2

D 12.25π cm^2

2 If the radius of a circle is increased by a factor of x, then the area is increased by a factor of:

A x

B $2x$

C x^2

D π

3 The areas of two circles have the same ratio as:

A their radii

B π

C their circumferences

D none of these

4 The area of a circle whose diameter is d equals:

A πd^2 units^2

B $\frac{1}{4}\pi d^2$ units^2

C $2\pi d$ units^2

D $\frac{1}{2}\pi d^2$ units^2

5 A circle is inscribed in a regular hexagon with four-centimeter sides. Find the area of the circle.

A 6π cm^2

B 12π cm^2

C 16π cm^2

D 20π cm^2

6 Find the area of the shaded region.

A 100 m^2

B 25π m^2

C $(12.5\pi - 24)$ m^2

D $(25\pi - 24)$ m^2

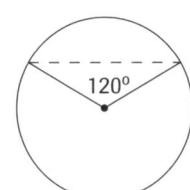

8 m

10 m

For items 7 and 8, refer to this diagram.

120°

7 The circumference is 20π centimeters. Find the area of the sector.

A $\frac{100\pi}{3}$ cm^2

B 100π cm^2

C 400π cm^2

D 200π cm^2

8 The circumference is 20π centimeters. Find the area of the segment.

A $(\frac{100\pi}{3} - 25\sqrt{3})$ cm^2

B $(100\pi - 25\sqrt{3})$ cm^2

C $(100\pi - 25)$ cm^2

D $(50\pi - 25\sqrt{3})$ cm^2

PRACTICE ANSWERS
Page 100

1. 78.5 in.^{2}
2. 530.9 in.^{2}
3. $12x$
4. 40π or about 125.6 in.^{2}
5. about 21.5 in.^{2}
6. 5 in.
7. $6\sqrt{3}$ or about 10.39 in.^{2}
8. 13.1 in.^{2}
9. about 2.3 in.

TEST PREP ANSWERS
Page 101

1. D
2. C
3. D
4. B
5. B
6. C
7. A
8. A

Name _____ Date _____

Square Measurement in Irregular Regions

Find the areas of the shaded figures.

1.

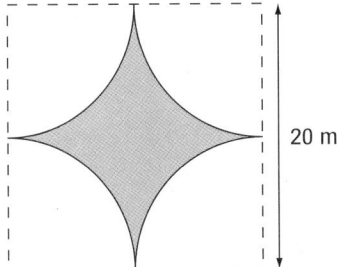

20 m

_____

2.

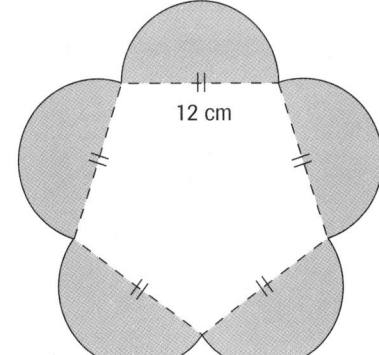

12 cm

_____

3.

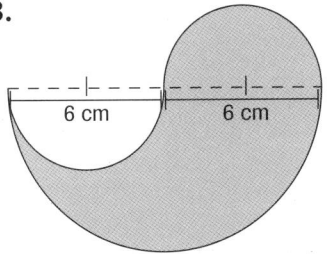

6 cm   6 cm

_____

4.

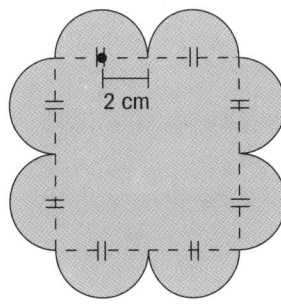

2 cm

_____

5.

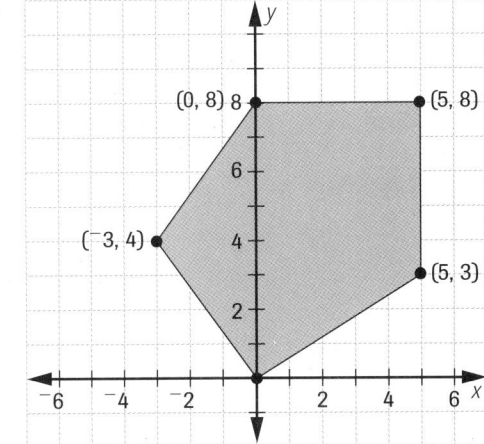

(0, 8) 8   (5, 8)

(⁻3, 4)

(5, 3)

_____

6. **More Help** See 131, 152, 238

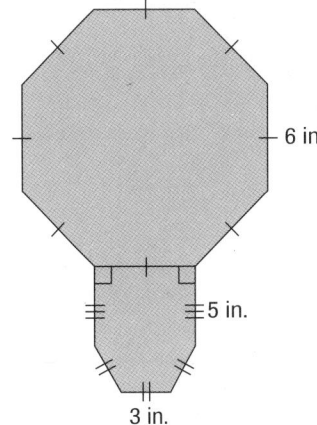

6 in.

5 in.

3 in.

_____

193

Name _____ Date _____

Square Measurement in Irregular Regions

Directions: Mark the letter of the best answer to each question. Use your calculator if necessary to find the area of each figure. All answers are in square units.

1.

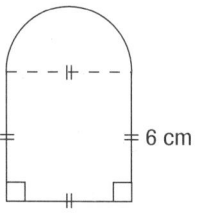

6 cm

A. $36 + 9\pi$

B. $24 + 4.5\pi$

C. $12 + 9\pi$

D. $36 + 4.5\pi$

2.

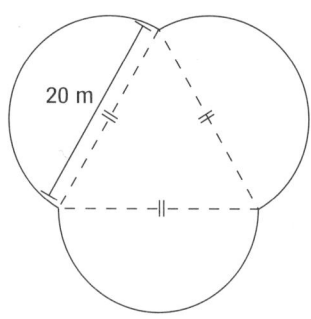

20 m

A. $100\pi + 100\sqrt{3}$

B. $100\pi + 100$

C. $150\pi + 100\sqrt{3}$

D. $150\pi + 100$

3.

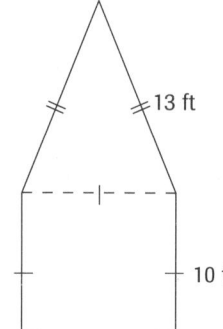

13 ft

10 ft

A. 160

B. 220

C. 170

D. 200

4.

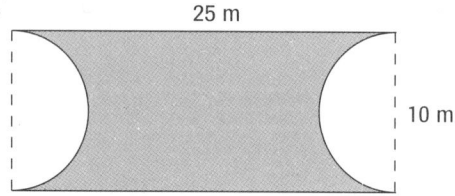

25 m

10 m

A. $625 - 25\pi$

B. $250 - 25\pi$

C. $625 + 25\pi$

D. $250 + 25\pi$

5.

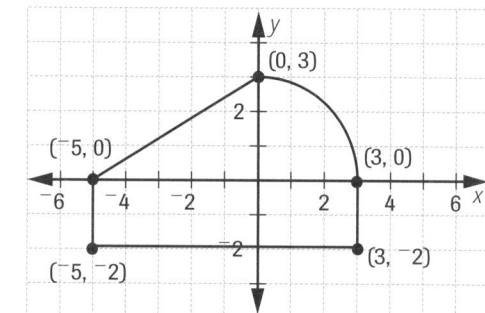

A. about 7.1

B. about 23.5

C. about 27.9

D. about 30.6

6.

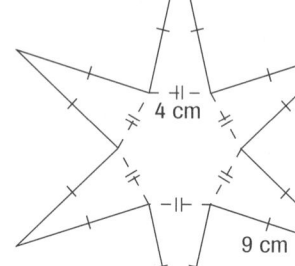

4 cm

9 cm

A. about 98.7

B. about 132.1

C. about 146.9

D. about 150.2

PRACTICE ANSWERS
Page 103

1. $400 - 100\pi$ or about 86 m^2
2. 90π or about 282.6 cm^2
3. 18π or about 56.52 cm^2
4. $64 + 16\pi$ or about 114.24 cm^2
5. about 44.5 units^2
6. about 215.51 in.^{2}

TEST PREP ANSWERS
Page 104

1. D
2. C
3. A
4. B
5. D
6. C

Name_____ Date_____

Square Measurement in Solids

Draw and/or add auxiliary lines to diagrams to help solve these problems. You may wish to use a calculator.

196

1. Find the surface area.

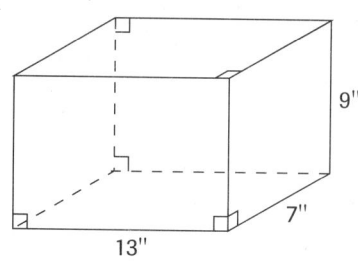

_____

2. A large room has a floor with dimensions 15 feet by 25 feet and a height of 10 feet. A gallon of paint covers about 400 square feet. If the walls of the room are to be painted with two coats, how many gallons of paint will be needed? Ignore the doors and windows.

_____

197

3. Give the exact surface area of the cylinder.

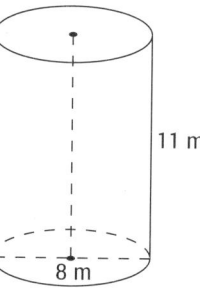

_____

4. A tennis ball has a diameter of about 2.5 inches. A can of three tennis balls is sold in a cylindrical can as shown. Find the surface area of the can without the lid.

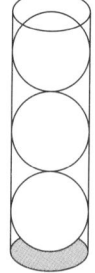

_____

198

5. Give the exact surface area of the cone.

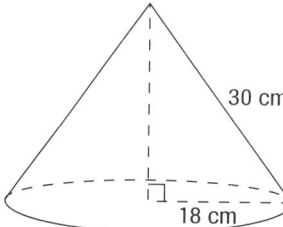

_____

Name _____ Date _____

6. If the lateral area of a right circular cone is 64π square meters and the radius of its base is 4 meters, find the length of the altitude.
 • **MORE HELP** See 152

_____

7. Find the surface area of the pyramid. • **MORE HELP** See 182

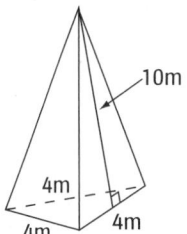

_____

8. Find the surface area of the figure. • **MORE HELP** See 196

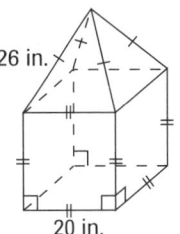

199

_____

9. Find the surface area of the sphere. Round to the nearest hundredth of a square centimeter.

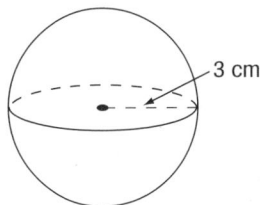

201

_____

10. Earth has a radius of about 3964 miles at the equator. Find the approximate area of Earth's surface.

_____

11. Two similar pyramids have volumes of 512 cubic centimeters and 729 cubic centimeters. Find the ratio of their total surface areas. • **MORE HELP** See 211

202

_____

12. In the Olympics, the official archery target has an outer circumference of 160π cm. The circumference of the bull's eye is 8π cm. Find the probability that the archer does not hit the bull's eye. • **MORE HELP** See 190

203

_____

Name _____ Date _____

Square Measurement in Solids

Directions: Circle the letter of the best answer to each question. You may wish to use a calculator for some exercises.

For exercises 1–3, find the total surface area of the figure shown.

1.

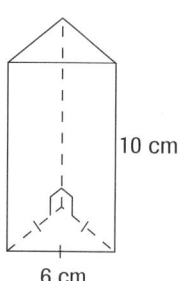

    A. $180 + 36\sqrt{3}$ cm²

    B. $180 + 18\sqrt{3}$ cm²

    C. 180 cm²

    D. $240 + 18\sqrt{3}$ cm²

2.

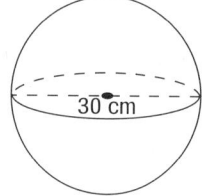

    A. 300 ft²

    B. $100 + 25\sqrt{3}$ ft²

    C. $100 + 75\sqrt{3}$ ft²

    D. $75\sqrt{3}$ ft²

3.

    A. 3375π cm²

    B. 1125π cm²

    C. 900 cm²

    D. 900π cm²

4. If a cube has a volume of 343 cubic centimeters, the total surface area is:

    A. 294 cm²

    B. 111 cm²

    C. 84 cm²

    D. 196 cm²

5. Each of the six edges of a triangular pyramid is 10 feet long. The total surface area is:

    A. $300\sqrt{3}$ ft²

    B. 100 ft²

    C. $100\sqrt{3}$ ft²

    D. 300 ft²

6. A manufacturer makes soup cans. Each can has a radius of 6 centimeters and a height of 14 centimeters. The total amount of metal needed to make one can is about:

    A. about 226 cm²

    B. about 527 cm²

    C. about 754 cm²

    D. about 1000 cm²

7. Find the surface area of the sugar cone shown below if the height of the cone is 4.5 inches and the diameter of the base is two inches *Remember, a sugar cone has no base.* • **MORE HELP** See 152

    A. about 4.6 in.²

    B. about 14.5 in.²

    C. about 10.6 in.²

    D. about 17.6 in.²

8. A dart lands randomly on the board shown below. Find the probability that the dart lands in the inner circle.

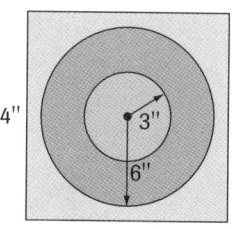

    A. about 0.428

    B. about 0.214

    C. about 0.144

    D. about 0.5

PRACTICE ANSWERS
Page 106

1. 542 in.^{2}
2. 4 gallons
3. 120π m^2
4. about 63.78 in.^{2}
5. 864π cm^2

Page 107

6. about 15.49 m
7. $60 + 4\sqrt{3}$ m^2
8. 2960 in.^{2}
9. 113.04 cm^2
10. 197,358,998 mi^2
11. 64:81
12. 0.9975

TEST PREP ANSWERS
Page 108

1. B
2. A
3. D
4. A
5. C
6. C
7. B
8. C

Name _____ Date _____

Cubic Measurement

Draw or add auxiliary lines to diagrams to help you solve these problems.
Use a calculator if you need one.

206

1. The cylinder and the square prism shown
   have bases which have the same area. Can
   Cavalieri's Principle be applied to find the
   volume of the cylinder? If so, find the volume
   and explain your answer.

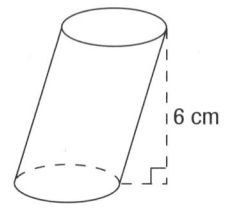 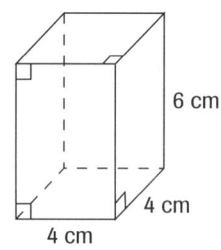

_____

_____

207

2. Find the volume of this prism.

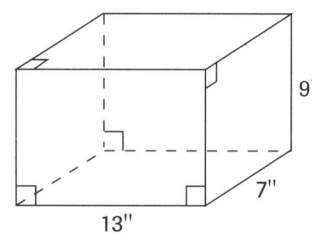

_____

3. A swimming pool has dimensions 12 × 10 × 6 feet. How many gallons of water
   are needed to fill the pool? One cubic foot equals 7.48 gallons of water.

_____

208

4. Find the exact volume of the cylinder.

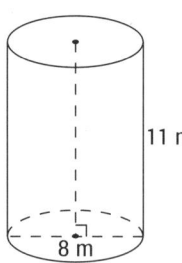

_____

5. The sides of a rectangle are 10 inches and 4 inches. Find the volume of a cylinder which is
   generated by rotating the rectangle about the 10-inch side.

_____

209

6. Find the exact volume of the pyramid.

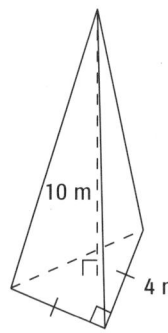

_____

Name _____ Date _____

7. Find the exact volume of the cone. • **MORE HELP** See 152

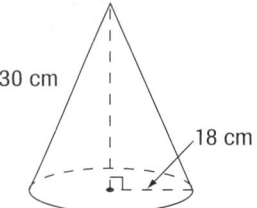

_____

8. The truncated cone is formed by bisecting the
   12-centimeter altitude of a cone with a plane
   parallel to its base. Find the exact volume of
   the truncated cone.

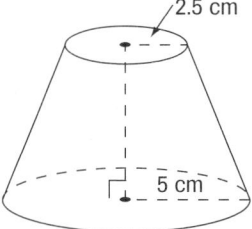

_____

9. The pyramids of Egypt are regular square pyramids. The height of one is 471 feet
   and each edge of the base is 707.75 feet. Find the volume.

_____

10. Find the volume of this figure. Round your answer
    to the nearest tenth. • **MORE HELP** See 207, 238

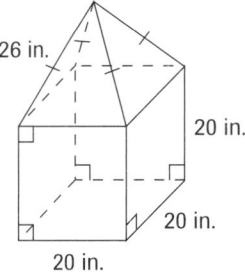

210

_____

11. Find the exact volume of the sphere.

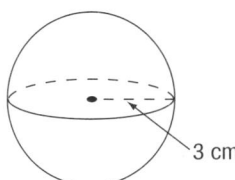

_____

12. A sphere with a 6-inch radius is inscribed in a cylinder. Find the ratio of the volume
    of the sphere to the volume of the cylinder. • **MORE HELP** See 208

_____

Name_____ Date_____

Cubic Measurement

Directions: Fill in the circle beside the best answer to each question.

1. Find the volume of the rectangular prism.

   A. 420 cm

   B. 420 cm³

   C. 420 cm²

   D. none of the above

2. Find the exact volume.

   A. 1000 ft³

   B. $\frac{500}{3}$ ft³

   C. $500\sqrt{3}$ ft³

   D. $\frac{500\sqrt{3}}{3}$ ft³

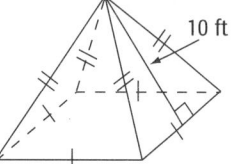

3. Find the exact volume.

   A. 4500π cm³

   B. 36,000π cm³

   C. 3600 cm³

   D. 27,000π cm³

4. How much wax is needed to make a candle with a hexagonal base and a height of 9 inches? Each side of the base is three inches long.

   A. about 210.4 in.³

   B. about 243 in.³

   C. about 140.3 in.³

   D. about 81 in.³

5. A cone is generated by revolving a right triangle with legs 10 inches and 12 inches, using the 12-inch side as the axis. Find of the volume of this cone.

   A. 400π in.³

   B. 400 in.³

   C. $\frac{400}{3\pi}$ in.³

   D. $\frac{400}{3}$ in.³

6. The ratio of the altitudes of two similar pyramids is 1:3. The volume of the larger pyramid is 400 cubic inches. What is the volume of the smaller pyramid?

   A. about 14.8 in.³

   B. about 44.4 in.³

   C. about 133.3 in.³

   D. about 1200 in.³

7. A plastic pipe is used for sewage. The outside diameter is two feet and the inside diameter is 1.8 feet. How much plastic is needed to make a section 16 feet in length?

   A. about 40.1 ft³

   B. about 38.2 ft³

   C. about 9.5 ft³

   D. about 0.38 ft³

PRACTICE ANSWERS
Page 113

1. yes; 96 cm³; The solids have the same height and their cross sectional areas are the same at every level.

2. 819 cm³

3. 5385.6 gallons

4. 176π m³

5. 160π or about 502.4 in.³

6. $26\frac{2}{3}$ m³

Page 114

7. 2592π cm³

8. 87.5π cm³

9. about 78,642,879.8 ft³

10. 16,727 cm³

11. 36π cm³

12. 2:3

TEST PREP ANSWERS
Page 112

1. B

2. D

3. A

4. A

5. A

6. A

7. C

Fun at Math Camp

OBJECTIVES
- Compute the area of rectangles of fixed perimeter
- Graph ordered pairs

MATERIALS
- Perimeter pieces: (straws, paper clips, coffee stirrers)

- **TIME**
- 30 minutes

TEACHER NOTES

- In this activity, students calculate the area of all possible rectangles that have a perimeter of 24 units and whole-number dimensions.

- If necessary, encourage students to use manipulatives to model the problem. Each pair of students will need 24 perimeter pieces.

- If needed, help students get started with the table of values.

- Have students visualize what the rectangle looks like as the area increases, and then begins to decrease. Maximum area is achieved when the figure is a square.

EXTENSIONS

- Encourage students to write an algebraic equation for each graph. The equations are

  1. $y = \dfrac{x(24 - 2x)}{2}$

  2. $y = x(24 - 2x)$

- Change the initial perimeter. For instance, build rectangles with a fixed perimeter of 36 or 48 units. Can students generalize any patterns?

- Change the problem so that the area is fixed, say 24 square units. What are the different rectangles that can be formed, and when is there a maximum perimeter? Consider only whole-number dimensions.

ANSWERS

1.

Width	Length	Area
1	11	11
2	10	20
3	9	27
4	8	32
5	7	35
6	6	36
7	5	35
8	4	32
9	3	27
10	2	20
11	1	11

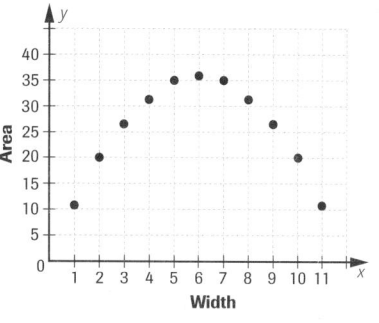

2. width = 6; length = 6

3.

Width	Length	Area
1	22	22
2	20	40
3	18	54
4	16	64
5	14	70
6	12	72
7	10	70
8	8	64
9	6	54
10	4	40
11	2	22

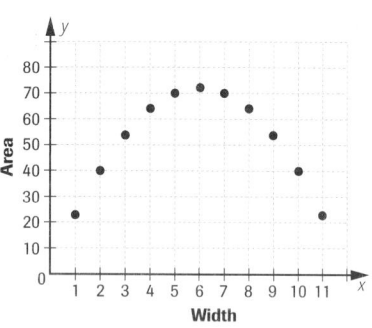

4. width = 6; length = 12

5. Answers will vary. The two graphs are parabolas. Each has the same domain values, [1, 11]. Both graphs have a maximum value at $x = 6$. The graphs differ in their maximum values. The first graph shows a maximum value of 36, while the second graph has a maximum value of 72.

Name_____ Date_____

Ordered pairs and
   Locating Points: 88

Perimeter of Polygons:
   170

Area of a Rectangle
   180

Fun at Math Camp

Two counselors at Summer Math Camp have come up with a new game. Each camper is given 24 congruent bamboo rods. The goal is to make a rectangle using all 24 rods. Make the rectangle of greatest area and you win!

1. Since you're at math camp, use your math skills and fill in the table below. Then, make the counselors smile and graph the results. The ordered pairs are (Width, Area).

Width	Length	Area
1		
2		
3		
4		
5		
6		
7		
8		
9		
10		
11		

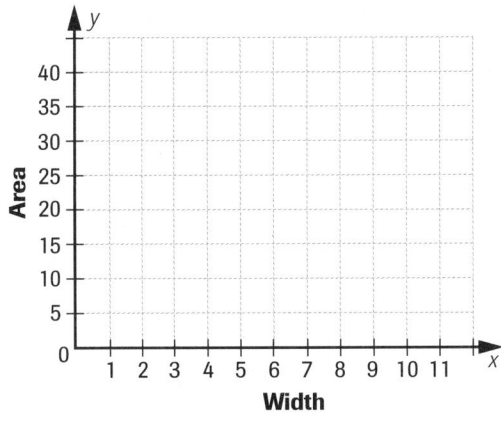

2. What dimensions will allow for the greatest area? _____

3. The rules have changed. The counselors said that you could build the rectangle along the edge of the riverbank (call that the length). Now you only need rods on three sides of your rectangle (two widths and a length). Fill in the table and graph the results.

Width	Length	Area
1		
2		
3		
4		
5		
6		
7		
8		
9		
10		
11		

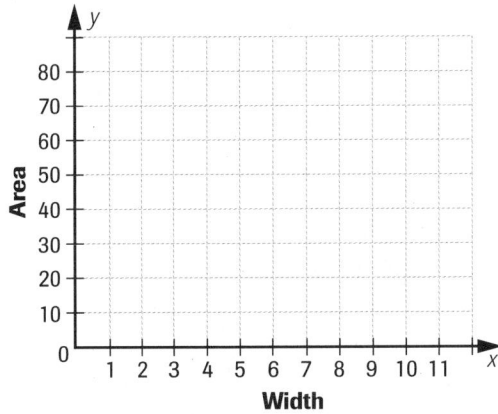

4. What are the dimensions of the rectangle of greatest area now?

   _____

5. How are the two graphs alike? How are they different?

   _____

   _____

Name_____ Date_____

Ratios, Rates, and Proportions

214

1. Tom is 5'3" tall; Clara is 4'10" inches tall. How much taller is Tom than Clara is? _____

2. How many times as fast as a propeller plane at 266 mph is a jet at 625 mph? _____

214

For exercises 3–7, refer to the diagram.

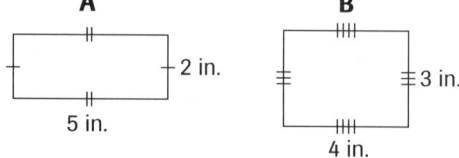

3. What is the ratio of the width to the length

   of rectangle A? _____

4. Find the ratio of the area of A to the area of B. _____

5. Find the ratio of the perimeter of A to the perimeter of B. _____

6. If you doubled one of the dimensions of A would you double the area? _____

7. If you doubled one of the dimensions of A would you double the perimeter? _____

215

For exercises 8–13, refer to the art.

Form of Ratio	Neal's Snares to Nicki's Snares	Neal's Tom-toms to all His Drums
8. Use *to*		
9. Use a *colon*		
10. Use *fraction form*		
11. Use *decimal form*		

12. If Nicki wants to make the ratio of her snares to her bass drums 5:3,

    what changes does she need to make? _____

13. Once the changes for exercise 12 are made, what will be the ratio of Nicki's snares

    to her Tom-toms? _____

Name _____ Date _____

216

Ms. Barton's math class has 10 boys and 12 girls. Use this fact to answer exercises 14–16.

14. What fraction of the class is boys? _____

15. What fraction of the class is girls? _____

16. What is the ratio of boys to girls in Ms. Barton's math class? _____

17. Pat eats 20 pancakes in five minutes. What is his rate per minute of pancake eating?

_____

217

18. Nicki can sustain a 40 beat drum roll for five seconds. Find her rate in beats per second.

_____

19. Neal's family's SUV can travel 350 miles on 15 gallons of gas. Find the SUV's rate of gas

consumption in miles per gallon. _____

20. Explain the statement, *The product of the means is equal to the product of the extremes.*

219

_____

_____

_____

Solve for x.

221

21. $\frac{4}{3} = \frac{x}{12}$ _____

22. $\frac{5}{x} = \frac{6}{10}$ _____

23. $\frac{x}{1} = \frac{5}{10}$ _____

24. $\frac{x+1}{3} = \frac{9}{6}$ _____

25. $\frac{3}{x-4} = \frac{12}{x+1}$ _____

26. $\frac{x}{x+2} = \frac{1}{x}$ _____

27. A model of the Bell X-1 is built to the scale
of 1 in. : 1.5 ft and the wingspan of the model
is 13.7 in. What is the wing span of the actual plane? _____

28. What are the measures of two supplementary angles that are in the ratio of 5:7?
- **MORE HELP** See 069

_____

Name_____ Date_____

Ratios, Rates, and Proportions

Directions: Mark the letter beside the best answer to each question.

1. In Timon's bag there are four red marbles and eight blue marbles. What is the ratio of red marbles to all the marbles in the bag?

   A. 4:8   **C.** 4:12

   B. 12:4   **D.** 8:12

2. Ms. Pulcort's math class has 11 boys and seven girls. Mr. Gomez's math class has eight girls and 15 boys. Which class has the largest ratio of girls to boys?

   A. Ms. Pulcort

   B. Mr. Gomez

   C. Neither; both are equal

   D. Cannot determine

3. You have a 3" by 5" picture to enlarge. You ask the photo shop to double each dimension. What is the ratio of the area of the enlarged photo to the area of the original?

   A. 2:1   **C.** 4:1

   B. 3:1   **D.** 8:1

4. Solve for x. $\frac{x}{x+1} = \frac{x+2}{x+4}$

   A. $x = 2$ **C.** $x = 4$

   B. $x = 3$ **D.** $x = 5$

Use this information for exercises 5–6: When Matt makes chocolate chip cookies he usually uses $\frac{1}{2}$ cup butter to 2 cups flour. Trying for a tastier cookie, he wants to increase the butter and decrease the flour by the same amount so that the ratio of butter to flour is 2:3.

5. Which proportion describes this best?

   A. $\frac{1}{2}x{:}2x = 2{:}3$ **C.** $\frac{1}{2}{:}2 = x{:}3$

   B. $\frac{\frac{1}{2}+x}{2-x} = 2{:}3$ **D.** $\frac{\frac{1}{2}-x}{2+x} = 2{:}3$

6. By how much should Matt increase the butter and decrease the flour?

   A. $\frac{1}{8}$ cup

   B. $\frac{1}{2}$ cup

   C. 1.5 cups

   D. $\frac{3}{4}$ cup

7. Two complementary angles are in the ratio of 4:1. What are their measures?

   A. 22.5° and 67.5°

   B. 15° and 75°

   C. 30° and 60°

   D. 18° and 72°

8. Anil rows at the rate of 15 meters per minute. How far will he travel in $\frac{1}{2}$ hour?

   A. 450 m   **C.** 75 m

   B. 150 m   **D.** 7.5 m

9. If a stock car model is built to the scale of 1 cm : 2.5 ft and the model measures 7.7 centimeters long, how long will the actual stock car be?

   A. 15 ft   **C.** 19.25 ft

   B. 17 ft   **D.** 3.08 m

10. What is the ratio of the area of the triangle to the area of the rectangle?

    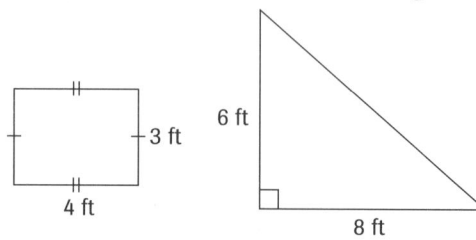

    A. 1:2   **C.** 4:1

    B. 1:4   **D.** 2:1

PRACTICE ANSWERS
Page 116

1. 5 in.
2. about 2.35 times as fast
3. 2:5
4. 5 to 6
5. $\frac{14}{14}$ or 1:1
6. yes
7. no
8. 4 to 3; 3 to 9
9. 4:3; 3:9
10. $\frac{4}{3}$; $\frac{3}{9}$
11. $1.3\overline{3}$; $0.3\overline{3}$
12. Add two more snares and one more bass drum.
13. 5:5

Page 117

14. $\frac{10}{22}$ or $\frac{5}{11}$
15. $\frac{12}{22}$ or $\frac{6}{11}$
16. 10:12 or 5:6
17. 4 pancakes per minute
18. 8 beats per second
19. $23\frac{1}{3}$ miles per gallon
20. If $a{:}b = c{:}d$, then $bc = ad$; b and c are called the means, a and d are called the extremes.
21. $x = 16$
22. $x = 8.3\overline{3}$
23. $x = 0.5$
24. $x = 3.5$
25. $x = 5.6\overline{6}$
26. $x = 2$ or $x = {}^-1$
27. 20.55 ft
28. 75° and 105°

TEST PREP ANSWERS
Page 118

1. C
2. A
3. C
4. A
5. B
6. B
7. D
8. A
9. C
10. D

Name _____ Date _____

Similar Polygons

222'

True or False?

1. Similar polygons are the same shape but not necessarily the same size. _____

2. A triangle cannot be similar to a rectangle. _____

3. Every pentagon is similar to every other pentagon. _____

4. If two polygons are similar, then their corresponding angles are congruent and their

   corresponding sides are in the same ratio. _____

5. If $\triangle ABC \sim \triangle DEF$ then $\frac{AB}{DE} = \frac{BC}{EF} = \frac{AC}{DF}$. _____

Determine whether the polygons are similar.

6.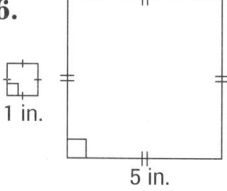

7.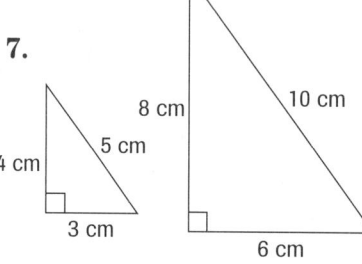

8.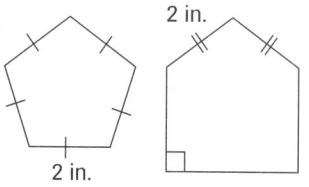

_____   _____   _____

224

Find the missing measures in these similar polygons.

9. Given that $\triangle ABC \sim \triangle DEF$, find x and y.

_____

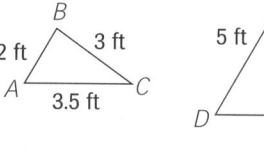

For exercises 10–11, compare
similar pentagons *PENTA* and *LQMTB*.

10. Find values for a, b, c, and d.

_____

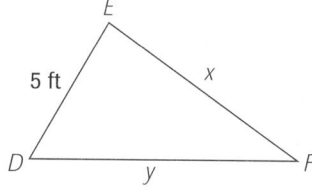

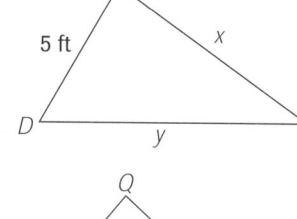

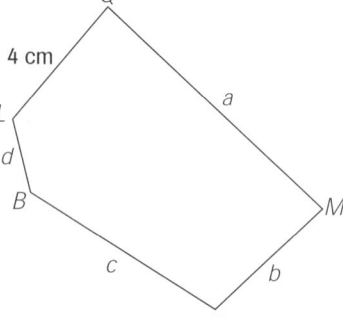

11. What is the ratio of the perimeter of *PENTA* to
    the perimeter of *LQMTB*?

_____

12. An 8" by 12" photo is reduced 70% to fit into a news column.

    What are the dimensions of the reduced photo? _____

Name _____ Date _____

13. a. How do you know that $\triangle XYZ \sim \triangle QPZ$?

227

_____

_____

_____

_____

_____

_____

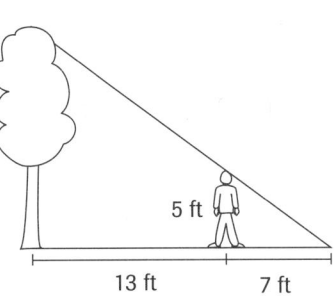

b. What is the value of XZ? _____

c. What is the value of XY? _____

14. Tom is 5 feet tall and he casts a 7-foot shadow.
The shadow of the tree is 20 feet.

How tall is the tree? _____

15. Prove that $\triangle ABC \sim \triangle DBA$

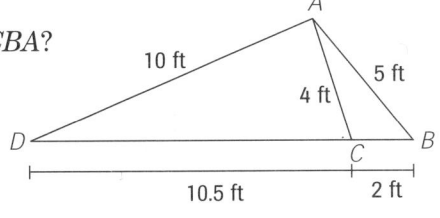

228

Proof

Given:

Prove:

Statements   **Reasons**

_____

_____

_____

_____

_____

_____

16. How do you know that you can use the
SSS Similarity Postulate to show that $\triangle ABD \sim \triangle CBA$?

230

_____

_____

_____

_____

_____

Name_____ Date_____

17. Given: $\triangle PDQ \sim \triangle SNT$ with side lengths shown in a–c
Find: Two possible sets of side-lengths for $\triangle SNT$ where one is the result of an enlargement and one is a reduction.

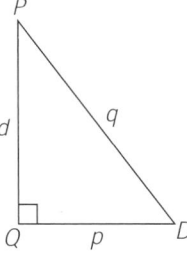
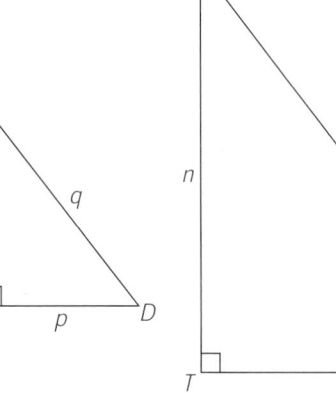

a. $p = 5$, $d = 12$, $q = 13$

_____

b. $p = 7$, $d = 24$, $q = 25$

_____

c. $p = 8$, $d = 15$, $q = 17$

_____

232

18. Find values for CE and DE.

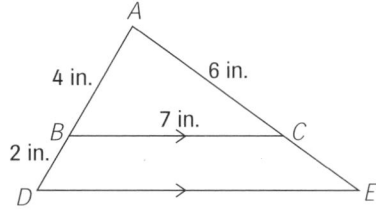

_____

19. Find values for AD, DE, and EC. • **MORE HELP** See 153

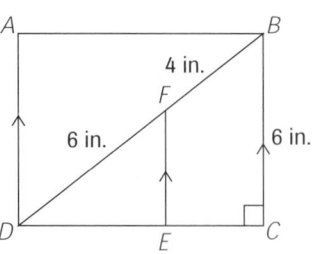

_____

233

20. What is the value of x?

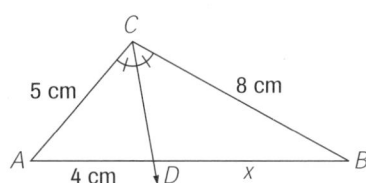

_____

Name _____ Date _____

Similar Polygons

Directions: Fill in the letter of the correct answer. Use the same diagram for exercises 1 and 2.

1 $\overline{BD}$ is the altitude of right $\triangle ABC$. Which statement is true?

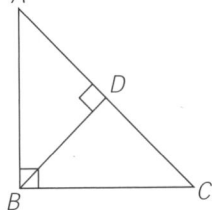

- **A** $\triangle ABC \sim \triangle ADB$
- **B** $\triangle ABC \sim \triangle ABD$
- **C** $\triangle ABC \sim \triangle BAD$

2 If $AB = 8$ units and $BC = 6$ units, then $DB = \underline{?}$ units.

- **D** 6.4
- **E** 4.8
- **F** 5.2

3 Solve for x and y.

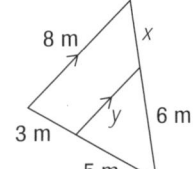

- **A** $x = 3.6$ m; $y = 5$ m
- **B** $x = 3$ m; $y = 4$ m
- **C** $x = 3.6$ m; $y = 4.8$ m

4 The perimeter of $\triangle ABC$ is 33 units. Find AD.

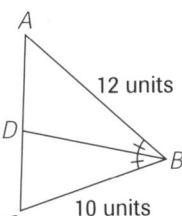

- **D** 4
- **E** 5
- **F** 6

5 Solve for x.

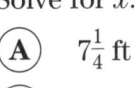

- **A** $7\frac{1}{4}$ ft
- **B** 2.8 ft
- **C** $2\frac{2}{7}$ ft

6 $PQRS \sim TUVW$. If $PQ = 11$ cm, $TW = 11$ cm, and $TU = 15$ cm, then $PS = \underline{?}$

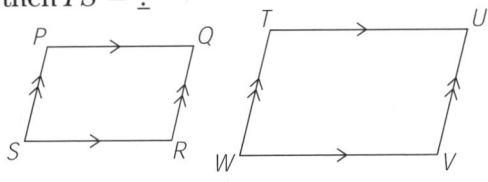

- **D** about 8 cm
- **E** about 7 cm
- **F** about 9 cm

7 Shelly wants to know how tall his house is. He stands in the shadow until his shadow falls to the edge of the house's shadow. He is 5 ft 3 in. tall. The shadow of the house is 80 ft while his shadow is 20 ft. How tall is the house?

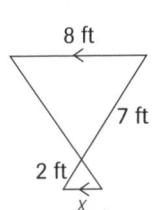

- **A** 60 ft
- **B** 21 ft
- **C** 26 ft

For exercises 8 and 9, use rectangle $ABCD$.

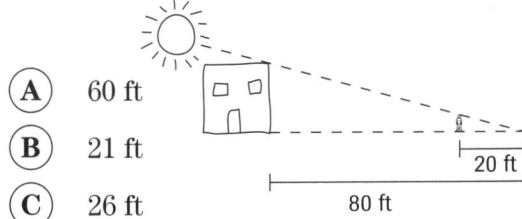

8 Find AE.

- **D** 4 in.
- **E** 5 in.
- **F** 6 in.

9 Find HD.

- **A** 4 in.
- **B** 5 in.
- **C** 6 in.

PRACTICE ANSWERS
Page 120

1. true

2. true

3. false

4. true

5. true

6. yes

7. yes

8. no

9. $x = 7.5$ units; $y = 8.75$ units

10. $a = 8$, $b = 4$, $c = 6$, $d = 2$

11. 1:2

12. 2.4 in. by 3.6 in.

Page 121

13. **a.** *One possible answer:* $\overline{XQ}$ and $\overline{PY}$ serve as transversals cutting parallel lines, so $\angle X \cong \angle Q$ and $\angle Y \cong \angle P$ making the triangles congruent by the AA Similarity Postulate.

   b. $XZ = 7.5$ cm

   c. $XY = 6.25$ cm

14. about 14.29 ft

15. **Proof**

Statements	Reasons
1 $AB = 2$; $DB = 6$; $BC = \frac{2}{3}$; $AD = 4.5$	Given
2 $\frac{AB}{DB} = \frac{2}{6}$ $\frac{BC}{BA} = \frac{\frac{2}{3}}{2}$	Substitution; def. of proportion
3 $\angle B \cong \angle B$	Reflexive Prop. of $\cong$ (T105)
4 $\triangle ABC \sim \triangle DBA$	SAS ~ Postulate (P21)

16. You have the measures of all of the sides; corresponding sides are proportional:
$$\frac{5}{2} = \frac{12.5}{5} = \frac{10}{4} = \frac{2.5}{1}$$

Page 122

17. Answers may vary. Samples are given.

   a. 10 units, 24 units, 26 units or 2.5 units, 6 units, 6.5 units

   b. 14 units, 48 units, 50 units or 3.5 units, 12 units, 12.5 units

   c. 16 units, 30 units, 34 units or 4 units, 7.5 units, 8.5 units

18. $CE = 3$ in., $DE = 10.5$ in.

19. $AD = 6$ units, $DE = 4.8$ units, $EC = 3.2$ units

20. $x = 6.4$ cm

TEST PREP ANSWERS
Page 123

1. A

2. E

3. A

4. F

5. C

6. D

7. B

8. E

9. C

Name _____ Date _____

Right Triangles

You may wish to draw or add auxiliary lines to diagrams and use a calculator to solve these problems.

235

1. $\overline{LP}$ is an altitude to the hypotenuse. Find x, y, and z.

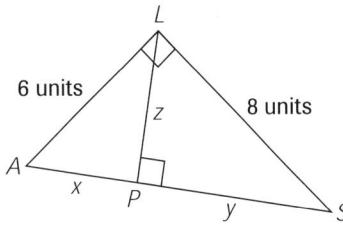

_____

2. *ABCD* is a rectangle. Find *AC* and *BE*. • **MORE HELP** See 152

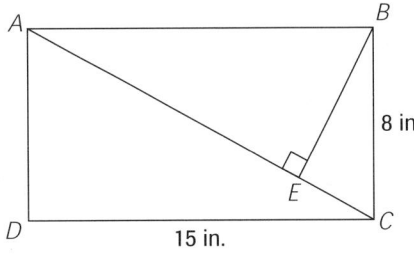

_____

236

3. In $\triangle PRT$, $PT = 50$ and $RT = 14$, find *ST*.

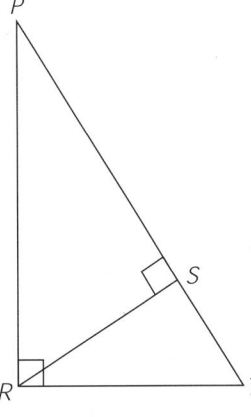

_____

4. Suppose Carlie wants to estimate the height of a tree in the park. She lines up the top and base of the tree at a distance of 15 feet with adjacent sides of an index card. From the ground to her eye is is 5'3" (5.25 ft). How tall is the tree?

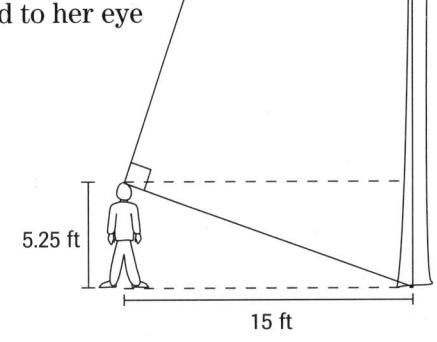

_____

Name _____ Date _____

5. In square *SQUA* find the length of diagonal *SU*.

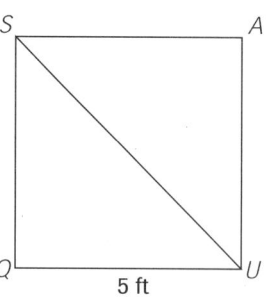

_____

For exercises 6–8, assume *SQUA* is a square. The inner squares are formed by joining the midpoints of sides.

6. If *SQ* = 8, what is the area of the shaded square?

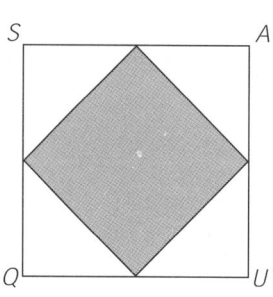

_____

7. If joining the midpoints of the shaded square formed one more square, how long would each side be? What would be the area of this new square?

_____

8. Can you identify a pattern that will allow you to predict without computing the area of the sixth square?

_____

9. Suppose the pitch of a symmetrical roof on a house that is 12 meters wide is 45°. What is the length of the rafter, *TU*, to the nearest tenth of a meter?

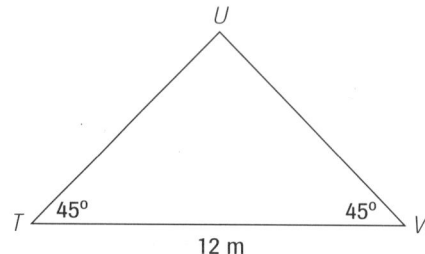

_____

Name _____ Date _____

10. △XYZ is equilateral. $\overline{XN}$ is an altitude.

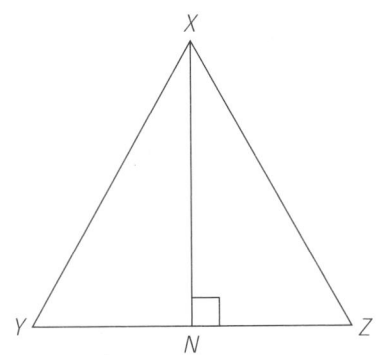

a. Write the measures of the angles of △XNZ.

_____

b. If $XZ = 10$ cm, find NZ and XN.

_____

c. What is the area of △XYZ?

_____

_____

11. In △PNB m∠B = 60° and NB = 6 meters. Use the diagram to help you find the exact measure of each segment.

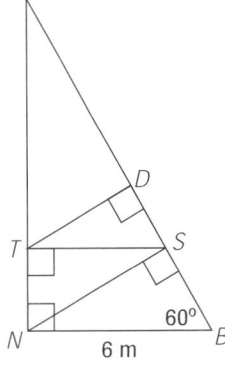

SB = _____   NS = _____

TN = _____   TS = _____

DS = _____   TD = _____

12. Suppose there is a 50-foot skateboard ramp with a 30° angle of elevation. How far above the ground is the top of the ramp?

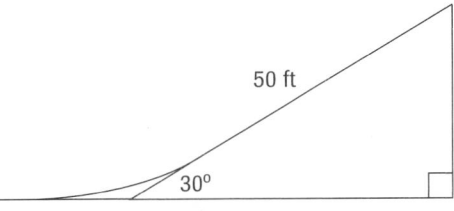

_____

13. If the length of apothem $\overline{OP}$ is $5\sqrt{3}$ cm, what is the perimeter of this regular hexagon?

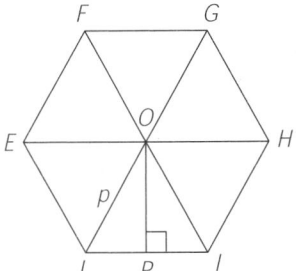

_____

Name_____ Date _____

Right Triangles

Directions: Mark the letter beside the best answer to each question.

1. Find the value of x.

   A. 5 in.

   B. 15 in.

   C. 13 in.

   D. 24 in.

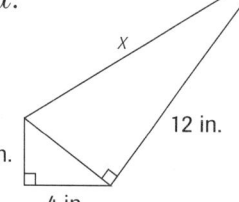

2. Find the value of x.

   A. $\sqrt{6}$ m

   B. $\sqrt{5}$ m

   C. 2 m

   D. $\sqrt{7}$ m

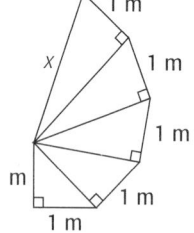

3. Find the value of EF. • **MORE HELP** See 139

   A. $5\sqrt{2}$ ft

   B. 5 ft

   C. $4.5\sqrt{2}$ ft

   D. $2.5\sqrt{2}$ ft

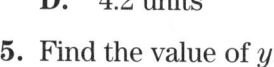

4. Find the value of x.

   A. 4.5 units

   B. 8 units

   C. 5 units

   D. 4.2 units

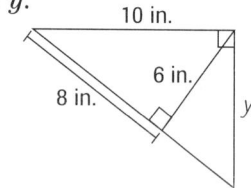

5. Find the value of y.

   A. 6 units

   B. 7.5 units

   C. 7 units

   D. 6.5 units

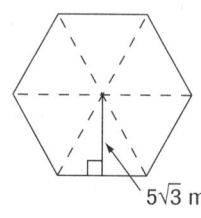

6. Find the area of this regular hexagon.
   Hint: Area of a regular polygon $= \frac{1}{2}$ apothem $\times$ perimeter.

   A. $50\sqrt{3}$ m²

   B. $60\sqrt{3}$ m²

   C. $150\sqrt{3}$ m²

   D. $300\sqrt{3}$ m²

7. Find the value of y.

   A. 3 yd

   B. 9 yd

   C. 7.5 yd

   D. 8 yd

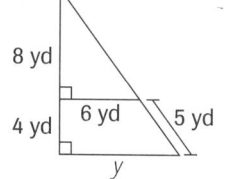

8. A man holds an avocado picking pole two feet from his body and uses it to cut the stem of an avocado 15 feet up in a tree. It falls to the ground 15 feet from the man. About how long is the picking pole?

   A. 16 ft

   B. 15 ft

   C. 17 ft

   D. 19 ft

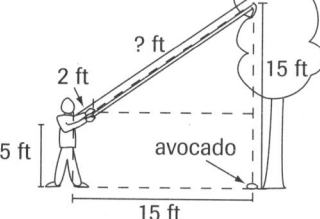

9. The perimeters of two similar 30°-60°-90° triangles are in the ratio of 3:4. The hypotenuse of the larger triangle is 100 centimeters. Find the length of the shorter leg of the smaller triangle.

   A. 50 cm

   B. $37.5\sqrt{3}$ cm

   C. 75 cm

   D. 37.5 cm

10. Find the perimeter of the triangle to the nearest tenth.

   A. 33.2 units

   B. 25.3 units

   C. 30.7 units

   D. 31.4 units

PRACTICE ANSWERS
Page 125

1. $x = 3.6$ units,
   $y = 6.4$ units,
   $z = 4.8$ units
2. $AC = 17$ in.; $BE \approx 7.1$ in.
3. $ST = 3.92$ m
4. about 48.11 ft

Page 126

5. $SU = 5\sqrt{2}$ ft
6. 32 ft²
7. 4 ft; 16 ft²
8. The pattern is: each square has half the area of the previous one. The area of the sixth square is 2 ft².
9. 8.5 m

Page 127

10. a. 30°–60°–90°
    b. $NZ = 5$ cm;
       $XN = 5\sqrt{3}$ cm
    c. $25\sqrt{3}$ cm²
11. $SB = 3$ m; $NS = 3\sqrt{3}$ m;
    $TN = 1.5\sqrt{3}$ m;
    $TS = 4.5$ m;
    $DS = 2.25$ m;
    $TD = 2.25\sqrt{3}$ m
12. 25 ft
13. 60 cm

TEST PREP ANSWERS
Page 128

1. C
2. A
3. D
4. A
5. B
6. C
7. B
8. A
9. D
10. C

Name_____ Date_____

Trigonometry

241 Write the proper ratio.

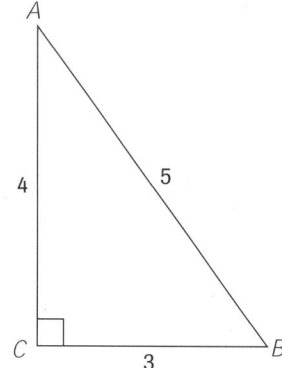

1. sin ∠A _____

2. sin ∠B _____

3. cos ∠A _____

4. cos ∠B _____

5. tan ∠A _____

6. tan ∠B _____

Use these triangles to find each ratio. • **MORE HELP** See 152-153

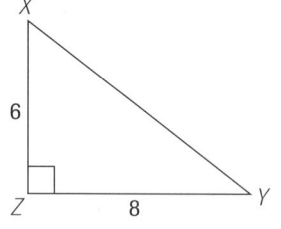
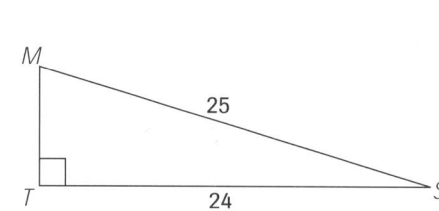
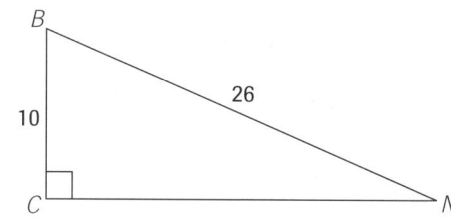

7. sin ∠X _____ **8.** cos ∠Y _____

9. tan ∠X _____ **10.** sin ∠S _____

11. tan ∠M _____ **12.** cos ∠N _____

13. sin ∠N _____ **14.** tan ∠B _____

243 Use the inverse function on your calculator
(in degree mode) or the Table of Trigonometric
Functions to solve exercises 15–17. Round to the
nearest degree.

15. What is the measure of ∠A? _____

16. What is the measure of ∠B? _____

17. What is the measure of ∠Q? _____

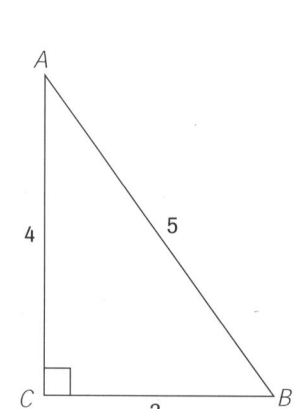
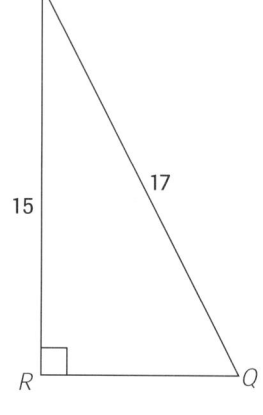

Name _____ Date _____

For exercises 18–19, write the measure of each angle in these two triangles.

- **MORE HELP** See 238-239

243

18.

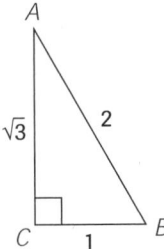

19.

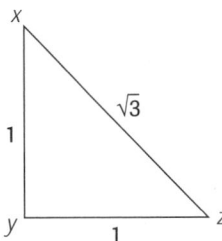

_____   _____

For exercises 20–22, make a labeled sketch of the problem. Write and solve an equation to answer the question.

245

20. Pedro's grandmother needs a handicap ramp to walk into her house. If her front door is six feet above the ground and she cannot walk at an incline of more than 20°, how long does the ramp need to be?

Labeled Sketch:

Equation:

Answer: _____

246

21. To the nearest 0.01 degree, what angle of descent (angle of depression) must a plane 50 horizontal miles from the airport and at an altitude of 20,000 feet make for its final approach?

Labeled Sketch:

Equation:

Answer: _____

Name _____ Date _____

248

22. A boat is caught in a storm at Point *A*. It is sending a distress signal to two Coast Guard Stations, at Points *B* and *C*, that are 50 miles apart on land. If m∠*ABC* = 31° and m∠*BAC* = 54°, find the station closest to the boat. About how far must a rescue boat travel to reach the distressed boat?

Labeled Sketch:

Equation:

Answer: _____

249

For exercises 23–24, use the Law of Cosines or any other method that works.

23. Find approximate values for *a* and *b*.

$a \approx$ _____

$b \approx$ _____

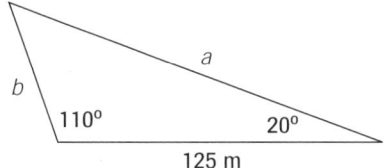

24. Find an approximate value for *c*.

$c \approx$ _____

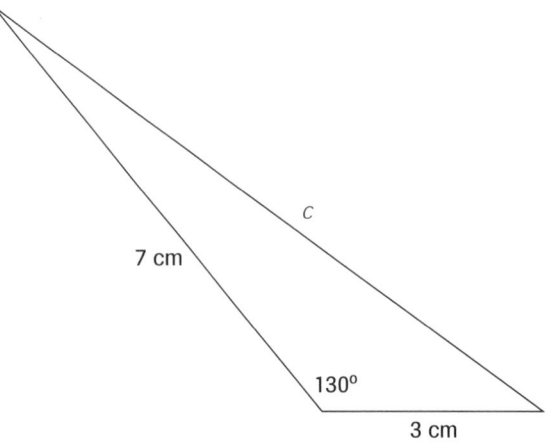

Name _____ Date _____

Trigonometry

Directions: Solve each problem. Mark your answer.

(1) What equation could you use to solve for x?

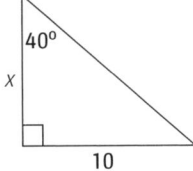

- **A** $\tan 50° = \frac{x}{10}$
- **B** $\sin 50° = \frac{x}{10}$
- **C** $\cos 50° = \frac{x}{10}$

(2) About how tall is the tree?

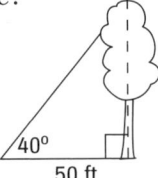

- **A** 38 ft
- **B** 50 ft
- **C** 42 ft

(3) If $\sin G = 0.5$, find $m\angle G$.

- **A** 45°
- **B** 30°
- **C** 60°

(4) A 50-foot ladder leans against a wall at a 60° angle. About how far up the wall does the ladder reach?

- **A** about 25 feet
- **B** about 32 feet
- **C** about 43 feet

(5) What equation could you use to solve for x?

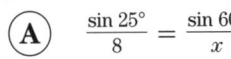

- **A** $\frac{\sin 25°}{8} = \frac{\sin 60°}{x}$
- **B** $\frac{\sin 60°}{8} = \frac{\sin 25°}{x}$
- **C** $x^2 = y^2 + z^2 - 2xy \cos 25°$

(6) Find the measure of $\angle A$ to the nearest degree.

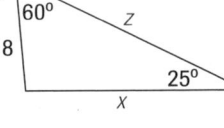

- **A** 28°
- **B** 30°
- **C** 32°

(7) If $\sin N = \frac{5}{13}$, what is $\cos N$? Draw the triangle and explain your reasoning.

- **A** $\frac{12}{13}$
- **B** $\frac{13}{5}$
- **C** $\frac{5}{12}$

_____

_____

(8) An airplane is flying at an altitude of 30,000 feet, approaching O'Hare Airport. Its angle of descent (angle of depression) is 5° and it will not need to change this angle before touching down. What is the horizontal distance to the point of touchdown?

- **A** about 65 miles
- **B** about one mile
- **C** about six miles

(9) Two fire towers, A and B, are 25 miles apart. Both spot a fire at point C. Find the distance, to the nearest mile, from each tower to the fire if $m\angle CAB = 110°$ and $m\angle ABC = 20°$.

- **A** 33 miles and 9 miles
- **B** 31 miles and 11 miles
- **C** 29 miles and 12 miles

(10) Romeo gazes at the top of Juliet's head at an angle of elevation of 42°. His eyes are 5.5 feet from the ground; he is 10 feet from the castle, and Juliet's balcony is ten feet above the ground. How tall is Juliet?

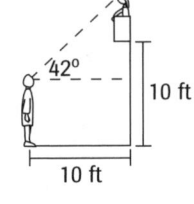

- **A** about 9 feet
- **B** about 4.5 feet
- **C** about 5 feet

PRACTICE ANSWERS
Page 130

1. $\frac{3}{5}$

2. $\frac{4}{5}$

3. $\frac{4}{5}$

4. $\frac{3}{5}$

5. $\frac{3}{4}$

6. $\frac{4}{3}$

7. $\frac{8}{10}$

8. $\frac{8}{10}$

9. $\frac{8}{6}$

10. $\frac{7}{25}$

11. $\frac{24}{7}$

12. $\frac{24}{26}$

13. $\frac{10}{26}$

14. $\frac{24}{10}$

15. about 37°

16. about 53°

17. about 62°

Page 131

18. m∠A = 30°,
    m∠B = 60°, m∠C = 90°

19. m∠X = m∠Z = 45°,
    m∠Y = 90°

20. 17.54 ft

21. about 4.33°

Page 132

22. Station C, about
    32 miles

23. $a = 153.34$ m,
    $b = 55.81$ m

24. 9.22 cm

TEST PREP ANSWERS
Page 133

1. C

2. C

3. B

4. C

5. A

6. A

7. A

8. A

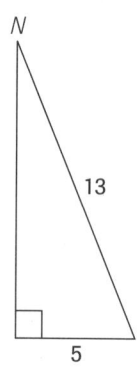

Sin N is the ratio of the side opposite ∠N to the hypotenuse. The Pythagorean Theorem says that the side adjacent must be 12. Thus cos $N = \frac{12}{13}$.

9. B

10. B

Name _____ Date _____

Geometric Connections

1. What happens when you compare ratios of successive terms of the Fibonacci Sequence?

   251

   _____

   _____

2. Think of any two numbers, x and y, with $x < y$. Use them to start a sequence that follows the rule for the Fibonacci Sequence. After you have ten terms in the sequence, compare ratios of successive terms. What happened?

   _____

   _____

3. Construct a golden rectangle from four-inch square $AEFD$ by finding the midpoint, M, of segment AE. Use point M as the center and the distance MF as the radius to draw an arc that intersects an extension of $\overline{AE}$. Label the point of intersection B. Construct a perpendicular at B and draw $\overline{BC}$ on this perpendicular such that $BC = AD$, then connect F and C. $ABCD$ and $EBCF$ are golden rectangles. In square $AEFD$, draw a quarter circle using F as center.

   253

   a. Form square $EBIG$ by copying $\overline{BE}$ onto $\overline{EF}$ and $\overline{BC}$, then connecting the new endpoints, G and I. In square $EBIG$, draw a quarter circle using G as center.
   b. In golden rectangle $GICF$, repeat, forming square $HICJ$ and draw a quarter circle using H as center.
   c. Repeat to form at least two more squares containing quarter circles.

Name _____ Date _____

Geometric Connections

Directions: Draw or enhance a diagram, show your work, and explain your reasoning.

Use this diagram for exercises 1–4.

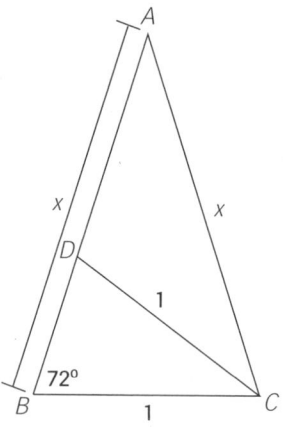

1. Solve for x and explain how x is related to the golden ratio.

Explanation: _____

_____

_____

_____

$x =$ _____

2. Use similar triangles to prove that $\overline{AB}$ is divided into two lengths that form a Golden Ratio.

_____

_____

_____

_____

_____

_____

3. Substitute into the ratio derived in exercise 2 to compute the value of the Golden Ratio.

You may need to use the quadratic formula: if $ax^2 + bx + c = 0$, then

$$x = \frac{-b \pm \sqrt{b^2 - 4ac}}{2a}.$$

_____

_____

_____

_____

_____

4. Draw a regular pentagram by extending the sides of a regular pentagon with sides of one unit. Prove that the one of the triangles which forms a point is congruent to $\triangle ABC$ at the top of the page.

_____

_____

_____

_____

5. Calculate the perimeter of the regular pentagram in exercise 4.

_____

PRACTICE ANSWERS
Page 135

1. $ABCD$ $\dfrac{2\sqrt{5}+2}{4} = \dfrac{(1+\sqrt{5})}{2}$

$EBCF$ $\dfrac{4}{2\sqrt{5}-2} = \dfrac{(1+\sqrt{5})}{2}$

$GICF$ $\dfrac{2\sqrt{5}-2}{6-2\sqrt{5}} = \dfrac{(1+\sqrt{5})}{2}$
and so on

The ratios approach the golden ratio $\dfrac{(1+\sqrt{5})}{2}$.

2. The ratios approach the golden ratio.

3.

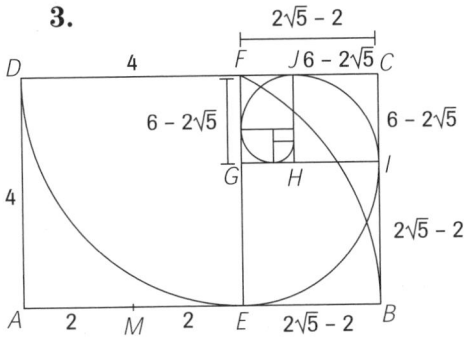

TEST PREP ANSWERS
Page 136

1. By drawing an altitude from A to BC and using trigonometry, $x \approx 1.618$.

2. Proof:

Since $\overline{AC} \cong \overline{BC}$ then $m\angle ACB = 72°$ and $m\angle BAC = 36°$.
$\overline{BC} \cong \overline{DC}$, then $m\angle BDC = 72°$ and $m\angle BCD = 36°$.
$m\angle ACD - m\angle BCD = m\angle ACD = 36°$.
$\triangle ABC \sim \triangle CDB$ by the AA $\sim$ Postulate (P21). Therefore $\dfrac{AB}{CD} = \dfrac{BC}{DB}$. Note that since $BC = DC = AD = 1$ and $AD + DB = AB$, this ratio is equivalent to $\dfrac{AB}{AD} = \dfrac{AD}{DB}$ which satisfies the definition of the Golden Ratio.

3. Substituting the values of the segments, we obtain:

$$\frac{x}{1} = \frac{1}{x-1}$$
$$x^2 - x = 1$$
$$x^2 - x - 1 = 0$$
$$x = \frac{1 \pm \sqrt{1 - 4(1)(^-1)}}{2(1)}$$
$$x = \frac{1+\sqrt{5}}{2},$$

approximately 1.618

(note: since x is a length, the negative value is meaningless)

4. Each interior angle of a regular pentagon measures $\dfrac{180°(5-2)}{5} = 108°$. This means that the exterior angles measure 72°. The ASA $\cong$ Theorem (T108) says that the points are congruent to the triangle at the top of the page.

5. $5 + \sqrt{5}$ units

Geometry at the Movies

OBJECTIVES
- Solve proportions
- Convert units of measure
- Compute with mixed measures
- Apply relationships in right isosceles triangles
- Compute perimeter, area, and volume

MATERIALS
none

TIME
- 30 minutes

TEACHER NOTES
In this activity, students apply a scale factor to find the dimensions of enlarged figures.

- Remind students how to set up a proportion.
$$\frac{\text{original dimension}}{\text{new dimension}} = \frac{1}{24}$$

- Remind students to write their new dimensions using an appropriate unit.

EXTENSIONS
- Encourage students to use their knowledge of scale factors and how they relate to linear, square, and cubic units of measure.

- Have students make a prop for the movie using a scale factor of about $\frac{1}{24}$. Suggest an item such as a paper clip, small eraser, or dime.

- Students can read about the making of the movie King Kong at www.pbs.org/wgbh/nova/specialfx/kingkong

- After students have answered exercise 7, ask them how many king-size sheets it would take to make one tissue. (4)

ANSWERS
1. $d = 15$ inches $= 1.25$ feet

   $l = 180$ inches $= 15$ feet

2. 10 feet by 16 feet by 1 foot

3. leg $= 8$ feet

4. 10 feet by 11 feet by $\frac{3}{4}$ feet

5. 16 feet by 18 feet

6. about 11.3 feet

7. area $= 288$ ft²; no, a king-size sheet is not wide or long enough

8. volume $= 82.5$ ft³

9. 4.5 in.; no, it will barely be a step up for Matt

Name _____ Date _____

Solving Proportions:
221

Similar Polygons: 222

Isosceles Right
Triangles: 238

Geometry at the Movies

How did they do that? This is a familiar question for a movie audience these days. The short answer, of course, is special effects. A more complete answer is … geometry!

Welcome to the set of *Inside a Desk*, a movie mystery. You've been hired by the studio to create the props for this movie about the case of a missing homework assignment. The director wants Matthew, the movie's star, to be able to walk around inside his desk to search for the homework that he claims someone has hidden.

To create the movie stage all of the props must be enlarged so that Matthew, his usual size, may walk around and appear to be a miniature person inside a desk. The scale factor that will be used for the movie is $\frac{1}{24}$, meaning the ratio of the original dimensions to enlarged dimensions is 1:24.

Break a leg and get to work. Label your answers with appropriate units.

In the table are a few common items that you know will be needed on the set. Determine the dimensions for each of the props.

Desk Item	Original Dimensions	New Dimensions
1. new pencil	$\frac{5}{8}$ in. diameter by $7\frac{1}{2}$ in. long	
2. paperback book	5 in. wide, 8 in. long, $\frac{1}{2}$ in. thick	
3. half a bologna sandwich	right triangle with a leg 4 in. long.	
4. CD case	5 in. by 5.5 in. by $\frac{3}{8}$ in.	
5. a tissue	8 inches by 9 inches	

6. Find the length of the hypotenuse of the BIG sandwich in exercise 3.

_____

7. Find the area of a new tissue. Could you use a king-size flat sheet (108" × 102") as the new tissue? Explain.

_____

8. What is the volume of the new CD case? (Perhaps that is where the homework is hiding.)

_____

9. In one scene Matt jumps up on top of a piece of gum. Actual chewing gum is $\frac{3}{16}$ in. thick. Will this be a difficult jump for Matt? Explain.

_____

Name _____ Date _____

Properties of Congruence

256

In exercises 1–2, identify the six pairs of corresponding parts of the congruent triangles.

1.

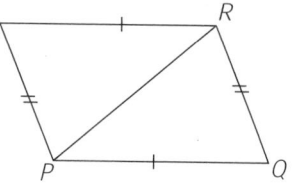

2.

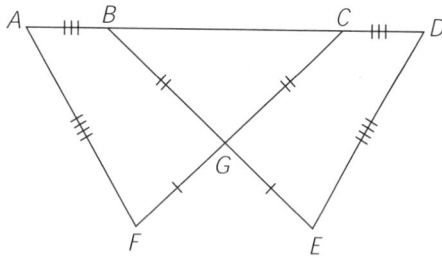

In exercises 3–4, the triangles are congruent. Find the values of x, y, and z.

3.

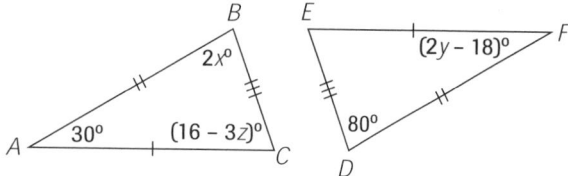

4.

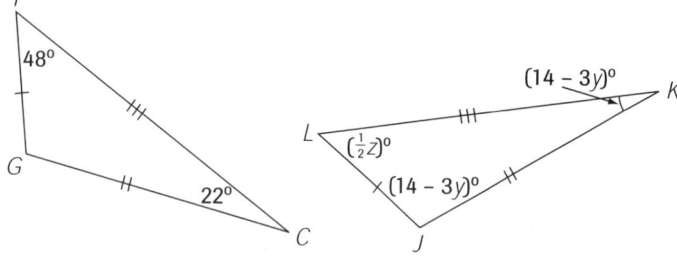

5. The quadrilaterals are congruent.
Find the values of x, y, z, and t.

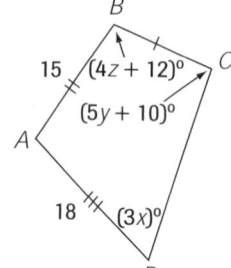
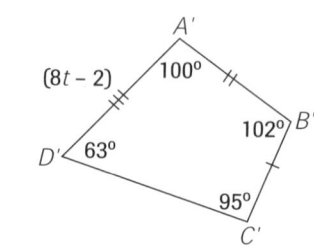

Name _____ Date _____

Decide whether the following figures and their relations satisfy the properties. If yes, write a statement illustrating this. If no, explain why not. An example is shown.

257–258

	Figures	Relation	Reflexive	Symmetric	Transitive	Equivalence Relation
Ex.	lines	is $\perp$ to	No A segment cannot be $\perp$ to itself.	Yes If $l_1 \perp l_2$, then $l_2 \perp l_1$	No 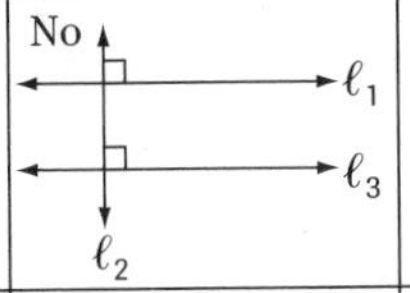	No relation is neither reflexive nor transitive
6.	angles	is less than				
7.	angles	is the complement of				
8.	angles	is adjacent to				
9.	angles	forms a linear pair				
10.	triangles	is similar to				
11.	polygons	is congruent to				
12.	lines	intersects				
13.	lines	is parallel to				
14.	planes	is parallel to				

Name_____ Date_____

Properties of Congruence

Directions: Fill in the circle beside the best answer to each question.

1. In the congruent triangles shown below, which angle corresponds to ∠R?

○ **A.** ∠U

○ **B.** ∠V

○ **C.** ∠1

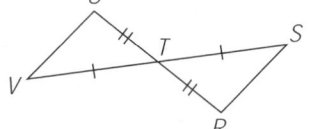

2. In the congruent triangles shown, which side corresponds to $\overline{MO}$?

○ **A.** $\overline{TP}$

○ **B.** $\overline{NO}$

○ **C.** $\overline{NP}$

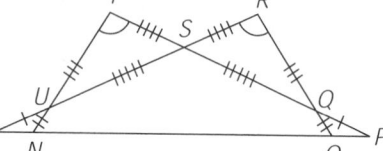

3. The triangles shown are congruent. Find the value of *x*.

○ **A.** 43.3

○ **B.** 10

○ **C.** 16.6

 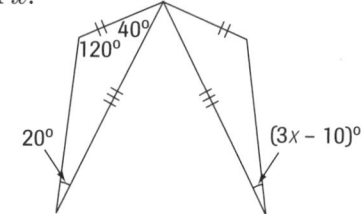

4. The quadrilaterals shown are congruent. Find the value of *x*.

○ **A.** 1.25

○ **B.** 2.25

○ **C.** 2

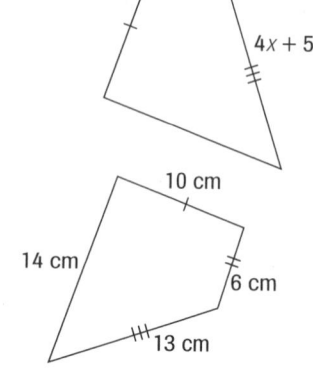

In exercises 5–13, identify the statement as an example of one of the following properties:

A. reflexive

B. symmetric

C. transitive

5. $\overline{PQ} \cong \overline{PQ}$

○ **A.**   ○ **B.**   ○ **C**

6. If *MN* = *TR*, and *TR* = *AB*, then *MN* = *AB*.

○ **A.**   ○ **B.**   ○ **C**

7. If ∠A ≅ ∠B, then ∠B ≅ ∠A.

○ **A.**   ○ **B.**   ○ **C**

8. If △DEF ≅ △PZR, then △PZR ≅ △DEF.

○ **A.**   ○ **B.**   ○ **C**

9. If m∠Z = m∠T and m∠2 = m∠T, then m∠Z = m∠2.

○ **A.**   ○ **B.**   ○ **C**

10. If *DE* + *EF* = *DF*, then *DF* = *DE* + *EF*.

○ **A.**   ○ **B.**   ○ **C**

11. △MNO ≅ △MNO

○ **A.**   ○ **B.**   ○ **C**

12. If m∠A + m∠B = m∠1 + m∠2 and m∠A + m∠B = m∠C, then m∠1 + m∠2 = m∠C.

○ **A.**   ○ **B.**   ○ **C**

13. ∠PZR ≅ ∠PZR

○ **A.**   ○ **B.**   ○ **C**

PRACTICE ANSWERS
Page 140

1. $\overline{SR} \cong \overline{QP}$, $\overline{PR} \cong \overline{RP}$,
   $\overline{SP} \cong \overline{QR}$,
   $\angle SPR \cong \angle QRP$,
   $\angle PSR \cong \angle RQP$,
   $\angle SRP \cong \angle QPR$
2. $\overline{AF} \cong \overline{DE}$, $\overline{AC} \cong \overline{DB}$,
   $\overline{FC} \cong \overline{EB}$,

Page 140 (cont.)

   $\angle AFC \cong \angle DEB$,
   $\angle FAC \cong \angle EDB$,
   $\angle ACF \cong \angle DBE$
3. $x = 40$, $y = 24$, $z = {}^{-}18$
4. $x = 4$, $y = {}^{-}32$, $z = 96$
5. $x = 21$, $y = 17$, $z = 22.5$,
   $t = 2.5$

TEST PREP ANSWERS
Page 142

1. A	2. C
3. B	4. C
5. A	6. C
7. B	8. B
9. C	10. B
11. A	12. C
13. A	

Page 141

	Figures	Relation	Reflexive	Symmetric	Transitive	Equivalence Relation
Ex.	lines	is $\perp$ to	No A segment cannot be $\perp$ to itself.	Yes If $l_1 \perp l_2$, then $l_2 \perp l_1$	No	No relation is neither reflexive nor transitive
6.	angles	is less than	No $m\angle A = m\angle A$	No if $m\angle A < m\angle B$ then $m\angle B > m\angle A$	Yes if $m\angle A < m\angle B$ and $m\angle B < m\angle C$ then $m\angle A < m\angle C$	No neither reflexive nor symmetric
7.	angles	is the complement of	No any angle other than $45°$ is not a complement of itself	Yes if $\angle A$ is complement to $\angle B$ then $\angle B$ is complement to $\angle A$	No if $\angle A$ is complement to $\angle B$ and $\angle B$ is complement to $\angle C$ then $m\angle A = m\angle C$	No neither reflexive nor transitive
8.	angles	is adjacent to	No $\angle A$ is not adjacent to itself	Yes if $\angle A$ is adjacent to $\angle B$ then $\angle B$ is adjacent to $\angle A$	No if $\angle A$ is adjacent to $\angle B$ and $\angle B$ is adjacent to $\angle C$ then $\angle A$ and $\angle C$ may not share a side	No neither reflexive nor transitive
9.	angles	forms a linear pair	No unless an angle measures $90°$, it cannot form a linear pair with itself	Yes if $\angle A$ and $\angle B$ form a linear pair then $\angle B$ and $\angle A$ form a linear pair	No if angles A and B and angles B and C form linear pairs then $m\angle A = m\angle C$	No neither reflexive nor transitive
10.	triangles	is similar to	Yes $\triangle ABC \approx \triangle ABC$	Yes if $\triangle ABC \approx \triangle DEF$ then $\triangle DEF \approx \triangle ABC$	Yes if $\triangle ABC \approx \triangle DEF$ and $\triangle DEF \approx \triangle GHI$ then $\triangle ABC \approx \triangle GHI$	Yes
11.	polygons	is congruent to	Yes $A \cong A$	Yes if $A \cong B$ then $B \cong A$	Yes if $A \cong B$ and $B \cong C$ then $A \cong C$	Yes
12.	lines	intersects	No a line has *all* points in common with itself	Yes if l_1 intersects l_2 then l_2 intersects l_1	No if l_1 intersects l_2 and l_2 intersects l_3 then l_1 and l_2 could be parallel	No neither reflexive nor transitive
13.	lines	is parallel to	No a line has *all* points in common with itself	Yes if $l_1 \parallel l_2$, then $l_2 \parallel l_1$	Yes if $l_1 \parallel l_2$ and $l_2 \parallel l_3$, then $l_1 \parallel l_3$	No not reflexive
14.	planes	is parallel to	No a plane has *all* points in common with itself	Yes if plane $A \parallel$ plane B then plane $B \parallel$ plane A	Yes if plane $A \parallel$ plane B and plane $B \parallel$ plane C then plane $A \parallel$ plane C	No not reflexive

Name _____ Date _____

Congruence of Polygons

In exercises 1–5, proofs are given. The same diagram, shown below, is used for each proof. From the following list of congruence postulates and theorems, choose the one that justifies the final statement in each proof.

A. SSS
B. SAS
C. ASA
D. AAS
E. H-L
F. H-A
G. L-L

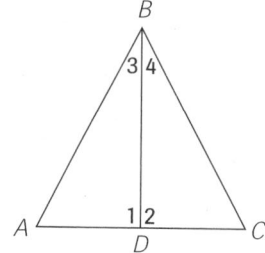

1. Proof

Given: $\overline{BD}$ is a median; $\overline{AB} \cong \overline{BC}$

Prove: $\triangle ADB \cong \triangle CDB$ • **MORE HELP** See 136

Statements	Reasons
❶ $\overline{AB} = \overline{BC}$	Given
❷ $\overline{BD}$ is a median	Given
❸ $\angle A \cong \angle C$	Base $\angle$s Theorem (T050)
❹ $AD = DC$; $\overline{AD} \cong \overline{DC}$	Def. of median; def. of $\cong$
❺ $\triangle ADB \cong \triangle CDB$	?

2. Proof

Given: $\overline{BD}$ is a median; $\overline{AB} \cong \overline{BC}$

Prove: $\triangle ADB \cong \triangle CDB$ • **MORE HELP** See 136

Statements	Reasons
❶ $\overline{BD}$ is a median	Given
❷ $AD = DC$; $\overline{AD} \cong \overline{DC}$	Def. of median; def. of $\cong$
❸ $\overline{AB} \cong \overline{BC}$	Given
❹ $\overline{BD} \cong \overline{BD}$	Reflexive prop. of $\cong$ (T105)
❺ $\triangle ADB \cong \triangle CDB$	?

3. Proof

Given: $\overline{BD}$ is an altitude; $\overline{AB} \cong \overline{BC}$

Prove: $\triangle ADB \cong \triangle CDB$

Statements	Reasons
❶ $\overline{BD}$ is an altitude	Given
❷ $\overline{AB} \cong \overline{BC}$	Given
❸ $\overline{BD} \perp \overline{AC}$	Def. of altitude
❹ $\angle 1$ and $\angle 2$ are rt. $\angle$s	Def. of $\perp$
❺ $\angle 1 \cong \angle 2$	All rt. $\angle$s $\cong$ (T020)
❻ $\angle A \cong \angle C$	Base $\angle$s Theorem (T050)
❼ $\triangle ADB \cong \triangle CDB$	?

Name _____ Date _____

4. Proof

Given: $\overline{AB} \cong \overline{BC}$; $\overline{BD}$ is an altitude

Prove: $\triangle ADB \cong \triangle CDB$

Statements	Reasons
❶ $\overline{AB} \cong \overline{BC}$	Given
❷ $\overline{BD}$ is an altitude	Given
❸ $\overline{BD} \perp \overline{AC}$	Def. of altitude
❹ $\angle 1$ and $\angle 2$ are rt. $\angle$s	Def. of $\perp$
❺ $\triangle ABD$ and $\triangle CBD$ are rt. $\triangle$s	Def. of rt. $\triangle$s
❻ $\overline{BD} \cong \overline{BD}$	Reflexive prop. of $\cong$ (T105)
❼ $\triangle ADB \cong \triangle CDB$	?

5. Proof

Given: $\overline{BD}$ is an angle bisector; $\overline{AB} \cong \overline{BC}$

Prove: $\triangle ADB \cong \triangle CDB$

Statements	Reasons
❶ $\overline{AB} \cong \overline{BC}$	Given
❷ $\overline{BD}$ is an $\angle$ bisector	Given
❸ $\angle 3 \cong \angle 4$	Def. of $\angle$ bisector
❹ $\angle A \cong \angle C$	Base $\angle$s Theorem (T050)
❺ $\triangle ADB \cong \triangle CDB$	?

Choose any style of proof for exercises 6-18.

261-270

6. Given: B is the midpoint of $\overline{AC}$; $\overline{AE} \cong \overline{DC}$; $\angle A \cong \angle C$

   Prove: $\triangle ABE \cong \triangle CBD$

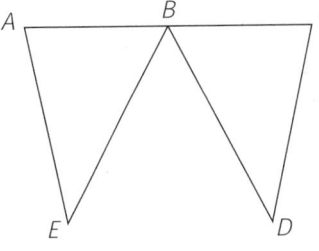

7. Given: $\angle B \cong \angle E$; C is the midpoint of $\overline{AD}$

   Prove: $\triangle ABC \cong \triangle DEC$

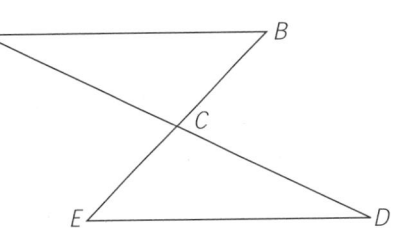

8. Given: $DC = AB$; $AD = BC$

   Prove: $\triangle DCB \cong \triangle BAD$

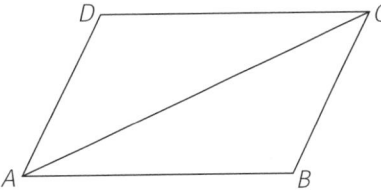

Name_____ Date_____

9. Given: $\overline{AB} \perp \overline{AE}$; $\overline{ED} \perp \overline{AE}$; $\overline{BC} \cong \overline{CD}$;
C is the midpoint of $\overline{AE}$
Prove: $\triangle BCA \cong \triangle DCE$

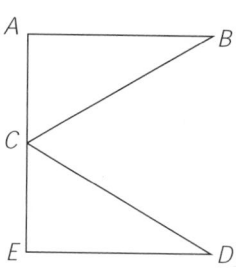

10. Given: $\angle 1$ is the complement of $\angle 2$; $\angle 3$ is the complement of $\angle 4$; $\overline{AB} \parallel \overline{CD}$
Prove: $\triangle ADB \cong \triangle CBD$

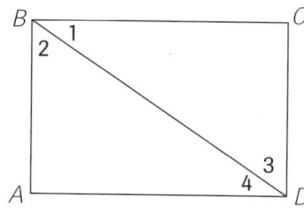

11. Given: $\triangle ABC$ is equilateral; $\overline{DB} \cong \overline{EC} \cong \overline{AF}$
Prove: $\triangle DBE \cong \triangle ECF \cong \triangle FAD$

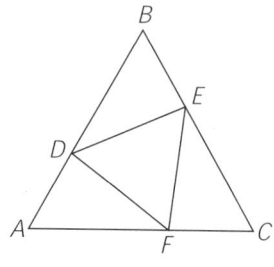

12. Given: $\angle 1 \cong \angle 2$; $\overline{DA} \cong \overline{EC}$
Prove: $\triangle DPA \cong \triangle EPC$

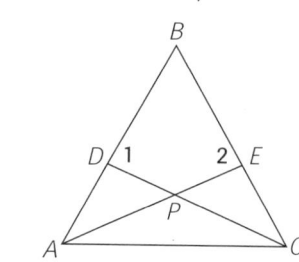

13. Given: $\angle 1 \cong \angle 2$; $\overline{AB} \parallel \overline{DC}$
Prove: $\triangle ABC \cong \triangle CDA$

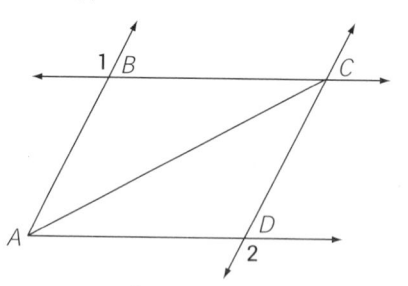

14. Look at the diagram. Decide whether the information given is sufficient to prove that $\triangle ABC \cong \triangle DEC$. Explain your answer.
Given: $\overline{AB} \cong \overline{DE}$; $\overline{CE} \cong \overline{BC}$

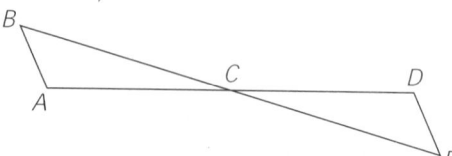

_____

_____

_____

Name _____ Date _____

Exercises 15–17 use the same diagram.

15. **Given:** $\overline{AC} \cong \overline{AB}$; $\angle 1 \cong \angle 2$; $\overline{IB} \cong \overline{CG}$
  Prove: $\triangle IHC \cong \triangle GFB$

16. **Given:** $AC = AB$; $AD = AE$; $IC = BG$
  Prove: $\triangle EBI \cong \triangle DCG$

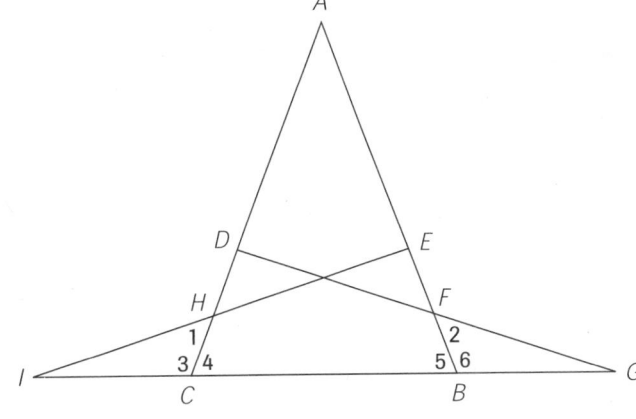

17. **Given:** $AB = AC$; $HC = FB$; $DH = EF$
  Prove: $DFBC \cong EHCB$

271-272

Exercises 18–19 use the same diagram.

18. **Given:** $\overline{BD} \perp \overline{AB}$; $\overline{DC} \perp \overline{AC}$; $\overline{EF} \perp \overline{AE}$;
  $\overline{FG} \perp \overline{AG}$; $\overline{BG}$ and $\overline{CE}$ bisect each other
  Prove: $ACDB \cong AEFG$

19. **Given:** A is a midpoint of $\overline{BG}$ and $\overline{CE}$; $ACDB$
  and $AEFG$ are kites; $\angle 2 \cong \angle 3$
  Prove: $ACDB \cong AEFG$ • **More Help** See 166

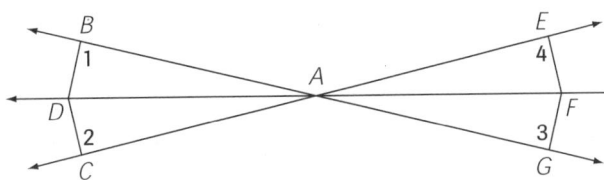

Name _____ Date _____

Congruence of Polygons

Directions: Fill in the circle beside the best answer to each question.

In exercises 1–4, the diagrams are marked with the given information. Choose the appropriate postulate or theorem which could be used to prove the triangles are congruent.

1.

○ **A.** SSS

○ **B.** SAS

○ **C.** AAS

○ **D.** ASA

2.

○ **A.** SSS

○ **B.** SAS

○ **C.** AAS

○ **D.** ASA

3.

○ **A.** H-A

○ **B.** L-L

○ **C.** H-L

○ **D.** not possible

4.

○ **A.** H-A

○ **B.** L-L

○ **C.** H-L

○ **D.** not possible

In exercises, 5–7, mark the diagram with the given information, then choose the postulate or theorem which could be used to prove the triangles are congruent.

5. Given: $\overline{AC}$ bisects $\angle BCD$; $\angle B \cong \angle D$
   Prove: $\triangle ABC \cong \triangle ADC$

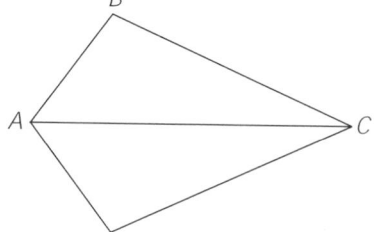

○ **A.** SSS

○ **B.** SAS

○ **C.** AAS

○ **D.** ASA

6. Given: $\overline{AF} \cong \overline{CD}$, $\overline{AB} \cong \overline{DE}$; $\overline{AB} \parallel \overline{DE}$
   Prove: $\triangle ABC \cong \triangle DEF$

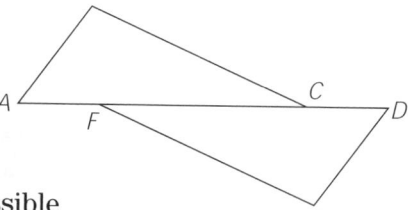

○ **A.** SSS

○ **B.** SAS

○ **C.** AAS

○ **D.** not possible

7. Given: $\overline{AE} \perp \overline{EC}$; $\overline{BD} \perp \overline{EC}$; $AP = BC$; $\overline{AB} \parallel \overline{EC}$
   Prove: $\triangle APE \cong \triangle BCD$

○ **A.** H-A

○ **B.** L-L

○ **C.** H-L

○ **D.** not possible

PRACTICE ANSWERS
Page 144

1. B

2. A

3. D

Page 145

4. E

5. C

Note: For exercises 6–18, we present sample two-column proofs, but students may choose other styles of proof instead. Alternative proofs for exercises 10, 12, 14, and 16 involve complements or supplements to congruent angles.

6. Proof

Statements	Reasons
❶ B is the midpt. of $\overline{AC}$	Given
❷ $\overline{AE} \cong \overline{DC}$, $\angle A \cong \angle C$	Given
❸ $\overline{AB} \cong \overline{BC}$	Def. of midpt.
❹ $\triangle ABE \cong \triangle CBD$	SAS $\cong$ Postulate (P23)

7. Proof

Statements	Reasons
❶ $\angle B \cong \angle E$	Given
❷ C is the midpt. of $\overline{AD}$	Given
❸ $\overline{AC} \cong \overline{CD}$	Def. of midpt.
❹ $\angle ACB \cong \angle DCE$	Vert. $\angle$s $\cong$ (T023)
❺ $\triangle ABC \cong \triangle DEC$	AAS $\cong$ Theorem (T109)

8. Proof

Statements	Reasons
❶ $DC = AB$, $AD = BC$	Given
❷ $\overline{DC} \cong \overline{AB}$; $\overline{AD} \cong \overline{BC}$	Def. of $\cong$
❸ $\overline{DB} \cong \overline{DB}$	Reflexive Prop. of $\cong$ (T105)
❹ $\triangle DCB \cong \triangle BAD$	SSS $\cong$ Postulate (P22)

Page 146

9. Proof

Statements	Reasons
❶ $\overline{AB} \perp \overline{AE}$	Given
❷ $\overline{ED} \perp \overline{AE}$	Given
❸ $\overline{BC} \cong \overline{CD}$	Given
❹ C is midpt. of $\overline{AE}$	Given
❺ $\angle BAC$ and $\angle DEC$ are rt. $\angle$s	$\perp$ lines $\Rightarrow$ 4 rt. $\angle$s (T011)
❻ $\triangle BCE$ and $\triangle DCE$ are rt. $\triangle$s	Def. of rt. $\triangle$
❼ $\overline{CE} \cong \overline{CA}$	Def. of midpt.
❽ $\triangle BCA \cong \triangle DCE$	H-L $\cong$ theorem (T110)

10. Proof

Statements	Reasons
❶ $\angle 1$ is complement of $\angle 2$	Given
❷ $\angle 3$ is complement of $\angle 4$	Given
❸ $\overline{AB} \parallel \overline{CD}$	Given
❹ $\angle 2 \cong \angle 3$, $m\angle 2 = m\angle 3$	Alt. Int. $\angle$s Theorem (T027); def. of $\cong$
❺ $m\angle 1 + m\angle 2 = 90^\circ$; $m\angle 3 + m\angle 4 = 90^\circ$	Def. of Complementary $\angle$s
❻ $m\angle 1 + m\angle 2 = m\angle 3 + m\angle 4$	Substitution
❼ $m\angle 1 = m\angle 4$; $\angle 1 \cong \angle 4$	Subtraction Prop. of =; def. of $\cong$
❽ $\overline{BD} \cong \overline{BD}$	Reflexive Prop. of $\cong$ (T105)
❾ $\triangle ADB \cong \triangle CBD$	ASA $\cong$ Theorem (T108)

11. Proof

Statements	Reasons
❶ $\triangle ABC$ is equilateral	Given
❷ $\overline{DB} \cong \overline{EC} \cong \overline{AF}$; $DB = EC = AF$	Given; def. of $\cong$
❸ $\overline{AB} \cong \overline{AC} \cong \overline{BC}$; $AB = AC = BC$	Def. of equilateral; def. of $\cong$
❹ $\angle A \cong \angle B \cong \angle C$	Base $\angle$s Theorem (T050)
❺ $AB = AD + DB$; $AC = AF + FC$; $BC = BE + EC$	Seg. + Postulate (P09)
❻ $AD + DB = AF + FC$ $BE + EC$	Substitution
❼ $BE = FC = AD$	Subtraction Prop. of =
❽ $\overline{BE} \cong \overline{FC} \cong \overline{AD}$	Def. of $\cong$
❾ $\triangle DBE \cong \triangle ECF \cong \triangle FAD$	SAS $\cong$ Postulate (P23)

12. Proof

Statements	Reasons
❶ $\angle 1 \cong \angle 2$	Given
❷ $\overline{DA} \cong \overline{EC}$	Given
❸ $m\angle 1 + m\angle ADC = 180^\circ$, $m\angle 2 + m\angle CEA = 180^\circ$	Linear pair Postulate (P14)
❹ $m\angle 1 + m\angle ADC = m\angle 2 + m\angle CEA$	Substitution
❺ $m\angle 1 = m\angle 2$	Def of $\cong$
❻ $m\angle ADC = m\angle CEA$	Subtraction Prop. of =
❼ $\angle ADC \cong \angle CEA$	Def. of $\cong$
❽ $\angle DPA \cong \angle CPE$	Vert. $\angle$s $\cong$ (T023)
❾ $\triangle DPA \cong \triangle EPC$	AAS $\cong$ Theorem (T109)

13. Proof

Statements	Reasons
❶ $\angle 1 \cong \angle 2$	Given
❷ $\overline{AB} \parallel \overline{DC}$	Given
❸ $\angle 1 \cong \angle ABC$; $\angle 2 \cong \angle ADC$	Vert. $\angle$s $\cong$ (T023)
❹ $\angle BAC \cong \angle DCA$	Alt. Int. $\angle$s Theorem (T027)
❺ $\angle ABC \cong \angle ADC$	Transitive Prop. of $\cong$ (T107)
❻ $\overline{AC} \cong \overline{AC}$	Reflexive Prop. of $\cong$ (T105)
❼ $\triangle ABC \cong \triangle CDA$	AAS $\cong$ Theorem (T109)

14. No, not sufficient information available. (SSA is not a $\cong$ theorem.)

Page 147

15. Proof

Statements	Reasons
❶ $\overline{AC} \cong \overline{AB}$	Given
❷ $\angle 1 \cong \angle 2$	Given
❸ $\overline{IB} \cong \overline{CG}$; $IB = CG$	Given; def. of $\cong$
❹ $IC + CB = IB$, $GB + BC = GC$	Seg. + Postulate (P09)
❺ $IC + CB = GB + CB$	Substitution
❻ $CB = CB$	Reflexive Prop. =
❼ $IC = GB$	Subtraction Prop. of =
❽ $\angle 4 \cong \angle 5$; $m\angle 4 = m\angle 5$	Base $\angle$s Theorem (T050); def. of $\cong$
❾ $m\angle 3 + m\angle 4 = 180^\circ$, $m\angle 5 + m\angle 6 = 180^\circ$	Linear pair Postulate (P14)
❿ $m\angle 3 + m\angle 4 = m\angle 5 + m\angle 6$	Substitution
⓫ $m\angle 3 = m\angle 6$; $\angle 3 \cong \angle 6$	Subtraction Prop. of =; def. of $\cong$
⓬ $\triangle IHC \cong \triangle GFB$	AAS $\cong$ Theorem (T109)

16. Proof

Statements	Reasons
❶ $AC = AB$; $AD = AE$; $IC = BG$	Given
❷ $\angle 4 \cong \angle 5$	Base $\angle$s Theorem (T050)
❸ $AD + DC = AC$, $AE + EB = AB$	Seg. + Postulate (P09)
❹ $AD + DC = AE + EB$	Substitution
❺ $DC = EB$	Subtraction Prop of $\cong$
❻ $\overline{DC} \cong \overline{EB}$	Def. of $\cong$
❼ $CB = CB$	Reflexive Prop of =
❽ $IC + CB = CB + BG$	+ Prop. of =
❾ $IC + CB = \overline{IB}$; $CB + BG = CG$	Seg. + Postulate (P09)
❿ $IB = CG$; $\overline{IB} \cong \overline{CG}$	Substitution; def. of $\cong$
⓫ $\triangle EBI \cong \triangle DCG$	SAS $\cong$ Postulate (P23)

17. Proof

Statements	Reasons
❶ $AB = AC$; $HC = FB$; $DH = EF$	Given
❷ $\overline{AC} \cong \overline{AB}$, $\overline{HC} \cong \overline{BF}$	Def. of $\cong$
❸ $\angle 4 \cong \angle 5$	Base $\angle$s Theorem (T050)
❹ $\overline{CB} \cong \overline{CB}$	Reflexive Prop. of $\cong$ (T105)
❺ $DC = DH + HC$, $EB = EF + FB$	Segment + Postulate (P09)
❻ $DH + HC = EF + FB$	+ Prop of =
❼ $DC = EB$; $\overline{DC} \cong \overline{EB}$	Substitution; def. of $\cong$
❽ $DFBC \cong EHCB$	SASAS $\cong$ Theorem (T113)

18. Proof

Statements	Reasons
❶ $\overline{BG}$ and $\overline{CE}$ bisect each other	Given
❷ $\overline{AB} \cong \overline{AG}$, $\overline{AC} \cong \overline{AE}$	Def. of bisect
❸ $\overline{BD} \perp \overline{AB}$; $\overline{EF} \perp \overline{AF}$; $\overline{DC} \perp \overline{AC}$, $\overline{FG} \perp \overline{AG}$	Given
❹ $\angle 1, \angle 2, \angle 3, \angle 4$ are rt. $\angle$s	Def. of $\perp$
❺ $m\angle 1 = m\angle 2 = m\angle 3 = m\angle 4 = 90^\circ$	Def. of rt. $\angle$
❻ $\angle 1 \cong \angle 4 \cong \angle 2 \cong \angle 3$	Def. of $\cong$
❼ $\angle BAC \cong \angle EAG$	Vertical $\angle$s $\cong$ (T023)
❽ $ACDB \cong AEFG$	ASASA $\cong$ Theorem (T114)

19. Proof

Statements	Reasons
❶ A is the midpt. of $\overline{BG}$ and $\overline{CE}$	Given
❷ $\overline{BA} \cong \overline{AG}$; $\overline{CA} \cong \overline{AE}$	Def. of midpt.
❸ $ABCD$ and $AEFG$ are kites	Given
❹ $\angle 2 \cong \angle 3$	Given
❺ $\overline{AB} \cong \overline{AC}$; $\overline{AE} \cong \overline{AG}$	Def. of kite
❻ $\overline{AB} \cong \overline{AE}$; $\overline{AC} \cong \overline{AG}$	Transitive Prop. of $\cong$ (T107)
❼ $\angle 1 \cong \angle 2$; $\angle 3 \cong \angle 4$	Kite → exactly one pair of opp $\cong$ $\angle$s (T083)
❽ $\angle 1 \cong \angle 4$; $\angle 2 \cong \angle 3$	Transitive Prop. of $\cong$ (T107)
❾ $\angle BAC \cong \angle EAG$	Vertical $\angle$s $\cong$ (T023)
❿ $ACDB \cong AEFG$	ASASA $\cong$ Theorem (T114)

TEST PREP ANSWERS
Page 148
(see page 215 for answers)

Here We Grow

OBJECTIVES
- Observe the relationships among shapes
- Explore congruence and similarity
- Develop spatial reasoning skills

MATERIALS
- Graph paper (page 212) or dot paper
- Pattern Blocks (optional)

TIME
- 20–30 minutes

TEACHER NOTES
- In this activity students will explore how some shapes can be combined to form a shape similar to the original.

- Students should observe that for the shapes which can grow into similar shapes, it takes 4, 9, 16, or n^2 of the smaller shape to make a larger, similar shape. This relates to the theorem: *If two polygons are similar with corresponding sides in the ratio of a:b, then the ratio of their areas is a^2:b^2.* (T085)

- Drawing the shapes on graph or dot paper will help students make sure that the shapes are congruent.

- Some students may benefit from cutting out a few copies of each shape so that they may manipulate them in order to make a larger figure.

EXTENSIONS
- Have students investigate the perimeter and area of the original shape and the enlarged shape. If the perimeter doubled, the area quadrupled. If the perimeter increased by a factor of n, the area increased by a factor of n^2

- Have students investigate whether it is possible to grow trapezoids other than the one with congruent legs that are the same length as the short base, which is half the length of the long base. (It is not: in order to lay out the trapezoids keeping the relationships among the sides the same, the trapezoid must have legs the same length as the short base; in order to keep the bases of the new trapezoid proportional to the bases

of the old one, the short base must be half the length of the long one.)

- Encourage students to investigate the work of M. C. Escher. What role do transformations play in Escher's drawings?

ANSWERS

1. a.

b.

c.

d.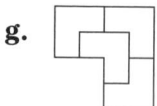

e.

f. Not possible

g.

h. Not possible

2. 4 is the expected answer; may be 9, 16, or n^2.

3. a.

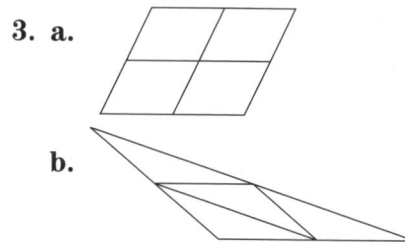

b.

Name _____ Date _____

Area of Similar
    Polygons: 186

Similar Polygons: 222

Tessellations: 296

Here We Grow

Two figures are congruent if they have the same shape and size. Two figures are similar if they are the same shape but not necessarily the same size. Some congruent shapes, when placed next to each other, *grow* into a larger shape that is similar to the original shapes.

Example: □ + □ + □ + □ = ⊞

1. Decide whether each of the following shapes can *grow* into a larger shape similar to the original. You may wish to sketch your solution on graph paper.

   a. right triangle

   b. isosceles triangle

   c. rectangle

   d. isosceles trapezoid with legs and
       short base $\frac{1}{2}$ as long as the long base

   e. rhombus

   f. quarter circle

   g. $\frac{3}{4}$ square

   h. pentagon with two right angles

2. For the shapes that did grow in exercise 1, how many smaller shapes did it take to make a larger, similar shape?

   _____

3. Reverse the process. Divide the shapes below into figures similar to the original.

   a. parallelogram   b. obtuse isosceles triangle

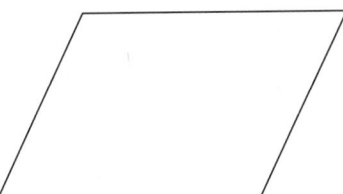

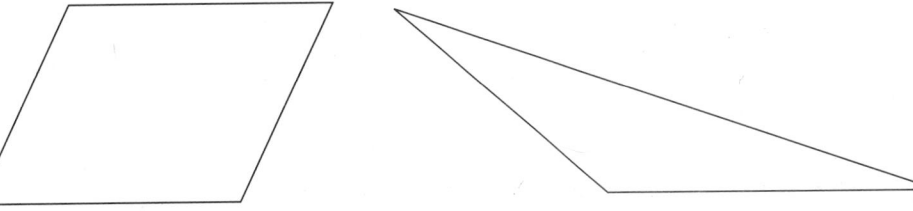

Name_____ Date_____

Rigid Transformations

274

For exercises 1–2, indicate which of the following transformations are NOT isometries.

1. _____

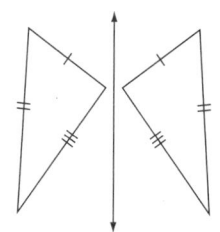
A.

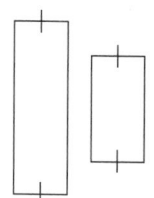
B.

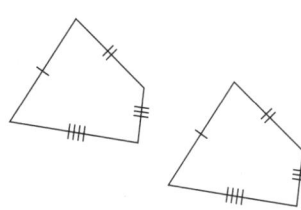
C.

2. _____

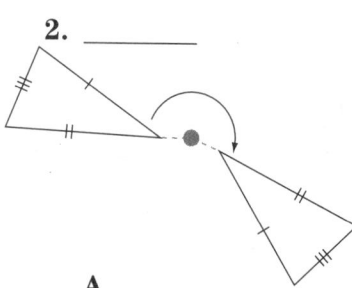
A.

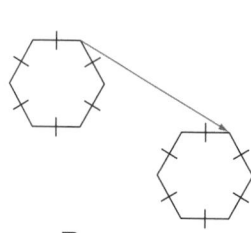
B.

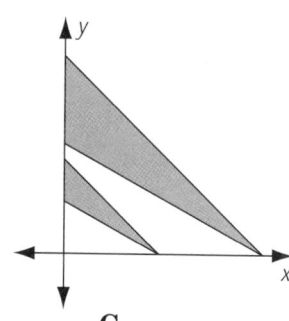
C.

For exercises 3–4, the transformations are isometries. Find the values of x and y.

3.

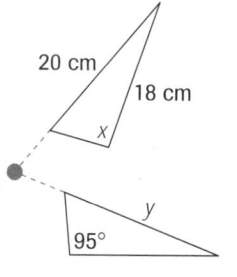

_____

4.

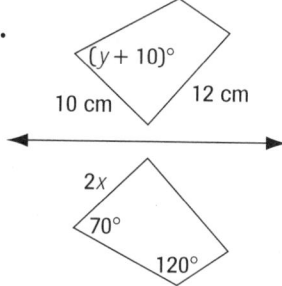

_____

For exercises 5–9, give the coordinates of the image of $A(^-2, 4)$.

277

5. Reflected over the x-axis._____

6. Reflected over the y-axis._____

7. Reflected over the line $y = x$._____

281

8. Rotated 90° clockwise about the origin._____

9. Rotated 180° clockwise about the origin._____

Name _____ Date _____

278

10. Draw the reflection of △ABC over the y-axis. Label the vertices.• MORE HELP See 275

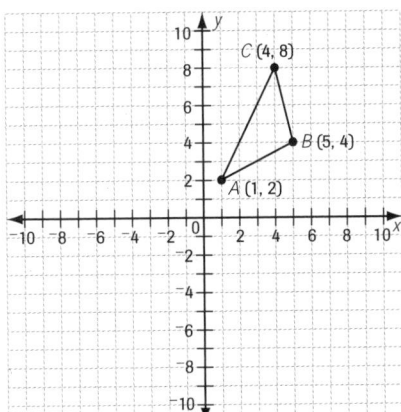

11. Sketch and label ABCD and its reflection over the line x = 1.

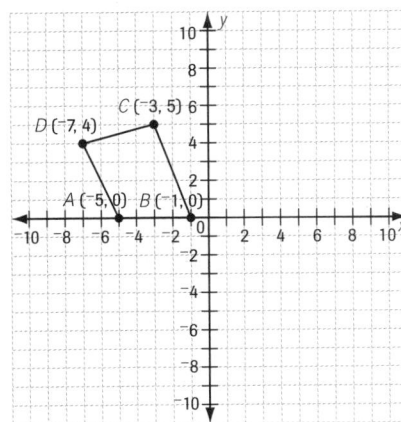

279

Do the figures in exercises 12–14 have line symmetry? If yes, give the number of lines of symmetry.

12. isosceles triangle

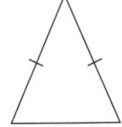

_____

13. parallelogram

_____

14. regular hexagon

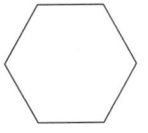

_____

281

15. Sketch and label the rotation 90° clockwise about the origin of ABCD.

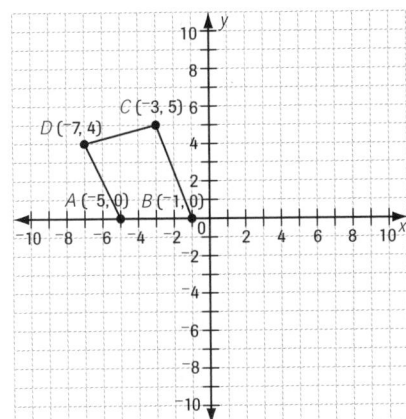

16. △ABC is the preimage. Draw the 180° clockwise rotation about the origin.

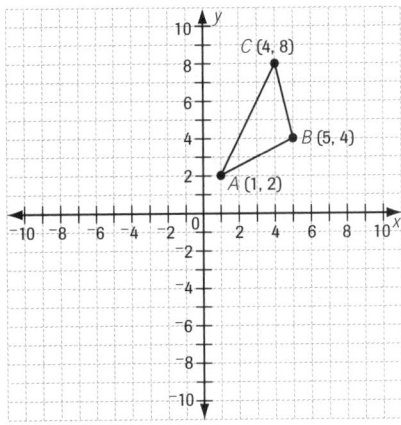

Name _____ Date _____

284

17. Sketch the image of △*TRS* after these two reflections. Describe this composition as a rotation.

Reflection: over the *y*-axis

Reflection: over the *x*-axis

_____

_____

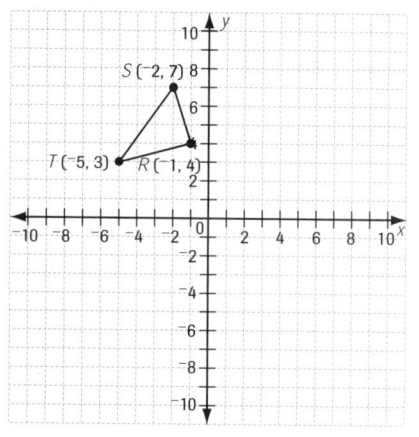

285

Do the figures in exercises 18–20 have rotational symmetry? If yes, describe the rotation.

18. rectangle   **19.** regular octagon   **20.** isosceles trapezoid

   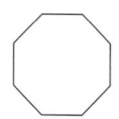   

_____   _____   _____

21. Sketch the image of △*TRS* after these two reflections. Describe this composition as a translation.

Reflection: over the *x*-axis

Reflection: over the line $y = {}^-3$

_____

_____

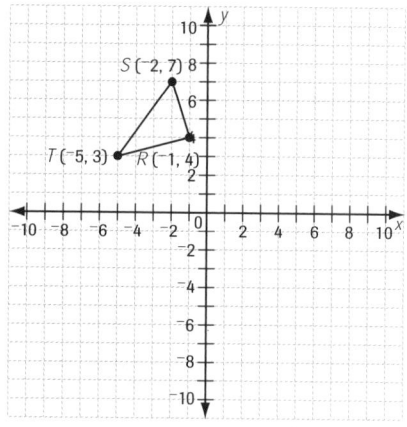

289

22. △*ABC* is the preimage. Draw the translation $(x, y) \rightarrow (x - 5, y + 1)$.

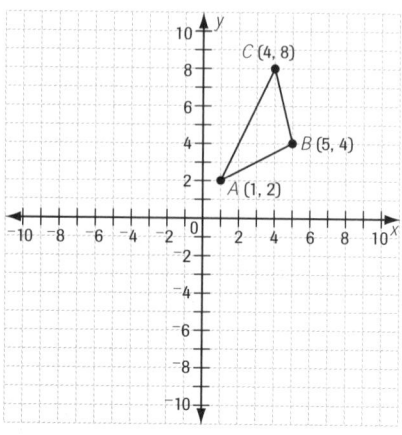

Name _____ Date _____

23. Draw and label $A'B'C'D'$ using the translation defined by the rule
$(x, y) \rightarrow (x + 7, y - 5)$.

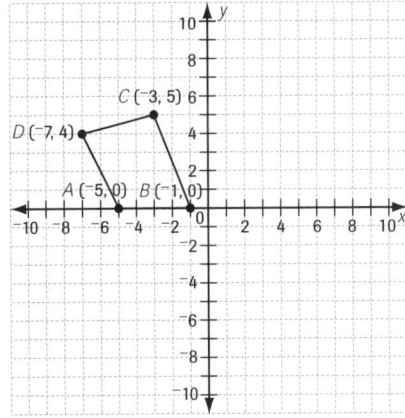

For exercises 24–25, use these matrices to determine the translation.

$$
\begin{matrix} P & Q & R \end{matrix}
$$
$$
\begin{bmatrix} ^-1 & 3 & 6 \\ 4 & 2 & ^-5 \end{bmatrix} + \begin{bmatrix} ^-1 & ^-1 & ^-1 \\ 3 & 3 & 3 \end{bmatrix}
$$

24. Give the vertices of $\triangle PQR$. _____

25. Give the coordinates of the image's vertices after the translation.

_____

26. Give the coordinates of the image of $A(^-2, 4)$ after this glide reflection.

Translation: $(x, y) \rightarrow (x + 5, y - 1)$

Reflection: over the x-axis

_____

27. Sketch the image of $\triangle MNO$ after this glide reflection.

Translation: $(x, y) \rightarrow (x - 6, y + 5)$

Reflection: over the y-axis

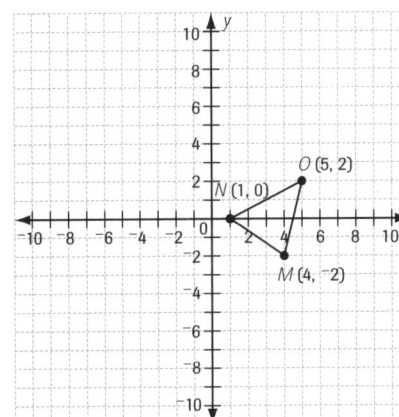

Name _____ Date _____

Rigid Transformations

Directions: Write the letter of the best answer.

For exercises 1–11, decide whether the statement is true or false. Write T for true and F for false.

_____ **1.** A translation preserves distance.

_____ **2.** A dilation is an isometry.

_____ **3.** All points in a rotation are moved the same distance.

_____ **4.** A reflection is an isometry.

_____ **5.** If $\triangle A'B'C'$ is the reflection of $\triangle ABC$ over a line, then $\triangle ABC$ is the reflection of $\triangle A'B'C'$ over the same line.

_____ **6.** An isosceles triangle has rotational symmetry.

_____ **7.** A square has eight lines of symmetry.

_____ **8.** An equilateral triangle has both line and rotational symmetry.

_____ **9.** A glide reflection is an isometry.

_____ **10.** The point of intersection of two lines of symmetry in any figure can be used as the center of rotation for that figure.

_____ **11.** If a figure is reflected over two parallel lines in succession, then the final image of the figure can be obtained from the preimage using a rotation.

For exercises 12–17, find the coordinates of the image, given the preimage and the transformation.

_____ **12.** $P(^-4, 6)$ is reflected over the x-axis.

    A $(4, 6)$ **B** $(4, ^-6)$ **C** $(^-4, ^-6)$

_____ **13.** $P(6, ^-2)$ is reflected over the y-axis.

    A $(^-6, ^-2)$ **B** $(6, 2)$ **C** $(^-6, 2)$

_____ **14.** $P(7, 6)$ is reflected over the line $y = x$.

    A $(^-7, ^-6)$ **B** $(6, 7)$ **C** $(^-6, ^-7)$

_____ **15.** $P(^-2, ^-3)$ is rotated about the origin 180°.

    A $(2, 3)$ **B** $(^-2, ^-3)$ **C** $(3, 2)$

_____ **16.** $P(3, 1)$ is translated according to the rule $(x, y) \rightarrow (x - 4, y + 2)$.

    A $(7, 3)$ **B** $(^-1, ^-1)$ **C** $(^-1, 3)$

_____ **17.** The image of $\overline{PQ}$ is defined by this glide reflection.

Translation: $(x, y) \rightarrow (x + 3, y - 2)$

Reflection: over the y-axis

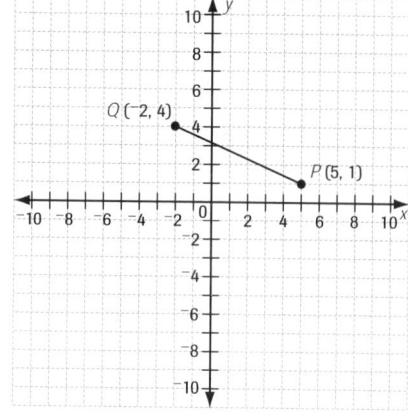

    A $P''(8, 1)$, $Q''(1, ^-2)$

    B $P''(^-8, 3)$, $Q''(^-1, 6)$

    C $P''(^-8, ^-1)$, $Q''(^-1, 2)$

PRACTICE ANSWERS

Page 152

1. B

2. C

3. $x = 95°$, $y = 20$ cm

4. $x = 5$ cm, $y = 60°$

5. $(^-2, ^-4)$

6. $(2, 4)$

7. $(4, ^-2)$

8. $(4, 2)$

9. $(2, ^-4)$

Page 153

10.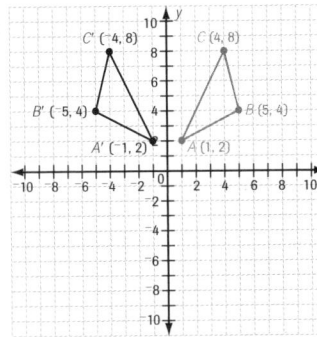

11.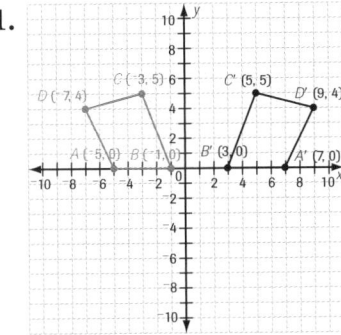

12. yes, 1

13. no

14. yes, 6

15.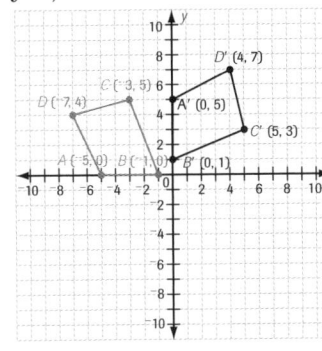

16.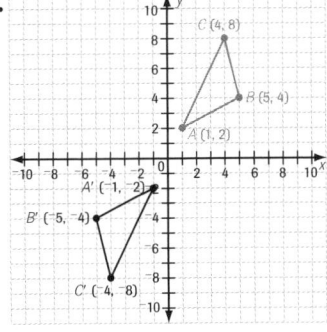

Page 154

17. $R''(1, ^-4)$, $S''(2, ^-7)$, $T''(5, ^-3)$; rotation 180° clockwise about origin

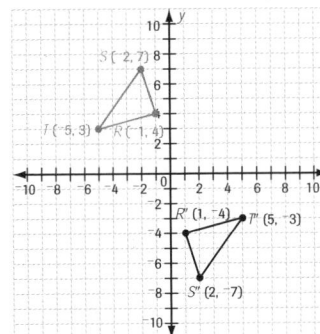

18. yes, 180°

19. yes, any multiple of 45°

20. no

21. $R''(^-1, ^-2)$, $S''(^-2, 1)$, $T''(^-5, ^-3)$; translation $(x, y) \rightarrow (x, y - 6)$

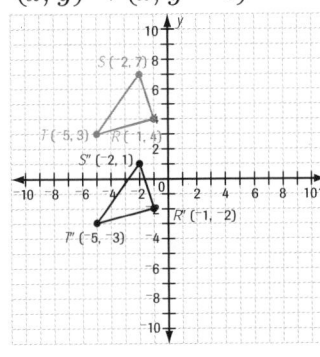

22.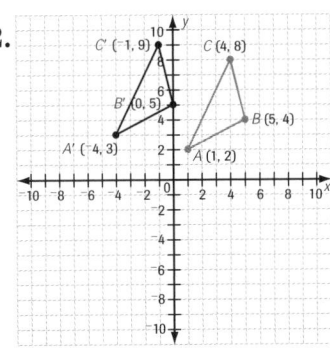

Page 155

23.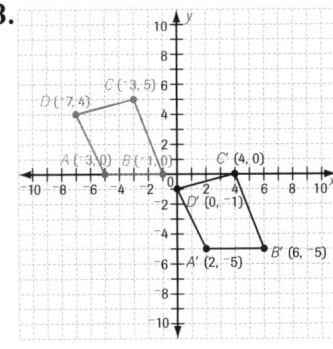

24. $P(^-1, 4)$, $Q(3, 2)$, $R(6, ^-5)$

25. $P'(^-2, 7)$, $Q'(2, 5)$, $R'(5, ^-2)$

26. $(3, ^-3)$

27. $M''(2, 3)$, $N''(5, 5)$, $O''(1, 7)$

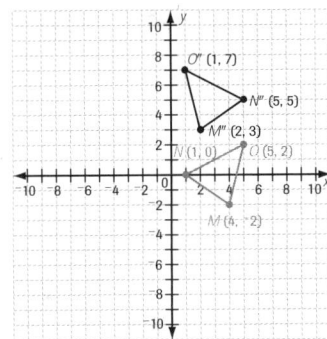

TEST PREP ANSWERS

Page 156

1. T   2. F

3. F   4. T

5. T   6. F

7. F   8. T

9. T   10. T

11. F   12. C

13. A   14. B

15. A   16. C

17. C

Name _____ Date _____

Non-Rigid Transformations

For exercises 1–3, $\triangle TRS$ is mapped onto $\triangle T'R'S'$ by a dilation with center C.
The ratio of $C'T'$ to CT is given. Is the dilation a reduction or an enlargement?

1. $\frac{8}{3}$ _____ **2.** $\frac{2}{5}$ _____ **3.** $\frac{1}{2}$ _____

For exercises 4–6, $\triangle MNO$ is mapped onto $\triangle M'N'O'$ by a dilation with center C.
$MN = 10$ cm, $NO = 12$ cm, and $MO = 15$ cm. The scale factor, k, is given.
Find the length of the indicated segment.

4. $k = \frac{3}{4}$, find $M'N'$. _____

5. $k = 2$, find $M'O'$. _____

6. $k = \frac{8}{5}$, find $N'O'$. _____

For exercises 7–8, identify the dilation, then find its scale factor and the values of x and y.

7.

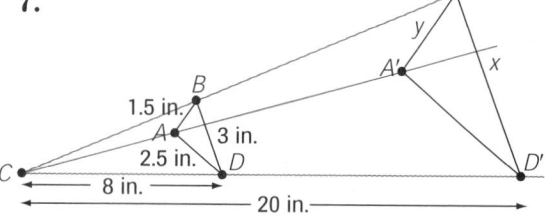

_____

_____

8.

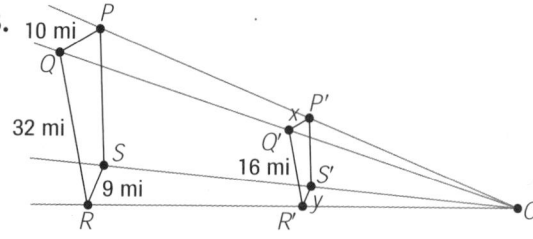

_____

_____

For exercises 9–10, use the origin as the center of the dilation with the given scale factor.
Find the coordinates of the vertices and sketch the image.

9. $k = \frac{3}{2}$

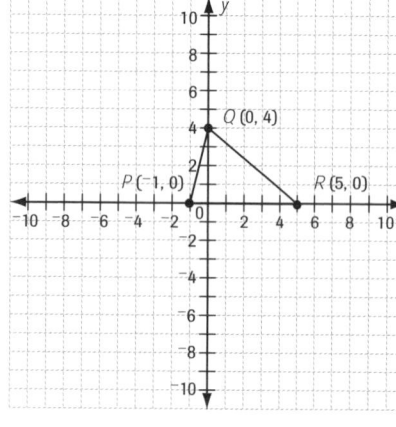

10. $k = \frac{1}{2}$

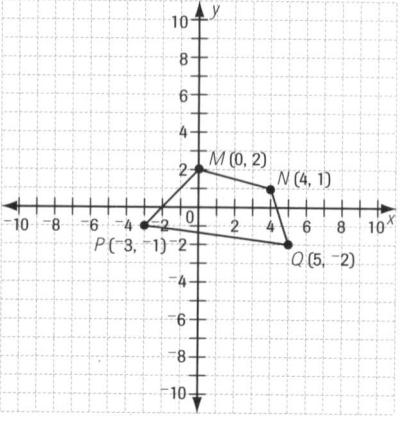

_____ _____

Name_____　Date_____

Non-Rigid Transformations

Directions: Mark the letter of the best answer.

For exercises 1–9, choose T if the statement is true or F if the statement is false.

1. A dilation is an isometry.

   T　　　F

2. If the scale factor in a dilation is less than one, then the dilation is a reduction.

   T　　　F

3. The scale factor in a dilation cannot equal one.

   T　　　F

4. A dilation is a rigid transformation.

   T　　　F

5. The preimage and image of a dilation are similar figures.

   T　　　F

6. The center of a dilation is the intersection of lines connecting corresponding points on the preimage and the image.

   T　　　F

7. The center of a dilation cannot be a point on the preimage.

   T　　　F

8. $\triangle RST$ is mapped onto $\triangle R'S'T'$ with center C; $CR' : CR = 3:5$. The dilation is an enlargement.

   T　　　F

9. The center of a dilation can be in the interior region of the preimage.

   T　　　F

10. $A(^-3, 2)$ is a preimage point in a dilation with scale factor $\frac{3}{2}$ and center at the origin. Find the coordinates of the corresponding image point.

    A $(\frac{^-9}{2}, 3)$　　**B** $(^-2, \frac{4}{3})$　　**C** $(2, \frac{^-4}{3})$

11. In a dilation with center at the origin, a point on the preimage is at $(^-3, 6)$ and the corresponding point on the image is at $(^-4, 8)$. Find the scale factor.

    A $\frac{3}{4}$　　　**B** $\frac{1}{2}$　　　**C** $\frac{4}{3}$

For exercises 12–14, $\triangle PQR$ is mapped onto $\triangle P'Q'R'$ by a dilation with center C and scale factor $\frac{4}{5}$. Find the length of the indicated segment.

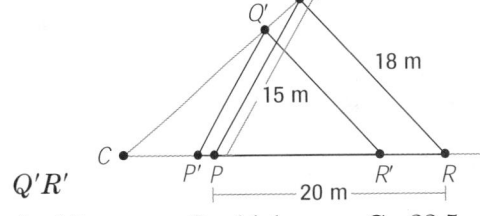

12. $Q'R'$

    A 12 m　　**B** 14.4 m　　**C** 22.5 m

13. $P'R'$

    A 12 m　　**B** 16 m　　**C** 18.75 m

14. $P'Q'$

    A 12 m　　**B** 16 m　　**C** 25 m

For exercises 15–18, find the value of the indicated variables in this dilation.

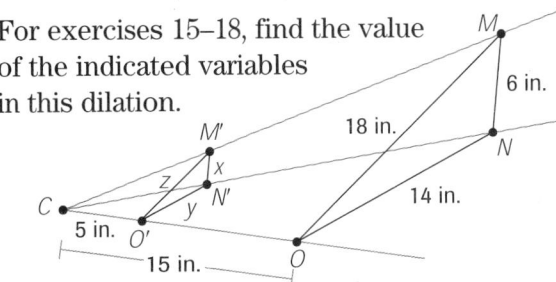

15. Find the scale factor.

    A $\frac{1}{3}$　　　**B** 3　　　**C** 0.3

16. Find x

    A 18 in.　　**B** 6 in.　　**C** 2 in.

17. Find y.

    A $4\frac{2}{3}$ in.　　**B** 6 in.　　**C** 2 in.

18. Find z.

    A $5\frac{2}{5}$ in.　　**B** 6 in.　　**C** 54 in.

PRACTICE ANSWERS
Page 158

1. Enlargement
2. Reduction
3. Reduction
4. 7.5 cm
5. 30 cm
6. 19.2 cm
7. Enlargement, $k = \frac{5}{2}$, $x = 7.5$ in. $y = 3.75$ in.
8. Reduction, $k = \frac{1}{2}$, $x = 5$ mi, $y = 4.5$ mi
9. $P'\ (^-1.5, 0), Q'(0, 6), R'(7.5, 0)$

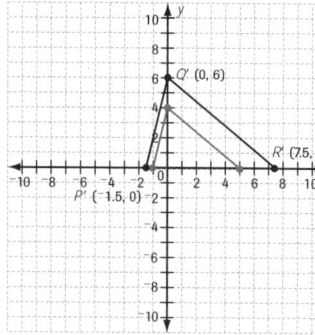

10. $P'(^-1.5, ^-0.5), M'(0, 1), N'(2, 0.5), Q'(2.5, ^-1)$

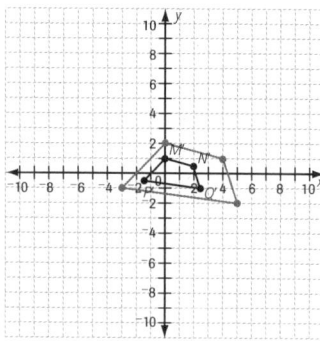

TEST PREP ANSWERS
Page 159

1. F
2. T
3. T
4. F
5. T
6. T
7. F
8. F
9. T
10. A
11. C
12. B
13. B
14. A
15. A
16. C
17. A
18. B

Name _____ Date _____

Transformation Patterns

For exercises 1–6, write the letter of the best description of the transformations in the frieze pattern.

A translation
B translation and 180° rotation
C translation and horizontal line reflection
D vertical line reflection

1.

_____

2.

_____

3.

_____

4.

_____

5.

_____

6.

_____

For exercises 7–10, use the given figure and transformation to sketch at least five figures in a frieze pattern.

7. Translation.

8. A Translation and 180° rotation.

9. Translation and horizontal line reflection.

10. Translation and vertical line reflection.

11. Expand the tessellation using at least six more regular hexagons and six more equilateral triangles.

12. Is the tessellation constructed in exercise 11 regular, semiregular or neither?_____

13. Determine whether these shapes can be used together 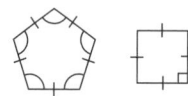 to create a tessellation. Explain your answer.

_____

_____

14. Create a tessellation using both of these figures. • **MORE HELP** See 131–132

15. Create your own tessellation, starting with any polygon. Follow the instructions in your handbook, item number 296.

Name_____ Date_____

Transformation Patterns

Directions: Write the letter of the best answer.

For exercises 1–4, refer to these friezes.

A

B

C

D

_____ **1.** Which frieze is a translation only?

_____ **2.** Which frieze is a translation with 180° rotation?

_____ **3.** Which frieze is a translation and horizontal line reflection?

_____ **4.** Which frieze is a vertical line reflection?

For exercises 5–9, choose the letter of the best description of the transformations in the frieze. There may be more than one answer.

A translation
B translation with 180° rotation
C translation and horizontal line reflection
D translation and vertical line reflection

_____ **5.** A V A V

_____ **6.** Z Z Z Z

_____ **7.** M M M M M / W W W W W

_____ **8.** ▲ V ▲ V ▲ V ▲

_____ **9.** (circles)

For exercises 10–18, write T if the statement is true; write F if the statement is false.

_____ **10.** Regular pentagons can be used to form a regular tessellation.

_____ **11.** In a tessellation, the sum of the angles at any vertex must be 180°.

_____ **12.** There are only three regular tessellations.

_____ **13.** A semiregular tessellation is formed using two or more regular polygons.

_____ **14.** Some tessellations have gaps where the polygons meet.

_____ **15.** Frieze patterns are classified according to the types of transformations used.

_____ **16.** Tessellations can be created using figures that are not polygons.

_____ **17.** A tessellation composed of a parallelogram and a triangle must be semiregular.

_____ **18.** M. C. Escher, a famous Dutch artist, was inspired by tile patterns in the Alhambra in Spain.

PRACTICE ANSWERS
Page 161

1. accept B or C
2. D
3. C
4. A
5. D
6. B

For exercises 7–11, answers will vary. Samples are given.

7.

8.

9.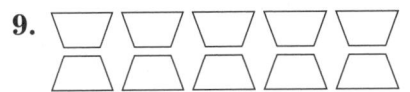

10.

11.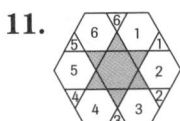

12. Semiregular

13. No, there is no combination of the interior angles of the two figures (108° and 90°) with a sum of 360°.

The sum of the angles at any vertex must be 360°.

14. Answers may vary. Sample answer:

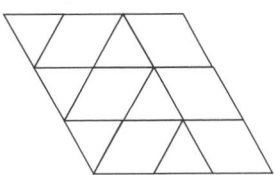

15. Answers may vary. Sample answer:

TEST PREP ANSWERS
Page 162

1. B
2. A
3. D
4. C
5. B
6. A or B
7. B or C
8. B or D
9. D
10. F
11. F
12. T
13. T
14. F
15. T
16. T
17. F
18. T

The Braille Code

OBJECTIVES
• Explore rotations and reflections within and between Braille letters
• Explore symmetry of Braille words

MATERIALS
none

TEACHER NOTES
• Most students will be familiar with the Braille system. Remind students that a blind person needs an orientation, just as sighted persons do, in order to read words.

• Introduce the topic by using a 3×2 matrix and asking students how many ways one or more dots could be arranged in the six locations (15).

```
① ④
② ⑤
③ ⑥
```

• Write the word *start* in Braille on the board.

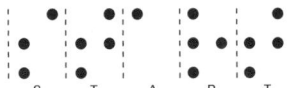

EXTENSIONS
• Have students research the origin of the Braille system or other similar coding systems such as UPC and zip code readers.

• Apply question 6 to block letters.

• Have students investigate the role of reflections in lettering on ambulances, or signs in alleyways where truck drivers use their mirrors to back up safely.

ANSWERS
1. t and x
2. k, l, o, r, w, x, y
3. c, g, x
4. 180° rotation: r to w
5. vertical line: d and f, e and i, h and j, r and w; horizontal line: m and u, n and z, p and v; diagonal line: none
6. sample answers: ox, row

Name _____ Date _____

The Braille Code

Louis Braille, blind since the age of 3, invented the first alphabet of raised dots in 1824. This system enables blind persons to read text with their fingertips.

The Braille letters use dots in a 3×2 matrix. Reflections and rotations play an important role in reading the Braille cell correctly. The letters shown here are lower case. To indicate an upper case letter, the dot in position 6 is placed just before the letter.

HANDBOOK
HELP

Rigid Transformations: 274

Reflections: 275

Rotations: 281

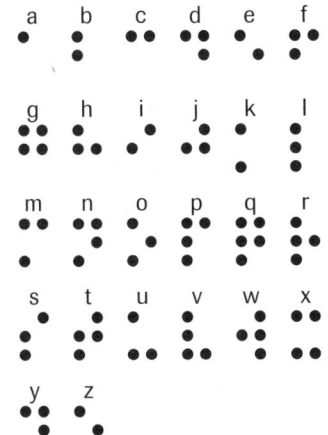

1. In block letters, *H* reads the same right side up and upside down. Which Braille letters have the property of 180° rotational symmetry?

   _____

2. In block letters, *H* has horizontal line symmetry. Which Braille letters have this property?

   _____

3. In block letters, *H* has vertical line symmetry. Which Braille letters have this same property?

   _____

4. Which Braille letters have rotations that are different Braille letters? Describe the rotation.

   _____

5. Which Braille letters have reflections that are different Braille letters? Describe the reflection. Example: *d* to *f* is vertical line reflection.

   _____

   _____

   _____

   _____

6. The Braille word ••• has vertical line symmetry. Find other Braille words that have symmetry.

   _____

Name _____ Date _____

Circle Relationships

For exercises 1–12, write *T* if the statement is true. Write *F* if the statement is false.

298 _____ **1.** The diameter of a circle is a line of symmetry for the circle. • **MORE HELP** See 279

298 _____ **2.** In any circle, one-half the diameter equals the radius.

299 _____ **3.** Any two circles with equal diameters are congruent.

300 _____ **4.** The center of a circle is the point of intersection for two concentric circles.

301 _____ **5.** If two coplanar circles are internally tangent, then they share the same center.

_____ **6.** If two coplanar circles are externally tangent, then they have no points in common.

_____ **7.** If two coplanar circles are internally tangent, then they have exactly one point in common.

302 _____ **8.** A circle can be inscribed in any isosceles trapezoid.

_____ **9.** If a line segment is drawn from the center of any regular hexagon to any vertex, this segment can be used as the radius of an inscribed circle.

_____**10.** In order for a circle to be inscribed in a triangle, the triangle must be equilateral.

_____**11.** If a circle is circumscribed about an equilateral triangle, then radii of the circle connect the center to each vertex of the triangle.

_____**12.** Archimedes used inscribed and circumscribed hexagons to approximate the value of π.

299 **13.** Sketch three congruent circles, each externally tangent to the other two. Connect the centers, forming a triangle. What is true about this triangle? Explain your answer.

_____

300 **14.** Sketch three concentric circles.

301 **15.** Sketch three circles with a common tangent where two of the circles are internally tangent and a third is externally tangent to the other two.

302 **16.** Sketch a heptagon inscribed in a circle.

302-303 **17.** Sketch a circle with an inscribed pentagon and a circumscribed square.

303 **18.** Sketch a circle circumscribed about a regular hexagon.

Name _____ Date _____

Circle Relationships

Directions: Write the letter of the best answer.

For exercises 1–11, match the diagrams to their descriptions. No letter can be used more than once.

A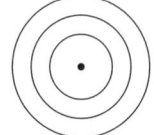

F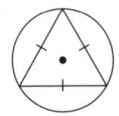

B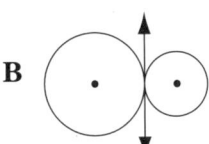

G

C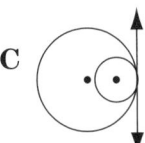

H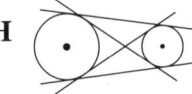

I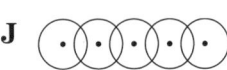

D

J

E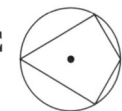

K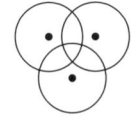

_____ **1.** a regular polygon inscribed in a circle

_____ **2.** externally tangent circles

_____ **3.** a circle inscribed in a triangle

_____ **4.** a circle inscribed in a regular quadrilateral

_____ **5.** externally tangent congruent circles

_____ **6.** concentric circles

_____ **7.** internally tangent circles

_____ **8.** intersecting circles

_____ **9.** intersecting circles with collinear centers

_____ **10.** non-intersecting circles with common tangents

_____ **11.** a polygon inscribed in a circle

For exercises 12–17, decide whether the statement is

 L always true

 M sometimes true

 N never true

_____ **12.** If two circles are congruent, then twice the diameter of one will equal the radius of the other.

_____ **13.** Two externally tangent circles are congruent.

_____ **14.** If a circle is inscribed in a square, then the diagonal of the square contains a diameter of the circle.

_____ **15.** If two circles are internally tangent, then the centers lie on a diameter of the larger circle.

_____ **16.** If a hexagon is inscribed in a circle, then all diagonals pass through the center of the circle.

_____ **17.** If a line of symmetry is drawn in a circle, then two semicircles are created.

PRACTICE ANSWERS
Page 166

1. T
2. T
3. T
4. F
5. F
6. F
7. T
8. F
9. F
10. F
11. T
12. T

13.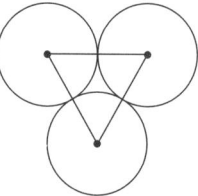

The triangle is equilateral because each side has a length of $2r$.

14.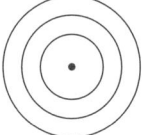

15.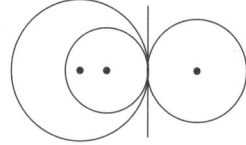

16.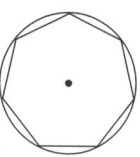

17.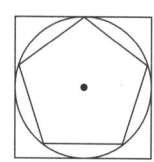

18.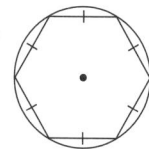

TEST PREP ANSWERS
Page 167

1. F
2. B
3. G
4. D
5. I
6. A
7. C
8. K
9. J
10. H
11. E
12. N
13. M
14. L
15. L
16. N
17. L

Name _____ Date _____

Segment and Line Relationships in Circles

For exercises 1–14, O is the center of the circle. Find the value of x.

306–307

1.

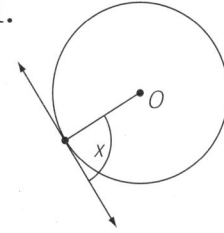

_____

2.

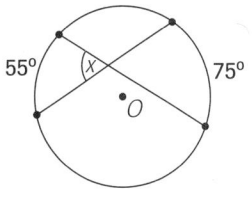

_____

3.

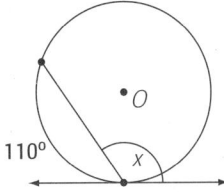

_____

306–307

4.

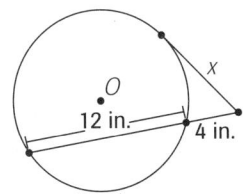

_____

5. • **MORE HELP** See 069

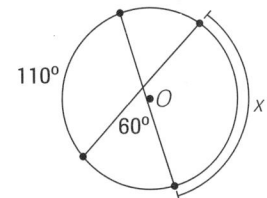

_____

6.

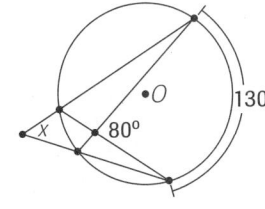

_____

308

7.

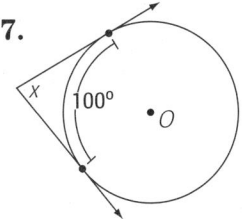

_____

8.

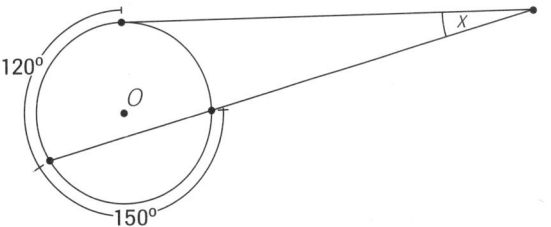

_____

9.

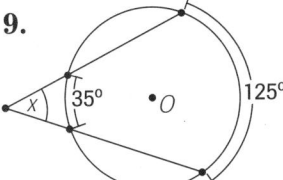

_____

10.

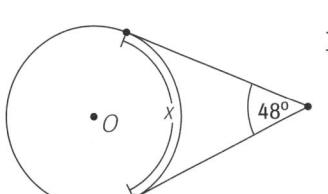

_____

11.

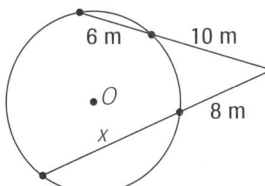

_____

307–308

12.

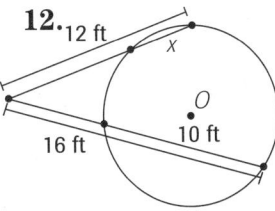

_____

13.

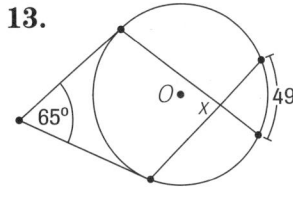

_____

14. • **MORE HELP** See 069

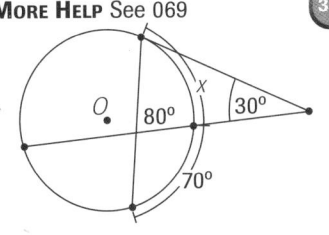

_____

Name _____ Date _____

15. **Given:** $\overline{AC} \cong \overline{CD}$; $\overline{AB}$ is a diameter of the circle

Prove: $\overline{BD} \cong \overline{AB}$ • **MORE HELP** See 270, 318

Statements	Reasons

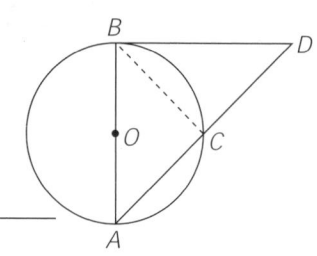

16. **Given:** B is the midpoint of $\overparen{ABC}$; $\overleftrightarrow{BD}$ is tangent to circle at B

Prove: $\overleftrightarrow{BD}$ is parallel to $\overline{AC}$ • **MORE HELP** See 077, 318

Statements	Reasons

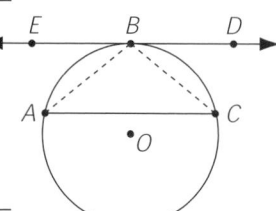

17. Find the measure of each numbered angle.
   • **MORE HELP** See 068, 132, 143

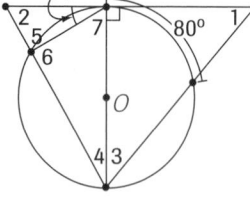

m∠1 = ____   m∠2 = ____

m∠3 = ____   m∠4 = ____

m∠5 = ____   m∠6 = ____

m∠7 = ____

18. Find the measure of each variable. • **MORE HELP** See 311

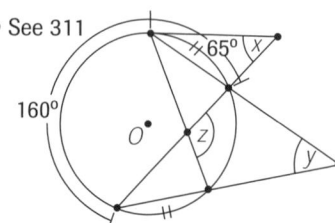

$x =$ ____

$y =$ ____

$z =$ ____

Name _____ Date _____

Segment and Line Relationships in Circles

Directions: Refer to the diagram, then compare the boxed quantities. Choose the letter of the best description of this comparison.

A the quantity in Column A is greater
B the quantity in Column B is greater
C the quantities are equal
D the relationship cannot be determined
from the given information

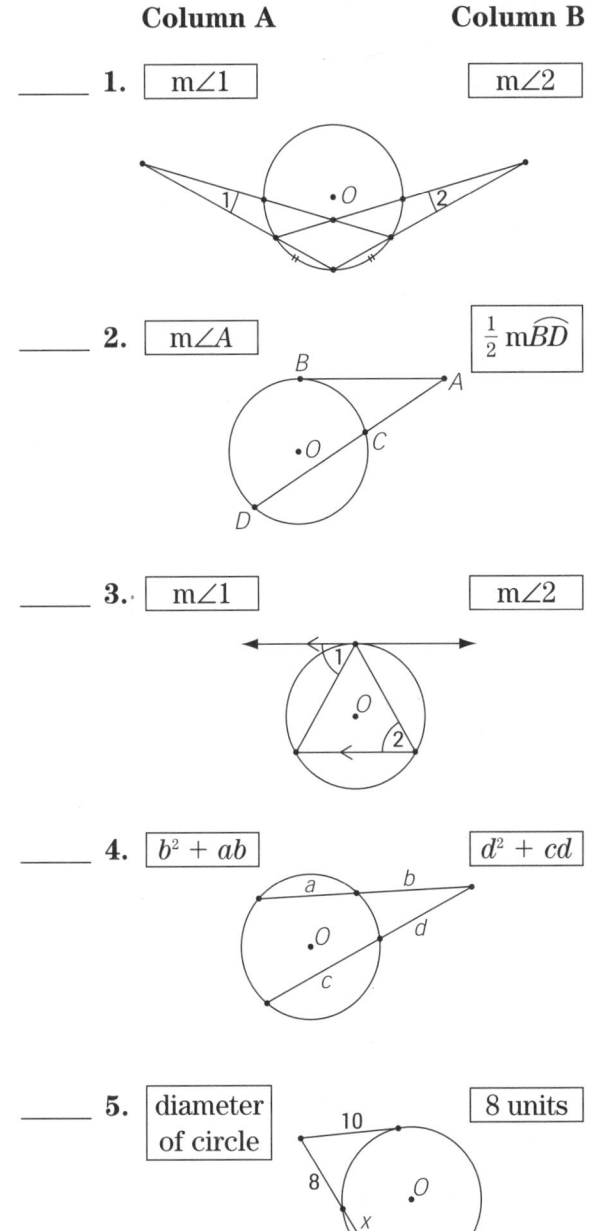

	Column A	**Column B**
_____ **1.**	m∠1	m∠2
_____ **2.**	m∠A	$\frac{1}{2}$ m$\widehat{BD}$
_____ **3.**	m∠1	m∠2
_____ **4.**	$b^2 + ab$	$d^2 + cd$
_____ **5.**	diameter of circle	8 units

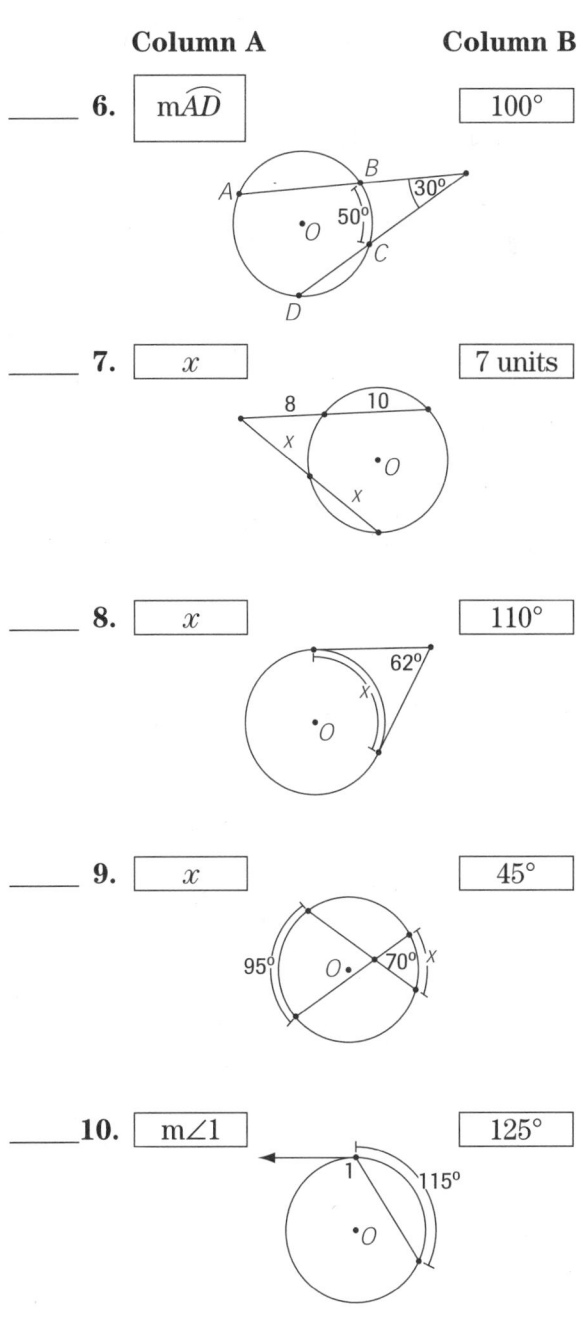

	Column A	**Column B**
_____ **6.**	m$\widehat{AD}$	100°
_____ **7.**	x	7 units
_____ **8.**	x	110°
_____ **9.**	x	45°
_____ **10.**	m∠1	125°
_____ **11.**	x	14 units

PRACTICE ANSWERS
Page 169

1. $90°$
2. $65°$
3. $125°$
4. 8 in.
5. $130°$
6. $50°$
7. $80°$
8. $15°$
9. $45°$
10. $132°$
11. 12 in.
12. 4 ft
13. $82°$
14. $70°$

Page 170

15. One possible proof:

Statements	Reasons
❶ $\overline{AC} \cong \overline{CD}$	Given
❷ $\overline{AB}$ is a diameter	Given
❸ $\widehat{ACB}$ is a semicircle	Def. of diameter
❹ $\angle ACB$ is a rt. $\angle$	$\angle$ inscribed in $\odot$ is rt. $\angle \leftrightarrow$ corresp. arc is semicircle (T140)
❺ $\overline{BC} \cong \overline{BC}$	Reflexive Prop. of $\cong$ (T105)
❻ $\triangle ABC \cong \triangle DBC$	L-L $\cong$ Theorem (T112)
❼ $\overline{BD} \cong \overline{AB}$	CPCTC

16. One possible proof:

Statements	Reasons
❶ B is the midpoint of $\widehat{ACB}$	Given
❷ $\overrightarrow{BD}$ is tangent to circle at B	Given
❸ $m\widehat{AB} = m\widehat{BC}$	Def. of midpoint
❹ $m\angle ABE = \frac{1}{2}m\widehat{AB}$, $m\angle BAC = \frac{1}{2}m\widehat{BC}$	$\angle$ inscribed in $\odot$ $\rightarrow$ measure is $\frac{1}{2}$ intercepted arc (T138)
❺ $m\angle ABE = m\angle BAC$	Substitution
❻ $\overrightarrow{BD}$ is parallel to $\overline{AC}$	Converse of Alt. Int. $\angle$s Theorem (T028)

17. $m\angle 1 = 50°$, $m\angle 2 = 60°$, $m\angle 3 = 40°$, $m\angle 4 = 30°$, $m\angle 5 = 90°$, $m\angle 6 = 90°$, $m\angle 7 = 60°$

18. $x = 47.5°$, $y = 45°$, $z = 115°$

TEST PREP ANSWERS
Page 171

1. D
2. B
3. C
4. C
5. D
6. A
7. A
8. A
9. C
10. B
11. A

Name _____ Date _____

Angle and Arc Relationships

For all of these exercises, the center of the circle is O.

310

1. For $\odot O$ name _____

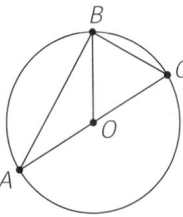

   a. a central angle

   b. an inscribed angle

   c. a minor arc

   d. a major arc

310-312
311-313

2.

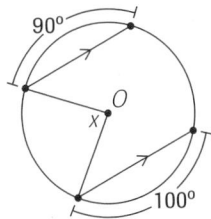

$x = $ _____

3.

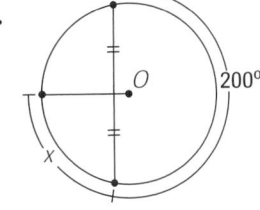

$x = $ _____

314

4.

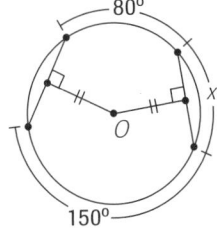

$x = $ _____

5.

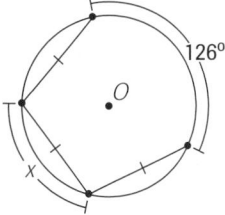

$x = $ _____

313, 315

6. For $\odot O$ name _____

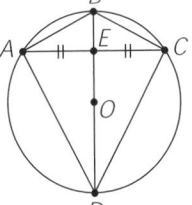

   a. two $\perp$ line segments

   b. two $\cong$ chords

   c. two $\cong$ inscribed angles

   d. two pairs $\cong$ arcs

310-316

7.

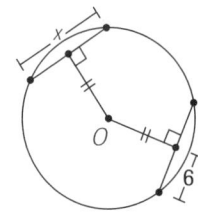

$x = $ _____

8.

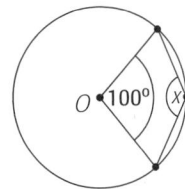

$x = $ _____

Name_____ Date_____

9.

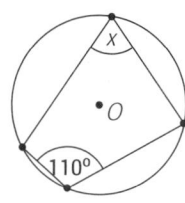

$x =$ _____

10.

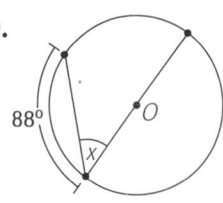

$x =$ _____

11.

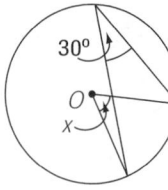

$x =$ _____

12.

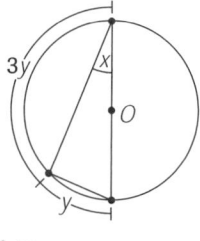

$x =$ _____

13.

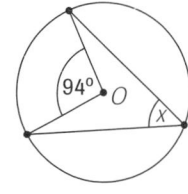

$x =$ _____

14.

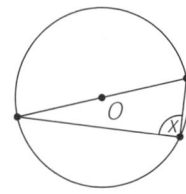

$x =$ _____

15. Chords $\overline{PR}$, $\overline{RS}$, and $\overline{SP}$ are equidistant from the center of $\odot O$.

Find the measure of $\angle PSR$. _____

16. Given: $\overline{QS} \perp \overline{PQ}$; $\overline{SR} \perp \overline{PR}$; P is the midpoint of $\overset{\frown}{QPR}$

Prove: $\overline{QS} \cong \overline{RS}$ • **More Help** See 268

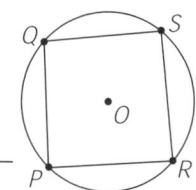

Statements   **Reasons**

_____

_____

_____

_____

_____

_____

_____

_____

_____

_____

_____

Name _____ Date _____

17. Given: Given: $\overarc{ABD} \cong \overarc{BDC}$

Prove: $\overline{AB} \cong \overline{DC}$

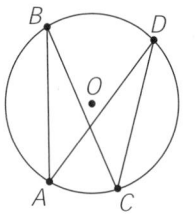

312, 314

Statements	Reasons
_____	_____
_____	_____
_____	_____
_____	_____
_____	_____
_____	_____
_____	_____

18. Refer to the diagram. • **MORE HELP** See 152-153

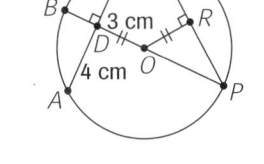

316

 a. $DC =$ _____   **b.** $PQ =$ _____   **c.** $PR =$ _____

 d. $OP =$ _____   **e.** $DB =$ _____

19. A central angle and an inscribed angle intercept the same arc. Find the ratio of the measure of the central angle to the measure of the inscribed angle. _____

311, 318

20. Refer to the diagram.

311–312, 318

 a. $m\angle BCD =$ _____   **b.** $m\overarc{DE} =$ _____   **c.** $m\overarc{BA} =$ _____

 d. $m\overarc{CD} =$ _____   **e.** $m\overarc{BC} =$ _____   **f.** $m\overarc{BCD} =$ _____

 g. $m\overarc{AE} =$ _____   **h.** $m\overarc{DEA} =$ _____   **i.** $m\overarc{BAE} =$ _____

 j. $m\overarc{ABC} =$ _____   **k.** $m\overarc{CDE} =$ _____

21. Refer to the diagram.

318

 a. $x =$ _____   **b.** $m\angle A =$ _____   **c.** $m\angle B =$ _____

 d. $m\overarc{AB} =$ _____   **e.** $m\angle BCA =$ _____   **f.** $m\angle BDA =$ _____

 g. $m\overarc{BCD} =$ _____

22. Refer to the diagram. • **MORE HELP** See 131

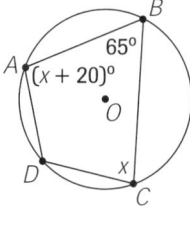

318–319

 a. $m\overarc{ADC} =$ _____   **b.** $m\angle D =$ _____   **c.** $m\overarc{ABC} =$ _____

 d. $m\angle C =$ _____   **e.** $m\angle A =$ _____   **f.** $m\overarc{BAD} =$ _____

 g. $m\overarc{BCD} =$ _____

Name_____ Date_____

Angle and Arc Relationships

Directions: Refer to the diagram, then compare the boxed quantities. Choose the letter of the best description of this comparison.

A the quantity in Column A is greater

B the quantity in Column B is greater

C the quantities are equal

D the relationship cannot be determined from the given information

Column A		Column B

____ **1.** $\boxed{\text{m}\angle 1}$ 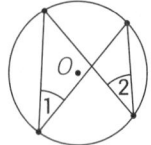 $\boxed{\text{m}\angle 2}$

____ **2.** $\boxed{\text{m}\widehat{ABC}}$ 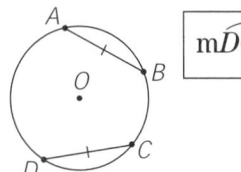 $\boxed{\text{m}\widehat{DCB}}$

____ **3.** $\boxed{x}$ 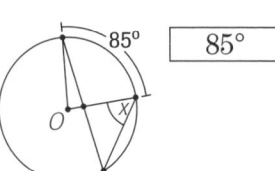 $\boxed{85°}$

____ **4.** $\boxed{PQ}$ 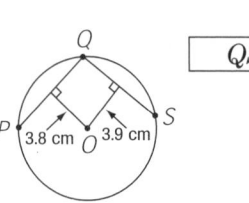 $\boxed{QS}$

____ **5.** $\boxed{DC}$ 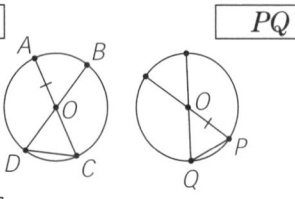 $\boxed{PQ}$

____ **6.** $\boxed{\text{m}\widehat{AB}}$  $\boxed{90°}$

Column A **Column B**

____ **7.** $\boxed{\text{m}\widehat{AB}}$ 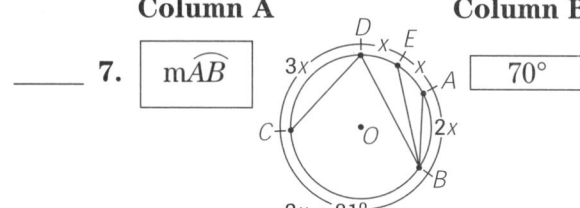 $\boxed{70°}$

____ **8.** $\boxed{\text{m}\angle C}$ 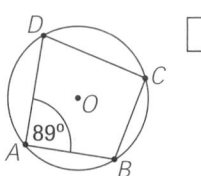 $\boxed{89°}$

____ **9.** $\boxed{117°}$ 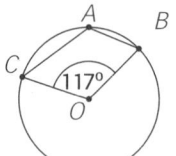 $\boxed{\text{m}\angle A}$

____ **10.** $\boxed{\text{m}\widehat{CB}}$ 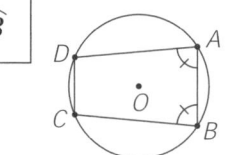 $\boxed{\text{m}\widehat{DA}}$

____ **11.** $\boxed{\begin{array}{c}\text{radius of}\\ \text{the circle}\end{array}}$ 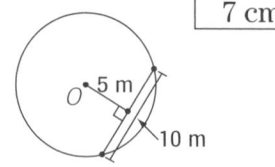 $\boxed{7\text{ cm}}$

____ **12.** $\boxed{x}$ 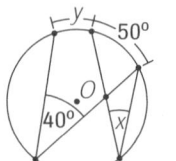 $\boxed{y}$

____ **13.** $\boxed{\begin{array}{c}\text{an inscribed}\\ \text{angle in}\\ \text{a circle}\end{array}}$ $\boxed{\begin{array}{c}\text{a central}\\ \text{angle in the}\\ \text{same circle}\end{array}}$

PRACTICE ANSWERS
Page 173

1. Either answer is acceptable
   a. ∠BOC, ∠BOA
   b. ∠BAC, ∠ABC
   c. $\overset{\frown}{BC}$, $\overset{\frown}{AB}$
   d. $\overset{\frown}{BCA}$, $\overset{\frown}{CAB}$
2. 85°
3. 80°
4. 65°
5. 78°
6. a. $\overline{BD} \perp \overline{AC}$
   b. Accept either $\overline{AD} \cong \overline{CD}$ or $\overline{AB} \cong \overline{BC}$
   c. Accept either ∠ADB ≅ ∠CDB or ∠CAD ≅ ∠ACD
   d. Accept either $\overset{\frown}{AD} \cong \overset{\frown}{CD}$ or $\overset{\frown}{AB} \cong \overset{\frown}{BC}$
7. 12 units
8. 130°

Page 174

9. 70°
10. 46°
11. 60°
12. 22.5°
13. 47°
14. 90°
15. 60°
16. One possible proof:

Statements	Reasons
❶ $\overline{QS} \perp \overline{PQ}$	Given
❷ $\overline{SR} \perp \overline{PR}$	Given
❸ P is the midpoint of $\overset{\frown}{QPR}$	Given
❹ $\overline{QP} \cong \overline{PR}$	2 minor arcs ≅ ↔ corresp. chords ≅ (T134)
❺ $\overline{PS} \cong \overline{PS}$	Reflexive prop. of ≅
❻ ∠PQS, ∠SRP are rt. ∠s	Def. of ⊥
❼ △PQS ≅ △PRS	H-L ≅ Theorem (T110)
❽ $\overline{QS} \cong \overline{RS}$	CPCTC

Page 175
17. One possible proof:

Statements	Reasons
❶ $\overset{\frown}{ABD} \cong \overset{\frown}{BDC}$	Given
❷ $\overset{\frown}{BD} \cong \overset{\frown}{BD}$	Reflexive prop. ≅
❸ m$\overset{\frown}{BD}$ = m$\overset{\frown}{BD}$	Def. of ≅
❹ m$\overset{\frown}{AB}$ + m$\overset{\frown}{BD}$ = m$\overset{\frown}{BD}$ + m$\overset{\frown}{DC}$	Arc + Postulate (P24); Substitution
❺ m$\overset{\frown}{AB}$ = m$\overset{\frown}{DC}$	Subtraction prop. of =
❻ $\overline{AB} \cong \overline{DC}$	2 minor arcs ≅ ↔ corresp. chords ≅ (T134)

18. a. 4 cm
    b. 8 cm
    c. 4 cm
    d. 5 cm
    e. 2 cm
19. 2:1
20. a. 90°
    b. 30°
    c. 0°
    d. 50°
    e. 130°
    f. 180°
    g. 120°
    h. 150°
    i. 150°
    j. 160°
    k. 80°
21. a. 40°
    b. 20°
    c. 20°
    d. 135°
    e. 67.5°
    f. 67.5°
    g. 120°
22. a. 130°
    b. 115°
    c. 230°
    d. 80°
    e. 100°
    f. 160°
    g. 200°

TEST PREP ANSWERS
Page 176

1. C
2. C
3. D
4. A
5. D
6. B
7. B
8. A
9. B
10. C
11. A
12. B
13. D

A Look From Space

OBJECTIVES
- Apply many properties of circles to solve a problem
- Review circumference and inverse trigonometric ratios

MATERIALS
- Scientific calculator or trigonometry table

TIME
- 30–40 minutes

TEACHER NOTES
- Satellites for telecommunications and television are of interest to most students. More and more students are familiar with needing good signals for cellular technology.

- This problem assumes satellites are in orbit above the equator. There will be some uncovered areas north and south of the range of these satellites.

- Remind students that the diagram is not drawn to scale. $\overrightarrow{SA}$ and $\overrightarrow{SB}$ are tangents.

- A scientific calculator will help students focus on the concept as opposed to the computation.

- For more information, see *Mission Mathematics: Linking Aerospace and the NCTM Standards*, from NCTM.

EXTENSIONS
- If the height of the satellite's orbit is increased to 1000 miles how does the required number of satellites change?

- The elevation of Mt. Whitney in California is 14,494 feet; Mt. Washington in New Hampshire is 6288 feet high. How far is the possible view from each mountaintop?

- Have students research geostationary orbits.

ANSWERS
1. 4600 miles

2. $\triangle OAS$ and $\triangle OBS$ are both right triangles. Each radius is perpendicular to the tangent at the point of tangency.

3. Each radius measures 4000 miles

4. Cos $\angle AOS = \frac{4000}{4600}$; m$\angle AOS \approx 29.59°$; m$\angle AOB \approx 59.18°$

5. $\left(\frac{59.18}{360}\right)(2\pi \cdot 4000) \approx 4130$ miles

6. $360° \div 59.18° \approx 6.08$; Students may suggest 6 or 7 satellites. Look for rational explanations.

7. 4817 miles for six satellites or 4129 miles for seven satellites

Name _____ Date _____

Circumference of
Circles: 176

Inverse Trigonometric
Ratios: 243

Special Segments in a
Circle: 305

Properties of
Tangents: 306

Arc Measure: 311

Trigonometric
Functions: 422

A Look From Space

Communications and television companies depend upon satellites orbiting the earth to transmit signals to customers on the ground. The companies try to cover as much area as possible with each satellite in their network so that they can launch and maintain a minimum number of satellites.

A new telecommunications company has hired you. Your first task is to determine the number of satellites needed by the company.

Earth's diameter is approximately 8000 miles. The satellite at point S moves in an equatorial orbit about 600 miles above Earth's surface, on a line through the center of the earth, point O. The satellite rotates once each day and appears to hover directly above a fixed point on Earth.

Not drawn to scale

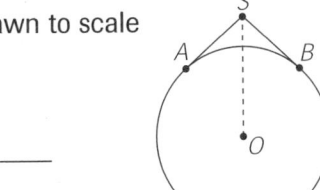

Show your work.

1. What is the measure of $\overline{OS}$? _____

2. Draw $\overline{OA}$ and $\overline{OB}$. What type of triangle is $\triangle OAS$? $\triangle OBS$? Explain.

3. What is the measure of $\overline{OA}$? _____ $\overline{OB}$? _____

4. Central $\angle AOB$ intercepts $\overset{\frown}{AB}$ which represents the points on earth that the satellite can see. What is the measure of $\angle AOB$? (Hint: determine m$\angle AOS$ first.)

5. What is the length of $\overset{\frown}{AB}$?

6. How many satellites would you recommend that your company launch in order to cover the whole circumference of the earth? Explain your recommendation.

7. Approximately how far apart would the satellites be in their circular orbit?

Name _____ Date _____

Classification of Solids

322

For exercises 1–6, classify the figure as a *polyhedron* or *not a polyhedron*. If the figure is a polyhedron, determine whether it is *convex* or *concave*.

1.

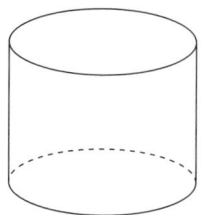

_____

2.

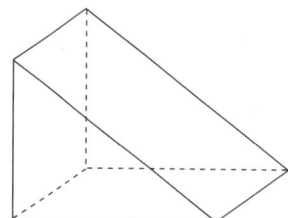

_____

3.

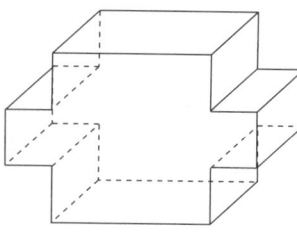

_____

4.

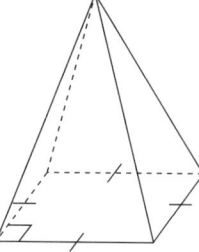

_____

5.

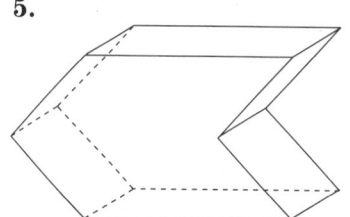

_____

6.

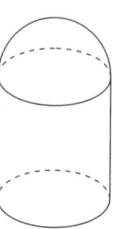

_____

323

For exercises 7–12, state the number of faces, vertices, and edges for the polyhedron.

7.

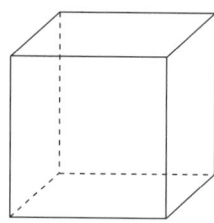

_____

8.

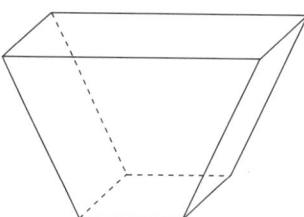

_____

9.

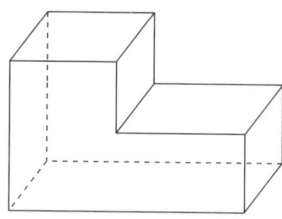

_____

10.

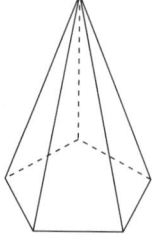

_____

11.

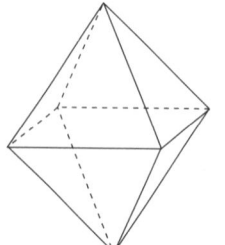

_____

12.

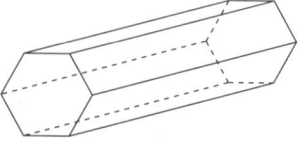

_____

Name _____ Date _____

For exercises 13–18, decide whether the statement is true or false.

_____13. Each face of a Platonic solid is a regular polygon.

_____14. Each face of an Archimedean solid is regular polygon.

_____15. There are fewer than ten Platonic solids.

_____16. There are fewer than ten Archimedean solids.

_____17. The prefix *icosa-* means twelve.

_____18. A *truncated* polyhedron has been cut in half.

For exercises 19–22, sketch an example of the prism.

19. right rectangular prism   **20.** oblique triangular prism

21. concave hexagonal prism   **22.** regular prism

For exercises 23–26, sketch an example of the pyramid.

23. square pyramid   **24.** oblique triangular pyramid

25. regular triangular pyramid   **26.** hexagonal pyramid

Name_____ Date_____

328-332 For exercises 27–35, write *True* if the statement is true. Write *False* if the statement is sometimes or always false. Rewrite false statements to make them true.

27. A cube is a regular polyhedron. _____

28. The base of a regular pyramid could be regular pentagon. _____

_____

29. A prismoid has parallel bases that are quadrilaterals. _____

_____

30. Euler's Theorem is valid for prismoids. _____

31. In an oblique cylinder, the altitude is the same as the distance between two corresponding points on the bases. _____

_____

32. The radius of a cylinder is equal to the radius of its base. _____

_____

33. In a cone, another word for *vertex* is *angle*. _____

34. In an oblique cone, the slant height varies, depending upon where you measure it.

_____

35. The center of a sphere is on the sphere. _____

330-332 For exercises 36–43, complete the sentence by filling in the correct word.

36. The bases of a cylinder are congruent and parallel _____.

37. The _____ of a cylinder is the perpendicular distance between the bases.

38. The lateral surface of a cylinder is the _____ surface.

39. The intersection of the base and the lateral surfaces of a cylinder or cone is called the _____.

40. In a(n) _____ cylinder, the segment joining the centers of the bases is not perpendicular to the bases.

41. In a right cone, the _____ intersects the base at its center.

42. The _____ height is the length of a segment from the vertex to any point on the lateral edge of a right cone

43. A great circle of a sphere has the same center and _____ as the sphere.

Name _____ Date _____

Classification of Solids

Directions: Fill in the circle next to the best answer. You will need a calculator or a table of square roots.

1. Which word *cannot* be used to describe the figure?

  ○ **A.** polyhedron

  ○ **B.** prism

  ○ **C.** convex

  ○ **D.** concave

2. Which solid is *not* a prism?

  ○ **A.** 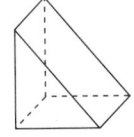   ○ **C.**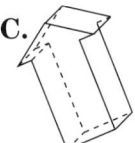

  ○ **B.** 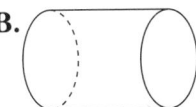   ○ **D.**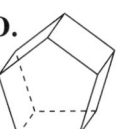

3. If a polyhedron has 12 vertices and 22 edges, how many faces does it have?

  ○ **A.** 10

  ○ **B.** 12

  ○ **C.** 14

  ○ **D.** cannot determine

4. Each face of this solid is an equilateral triangle. Select the best description for the solid.

  ○ **A.** pyramid

  ○ **B.** regular polyhedron

  ○ **C.** tetrahedron

  ○ **D.** hexahedron

5. Which figure is *not* a Platonic Solid?

  ○ **A.** 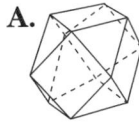   ○ **C.**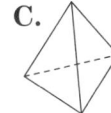

  ○ **B.** 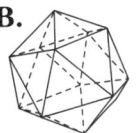   ○ **D.**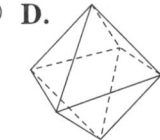

6. The diagonal of a rectangular prism with dimensions 8 centimeters by 4 centimeters by 6 centimeters

  ○ **A.** about 18 cm.

  ○ **B.** about 6 cm.

  ○ **C.** about 116 cm.

  ○ **D.** about 10.77 cm.

7. Which solid is oblique?

  ○ **A.** 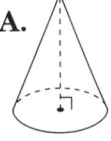   ○ **C.**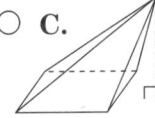

  ○ **B.**    ○ **D.**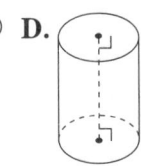

8. Identify the slant height of the cone.

  ○ **A.** $\overline{AC}$

  ○ **B.** $\overline{AB}$

  ○ **C.** $\overline{BC}$

  ○ **D.** $\overline{CD}$

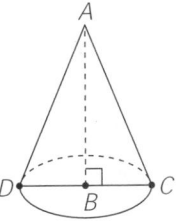

PRACTICE ANSWERS
Page 180

1. not a polyhedron
2. convex polyhedron
3. concave polyhedron
4. convex polyhedron
5. concave polyhedron
6. not a polyhedron
7. 6, 8, 12
8. 6, 8, 12
9. 8, 12, 18
10. 6, 6, 10
11. 8, 6, 12
12. 8, 12, 18

Page 181

13. T
14. T
15. T
16. F
17. F
18. F

For exercises 19–22, sketches may vary. Samples are shown.

19.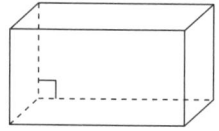

20.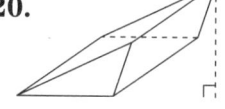

21.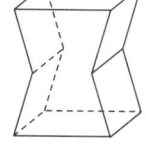

22.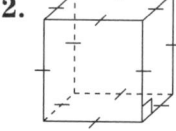

23.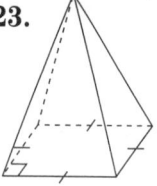

24.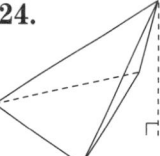

25.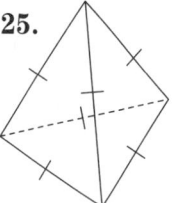

26.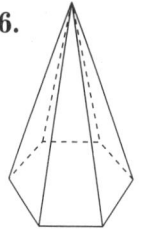

Page 182

27. true
28. true
29. false; A prismoid has parallel bases that <u>are not necessarily congruent</u>.
30. true
31. false; In a <u>right</u> cylinder, the altitude is the same as the distance between two corresponding points on the bases.
32. true
33. false; In a cone, another word for vertex is <u>apex</u>.

34. false; In an oblique cone, <u>there is no slant height</u>.
35. false; The center of a sphere is <u>in</u> the sphere.
36. circles
37. height
38. curved
39. base edge
40. oblique
41. altitude
42. slant
43. radius

TEST PREP ANSWERS
Page 183

1. C
2. B
3. B
4. D
5. A
6. D
7. C
8. A

Name_____ Date_____

Visualization of Solids

You will need graph paper and isometric dot paper.

334

For exercises 1–4, sketch the solid, using dotted lines to represent hidden portions.

1. a right circular cone

2. a rectangular prism

3. a square pyramid

4. a right circular cylinder

335

Make an isometric and an orthographic drawing of each solid.

5.

6.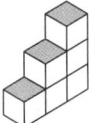

For exercises 7–8, name the shape that would be formed if each net were folded into a solid.

7.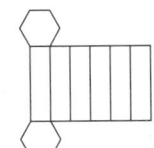

_____

8.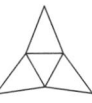

_____

336

For exercises 9–10, decide whether the figure is a net for a cube.

9.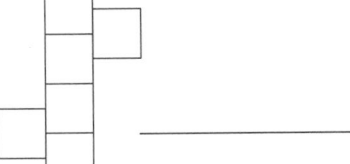

_____

10.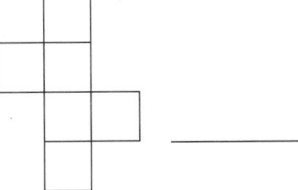

_____

337

For exercises 11–13, describe the cross section of the cube.

11.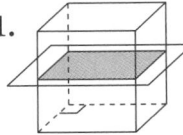

_____

12.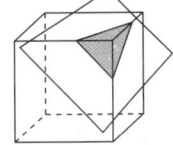

_____

13.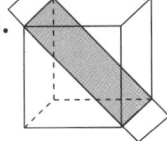

_____

338

For exercises 14–16, describe the cross section that results from the plane intersecting a double napped cone.

14.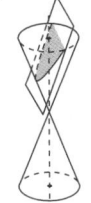

_____

15.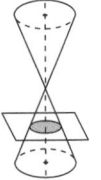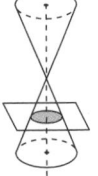

_____

16.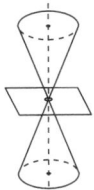

_____

Name_____ Date_____

Visualization of Solids

Directions: Write your answer in the space provided.

For exercises 1–5, decide whether the statement is true or false.

_____ **1.** An orthographic drawing shows the net that would fold into a solid.

_____ **2.** When solids are sketched, the hidden edges should appear as dashed lines.

_____ **3.** A plane can intersect a cube to form a pentagon.

_____ **4.** A plane can intersect a cube to form a regular hexagon.

_____ **5.** Any cross section of a sphere is called a great circle.

For exercises 6–13, match the net in Column A with the name of the solid into which it can be folded in Column B.

Column A	Column B

_____ **6.** 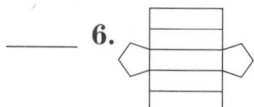   **A.** rectangular prism

_____ **7.** 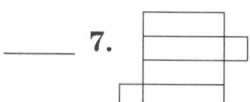   **B.** right triangular prism

_____ **8.** 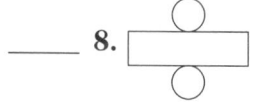   **C.** equilateral triangular prism

_____ **9.** 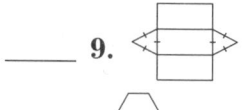   **D.** cone

_____ **10.** 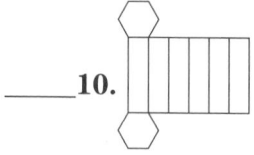   **E.** hexagonal pyramid

_____ **11.**    **F.** pentagonal prism

_____ **12.** 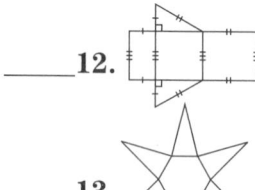   **G.** cylinder

_____ **13.** 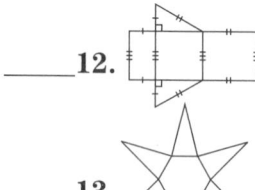   **H.** hexagonal prism

PRACTICE ANSWERS
Page 185

1.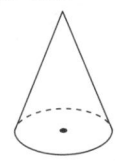

2.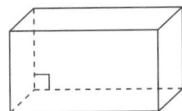

3.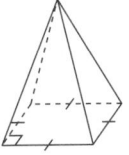

4.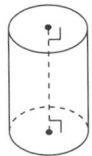

7. hexagonal prism
8. triangular pyramid
9. no
10. yes
11. square
12. equilateral triangle
13. rectangle
14. parabola
15. circle
16. point

TEST PREP ANSWERS
Page 186

1. F
2. T
3. T
4. T
5. F
6. F
7. A
8. G
9. C
10. H
11. D
12. B
13. E

5.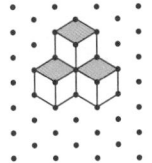

6.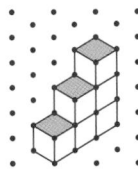

Build It Now!

OBJECTIVES
• Construct a solid from its net
• Investigate Euler's Theorem with the Platonic solids

MATERIALS
• Construction paper
• Tape
• Scissors

TEACHER NOTES
• This is a fun activity for most students. They enjoy the kinesthetic experience of creating a three-dimensional model from a two-dimensional net.

• Students may wish to leave tabs on their nets in order to make taping easier. A sample tetrahedron is shown.

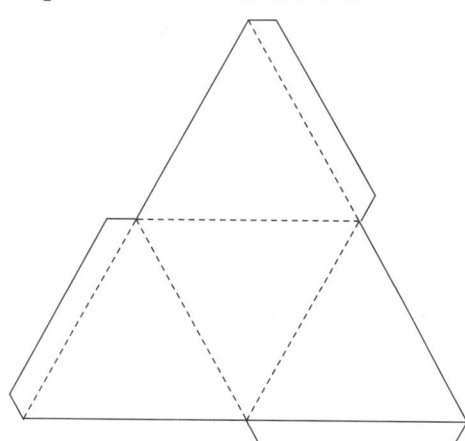

• If time is a constraint, you could enlarge the nets on a photocopier with the final version being copied onto stiffer paper.

EXTENSIONS
• Have students cut the solids out of colors that suggest the elements with which Plato associated them.

• Have students use the five solids to make a mobile. They can all be hung from one coat hanger, or use string and bamboo skewers to make a more traditional style mobile.

• Have students construct one or more of the Archimedean solids using similar templates.

ANSWERS

1.

2.
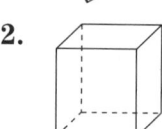

3.
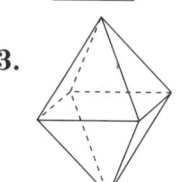

4.

5.
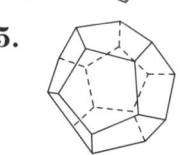

6.

	F	V	E
Tetrahedron	4	4	6
Hexahedron	6	8	12
Octahedron	8	6	12
Icosahedron	20	12	30
Dodecahedron	12	20	30

Name _____ Date _____

Euler's Theorem: 323
Platonic Solids: 324

Build It Now!

There are five regular polyhedrons, called Platonic solids after the Greek mathematician and philosopher Plato. Each solid is constructed using a single regular polygon with the same number of polygons meeting at each vertex.

Below are the nets for each of the solids. Plato named each solid and associated each with one of the four basic "elements" along with a fifth element.

Use the nets as maps to help make three-dimensional models of the solids. Trace each regular polygon onto stiff paper, cut out, and use as a template. Use your template to recreate, on construction paper, the net for each solid. Cut along solid lines and fold on dashed lines. Use tape to secure.

Regular Polygon Templates:

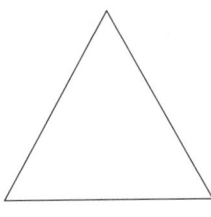

1. Tetrahedron (fire)   **2.** Cube (earth)   **3.** Octahedron (air)

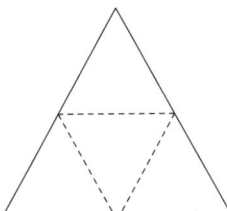
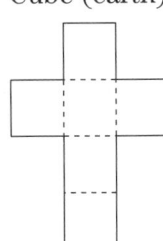
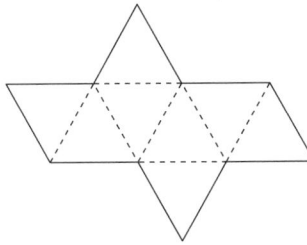

4. Icosahedron (water)   **5.** Dodecahedron (cosmos)

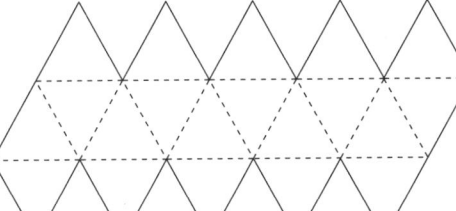
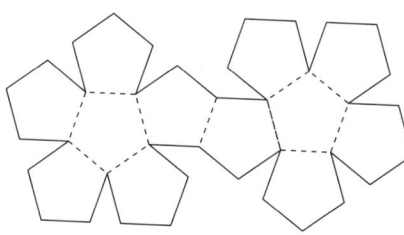

6. Record the number of faces, vertices, and edges for each of your polyhedrons to verify Euler's theorem.

	F	V	E
Tetrahedron			
Hexahedron			
Octahedron			
Icosahedron			
Dodecahedron			

Name _____ Date _____

Problem Solving Strategies

343-357 Solve each problem.

Remember the Plan
❶ Understand
❷ Plan
❸ Try
❹ Look Back

1. In a class of 26 students, a survey determined what vegetables the students like. The top three vegetables were spinach, broccoli, and carrots. The survey revealed that 16 students like spinach, two like only carrots and spinach, eight like only spinach, four like all three vegetables, two like only broccoli but eight included broccoli among their choices, and five like only carrots or only broccoli but not both. Determine how many students like carrots, how many like broccoli or spinach, and how many like broccoli or carrots but not spinach. Explain why the sum of the students making these three choices is not 26.

2. Place the numbers 1–8 in the squares so that no consecutive numbers (like 3 and 4) are located in adjacent squares horizontally, vertically, or diagonally.

3. The homemade cookies at the sandwich shop are a bargain at 35¢. A customer purchases a cookie and gives you a $1.00 bill. How many different ways can you give the customer change if you have quarters, dimes, and nickels? Which way uses the fewest coins? Which uses the most?

4. Your friend Sarah told you in an e-mail that she had won a dart game with a score of 73 and all 10 of the darts she threw hit the dartboard. You wonder if she had any bull's eyes (scored a 10). Did she? Explain.

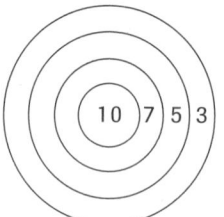

Name _____ Date _____

5. The organizers of a talent show wanted to feature a musician as the final act. Five musicians auditioned and each performed a different type of music. Read the clues and fill in the table to match each musician with the type of music.

- Abbi lives in the same town as both Bob and the country musician.
- The jazz musician auditioned before Ellie, who auditioned second.
- The country musician auditioned last, after Dion.
- The rock and roll musician followed Bob, who was the first to audition.
- Abbi left before Dion's audition, because she doesn't like the classical music that he sings.

	Abbi	Bob	Carla	Dion	Ellie
Blues					
Classical					
Country					
Jazz					
Rock & Roll					

6. Your friend was doodling in class and drew these figures on graph paper. If your friend keeps extending this pattern, how many small squares will there be in the ninth figure? What will be the perimeter of the ninth figure? Explain how you arrived at your answers.

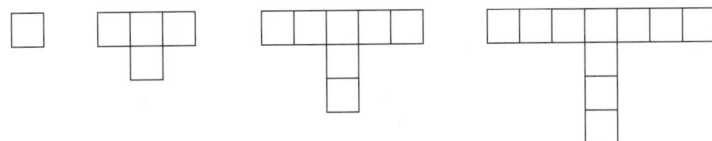

7. Beth, Kinsley, and Kori went shopping. Beth spent half of her money on a new pair of khaki pants, then she gave Kinsley $4.00 that she owed her. Beth spent $\frac{1}{4}$ of her remaining money on lunch. After lunch she spend $\frac{2}{3}$ of her remaining money on a new tank top. Finally, she spent $3.00 for a popcorn and soda. She went home with $4.00. How much money did she start the day with?

8. You save $2.00 the first day, $2.50 the second day, $3.00 the third day, $3.50 the fourth day. If you continue this pattern for 30 days, how much will you have saved?

Name _____ Date _____

9. You need to schedule a chess tournament among eight players. Each player must play each other player once. How many games must you schedule?

10. A luncheon special offers a two-item combination plate for $4.95. There are six items to select from: ravioli, lasagna, meatloaf, chili, potatoes, and green beans. How many different two-item combinations are possible?

11. At 7:45 A.M., you begin a 12-mile hike. At 8:20 A.M., you have walked one mile. If you can hike at the same rate the entire day, when will you finish your hike?

12. Show all of the different combinations of three even numbers with a sum of 20. (Consider $2 + 2 + 16$ to be the same as $2 + 16 + 2$.)

Name _____ Date _____

Problem Solving Strategies

Directions: Solve each problem. Show and explain your work.

1. The number of ants in your ant farm doubles every 10 days. On the sixty-first day there are 640 ants in the farm. How many ants did you start with? How many will you have on day 81?

2. A sock drawer contains 60 loose socks. Each sock is one of six colors. In the pre-dawn darkness, what is the minimum number of socks that must be taken from the drawer to ensure that two socks are the same color?

3. When the points scored by six basketball players during a tournament were arranged in order, the difference between any two consecutive totals was nine. The mean of the six players' points was 36.5. How many points did the highest scoring player score?

4. Herb, Irene, and Jon work in a bank. One is the manager, one is the assistant manager, and one is a teller. The teller, who is an only child, is the youngest. Irene, who is married to Jon's brother, is older than the manager is. Which jobs do Herb, Irene, and Jon have?

5. How many equilateral triangles whose vertices are dots can you draw on each triangular grid? (The triangles are not necessarily all the same size.)

```
    A              B              C
    •              •              •

•       •      •       •      •       •

    •   •   •          •   •   •

            •   •   •   •
```

6. Four people enter a race. Assuming no ties, how many different outcomes are possible for first place and second place?

PRACTICE ANSWERS
Page 190

1.
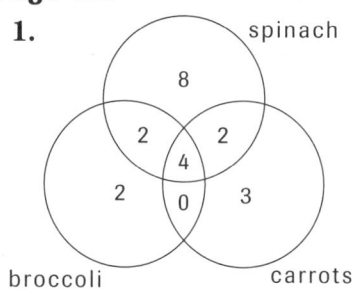

9 students like carrots

18 students like broccoli or spinach

0 students like broccoli or carrots but not spinach

There are not 26 responses because this diagram shows only the top three vegetables— the other five students had other favorite vegetables.

2. Sample Answer:

3	5

7	1	8	2

4	6

3. There are 14 ways to make 65¢ change.

Quarters	Dimes	Nickels	Total Coins
2	1	1	4 *
2	0	3	5
1	4	0	5
1	3	2	6
1	2	4	7
1	1	6	8
1	0	8	9
0	6	1	7
0	5	3	8
0	4	5	9
0	3	7	10
0	2	9	11
0	1	11	12
0	0	13	13**

* fewest coins

** most coins

4. She must have gotten at least one bull's eye because even ten 7s won't give a high enough score. Use *Guess, Check and Revise* to find three possible combinations: three 10s, five 7s, one 5, one 3; one 10, nine 7s; five 10s, four 5s, one 3.

Page 191

Solution methods will vary. Samples are provided.

5. Use the *Use Logical Reasoning* strategy.

	Abbi	Bob	Carla	Dion	Ellie
Blues	✔	X	X	X	X
Classical	X	X	X	✔	X
Country	X	X	✔	X	X
Jazz	X	✔	X	X	X
Rock & Roll	X	X	X	X	✔

6. Use the *Find and Use a Pattern* strategy. One way to describe the pattern is to think of adding a square on the left, right, and bottom. Three squares get added in each new figure, so for the ninth figure there would be $1 + 8(3) = 25$ squares. The perimeter follows the pattern 4, 10, 16, … and is increasing by six for each figure. The ninth figure would have a perimeter of $4 + 8(6) = 52$ units.

7. Use the *Work Backward* strategy or the *Model with an Equation* strategy.
$(\frac{1}{3})(\frac{3}{4})(\frac{B}{2} - 4) - 3 = 4$;
$B = 64$. She began the day with $64.

PRACTICE ANSWERS
Page 191
(continued on page 216)

Page 192
(see page 216 for answers)

TEST PREP ANSWERS
Page 193
(see page 217 for answers)

Name _____ Date _____

Problem Solving Skills

Show your work.
For exercises 1–3, refer to this problem.
Two sides of a right triangle measure 4 centimeters and 5 centimeters. What is the measure of the third side?

1. What do you need to know to solve this problem? _____

2. Is it possible to have more than one correct answer? Explain. _____

3. Solve the problem. _____

For exercises 4–6, refer to this problem.
The mean of three numbers is 20, the median is 15, and the range is 15.
What are the three numbers?

4. Can you estimate to solve this problem? Why or why not? _____

5. Could the numbers be 5, 15, and 20? Why or why not? _____

6. Solve the problem. _____

For exercises 7–9, refer to this problem.
The expression $\frac{5 \cdot 5 + 5}{5} - 5$ uses five 5s and has a value of one. Use five 5s to create a different expression with a value of five.

7. What do you need to know in order to solve this problem? _____

8. Is it possible to have more than one correct answer? Explain. _____

9. Solve the problem. _____

For exercises 10–18, refer to this table.

State	Land Area	Rank	2000 Population	Rank
Colorado	104,100 sq. mi.	8	4,301,261	24
Iowa	56,276 sq. mi.	26	2,926,324	30
Kansas	82,282 sq. mi.	15	2,688,418	32
Missouri	69,709 sq. mi.	21	5,595,211	17
Nebraska	77,359 sq. mi.	16	1,711,263	38
Oklahoma	69,903 sq. mi.	20	3,450,654	27
South Dakota	77,121 sq. mi.	17	754,844	46
Wyoming	97,819 sq. mi.	9	493,782	51

Source: 2000 Census data for all 50 states and District of columbia

For exercises 10–12, refer to this problem.
How many of the 50 states have a land area greater than the area of Wyoming?

10. What information do you need to know in order to answer this question? _____

11. Is it possible to have more than one answer to this question? Explain. _____

12. Solve the problem. _____

Name _____ Date _____

360

For exercises 13–15, refer to this problem.

Population density is the number of people per some unit of area. An example would be the number of people per square mile. For the Midwestern states listed, which state(s) have a population density greater than that of Kansas?

13. What operation is needed to solve this problem? _____

14. Is it possible to estimate to solve this problem? Explain why or why not. _____

_____

15. Solve the problem. _____

For exercises 16–18, refer to this problem.

The area of the District of Columbia is 68 square miles (rank = 51). In 2000, D. C. had a population of 572,059 (rank = 50). About how many people are there per square mile in the District of Columbia?

16. What do you need to do to solve this problem? _____

17. Use compatible numbers to estimate the population density. _____

_____

18. How do you think the population density of the District of Columbia compares to that of

the Midwestern states? Explain. _____

For exercises 19–21, refer to this problem.

Name the cylinder whose volume is approximately 50 cm³.

A.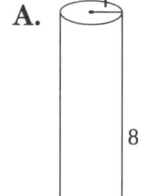

B.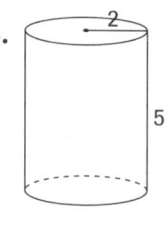

C.

19. What do you need to know in order to solve this problem? _____

20. Can you estimate to solve this problem? Why or why not? _____

_____

21. Name the cylinder. _____

_____

Name _____ Date _____

361

For exercises 22–23, refer to this problem.
Section 6.1 of the geometry text contains six pages. The sum of the page numbers in this section is 747. What are the page numbers for the six pages in this section?

22. Solve the problem. _____

23. Check your solution by using another method. _____

_____

For exercises 24–25, refer to this diagram.
• **MORE HELP** See 141, 152, 182

4 cm

24. Find the total area of the shaded equilateral triangles. _____

_____

25. Check your solution by using another method. _____

_____

For exercises 26–27, refer to this problem.
You are paid $8.50 an hour for moving 2" by 4" by 8' pieces of lumber from the showroom floor to the loading dock, a distance of 84 feet. A customer buys 18 pieces of the lumber worth $86.40. How long does it take you to move the lumber?

26. Do you have enough information to solve the problem? _____

27. If the answer to exercises 26 is *yes*, solve the problem. If *no*, identify the missing

information. _____

362

For exercises 28–29, refer to this problem.
One circle has a radius that is triple the radius of another circle. How do the areas of the two circles compare?

28. Do you have enough information to solve the problem? _____

29. If *yes*, solve the problem. If *no*, identify the missing information. _____

For exercises 30–31, refer to this problem.
The conversion formula for Centigrade to Fahrenheit is $F = \frac{9}{5}C + 32°$. Determine the temperature that's the same on both scales.

30. Do you have enough information to solve the problem? _____

31. If the answer to exercise 30 is *yes*, solve the problem. If *no*, identify the missing

information. _____

Name _____ Date _____

Problem Solving Skills

Directions: Select the most appropriate method to solve each problem. Then, if it is solvable, use any strategy to solve.

1. Use the numbers 1 through 6 so that the sum on each side of the triangle is the same.
  - **A.** Be ready for multiple answers.
  - **B.** Use an estimate.
  - **C.** Compute an exact answer.
  - **D.** not enough information

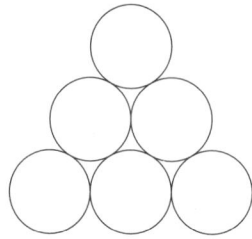

2. The number of units in the circumference of a given circle is equal to the number of units in its area. Find the radius of the circle.
  - **A.** Be ready for multiple answers.
  - **B.** Use an estimate.
  - **C.** Compute an exact answer.
  - **D.** not enough information

3. On a recent chapter test one student scored 15 points higher than the class mean. What was the lowest score?
  - **A.** Be ready for multiple answers.
  - **B.** Use an estimate.
  - **C.** Compute an exact answer.
  - **D.** not enough information

4. It takes approximately 45 seconds to fill the watering can, about 20 seconds to walk from the sink to the flower bed, and about 10 seconds to empty the can. How long will it take to water the garden if this requires refilling the watering can four times?
  - **A.** Be ready for multiple answers.
  - **B.** Use an estimate.
  - **C.** Compute an exact answer.
  - **D.** not enough information

5. Each letter represents a different digit. Name the digits that make the addition example a true equation.

DO
YOU
+ SEE
A SUM

  - **A.** Be ready for multiple answers.
  - **B.** Use an estimate.
  - **C.** Compute an exact answer.
  - **D.** not enough information

6. Seventy-eight percent of all people are gum-chewers, and 35 percent of all people are under the age of fifteen. Given that a person has been selected at random, what is the probability that the person is not a gum-chewer and is above age fifteen?
  - **A.** Be ready for multiple answers.
  - **B.** Use an estimate.
  - **C.** Compute an exact answer.
  - **D.** not enough information

PRACTICE ANSWERS
Page 195

1. You need to know which side is the hypotenuse so you can use the Pythagorean Theorem.

2. Yes; the hypotenuse could be 5 units long, so you would be solving for a leg; or the legs could 4 and 5 units long so you would be solving for the hypotenuse.

3. $\sqrt{41}$ cm or 3 cm

4. No; exact computation is needed to find the mean of 3 numbers.

5. no
$(5 + 15 + 20) \div 3 \neq 20$

6. 15, 15, 30

7. Answers may vary: you need to be familiar with basic operations and the order of operations

8. Yes; it is possible to write many different expressions that have a value of 5.

9. Sample answers:
$5 + \frac{5-5}{5 \div 5}$ or
$5 - \{5 - [5 - (5 - 5)]\}$

10. You need to know the land area rank of Wyoming.

11. No; states either have a land area greater than or less than Wyoming.

12. eight states

Page 196

13. division

14. Yes; estimate which states have a population to land area ratio of about 33 to 1 sq. mi or greater. You could also reason that if a state has a population greater than Kansas' and a smaller land area, the population density has to be greater.

15. Colorado, Iowa, Missouri, Oklahoma

16. division, estimation

17. Use compatible numbers: 560,000 people $\div$ 70 square miles $\approx$ 8000 people per square mile.

18. District of Columbia has a population density greater than any of the states listed because its population is about $\frac{1}{10}$ of that of the most populated state, but its area is $\frac{1}{1500}$ of the largest state.

19. You need to know how to compute the volume of a cylinder.

20. Yes. The problem gives an approximate volume.

21. cylinder C, because $\pi(4^2)(1) \approx 50$ cm³

Page 197

22. Possible solution method: $x + (x + 1) + (x + 2) + (x + 3) + (x + 4) + (x + 5) = 747$; $x = 122$. The pages are 122, 123, 124, 125, 126, and 127.

23. Possible solution method:
$747 \div 6 = 124.5$, so pages 124 and 125 are in the middle of the section. The six pages are 122, 123, 124 followed by 125, 126, 127.

24. Possible solution method: The center triangle has $\frac{1}{4}$ the area of the largest triangle and the smaller triangles each have $\frac{1}{16}$ the area of the largest triangle. So the shaded portion is $(\frac{1}{4} + \frac{3}{16})$(area of large triangle) = $\frac{7}{16}(\frac{4^2\sqrt{3}}{4}) = \frac{7\sqrt{3}}{4}$.

25. Possible solution method: Add the area of the middle triangle to 3(area of small triangles).
Shaded portion =
$\frac{2^2\sqrt{3}}{4} + 3(\frac{1^2\sqrt{3}}{4}) = \frac{7\sqrt{3}}{4}$

26. no

27. You need to know how long it takes you to make each trip from the showroom to the loading dock, and how many pieces of lumber you can carry on each trip.

28. yes

29. The ratio of area of larger circle to area of smaller circle is 9:1.

30. yes

31. $F = \frac{9}{5}C + 32°$,
so solve: $t = \frac{9}{5}t + 32$,
$\frac{-4}{5}t = 32$, $t = {}^-40$

TEST PREP ANSWERS
Page 198
(see page 218 for answers)

What's Cooking?

OBJECTIVE
• Use logical reasoning to solve a multiple-step problem

MATERIALS
none

TIME
• 30–40 minutes

TEACHER NOTES
• This is a problem that should be solved with a partner, although groups of 3 or 4 could also work together.

• The less said by the teacher, usually the better. If students ask whether steps can be performed simultaneously (i.e. preheat the oven while combining ingredients), you might want to respond with the question, "Is that reasonable?"

• Remind students that the solution must include the starting time.

EXTENSIONS
• Students can make a poster or overhead transparency and present their solutions to the class.

• Ask students to decide how different their solution would be if a friend helped them bake the cake.

ANSWERS
There are many correct answers, some more logical or efficient than others. Look to see whether the sequence is logical (i.e. steps 11 and 12 precede step 10). Steps 15 and 4 must be first and second respectively. Some students may elect to do step 14 at several points in the process.

Possible solution:

Step 15: get recipe (20)

Step 4: shop (45)

Step 12: melt shortening (4)

Step 11: beat eggs (during step 12)

Step 8: measure milk (during step 12)

Step 10: combine wet ingredients (5)

Step 17: prepare dry ingredients (10)

Step 7: combine ingredients (15)

Step 5: preheat oven (during step 7)

Step 9: prepare pans (2)

Step 13: pour batter (2)

Step 16: bake cake (45)

Step 1: remove cake (1)

Step 3: cool cake (30)

Step 2: mix frosting (during step 3)

Step 6: frost cake (10)

Step 14: clean up (15)

Total time = 3 hours 24 minutes; start working by 2:36 P.M.

Step 18: eat the cake after 6 P.M.

Name _____ Date _____

What's Cooking?

You have invited friends over to celebrate the beginning of spring vacation and you want to serve a cake for dessert. You want everything done by 6 P.M. so that you may enjoy your company.

Directions: Work with a partner. You will hand in a <u>time for starting the cake</u>, and an ordered step-by-step list of what activities are to be done. Give supporting rationale as necessary.

1. Remove cake from oven. Time 1 minute.

2. Mix the frosting. Time 10 minutes. (Frosting will harden if completed more than 10 minutes before use.)

3. Remove cake from pan and place on wire rack to cool. Time 30 minutes.

4. Go to store to buy ingredients. Time 45 minutes.

5. Preheat oven. Time 5 minutes.

6. Frost cake. Time 10 minutes.

7. Combine wet and dry ingredients and beat for 100 strokes. The ingredients must first be combined as wet and dry separately. Time 15 minutes.

8. Measure milk. Time 0.5 minutes.

9. Grease and flour baking pans. Time 2 minutes.

10. Combine milk, eggs, and shortening. Eggs, milk and shortening must be prepared before this step. Time 5 minutes.

11. Beat eggs. Time 2 minutes.

12. Measure and melt shortening. Time 4 minutes.

13. Pour batter into pans. Time 2 minutes.

14. Wash dishes and countertop. Time 15 minutes.

15. Look through cookbook and select a recipe. Time 20 minutes.

16. Put cake into oven and bake. Time 45 minutes.

17. Measure and sift dry ingredients. Time 10 minutes.

18. Eat the cake. Time 15 minutes.

Name _____ Date _____

Elliptic and Spherical Geometries

364

For exercises 1–5 complete the sentence by selecting a word from the list.

A. theorems	**B.** perpendicular	**C.** postulates	**D.** no
E. parallel	**F.** intersect	**G.** two	**H.** one

_____ **1.** Euclidean geometry is based upon a set of ___ formulated by Euclid over 2000 years ago.

_____ **2.** Euclid's fifth postulate is often referred to as the ___ postulate.

_____ **3.** In spherical geometry we assume that through a given point not on a line, you can draw ___ line(s) parallel to the given line.

_____ **4.** In Euclidean geometry we assume that through a given point not on a line, you can draw ___ line(s) parallel to the given line.

_____ **5.** Any two lines in spherical geometry will ___.

365

For exercises 6–11, decide whether each statement about spherical geometry is true or false.

_____ **6.** The plane in Euclidean geometry becomes a sphere in spherical geometry.

_____ **7.** Exactly one great circle passes through each pair of polar points.

_____ **8.** Two polar points determine exactly one line.

_____ **9.** Any two non-polar points determine exactly one line.

_____ **10.** Through a point not on a line, there are an infinite number of lines through the point perpendicular to the given line.

_____ **11.** All lines on a sphere are the same length.

For exercises 12–16, refer to sphere *S*.

12. Name a pair of polar points. _____

13. Name a pair of non-polar points. _____

14. m$\widehat{AB}$ + m$\widehat{BA'}$ = m_____.

15. Name a point between *C* and *A'*. _____

16. The length of $\widehat{ABA'B'}$ equals the length of what other line? _____

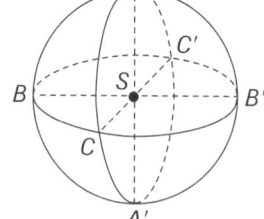

366

17. Explain why the sum of angles in a triangle in spherical geometry can be greater than 180°.

_____

367

18. In coordinate geometry, each coordinate represents a distance. What do coordinates in

spherical geometry represent? _____

_____

Name _____ Date _____

Elliptic and Spherical Geometries

Directions: Fill in the letter of the best answer.

1 Euclid's fifth postulate is called the

  A Perpendicular Postulate.

  B Parallel Postulate.

  C Distance Postulate.

2 The Spherical Parallel Postulate states that through a given point not on a given line, there is (are) ___ line(s) parallel to the given line.

  D no

  E one

  F two

3 In spherical geometry, two lines intersect in how many points?

  A one

  B two

  C infinitely many

4 The shortest distance between two points on a sphere is

  D not measurable.

  E a radius of a great circle.

  F an arc of a great circle.

5 Two endpoints of a diameter of a great circle are called

  A opposite points.

  B inverse points.

  C polar points.

6 On a sphere, vertical angles are

  D always congruent.

  E sometimes congruent.

  F never congruent.

7 On a sphere, lines are

  A always congruent.

  B sometimes congruent.

  C never congruent.

8 Through any two non-polar points, how many lines can be drawn?

  D none

  E one

  F two

9 You draw a triangle on a sphere with two vertices on the equator and the third vertex at the North Pole. The sum of the angles of this triangle is

  A less than 180°.

  B equal to 180°.

  C greater than 180°.

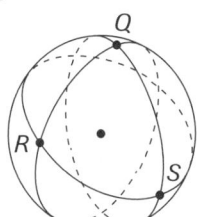

PRACTICE ANSWERS
Page 202

1. C
2. E
3. D
4. H
5. F
6. T
7. F
8. F
9. T
10. T
11. T
12. A and A', or B and B', or C and C'
13. Possible answer: A and B
14. m$\widehat{ABA'}$
15. A or C'
16. Possible answer: $\widehat{CBC'B'}$
17. Some lines intersect at right angles, so the angles of a triangle can have a sum of 270°
18. ρ is a distance but Φ and Θ are angles

TEST PREP ANSWERS
Page 203

1. B
2. D
3. B
4. F
5. C
6. D
7. A
8. E
9. C

Name _____ Date _____

Hyperbolic Geometry

For exercises 1–5, complete each sentence by selecting a word from the list.

A. theorem   **B.** perpendicular   **C.** postulates   **D.** one

E. parallel   **F.** intersecting   **G.** two   **H.** infinitely many

_____ **1.** In hyperbolic geometry we assume that through a given point not on a line, you can draw ___ line(s) parallel to the given line.

_____ **2.** In Euclidean geometry we assume that through a given point not on a line, you can draw ___ line(s) parallel to the given line.

_____ **3.** A line in hyperbolic geometry has endpoints that are ___ to the boundary circle at both endpoints.

_____ **4.** Euclidean geometry is based upon a set of ___ formulated by Euclid over 2000 years ago.

_____ **5.** Euclid's fifth postulate is often referred to as the ___ postulate.

For exercises 6–16, decide whether the statement about hyperbolic geometry is true or false.

_____ **6.** The plane from Euclidean geometry becomes the interior points of an infinitely large circle in hyperbolic geometry.

_____ **7.** Lines are the arcs formed on the circle.

_____ **8.** The Poincaré disk is one name for the circular plane.

_____ **9.** Henri Poincaré alone developed hyperbolic geometry.

_____ **10.** Lines in hyperbolic geometry have infinite length.

_____ **11.** Two perpendicular lines can be parallel to the same line.

_____ **12.** Angles on the Poincaré disk are acute or right, but not obtuse.

_____ **13.** The sum of the measures of the angles of a triangle is less than 180°.

_____ **14.** The Pythagorean Theorem is true for all triangles drawn on the Poincaré disk.

_____ **15.** It is possible to draw similar triangles in hyperbolic geometry.

_____ **16.** Two triangles in hyperbolic geometry with the same angle-sum have the same area.

Name _____ Date _____

Hyperbolic Geometry

Directions: Fill in the letter of the best answer for each question.

1 Euclid's fifth postulate is called the

    A   Intersection Postulate.

    B   Perpendicular Postulate.

    C   Parallel Postulate.

2 The Hyperbolic Parallel Postulate states that through a given point not on a given line, there is (are) ___ line(s) parallel to the given line.

    D   infinitely many

    E   no

    F   two

3 In hyperbolic geometry, all lines are

    A   infinitely long.

    B   parallel to each other.

    C   intersecting.

4 In hyperbolic geometry, angles formed by two lines are measured by

    D   the angles formed at the endpoints of the lines.

    E   the angles formed by the tangents to the arcs at their point of intersection.

    F   projecting the angle to be inscribed in the Poincaré disk.

5 In the diagram, lines *AP*, *BP*, and *CP* are all

    A   perpendicular at point *P*.

    B   congruent to one another.

    C   parallel to line ℓ.

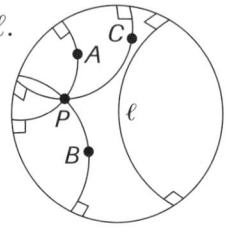

6 In hyperbolic geometry, similar triangles are

    D   defined the same as in Euclidean geometry.

    E   impossible.

    F   triangles with corresponding angles congruent.

7 In hyperbolic geometry, the Pythagorean Theorem is

    A   never true.

    B   sometimes true.

    C   always true.

8 As the area of a triangle increases, the sum of its angles

    D   increases.

    E   decreases.

    F   stays the same.

9 The sum of the measures of the angles of a triangle is

    A   greater than 180°.

    B   equal to 180°.

    C   less than 180°.

PRACTICE ANSWERS
Page 205

1. H
2. D
3. B
4. C
5. E
6. T
7. F
8. T
9. F
10. T
11. T
12. F
13. T
14. F
15. F
16. T

TEST PREP ANSWERS
Page 206

1. C
2. D
3. A
4. E
5. C
6. E
7. A
8. E
9. C

Take a Trip

TIME
• 30 minutes

OBJECTIVES
- Investigate great circles and distances on a sphere
- Use planar maps to plot an airplane route

MATERIALS
- Globe
- Yarn or string
- Clear tape

TEACHER NOTES
- Students should work with a partner on this application.

- Some yarn can stretch a bit so warn students not to pull or distort the length of yarn they are working with.

- Students may need assistance in locating Los Angeles and Moscow.

- In step 6, when students plot their route, there will be a curvature to the route. This is because, in the Mollweide Projection shown, great circles are projected into a curved line and the axes of symmetry of this map coincide with the Greenwich meridian and the equator. The route from Los Angeles to Moscow is not on the axis of symmetry.

EXTENSIONS
- Have students select two locations on the globe that are polar opposites. Compare the distance between these two locations with the distance around the equator.

- Have students use the Internet to look up the distance between Los Angeles and Moscow.

ANSWERS
1. answers may vary; approximately 51 inches on a 16-inch globe

2. answers may vary; approximately 493 miles per inch on a 16-inch globe

3. Possible answer: Fly from Los Angeles over northwest United States, western Canada, the Canadian Arctic, northern Greenland, northern Finland and to Moscow.

4. answers may vary; approximately $12\frac{3}{8}$ inches on a 16-inch globe

5. approximately 6100 miles

6. There should be a curvature to the route.

Name _____ Date _____

Ratios: 214

Solving Proportions: 221

Elliptic and Spherical Geometries: 364

Points, Lines, and Angles in Euclidean and Spherical Geometries: 365

Take a Trip

We are used to seeing the countries of the world displayed on a two-dimensional map like this one. The Earth, however, is pretty close to a sphere. When considering the distance, or airplane path, between two cities, you need to remember the Earth's shape.

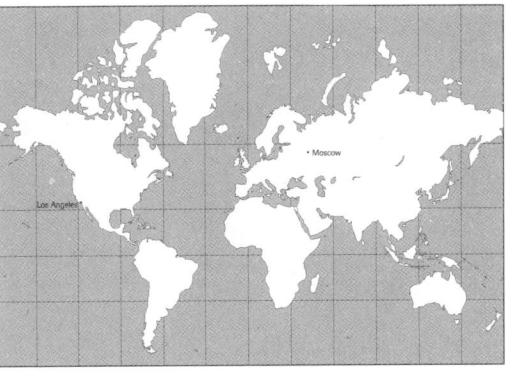

For this investigation you will need a globe, yarn or string, and tape.

1. Wrap the yarn around the globe at its equator to find the length of a great circle of your globe. Record the length of the string.

   _____ inches

2. The diameter of the earth is approximately 8000 miles. Use this information to determine a scale for one inch of your yarn.

   1 inch yarn = _____ miles

3. A pilot is flying from Los Angeles to Moscow. Use your yarn to show the shortest path for the pilot to fly. Use tape to hold the yarn in place. Describe the route.

   _____

   _____

   _____

4. Remove the yarn and measure it. _____ inches

5. Use the scale you determined in step 2 to calculate the approximate distance from Los Angeles to Moscow. _____ miles

6. Trace the same route on this planar map. Does the route appear to be straight?

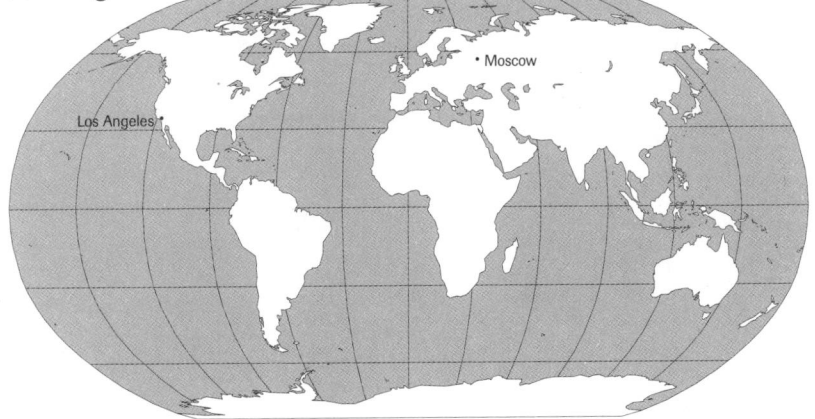

Name _____ Date _____

Name _____ Date _____

1.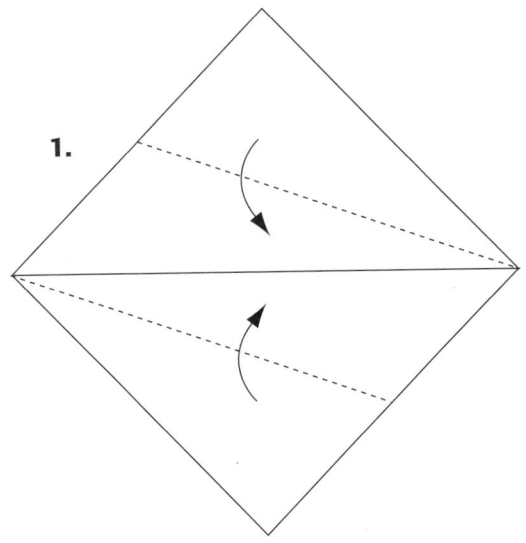

2.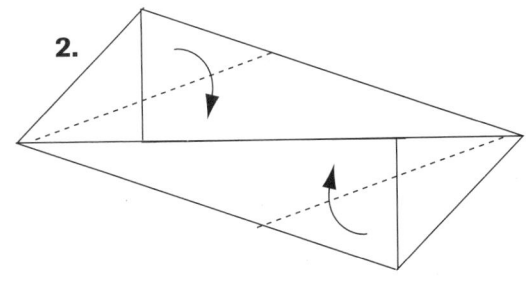

3.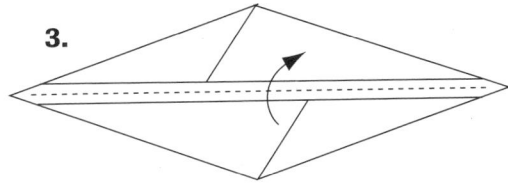

4.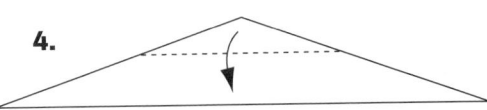

Do the same on the opposite side.

5.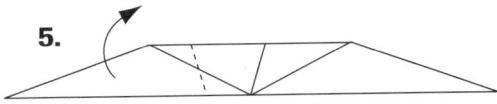

6.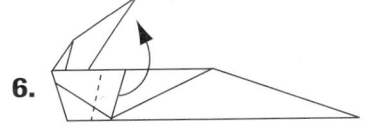

7.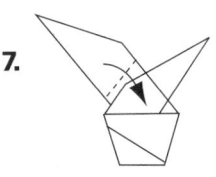

8.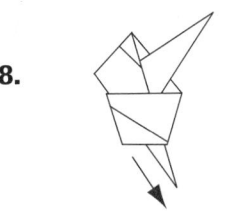

9.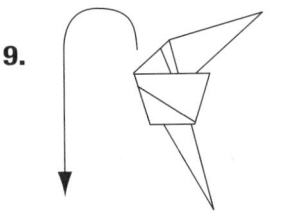

10.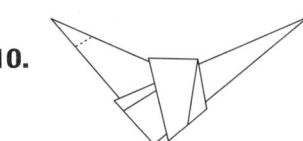

First, fold the "valley" lines
and make the face.

11.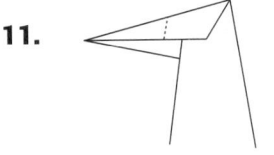

12.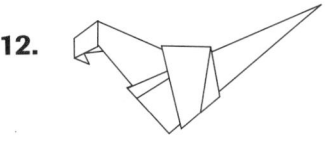

PRACTICE ANSWERS
Page 56

44.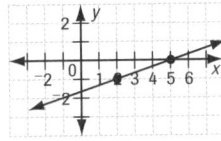

45.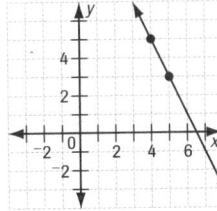

46.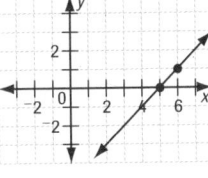

47.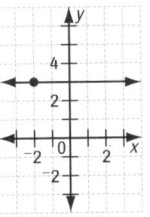

48.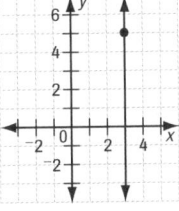

49.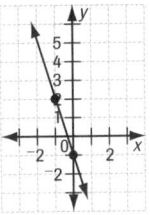

50.

51. $y = 3x - 2$

52. $y = \frac{-1}{2}x + 3$

53. $y = {}^{-}x + 1$

54. $y = \frac{-4}{3}x$

55. $y = \frac{1}{2}x$

56. $x = 1$

57. $y = {}^{-}2x + 8$

58. $y = \frac{-3}{2}x + 3$

59. $y = 6$

60. $k = 12$

61. $k = 1$

62. Given that the vertices of $\triangle ABC$ are $A(0, 0)$, $B({}^{-}6, {}^{-}2)$, and $C({}^{-}5, {}^{-}5)$. By the slope formula the slope of $\overline{AB} = \frac{1}{3}$ and the slope of $\overline{BC} = {}^{-}3$. Since $(\frac{1}{3})({}^{-}3) = {}^{-}1$, $\overline{AB} \perp \overline{BC}$. By the definition of $\perp$, $\angle ABC$ is a right $\angle$. Therefore, by the definition of right $\triangle$, $\triangle ABC$ is a right triangle.

TEST PREP ANSWERS
Page 57

1. F
2. F
3. F
4. T
5. F
6. T
7. T
8. T
9. F
10. F
11. C
12. A
13. C
14. C
15. A
16. B
17. A
18. B
19. C
20. A
21. C

APPLICATION ANSWERS
Page 88

1.

Polygon Name	Number of Sides	Number of ∠s	A. Sum of Interior ∠s	B. Sum of Exterior ∠s	C. One Interior ∠ of Regular Polygon	D. One Exterior ∠ of Regular Polygon
Triangle	3	3	180°	360°	60°	120°
Quadrilateral	4	4	360°	360°	90°	90°
Pentagon	5	5	540°	360°	108°	72°
Hexagon	6	6	720°	360°	120°	60°
Heptagon	7	7	900°	360°	128.6°	51.4°
Octagon	8	8	1080°	360°	135°	45°
Decagon	10	10	1440°	360°	144°	36°
n-gon	n	n	$(n-2)180$	360°	$\dfrac{(n-2)180}{n}$	$\dfrac{360}{n}$

2.

A.

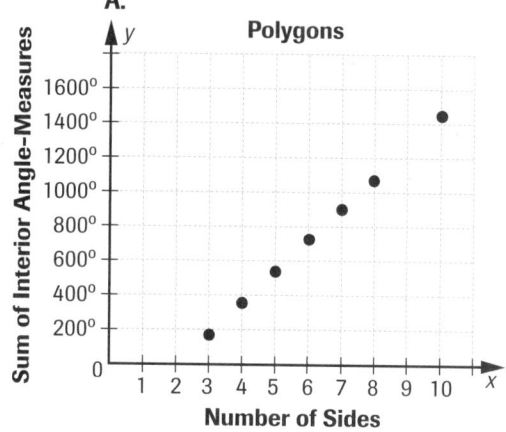

B.

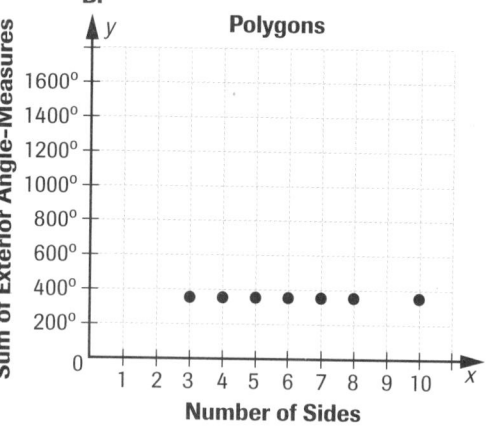

C.

D.

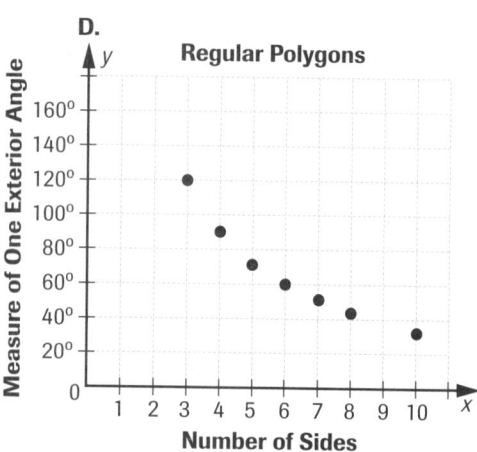

TEST PREP ANSWERS
Page 148

1. A   2. D
3. A   4. C

5. C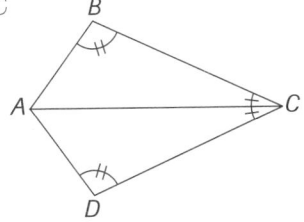

6. B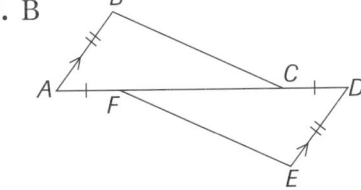

7. C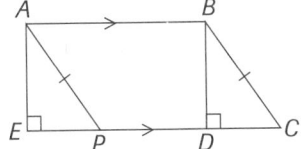

PRACTICE ANSWERS
Page 191 (continued)

8. Use the *Identify Subgoals* strategy.

Sum $= (2 + 3 + 4 + \ldots + 16) + (2.50 + 3.50 + 4.50 + \ldots + 16.50)$

$= 2(2 + 3 + 4 + \ldots + 16) + 15(0.50)$

$= 2(135) + 7.50$

$= \$277.50$

PRACTICE ANSWERS
Page 192

Solution methods will vary. Samples are provided.

9. Use the *Try a Simpler Problem* and *Find and Use a Pattern* strategies.

AB	BC
AC	BD
AD	BE
AE	BF
AF	BG
AG	BH
AH	

After you've paired Player A with all seven other players, you only have to pair Player B with six other players (*A vs B* has already been accounted for). This pattern will continue. Players must play $7 + 6 + 5 + 4 + 3 + 2 + 1 = 28$ games.

10. Use the *Account for All Possibilities* strategy.

RL	LM	MC	CP	PG
RM	LC	MP	CG	
RC	LP	MG		
RP	LG			
RG				

There are $5 + 4 + 3 + 2 + 1 = 15$ two-item combinations.

11. Use the *Model with an Equation* strategy. $\frac{35}{1} = \frac{x}{12}$. Solve for x, which will be a number of minutes; convert the minutes to hours and add to the starting time to get 2:45 P.M.

12. Use the *Account for All Possibilities* strategy. First, decide which even numbers can be addends in a three-addend sum of 20. Then take the largest of these (16) and find all combinations that work. Take the next smaller addend (14) and find all combinations that work. Continue until you reach the middle possible addend (8) and find all combinations that work. All smaller addends should already be accounted for using this method. There are eight possible combinations of addends.

$16 + 2 + 2 = 20$
$14 + 4 + 2 = 20$
$12 + 6 + 2 = 20$
$12 + 4 + 4 = 20$
$10 + 8 + 2 = 20$
$10 + 6 + 4 = 20$
$8 + 8 + 4 = 20$
$8 + 6 + 6 = 20$

TEST PREP ANSWERS
Page 193

Sample Solutions are provided.

1. Use the *Work Backward* strategy.

Day	1	11	21	31	41	51	61	71	81
Ants	10	20	40	80	160	320	640	1280	2560

$$\uparrow$$
START

2. Use the *Use Logical Reasoning* strategy: if the first six are all different in color, the seventh sock must match one of them.

3. Use the *Model with an Equation* strategy.

$$x + (x + 9) + (x + 18) + (x + 27) + (x + 36) + (x + 45) = 6(36.5)$$
$$6x + 135 = 219$$
$$6x = 84$$
$$x = 14$$

The highest scorer had $14 + 45 = 59$ points

4. Use the *Use Logical Reasoning* strategy. The teller is an only child so it's not Jon, who has a brother. The teller is the youngest so it can't be Irene, who is older than the manager. Therefore the teller must be Herb. Since Irene is older than the manager, she must be the assistant manager which leaves Jon as the manager.

5. Use the *Account for All Possibilities* strategy.

   A. 1

   B. 5

   C. 13

6. Use the *Account for All Possibilities* strategy. Separate into cases and list: *AB, AC, AD, BA, BC, BD, CA, CB, CD, DA, DB, DC*. There are 12 possible outcomes.

TEST PREP ANSWERS
Page 198

1. A; sample solution:

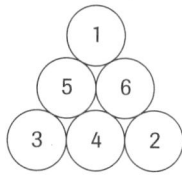

2. C; $r = 2$

3. D

4. B; about 6.3 minutes

5. A; two possible
   solutions: $25 + 957 + 688 = 1670$; $80 + 902 + 344 = 1326$

6. C; about 0.14

Reader's Choice
SPLIT EDITION

Reader's Choice

SPLIT EDITION

Sandra Silberstein
Barbara K. Dobson
Mark A. Clarke

Ann Arbor

THE UNIVERSITY OF MICHIGAN PRESS

Published in the United States of America by
The University of Michigan Press
Manufactured in the United States of America

2018   2017   2016   2015   6   5   4   3

Contents

Acknowledgments

When we stepped back from our work for this edition, we realized that a dominant theme had emerged: change in a globalized world. We could not escape the fact that the most salient feature of the era is the need to constantly negotiate one's identity in the face of shifting technological, cultural, and interpersonal realities. In this context, we appreciate all the more the constancy of institutional, collegial, and family support. We want to acknowledge here the unwavering patience and good will of Doug, Tom, and Patricia, who long ago stopped wondering if the conference call would ever be over. And, as has been the case for the past two editions, we depended heavily on the consummate professionalism of our editor, Kelly Sippell. Thank you, Kelly, for the intelligence, insight, creativity, and peerless dedication you bring to the project.

Ann Arbor, Denver, Seattle, January 2008

These are tender times. As we enter the new millennium, we are increasingly grateful for the love and support of those who live and work beside us and mindful of friends who are no longer here. This edition owes much to the leadership of Mary Erwin, who created an environment that permitted us to bear down on long-postponed tasks, and to Kelly Sippell, whose insightful contributions and personal commitment often reached the level of co-authorship.

Ann Arbor, Denver, Seattle, September 2001

As we enter our third decade of collaboration, we would like to thank spouses and children who have endured countless hours of conference calls and overnight-mail runs. Thanks are also due Sue Hodes and Sharon Tsutsui for thoughtful comments on this edition. And we are especially fortunate to have had the skilled and enthusiastic support of the University of Michigan Press: Associate Editor Chris Milton has been correcting us for as long as we can remember; Executive Editor LeAnn Fields first persuaded us that our sanity could withstand revision; Assistant Director Mary Erwin erased our memories of the first revision; and Director Colin Day has paid the bills.

Ann Arbor, Denver, Seattle, February 1994

We thank the many teachers who, over the years, have provided insights and suggestions for revision. To the roll call from the previous edition, we add the following names and apologize for any omissions: Sally Alexander, Kathryn Allahyari, Carol Deselams, Patricia A. Carrell, Joan Eisterhold, Pat Grogan, Liz Hamp-Lyons, Linda Hillman, Sara Klinghammer, Cherie Lenz-Hackett, Ellen Lipp, Daphne Mackey, Sharon Myers, Marnie Ramker, Sam Shepherd, Jerry Stanfield, Marianne Wieferich, Kay Winfield. We are grateful to our colleagues and to the dynamic context of TESOL reading pedagogy and research. Similarly, we continue to benefit from the contributions of our coauthors on the first edition, Margaret Baudoin Metzinger and Ellen Bober.

Special thanks to research assistants Elisabeth Mitchell, University of Washington, and Kathy Riley, University of Colorado at Denver, and to our colleagues at the University of Michigan Press.

Finally, we once again thank our families for continued support and patience toward a task that, no doubt, they hoped they had seen the last of.

Denver, Detroit, Seattle, June 1987

The successful completion of *Reader's Choice* is the result of the cooperation, confidence, and endurance of many people. The authors greatly appreciate the contributions of the individuals listed below. It is impossible to overestimate the importance of their efforts in helping us meet deadlines, their insights during classroom testing, and their encouragement through critique and rewrite sessions.

Heartfelt thanks, therefore to:

H. Douglas Brown, director of the English Language Institute (ELI), University of Michigan, whose assistance ranged from personal and professional advice to administrative and financial support. Professor Brown has consistently encouraged creativity and innovation at the ELI. His continued support of *Reader's Choice* ensured its successful completion.

Eleanor Foster, ELI administrative assistant and her capable secretarial and production staff: Elaine Allen, Ginny Barnett, Shelly Cole, Gail Curtis, Lynne Davis, Sue Feldstein, Martha Graham, Donna Head, Barbara Kerwin, Debbie Milly, Lisa Neff, Cathy Pappas, and Louisa Plyler.

George E. Luther and Roderick D. Fraser, ELI administrators, whose efforts made possible financial support and the classroom testing of *Reader's Choice*.

David P. Harris, director of the American Language Institute, Georgetown University; ELI authors Joan Morley and Mary Lawrence; Betsy Soden, ELI lecturer and reading coordinator; Carlos A. Yorio, professor of Linguistics, Toronto University—colleagues in English as a second language (ESL) whose critiques of early drafts proved invaluable.

ESL teachers whose patient and skillful use of the materials through numerous stages of development made detailed revisions and improvements possible—Honor Griffith and Lynne Kurylo of the University of Toronto; Betsy Berriman, Cristin Carpenter, Eve Daniels, Susan Dycus, Adelaide Heyde, Wayne Lord, Michele McCullough, Nancy Morrison, Syd Rand, and John Schafer of the English Language Institute.

And finally, thank you to Mario, Patricia, Tom, and Doug, friends and family for their patience and support; our parents and children, for whose pride and enthusiasm we are grateful; our students, whose insightful suggestions made revisions possible; and all the teachers and staff of the English Language Institute for providing an atmosphere which nurtures innovative teaching and creative materials development.

The authors wish to gratefully acknowledge grants from the English Language Institute and *Language Learning,* which provided funds for released time for several of the authors, and for secretarial and production assistance.

Ann Arbor, June 1977

Introduction for Students

Welcome to the fifth edition of *Reader's Choice*. This book has been written to meet the needs of teachers and students in a rapidly changing globalized world. The purpose of this introduction is to acquaint you with the book and with our approach to teaching reading in English to speakers of other languages.

We believe that reading is an active process in which effective readers bring their understanding of the world to bear on text. Whether reading a book or an article, an advertisement or a chart, or surfing the Internet—regardless of the content or form of the material—successful readers rely on an attitude of independence and the coordination of a number of skills and strategies. Efficient readers approach material with goals in mind, and they adjust their behavior accordingly. They develop expectations, and they read to confirm, reject, or adjust those expectations. Most of this is done without conscious attention to the process. The material in *Reader's Choice* gives you practice in this kind of independent, efficient, and critical reading.

We believe *Reader's Choice* is most effective when it is used in situations where curiosity and active participation are encouraged. It is a tool that will help you and your teachers develop a partnership for learning. You will see that we speak directly to students in the directions, exercises, and answer key (now not included in the book). To the extent possible, we have tried to permit you to get to know us and our approach to teaching and learning—and to living. We encourage you to take a playful approach to the readings and exercises in this book and to interact with the book and each other in ways that permit you, as individuals, to develop your own attitude and approach to learning.

When you look at the Contents page you will notice that there are three kinds of units in *Reader's Choice*. The odd-numbered units (1 through 5) contain language skills work. These exercises give you intensive practice in using word-, sentence-, and discourse-level reading strategies. The even-numbered units (2 through 6) contain reading selections that give you the opportunity to use the skills you have learned to interact with and evaluate the ideas of texts. Finally, Unit 7 consists of a longer, more complex reading selection.

Basic language and reading skills are introduced in early units and reinforced throughout the book. The large number of exercises provides opportunities for repeated practice. Do not be discouraged if you do not finish each exercise, if you have trouble answering specific questions, or if you do not understand everything in a particular reading. The purpose of the tasks in *Reader's Choice* is to help improve your problem-solving skills. For this reason, the process of attempting to answer a question is often as important as the answer itself.

Reader's Choice contains exercises that provide practice in both language and reading skills. In this Introduction, we will first provide a description of language skills exercises followed by a description of the reading skills work contained in the book.

Language Skills Exercises

Word Study Exercises

Upon encountering unfamiliar vocabulary in a passage, there are several strategies available to readers. First, you can continue reading, realizing that often a single word will not prevent understanding the general meaning of a selection. If further reading does not solve the problem, you can use one or more of three basic skills to arrive at an understanding of the unfamiliar word. You can use context clues to see if surrounding words and grammatical structures provide information about the unknown word. You can use word analysis to see if understanding the parts of the word leads to an understanding of the word. Or, you can use a dictionary to find an appropriate definition. *Reader's Choice* contains numerous exercises that provide practice in these three skills.

Word Study: Context Clues

Guessing the meaning of an unfamiliar word from **Context Clues** involves using the following kinds of information:

    a. knowledge of the topic about which you are reading

    b. knowledge of the meanings of the other words in the sentence (or paragraph) in which the word occurs

    c. knowledge of the grammatical structure of the sentences in which the word occurs

When these exercises appear in skills units, their purpose is to provide practice in guessing the meanings of unfamiliar words using context clues. Students should not necessarily try to learn the meanings of the vocabulary items in these exercises. The **Vocabulary from Context** exercises that accompany reading selections have a different purpose. Generally the first exercise should be done before a reading selection is begun and used as an introduction to the reading. The vocabulary items have been chosen for three reasons:

    a. because they are fairly common and therefore useful for students to learn

    b. because they are important for an understanding of the passage

    c. because their meanings are not easily available from the context in the selection

Word Study: Stems and Affixes

Another way to discover the meanings of unfamiliar vocabulary is to use word analysis, that is, to use knowledge of the meanings of the parts of a word. Many English words have been formed by combining parts of older English, Greek, and Latin words. For instance, the word *bicycle* is formed from the parts *bi,* meaning "two," and *cycle,* meaning "round" or "wheel." Often knowledge of the meanings of these word parts (along with context) can help the reader to guess the meaning of an unfamiliar word. Exercises in **Word Study: Stems and Affixes** provide practice in this skill at regular intervals throughout the book. The **Appendix** lists all of the stems and affixes that appear in these exercises.

Word Study: Dictionary Use

Sometimes the meaning of a single word is essential to an understanding of the total meaning of a selection. If context clues and word analysis do not provide enough information, it will be necessary to use a dictionary. The **Word Study: Dictionary Use** exercises in the skills units provide students with a review of the information available from dictionaries and practice in using a dictionary to obtain that information. The **Dictionary Study** exercises that accompany some of the reading selections require students to use the context of an unfamiliar vocabulary item to find an appropriate definition from the dictionary entries provided.

Sentence Study Exercises

Sometimes comprehension of an entire passage requires the understanding of a single sentence. **Sentence Study** exercises give students practice in analyzing the structure of sentences to determine the relationships of ideas within a sentence. You will be presented with a complicated sentence followed by tasks that require analyzing the sentence for its meaning. Often you will be required to use the available information to draw inferences about the author's message.

Paragraph Reading and Paragraph Analysis Exercises

These exercises give you practice at the paragraph level. Some of the paragraph exercises are designed to provide practice in discovering the general message. You will be asked to determine the main idea of a passage: that is, the idea that is the most important, around which the passage is organized. Other paragraph exercises are meant to provide practice in careful, detailed reading. You will be required not only to find the main idea of a passage but also to guess vocabulary from context, to answer questions about specific details in the paragraph, and to draw conclusions based on an understanding of the passage.

Discourse Focus

Effective reading requires the ability to select skills and strategies appropriate to a specific reading task. The reading process involves using information from the full text and knowledge of the world in order to interpret a passage. Readers use this information to make predictions about what they will find in a text and to decide how they will read. Sometimes we need to read quickly to obtain only a general idea of a text; at other times we read carefully, drawing inferences about the intent of the author. Discourse-level exercises introduce these various approaches to reading, which are then reinforced throughout the book. These reading skills are described in more detail in the discussion that follows.

Nonprose Reading

Throughout *Reader's Choice,* nonprose selections (a menu, bus schedule, road map, and charts and graphs) provide practice reading material that is not primarily arranged in sentences and paragraphs. It is important to remember that the same problem-solving skills are used to read both prose and nonprose material.

Reading Skills Exercises

Students will need to use all of their language skills in order to understand the reading selections in *Reader's Choice.* The book contains many types of selections on a wide variety of topics. These selections provide practice in using different reading strategies to comprehend texts. They also give practice in four basic reading skills: **skimming, scanning, reading for thorough comprehension,** and **critical reading.** An introduction to each of these is presented, with exercises, in Unit 1, and practiced throughout the even-numbered units.

Skimming

Skimming is quick reading for the general idea(s) of a passage. This kind of rapid reading is appropriate when trying to decide if careful reading would be desirable or when there is not time to read something carefully.

Scanning

Like skimming, **scanning** is also quick reading. However, in this case the search is more focused. To scan is to read quickly in order to locate specific information. When you read to find a particular date, name, or number, you are scanning.

Reading for Thorough Comprehension

Reading for thorough comprehension is careful reading in order to understand the full meaning of the passage. At this level of comprehension, the reader is able to summarize the author's ideas but has not yet made a critical evaluation of those ideas.

Critical Reading

Critical reading demands that readers make judgments about what they read. This kind of reading requires posing and answering questions such as, *Does my own experience support that of the author? Do I share the author's point of view? Am I convinced by the author's arguments and evidence?*

Of course, effective readers use combinations of these skills and strategies simultaneously. Systematic use of the exercises and readings in *Reader's Choice* will give you practice in the basic language and reading skills necessary to become a proficient reader. Additional suggestions for the use of *Reader's Choice* in a classroom setting are included in the To the Teacher section on the website: **www.press.umich.edu/esl/.**

What's New in This Edition?

Every unit in *Reader's Choice, 5th Edition,* has been updated and contains new material:

Globalization and Identity. The fifth edition of *Reader's Choice* engages complex issues of identity, particularly within our increasingly globalized world. Whether reading about language policy or international business or fiction highlighting multiculturalism, the activities in *Reader's Choice, 5th Edition,* create the linguistic and intellectual scaffolding that encourages meaningful interactions about our complex world. Even technical material includes thoughtful activities that place technology and science within a social context.

Visual Literacy: Students in the twenty-first century are confronted with a dizzying array and combination of print and graphics. The average commercial web page, for example, contains more links to information than does the table of contents of the average ESOL textbook. Throughout this edition are activities that develop strategies for gleaning information from combinations of text and graphics. This is especially true in the **Web Work.**

Web Work. Extensive Web Work appears in two skills units—all of it new. Additional new web-based activities are sprinkled throughout the book, accompanying other skills-unit activities and reading selections. While these present some of the intricacies of the Internet, their primary purpose is broader: to introduce and provide practice in decision-making strategies for effective reading. Whether accessing a travel site or reading highly technical material, the ability of students to evaluate information sources is nowhere more crucial than on the Internet, and these activities highlight critical reading skills. Because the current generation of students is familiar with the Internet, we spend less time introducing the basics and provide more options for students to do Internet-based research. *Reader's Choice, 5th Edition,* provides reproductions of web pages, and for students and teachers who want to go beyond this, allows for work on the *Reader's Choice* companion website (**www.press.umich.edu/esl/readerschoice/**) and other online resources.

New Readings. Five new reading selections respond to the changing environment faced by our students. These are often part of thematically linked sets of passages. Topics take up issues of globalization in a multicultural, multigenerational world, engaging issues from educational policy to economics and business to new fiction that expands the range of cultural experiences reflected in the text.

New Longer Reading. Unit 7 comprises a full short story by Jhumpa Lahiri, from her Pulitzer Prize–winning book, *Interpreter of Maladies.* The story, "The Third and Final Continent," is the genesis of her novel, *The Namesake.* Students may be familiar with the movie by the same name that is based on it. The rich and moving story details a modern journey across continents. Both immigrant and international students will find much to identify with.

Additional Vocabulary. The new reading selections bring with them extensive additional vocabulary work. New lexical items are often topically related across a series of linked readings. Items are introduced and practiced in a variety of formats, always reinforcing both the given item and more general literacy and acquisition skills. In both the skills units and readings, additional dictionary work, particularly examples of web-based information, has been added. Some of the Vocabulary Review activities included in previous editions are now featured on the *Reader's Choice* companion website.

Additional Skills. *Reader's Choice, 5th Edition,* includes additional skills work. Paragraph Main Idea work now requires students to read longer passages, creating prose summaries. Throughout the book, students transfer data from prose to tables and from graphs to prose; throughout, students read to write.

Updating. All the skills and reading selection units have been updated. Throughout the text are new items along with expanded and updated introductions and activities.

What Hasn't Changed?

Language Work. The odd-numbered skills units continue to provide the intensive language-based reading practice that teachers and students have come to rely on.

Authentic Reading. The text continues to provide authentic reading passages and tasks. From the menu to the Internet to textbooks to science reporting to fiction, the fifth edition of *Reader's Choice* continues to provide realistic literacy tasks.

Integrated Skills. The activities in *Reader's Choice* encourage integrated skills work with a focus on reading. The text provides thoroughgoing opportunities for speaking, listening, and writing in the context of the issues raised in the readings. At the core are literate activities that afford opportunities for task-based work.

Respect for the Students. Throughout *Reader's Choice,* students are addressed as intelligent language users who bring to their tasks a great deal of knowledge about learning and about the world. Instructions explain to students the rationale for activities and provide options for productive ways to approach the task at hand.

High-Quality Work. In all activities, students are stretched to interact with texts in challenging and meaningful ways. The book assumes intelligent, engaged students who will be stimulated to do their best work.

Humor and Whimsy. Throughout the text we continue to provide light-hearted moments. In the fifth edition, we have sprinkled the Internet convention of the winking face to key some of those moments. ☺

Discourse Focus
Reading for Different Goals—Web Work

Before You Begin
1. Do you read a menu the same way you read a textbook?
2. If not, what are the differences?

Efficient readers read differently depending on what they are reading and their goals. There are four basic types of reading behaviors or skills: **skimming, scanning, reading for thorough comprehension,** and **critical reading.** Each is explained below, and exercises are provided to give you practice in each of these. The exercises below are also designed to introduce reading strategies on the Internet. To work on these activities, you may either use the web pages reproduced on pages 2 and 3 or, if you are online, your teacher may want you to use the *Reader's Choice* website to work on the exercises in this section: **www.press.umich.edu/esl/readerschoice/.**

Skimming

Skimming is quick reading for general ideas. When you skim, you move your eyes quickly to acquire a basic understanding of the text. You do not read everything, and you do not read carefully. You read quickly such things as the title and subtitles and topic sentences. You also look at pictures, charts, graphs, icons, etc., for clues to what the text is about.

Use the web page from **CNN.com** (pages 2–3) and the related links to answer the following questions. Move quickly from the questions to the web page. Do not write out your answers completely; just make notes that will help you remember your answers. Your teacher may want to read the questions aloud as you skim to find the answers.

1. Have you ever visited this website before? What kind of information would you expect to find here?

   _____

2. How is the web page on pages 2–3 organized? For example, what kind of information do you find in the columns on the sides of the page? What else is on the page? _____

   _____

3. Notice that there is a news story in the middle the web page. Look quickly at the story and the related illustration (page 2) and map (page 3).

   • In a few words, what is the story about? _____

   _____

   • What information do you find in the illustration and map? _____

   _____

1

Web CNN News CNN Videos `SEARCH`

HOME WORLD U.S. POLITICS ENTERTAINMENT HEALTH TECH TRAVEL LIVING BUSINESS SPORTS TIME.COM   CNN VIDEO I-REPORT RSS FEEDS
Personalize Your Weather   International Edition

RESOURCES
- World Weather
- CNNMoney International
- CNN International
- TIME Asia
- TIME Europe
- International News Safety Institute
- Council on Foreign Relations
- Election Watch

EUROPE
More Europe News
MOSCOW, RUSSIA:
Search for Russian miners
LONDON, ENGLAND:
Slave ship log book up for auction

ASIA
More Asia News
DERA ISMAIL KHAN, PAKISTAN:
Pakistan border clashes 'kill 30'
BEIJING, CHINA:
China plans to develop large jets

AFRICA
More Africa News
CONAKRY, GUINEA:
Bridge collapse kills 65
KINSHASA, CONGO:
U.N. deploys to separate rival forces
CAPE TOWN, SOUTH AFRICA:
African nations take on Zimbabwe problem

Controversial Skywalk in Place Over Grand Canyon

Story Highlights

- Walkway over Grand Canyon to be unveiled Tuesday; opens to public next week
- Glass-floored Skywalk lets visitors look 4,000 feet straight down to canyon floor
- Cost: $75 and up, including fee to get on Hualapai reservation
- Concerns raised about tribal burial sites, tourist glitz in natural wonder

(1) HUALAPAI INDIAN RESERVATION, Arizona (AP)—Visitors who have marveled at the Grand Canyon's vistas will now have a dizzying new option: a glass-bottom observation deck allowing them to gaze into the chasm beneath their feet.

(2) The Skywalk, which will be unveiled Tuesday, is being touted as an engineering marvel. The glass-and-steel horseshoe extends 70 feet beyond the canyon's edge with no visible supports above or below.

(3) Visitors will be able to see 4,000 feet straight down to the canyon floor, a vantage point more than twice as high as the world's tallest buildings.

(4) Hualapai Indians, who live near the rim about 90 miles west of the national park, allowed a Las Vegas developer to build the $30 million Skywalk in hopes of creating a unique attraction on their side of the canyon.

(5) Tribal leaders are betting that people will flock here, braving the rugged terrain—including a twisty ride through unpaved roads — to walk its transparent surface. The Skywalk, they hope, will become the centerpiece of a budding tourism industry that includes helicopter tours, river rafting, a cowboy town and a museum of Indian replica homes.

(6) It's scheduled to open to the public on March 28. The fee for the Skywalk will be $25; visitors will pay an additional fee to enter the Hualapai reservation. Tours on the reservation start at $50.

(7) The Skywalk has sparked debate on and off the reservation. Many

Visit The Grand Canyon
Review of Grand Canyon Attractions Activities, Lodging, Tours.
www.familyvacation destination.org

Meet Hiking Singles
View Photo Profiles. Local Singles into Hiking. Join Now for Free.
www.Fitness-Singles.com

RV Travel— Grand Canyon
Plan your family RVing adventure with Funroads tips, links, guides
www.funroads.com/travel/rv

Grand Canyon Tours
Experience the Grand Canyon. Find the perfect tour from our list

MIDDLE EAST
More Middle East News
BAGHDAD, IRAQ:
Iraqi forces raid Sunni lawmaker's home
UNITED NATIONS:
Iraq announces reconstruction plan

AMERICAS
More Americas News
GUATEMALA CITY, GUATEMALA:
Police arrest assassination suspects
PANAMA CITY, PANAMA:
Panama seizes 21.4 tons of cocaine
RIO DE JANEIRO, BRAZIL:
Italian arrested for 1970s killings

U.S.
More U.S. News
MCGRADY, NORTH CAROLINA:
Boy Scout found weak, hungry and thirsty

Hualapai (pronounced WALL-uh-pie) worry about disturbing nearby burial sites, and environmentalists have accused the tribe of transforming the majestic canyon into a tourist trap.

(8) Hualapai leaders say they weighed those concerns for years before agreeing to build the Skywalk. With a third of the tribe's 2,200 members living in poverty, the tribal government decided it needs the tourism dollars.

(9) "When we have so much poverty and so much unemployment, we have to do something," said Sheri Yellowhawk, a former tribal councilwoman overseeing the project. "It sounded like a good idea."

(10) Las Vegas businessman David Jin fronted the money to build the Skywalk. Yellowhawk said Jin will give it to the Hualapai in exchange for a cut of the profits.

(11) Construction crews spent two years building the Skywalk. They drilled steel anchors 46 feet into the limestone rim to hold the deck in place. Earlier this month, they welded the Skywalk to the anchors after pushing it past the edge using four tractor trailers and an elaborate system of pulleys.

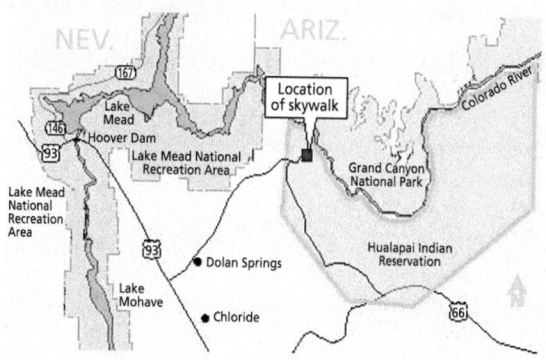

Canyon View

Tourists to the west rim of the Grand Canyon will pay $25 to stroll on a glass walkway overlooking the canyon.

PAM KILLINSWORTH/REVIEW JOURNAL

Grand Canyon Skywalk

- Hualapai Indian Reservation
- Juts out about 70 feet into the canyon, 4000 ft above the Colorado River
- Will accommodate 120 people comfortably (How comfortable would YOU be?)
- Built with more than a million pounds of steel beams and includes dampeners that minimize the structure's vibration
- Designed to hold 72 millions pounds, withstand an 8.0 magnitude earthquake 50 miles away, and withstand winds in excess of 100 mph
- Has a glass bottom and sides . . . four inches thick

(12) Architect Mark Johnson said the Skywalk will support the weight of a few hundred people and withstand canyon winds of 100 mph. The observation deck has been embedded with shock absorbers to keep it from wobbling like a diving board as people walk on it.

(13) Hualapai leaders were to be the first to set foot on the Skywalk on Tuesday. They've hired former astronauts Buzz Aldrin and John Herrington to join them. The astronauts were expected to help christen the deck during a brief ceremony.

(14) Herrington was chosen in part because he's a registered Chickasaw Indian. Aldrin said he agreed to attend after reading about the project. And, as the Apollo 11 astronaut famous for walking on the moon, Aldrin said he has no fear of heights.

LANGUAGES
CNN.com can be read in:

أخبار بالعربية
日本語ニュース
한국어 뉴스

RESOURCES
- World Weather
- CNNMoney International
- TIME Asia
- TIME Europe
- International News Safety Institute
- Council on Foreign Relations
- Election Watch

Scanning

Scanning is also quick reading, but when you scan, you are looking for information to answer a specific question. You are usually looking for a number or a word or the name of something. When you scan, you usually take the steps that follow.

1. Decide exactly what information you are looking for and what form it is likely to take. For example, if you wanted to know how much something cost, you would be looking for a number. If you wanted to know when something will start, you would be scanning for a date or a time. If you wanted to know who did something, you would be looking for a name.

2. Next, decide where you need to look to find the information. You would turn to the sports section of the newspaper to discover who won a baseball game, and you would scan the C section of the phone book for the phone number of Steven Cary.

3. Move your eyes quickly down the page until you find what you want.

4. When you find what you need, you usually stop reading.

The following questions give you practice in scanning. Use the web page from **CNN.com** (pages 2–3) to answer the questions.

1. If you wanted to return to the main CNN site, where would you click? _____

2. Where would you click if you were planning a trip to Montreal and wanted information about the weather? _____

3. Where would you click if you wanted to read the'news in Japanese? _____

4. Where would you look for stories about China? _____

5. If you wanted to read about sports after finishing this story, where would you click? _____

For the following questions, quickly scan information about the Grand Canyon Skywalk (pages 2 and 3).

6. How high is the Skywalk? _____

7. How far out from the Canyon Wall does it extend? _____

8. How much does it cost to visit the Skywalk? _____

9. Where is the Skywalk located?

   • In which state is it located? _____

   • Which side of the Grand Canyon is it on? _____

   • Which Indian Reservation do you have to enter to get there? _____

Reading for Thorough Comprehension

When you read for thorough comprehension, you try to understand the full meaning of the reading. You want to know the details as well as the general meaning of the selection. When you have thoroughly comprehended a text, you have done the following things.

1. You have understood the main ideas and the author's point of view.

2. You have understood the relationships of ideas in the text, including how they relate to the author's purpose.

3. You have understood most of the concepts in the passages as well as the vocabulary. This may require you to guess the meanings of unfamiliar words from context or to look up words in the dictionary.

4. You have begun to note that some of the ideas and points of view that were not mentioned were, however, implied by the author. This is called **drawing inferences.** It is the beginning of **critical reading,** which will be the focus of the next activity.

The following questions give you practice in reading for thorough comprehension. To answer these, read the entire article, "Controversial Skywalk in Place Over Grand Canyon." Answer the questions according to your understanding of the article and the accompanying illustration and map (pages 2 and 3). Your teacher may want you to work on these individually, in small groups, or in pairs. True/False items are indicated by a T / F before the statement.

1. What word in Paragraph 2 tells you the shape of the Skywalk?

2. (T)/ F   The Skywalk floor is made of glass.

3. T /(F)   The Skywalk was built by the Hualapai Indian tribe.

4. (T)/ F   Both Indians and environmentalists have concerns about the Skywalk.

5. T /(F)   The Skywalk has already made the tribe wealthy.

6. In Paragraph 10, what do you think *fronted* means? _____ sen D gnate d er _____

7. T /(F)   Businessman David Jin will receive all of the profits from the Skywalk.

8. Why were two astronauts chosen to be among the first to walk on the Skywalk?
   _____ Because thay may help christen the deck during a brief ceremony. _____

Critical Reading

When reading critically, we draw conclusions and make judgments about the reading. We ask questions such as, "What inferences can be drawn from this? Do I agree with this point of view?" We often do this when we read, but in some cases it is more important than others, as, for example, when authors give opinions about important issues or when you are trying to make a decision.

Use the web page from **CNN.com** (pages 2–3) to answer the following critical reading questions. Some questions require an opinion; be prepared to defend your choices. For statements preceded by T / F / N, circle T if the statement is true, F if the statement is false, and N if there is not enough information for us to know if the statement is true or false.

1. Who would be likely to use this website? Would you bookmark this site on your own computer?

   _____

2. Would you come to this site if you were interested in buying or selling a used car? _____

3. T / F / N   This website contains only news stories.

4. If you were interested in the elections in your home country, would you click Election Watch under Resources? Why or why not? _____

   _____

Use information about the Grand Canyon Skywalk (pages 2 and 3) to answer the following questions. Some questions may have more than one correct answer. Others require an opinion. Be prepared to defend your choices.

5. Why do you think the observation deck is called the Skywalk? _Because it is_
   located up the montain up to 4000 feets

6. T / F /(N) The Grand Canyon can be very windy.

7. Why do you think the Hualapai Indians allowed the Skywalk to be built? _Because they_
   hope to creat a unique attraction on their side of the canyon

8. T /(F)/ N If you visited the Skywalk today, you would find helicopter tours, river rafting, a cowboy town, and museum nearby.

9. Why do you think David Jin financed the Skywalk? _____Yes_____

10. (T)/ F / N The Skywalk is a good thing for the Hualapai Indians.

11. T /(F)/ N If you're afraid of high places, you'll find the Skywalk exciting.

12. Would you visit the Skywalk? Why or why not? _no, I do not like high_
    places

Nonprose Reading
Menu

Nonprose writing consists of disconnected words and numbers instead of the sentences and paragraphs you usually learn to read. Each time you need information from a train schedule, a graph, a menu, an ad, or the like, you must read nonprose material. This exercise and similar exercises that begin subsequent units will help you practice the problem-solving skills you will need in order to read nonprose texts.

Between pages 8 and 9 is a menu such as you might find in a restaurant in the U.S. or Canada.

Before You Begin

1. Quickly skim* the menu. What is your first impression of this restaurant? What kind of restaurant is it?

2. Is this a restaurant that you think you would like to go to for lunch? Why or why not?

Scanning

The questions below are designed to help you quickly become more acquainted with this menu so that you would be able to order a meal. They are the kind of questions that you might have when you order from a menu for the first time. Scan the menu to answer the questions. You do not need to understand every word on the page. <u>Note</u>: Not all questions have a single correct answer. The answer to some questions may be "We don't know; the menu doesn't give this information." Other questions may have more than one answer. Do not go on to Reading for Details (page 9) until you have checked your answers.

1. Does this restaurant serve breakfast, lunch, and dinner?

   _____

2. Does this restaurant serve alcoholic drinks? How do you know?

   _____

3. Does this restaurant serve desserts? How do you know?

   _____

4. Does this restaurant serve hot sandwiches? How do you know?

   _____

5. If you don't want to eat pork, list some entries you would avoid.

   _____

6. If you don't want to eat meat or fish, what are some items you could order at this restaurant?

   _____

---

*For an introduction to skimming, see page 1.

7. If your five-year-old niece wanted to eat meat, which dish(es) should she order?

_____

8. You want to buy an Artisan Bread. What do you think *Miche, Baguette, Loaf,* and *Demi* refer to?

_____

9. Could you have eggs for breakfast? _____

10. It's 1:00 in the afternoon. Could you order a Four-Cheese Soufflé? _____

11. Is tax included in the prices on this menu? _____

12. Is a tip for the server included in the prices on this menu? _____

13. a. How much does a Smoked Turkey Breast sandwich with cheese cost? _____

    b. You want to order from the You Pick Two section of the menu. How much would you pay if you wanted a half Mediterranean Veggie sandwich with soup in a bread bowl?

_____

14. If you wanted a salad with chicken, which dish(es) could you order?

_____

15. a. What does a bagel look like? _____

    b. At Panera, bagels can come with Flavorful Spreads. What do you think a *spread* is?

_____

16. a. If you wanted a hot drink with no caffeine, what could you order?

    b. Could you order iced tea at Panera?

_____

Web Work

1. These days, a business decision faced by cafés like Panera is whether or not to offer their customers free Wi-Fi (wireless access to the Internet). If they do, some people will set up their "offices" in the cafe and spend all day there.

    a. Develop an oral or written proposal to a café about what its Wi-Fi policy should be. Your teacher may want you to work alone or with your classmates (in a café or in class). Consider advantages and disadvantages for the company of offering free Wi-Fi. Be sure to consider the issue from the customer's point of view: What are advantages and disadvantages of working in a café? Will customer advantages help the restaurant?

    b. Check Panera's website (**www.panerabread.com**) to see what the company's policy is. Did it adopt your proposal?

Reading for Details

Indicate if each statement is True (T) or False (F).

1. _____ Tuna is the only fish served in this restaurant.

2. _____ You can have a pizza and salad for lunch.

3. _____ You can arrange to have your food ready for you when you arrive.

4. _____ This restaurant serves hot soups in a bowl made of bread.

5. _____ Half a Tuscan Chicken sandwich and a bowl of Low-Fat Vegetarian soup costs $7.19.

6. _____ If you have $7.00, you can afford a Three-Cheese Pizza.

7. _____ If you order a Caesar Salad, bread comes with it at no extra cost.

8. _____ It's Tuesday; you can order Boston Clam Chowder with your salad.

9. _____ After 4:00, you can order a dinner salad with your Tuscan Chicken sandwich.

10. _____ None of the food in this restaurant contains any trans fat.

11. _____ If you were hosting a party, you could have Panera bring the food.

Critical Reading

The following questions require drawing inferences and giving your own opinion.

1. Would you take your family to this restaurant for a birthday dinner? Why or why not? _____

   _____

2. You have $10.00 to spend. What would you order? (Make sure to save enough for tax and perhaps a tip.) _____

   _____

3. If you were on a diet, which dishes might you order? Would you order the Lower-Carb Bread? Why or why not? _____

   _____

4. Many restaurants make up their own names for menu items. Panera calls its pizza *Crispani*. Why do you think the company invented that name? _____

5. Look at the back of the menu, at the section called Operation Dough-Nation.

   a. This is a *pun*, a type of word play. What are two different meanings of the word *dough?* What is a *donation?* What is the pun? _____

   _____

   b. T / F Panera gives a portion of each sale to the local community.

   c. Panera says, "With your help, we can make a difference." What does the company mean by that? Do you think that companies like Panera can make a difference? Why or why not?

   _____

   _____

Word Study
Context Clues

Efficient reading requires the use of various problem-solving skills. For example, it is impossible for you to know the exact meaning of every word you read, but by developing your guessing ability, you will often be able to understand enough to arrive at the total meaning of a sentence, a paragraph, or an essay. Context Clues exercises are designed to help you improve your ability to guess the meaning of unfamiliar words by using context clues. (Context refers to the sentence and paragraph in which a word occurs.) In using the context to decide the meaning of a word, you have to use your knowledge of grammar and your understanding of the author's ideas. Although there is no formula that you can memorize to improve your ability to guess the meanings of unfamiliar words, you should keep the following points in mind.

1. Use the meanings of the other words in the sentence (or paragraph) and the meaning of the sentence as a whole to reduce the number of possible meanings.

2. Use grammar and punctuation clues that point to the relationships among the various parts of the sentence.

3. Be content with a general idea about the unfamiliar word; the exact definition or synonym is not always necessary.

4. Learn to recognize situations in which it is not necessary to know the meaning of the word.

The explanations given on page 11 for each sentence in the example exercise show how context clues can be used to guess the meaning of unfamiliar words.

Example

Each of the sentences in this exercise contains a blank in order to encourage you to look only at the context provided as you attempt to determine the possible meanings of the missing word. Read each sentence quickly, and supply a word for each blank. There is no single correct answer. Use context clues to help you provide a word that is appropriate in terms of grammar and meaning.

1. I removed the _____ from the shelf and began to read.

2. Harvey is a thief; he would _____ the gold from his grandmother's teeth and not feel guilty.

3. Our uncle was a _____, an incurable wanderer who never could stay in one place.

4. Unlike his brother, who is truly a handsome person, Hogartty is quite _____.

5. The Asian _____, like other apes, is specially adapted for life in trees.

6. But surely everyone knows that if you step on an egg, it will _____.

7. Mary got a new _____ for her birthday. It is a sports model—red with white interior and bucket seats.

Explanation

1. I removed the _____ from the shelf and began to read.

   book
   magazine
   paper
   newspaper

   The number of things that can be taken from a shelf and read is so few that the word *book* probably jumped into your mind at once. Here, the association between the object and the purpose for which it is used is so close that you have very little difficulty guessing the right word.

2. Harvey is a thief; he would _____ the gold from his grandmother's teeth and not feel guilty.

   steal
   take
   rob

   Harvey is a thief. A thief steals. The semicolon (;) indicates that the sentence that follows contains an explanation of the first statement. Further, you know that the definition of *thief* is a person who steals.

3. Our uncle was a _____, an incurable wanderer who never could stay in one place.

   nomad
   roamer
   traveler
   drifter

   The comma (,) following the blank indicates a phrase in apposition, that is, a word or group of words that could be used as a synonym of the unfamiliar word. The words at the left are all synonyms of *wanderer*.

4. Unlike his brother, who is truly a handsome person, Hogartty is quite _____.

   ugly
   homely
   plain

   Hogartty is the opposite of his brother, and since his brother is handsome, Hogartty must be ugly. The word *unlike* signals the relationship between Hogartty and his brother.

5. The Asian _____, like other apes, is specially adapted for life in trees.

   gibbon
   monkey
   chimp
   ape

   You probably didn't write *gibbon*, which is the word the author used. Most native speakers wouldn't be familiar with this word either. But since you know that the word is the name of a type of ape, you don't need to know anything else. This is an example of how context can teach you the meanings of unfamiliar words.

6. But surely everyone knows that if you step on an egg, it will _____.

   break

   You recognized the cause and effect relationship in this sentence. There is only one thing that can happen to an egg when it is stepped on.

7. Mary got a new _____ for her birthday. It is a sports model, red, with white interior and bucket seats.

   car

   The description in the second sentence gave you all the information you needed to guess the word *car*.

EXERCISE 1

In the following exercise, do NOT try to learn the italicized words. Concentrate on developing your ability to guess the meanings of unfamiliar words using context clues. Read each sentence carefully and write a definition, synonym, or description of the italicized word on the line provided.

1. _____ We watched as the cat came quietly through the grass toward the bird. When it was just a few feet from the victim, it gathered its legs under itself and *pounced*.

2. _____ Some people have no difficulty making the necessary changes in their way of life when they move to a foreign country; others are not able to *adapt* as easily to a new environment.

3. _____ In spite of the fact that the beautiful *egret* is in danger of dying out completely, many clothing manufacturers still offer handsome prices for their long, elegant tail feathers, which are used as decorations on hats.

4. _____ When he learned that the club was planning to admit women, the colonel began to *inveigh against* all forms of liberalism; his shouting attack began with universal voting and ended with a protest against divorce.

5. _____ The snake *slithered* through the grass.

6. _____ The man thought that the children were defenseless, so he walked boldly up to the oldest and demanded money. Imagine his surprise when they began to *pelt* him with rocks.

7. _____ Experts in *kinesics*, in their study of body motion as related to speech, hope to discover new methods of communication.

8. _____ Unlike her *gregarious* sister, Jane is a shy, unsociable person who does not like to go to parties or to make new friends.

9. _____ After a day of skiing, Harold is *ravenous*. Yesterday, for example, he ate two bowls of soup, salad, a large chicken, and a piece of chocolate cake before he was finally satisfied.

10. _____ After the accident, the ship went down so fast that we weren't able to *salvage* any of our personal belongings.

Word Study
Dictionary Use

Before You Begin

1. When do you use a dictionary?

2. What kind of information does it give you?

3. When reading English, do you use a monolingual (English-English) or bilingual dictionary?

4. What are the advantages and disadvantages of a bilingual dictionary? Of a monolingual dictionary?

5. Are there times when you do not know what a word means and you do not use a dictionary?

The dictionary provides many kinds of information about words. Below is an excerpt from an English language dictionary. Study the entry carefully; notice how much information the dictionary presents under the word *prefix*.

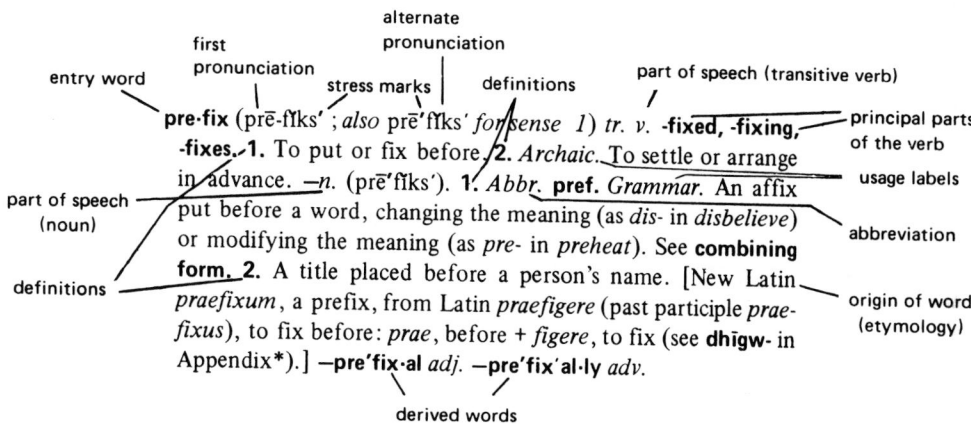

Other dictionaries may use a different system of abbreviations or different pronunciation symbols. It is important for you to become familiar with your English dictionary and with the symbols it uses. Look up *prefix* in your dictionary, and compare the entry to the entry shown above. Discuss any differences that you find.

Dictionaries are also available on the Internet. On page 14 is the first of several different dictionaries' entries for *prefix* that you would find on the website **www.dictionary.com.**

Results for: *prefix*

Dictionary.com Unabridged (v 1.1)

pre·fix 🅿 ◀)) *n.* ˈpri fɪks; *sv.* ˈpri fɪks, priˈfɪks—Show Spelled Pronunciation [*n.* **pree**-fiks; *v.* **pree**-fiks, pree-**fiks**] Pronunciation Key—Show IPA Pronunciation

–noun
1. *Grammar.* an affix placed before a base or another prefix, as *un-* in *unkind*, *un-* and *re-* in *unrewarding.*
2. something prefixed, as a title before a person's name.

–verb (used with object)
3. to fix or put before or in front: *to prefix an impressive title to one's name.*
4. *Grammar.* to add as a prefix.
5. to fix, settle, or appoint beforehand.

[Origin: 1375–1425; (v.) late ME *prefixen* < MF *prefixer* < L *praefixus,* ptp. of *praefīgere* to set up in front; see PRE-, FIX; (n.) < NL *praefixum,* neut. of *praefixus*]

—Related forms
pre·fix·a·ble, *adjective*
pre·fix·al 🅿 ◀)) ˈpri fɪk səl, priˈfɪk - Show Spelled Pronunciation [**pree**-fik-s*uh*l, pree-**fik**-] Pronunciation Key - Show IPA Pronunciation, *adjective*
pre·fix·al·ly, *adverb*
pre·fix·ion 🅿 ◀)) priˈfɪk ʃən - Show Spelled Pronunciation [**pree**-fik-sh*uh*n] Pronunciation Key -

EXERCISE 1

Use the sample entries from the print and online dictionaries above and the print dictionary page (page 17), and your own dictionary to discuss this exercise. Your teacher may want you to work alone, in pairs, or in small groups.

1. When a dictionary gives more than one spelling or pronunciation of a word, which one should you use?

2. Look at the sample print and electronic entries for *prefix.*

   a. How many syllables are in *prefix?* _____

   b. What symbol is used to separate the syllables? _____

3. Notice that *prefix* can be pronounced with the stress on either syllable when used as a verb.

    a. Which syllable is stressed in the first pronunciation of the verb *prefix?* _____

    b. Which syllable is stressed when *prefix* is used as a noun? _____

    c. Practice pronouncing *prefix* with the stress on the first and on the second syllable.

4. a. Where is the pronunciation guide on page 17? _____

    b. Where is it in **dictionary.com**? _____

    c. Where is it in your dictionary? _____

    d. What is the key word in the pronunciation guide on page 17 that shows you how to pronounce the e in the first pronunciation of *prefix?* _____

    e. What would you do to see the pronunciation guide used in **dictionary.com**? _____
    _____

5. a. How many different meanings are given in the entry from the print dictionary for the verb *prefix?* How many are there in the entry from **dictionary.com**? _____

    b. How many different meanings are there in the entry from the print dictionary entry for the noun *prefix?* How many are there in the entry from **dictionary.com**? _____

6. a. Look at the entry for *prefix* from the print dictionary. What are *derived words?*
    _____

    b. What term from the online dictionary entry means the same thing as *derived words?*
    _____

7. a. According to the print dictionary entry, what is the meaning of the Latin root from which *pre-* has developed? _____

    b. Where would you find this information in the **dictionary.com** entry? _____

8. Dictionary entries sometimes include usage labels such as *archaic, obsolete, slang, colloquial, poetic, regional,* and *informal.* Why are these labels useful? _____

9. If you needed to cite the dictionary definition of *prefix* in the bibliography of an academic paper you were writing, how would you find out the proper form to use? _____
_____

EXERCISE 2

In this exercise you may either scan a page of a printed dictionary (on page 17) or use the website **www.dictionary.com** to find answers to specific questions. Read each question, find the answer as quickly as possible, and then write it in the space provided. These questions will introduce you to several kinds of information to be found in a dictionary.

1. a. Would you find the word *glory* on the print dictionary page shown on page 17? _____

   b. How would you find the word *glory* in **www.dictionary.com**?

   _____

2. How many syllables are there in *glossolalia?* _____

3. Which syllable is stressed in the word *glutamic?* _____

4. What are the key words that tell you how to pronounce the *o* in the first pronunciation shown for *glycerol?* _____

5. What is the first way shown to spell the plural of *glottis?* _____

6. What is the past tense of *to glue?* _____

7. What is the adverb derived from *glower?* _____

8. What word must you look up to find *glossographer?* _____

9. For whom was *gloxinia* named? _____

10. From what two languages has *glucose* developed? _____

11. Is the intransitive verb (a verb used without an object) *gloze* commonly used today? _____

12. How many synonyms are listed for the word *glum?* Why are these words defined here?

    _____

13. When was Christoph Willibald Gluck born? _____

14. What is the population of Gloucester, Massachusetts? _____

15. List five different kinds of information you can find in a dictionary?

    1. _____   3. _____   5. _____

    2. _____   4. _____

16. How do print dictionaries compare with online dictionaries? Which type of dictionary do you prefer? In the table, put a check (✓) in the appropriate column to show which type of dictionary you think is better. Be prepared to defend your answers using examples from Exercises 1 and 2.

	Print Dictionary	**Electronic Dictionary**
More convenient		
More information		
More trustworthy information		
More up-to-date information		
Easier and faster to use		
Easier to read		
Less expensive		

in the margin or between lines of a text or manuscript. **2.** An expanded version of such notes; a glossary. **3.** A purposefully misleading interpretation or explanation. **4.** An extensive commentary, often accompanying a text or publication. —*v.* **glossed, glossing, glosses.** —*tr.* **1.** To provide (a text) with glosses. **2.** To give a false interpretation to. —*intr.* To make glosses. [Middle English *glose,* from Old French, from Medieval Latin *glōsa,* from Latin *glōssa,* word that needs explanation, from Greek *glōssa,* tongue, language. See **glōgh-** in Appendix.*] —**gloss′er** *n.*

gloss. glossary.

glos·sal (glôs′əl, glŏs′-) *adj.* Of or pertaining to the tongue. [From Greek *glōssa,* tongue. See **gloss** (explanation).]

glos·sa·ry (glôs′ə-rē, glŏs′-) *n., pl.* **-ries.** *Abbr.* **gloss.** A collection of glosses, such as a vocabulary of specialized terms with accompanying definitions. [Latin *glossārium,* from *glōssa,* GLOSS (explanation).] —**glos·sar′i·al** (glô-sâr′ē-əl, glŏ-) *adj.* —**glos·sar′i·al·ly** *adv.* —**glos′sa·rist** *n.*

glos·sog·ra·phy (glô-sŏg′rə-fē, glŏ-) *n.* The writing and compilation of glosses or glossaries. [Greek *glōssa,* tongue, language, GLOSS (explanation) + -GRAPHY.] —**glos·sog′ra·pher** *n.*

glos·so·la·li·a (glôs′ō-lā′lē-ə, glŏs′-) *n.* **1.** Fabricated nonmeaningful speech, especially as associated with certain schizophrenic syndromes. **2.** The **gift of tongues** *(see).* [New Latin *glossolalia,* from (New Testament) Greek *glōssais lalein,* "to speak with tongues" : *glossa,* tongue (see **glōgh-** in Appendix*) + *lalein,* to talk, babble (see **la-** in Appendix*).]

glos·sol·o·gy (glô-sŏl′ə-jē, glŏ-) *n. Obsolete.* Linguistics. [Greek *glōssa,* tongue, language, GLOSS (explanation) + -LOGY.] —**glos·sol′o·gist** *n.*

gloss·y (glôs′ē, glŏs′ē) *adj.* **-ier, -iest.** **1.** Having a smooth, shiny, lustrous surface. **2.** Superficially attractive; specious. —*n., pl.* **glossies.** *Photography.* A print on smooth, shiny paper. Also called "glossy print." —**gloss′i·ly** *adv.* —**gloss′i·ness** *n.*

glost (glôst, glŏst) *n.* **1.** A lead glaze used for pottery. **2.** Glazed pottery. [Variation of GLOSS (sheen).]

glot·tal (glŏt′l) *adj.* **1.** Of or relating to the glottis. **2.** *Phonetics.* Articulated in the glottis. [From GLOTTIS.]

glottal stop. *Phonetics.* A speech sound produced by a momentary complete closure of the glottis, followed by an explosive release.

glot·tis (glŏt′ĭs) *n., pl.* **-tises** or **glottides** (glŏt′ə-dēz′) **1.** The space between the vocal cords at the upper part of the larynx. **2.** The vocal structures of the larynx. [New Latin, from Greek *glōttis,* from *glōtta, glōssa,* tongue, language. See **glōgh-** in Appendix.*]

Glouces·ter (glôs′tər, glŏs′-). **1.** Also **Glouces·ter·shire** (-shĭr, -shər). *Abbr.* **Glos.** A county of south-central England, 1,257 square miles in area. Population, 1,034,000. **2.** The county seat of this county. Population, 72,000. **3.** A city, resort center, and fishing port of Massachusetts, 27 miles northeast of Boston. Population, 26,000.

glove (glŭv) *n.* **1. a.** A fitted covering for the hand, usually made of leather, wool, or cloth, having a separate sheath for each finger and the thumb. **b.** A gauntlet. **2. a.** *Baseball.* An oversized padded leather covering for the hand, used in catching balls; especially, one with more finger sheathes than the catcher's or first baseman's mitt. **b.** A **boxing glove** *(see).* —**hand in glove.** In a close or harmonious relationship. —*tr.v.* **gloved, gloving, gloves.** **1.** To furnish with gloves. **2.** To cover with or as if with a glove. [Middle English *glove,* Old English *glōf.* See **lep-²** in Appendix.*]

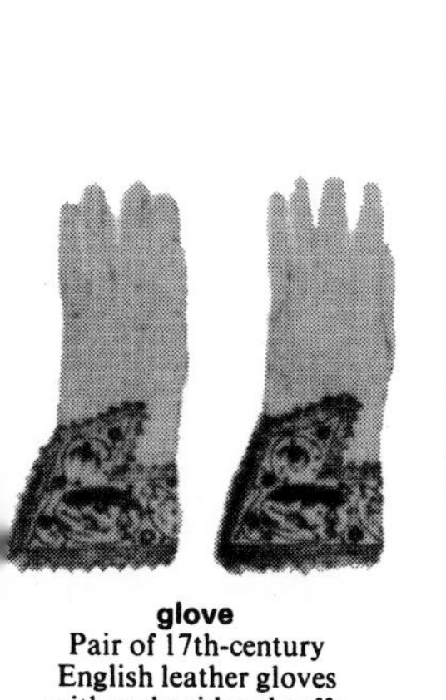

glove
Pair of 17th-century English leather gloves with embroidered cuffs

glove compartment. A small storage container in the dashboard of an automobile.

glov·er (glŭv′ər) *n.* One who makes or sells gloves.

glow (glō) *intr.v.* **glowed, glowing, glows.** **1.** To shine brightly and steadily, especially without a flame: *"a red bed of embers glowing in the furnace"* (Richard Wright). **2.** To have a bright, warm color, usually reddish. **3. a.** To have a healthful, ruddy coloration. **b.** To flush; to blush. **4.** To be exuberant or radiant, as with pride. —*n.* **1.** A light produced by a body heated to luminosity; incandescence. **2.** Brilliance or warmth of color, especially redness: *"the evening glow of the city streets when the sun has gone behind the tallest houses"* (Sean O'Faolain). **3.** A sensation of physical warmth. **4.** A warm feeling of passion or emotion; ardor. —See Synonyms at **blaze.** [Middle English *glowen,* Old English *glōwan.* See **ghel-²** in Appendix.*]

glow·er (glou′ər) *intr.v.* **-ered, -ering, -ers.** To look or stare angrily or sullenly; to frown. —*n.* An angry, sullen, or threatening stare. [Middle English *glo(u)ren,* to shine, stare, probably from Scandinavian, akin to Norwegian dialectal *glora.* See **ghel-²** in Appendix.*] —**glow′er·ing·ly** *adv.*

glow·ing (glō′ĭng) *adj.* **1.** Incandescent; luminous. **2.** Characterized by rich, warm coloration; especially, having a ruddy, healthy complexion. **3.** Ardently enthusiastic or favorable.

glow plug. A small heating element in a diesel engine cylinder used to facilitate starting.

glow·worm (glō′wûrm′) *n.* A firefly; especially, the luminous larva or wingless, grublike female of a firefly.

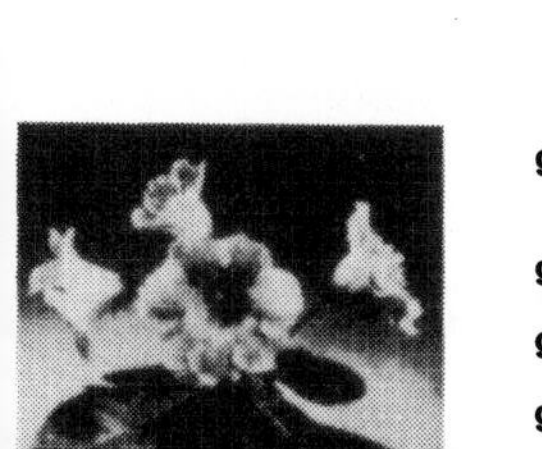

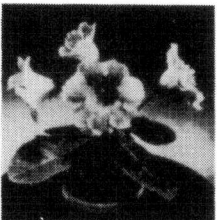

gloxinia
Sinningia speciosa

glox·in·i·a (glŏk-sĭn′ē-ə) *n.* Any of several tropical South American plants of the genus *Sinningia;* especially, *S. speciosa,* cultivated as a house plant for its showy, variously colored flowers. [New Latin, after Benjamin Peter *Gloxin,* 18th-century German botanist and physician.]

gloze (glōz) *v.* **glozed, glozing, glozes.** —*tr.* To minimize or underplay; to gloss. Used with *over.* —*intr. Archaic.* To use flattery or cajolery. [Middle English *glosen,* to gloss, falsify, flatter, from Old French *glosser,* from *glose,* GLOSS (explanation).]

Gluck (glŏŏk), **Christoph Willibald.** 1714–1787. German composer of operas.

glu·cose (glōō′kōs′) *n.* **1.** A sugar, **dextrose** *(see).* **2.** A colorless to yellowish syrupy mixture of dextrose, maltose, and dextrins with about 20 per cent water, used in confectionery, alcoholic fermentation, tanning, and treating tobacco. [French, from Greek *gleukos,* sweet new wine, must. See **dlku-** in Appendix.*]

glu·co·side (glōō′kə-sīd′) *n.* A **glycoside** *(see),* the sugar component of which is glucose. —**glu′co·sid′ic** (-sĭd′ĭk) *adj.*

glue (glōō) *n.* **1.** An adhesive substance or solution; a viscous substance used to join or bond. **2.** An adhesive obtained by boiling animal **collagen** *(see)* and drying the residue. In this sense, also called "animal glue." —*tr.v.* **glued, gluing, glues.** To stick or fasten together with or as if with glue. [Middle English *gleu,* glue, birdlime, gum, from Old French *glu,* from Late Latin *glūs* (stem *glūt-*), from Latin *glūten.* See **gel-¹** in Appendix.*]

glum (glŭm) *adj.* **glummer, glummest.** **1.** In low spirits; dejected. **2.** Gloomy; dismal. [From Middle English *glomen, gloumen,* to look sullen, GLOOM.] —**glum′ly** *adv.* —**glum′ness** *n.*

Synonyms: *glum, gloomy, morose, dour, saturnine.* These adjectives mean having a cheerless or repugnant aspect or disposition. *Glum* implies dejection and silence, and more often than the other terms refers to a mood or temporary condition rather than to a person's characteristic state. *Gloomy* differs little except in being more applicable to a person given to somberness or depression by nature. *Morose* implies sourness of temper and a tendency to be uncommunicative. *Dour* especially suggests a grim or humorless exterior and sometimes an unyielding nature. *Saturnine* suggests severity of aspect, extreme gravity of nature, and often a tendency to be bitter or sardonic.

glu·ma·ceous (glōō-mā′shəs) *adj.* Having or resembling a glume or glumes.

glume (glōōm) *n. Botany.* A chaffy basal bract on the spikelet of a grass. [New Latin *gluma,* from Latin *glūma,* husk. See **gleubh-** in Appendix.*]

glut (glŭt) *v.* **glutted, glutting, gluts.** —*tr.* **1.** To fill beyond capacity; satiate. **2.** To flood (a market) with an excess of goods so that supply exceeds demand. —*intr.* To eat excessively. —See Synonyms at **satiate.** —*n.* **1.** An oversupply. **2.** The act or process of glutting. [Middle English *glotten, glouten,* probably from Old French *gloutir,* to swallow, from Latin *gluttīre.* See **gwel-⁵** in Appendix.*]

glu·tam·ic acid (glōō-tăm′ĭk) *n.* An amino acid present in all complete proteins, found widely in plant and animal tissue, and having a salt, sodium glutamate, that is used as a flavor-intensifying seasoning. [GLUT(EN) + AM(IDE) + -IC.]

glu·ta·mine (glōō′tə-mēn′, -mĭn) *n.* A white crystalline amino acid, $C_5H_{10}N_2O_3$, occurring in plant and animal tissue and produced commercially for use in medicine and biochemical research. [GLUT(EN) + AMINE.]

glu·ten (glōōt′n) *n.* A mixture of plant proteins occurring in cereal grains, chiefly corn and wheat, and used as an adhesive and as a flour substitute. [Latin *glūten,* glue. See **gel-¹** in Appendix.*] —**glu′te·nous** *adj.*

gluten bread. Bread made from flour with a high gluten content and low starch content.

glu·te·us (glōō′tē-əs, glōō-tē′-) *n., pl.* **-tei** (-tē-ī′, -tē′ī′). Any of three large muscles of the buttocks: **a.** *gluteus maximus,* which extends the thigh; **b.** *gluteus medius,* which rotates and abducts the thigh; **c.** *gluteus minimus,* which abducts the thigh. [New Latin, from Greek *gloutos,* buttock. See **gel-¹** in Appendix.*] —**glu′te·al** *adj.*

glu·ti·nous (glōōt′n-əs) *adj.* Resembling or of the nature of glue; sticky; adhesive. [Latin *glūtinōsus,* from *glūten,* glue. See **gel-¹** in Appendix.*] —**glu′ti·nous·ly** *adv.* —**glu′ti·nous·ness, glu′ti·nos′i·ty** (-ŏs′ə-tē) *n.*

glut·ton¹ (glŭt′n) *n.* **1.** One that eats or consumes immoderately. **2.** One that has inordinate capacity to receive or withstand something: *a glutton for punishment.* [Middle English *glotoun,* from Old French *gluton, gloton,* from Latin *gluttō.* See **gwel-⁵** in Appendix.*] —**glut′ton·ous** *adj.* —**glut′ton·ous·ly** *adv.*

glut·ton² (glŭt′n) *n.* A mammal, the **wolverine** *(see).* [From GLUTTON (eater), translation of German *Vielfrass,* "great eater."]

glut·ton·y (glŭt′n-ē) *n.* Excess in eating or drinking.

glyc·er·ic acid (glĭ-sĕr′ĭk, glĭs′ər-). A syrupy, colorless compound, $C_3H_6O_4$. [From GLYCERIN.]

glyc·er·ide (glĭs′ə-rīd′) *n.* An ester of glycerol and fatty acids. [GLYCER(IN) + -IDE.]

glyc·er·in (glĭs′ər-ĭn) *n.* Glycerol. [French, from Greek *glukeros,* sweet. See **dlku-** in Appendix.*]

glyc·er·ol (glĭs′ə-rôl′, -rōl′, -rŏl′) *n.* A syrupy, sweet, colorless or yellowish liquid, $C_3H_8O_3$, obtained from fats and oils as a by-product of the manufacture of soaps and fatty acids, and used as a solvent, antifreeze and antifrost fluid, plasticizer, and sweetener, and in the manufacture of dynamite, cosmetics, liquid soaps, inks, and lubricants. [GLYCER(IN) + -OL.]

glyc·er·yl (glĭs′ər-əl) *n.* The trivalent glycerol radical CH_2CHCH_2. [GLYCER(IN) + -YL.]

gly·cin (glī′sĭn) *n.* Also **gly·cine** (-sēn′, -sĭn). A poisonous compound, $C_8H_9NO_3$, used as a photographic developer. [From GLYCINE.]

gly·cine (glī′sēn′, -sən) *n.* **1.** A white, very sweet crystalline amino acid, $C_2H_5NO_2$, the principal amino acid occurring in sugar cane, derived by alkaline hydrolysis of gelatin, and used in biochemical research and medicine. **2.** Variant of **glycin.** [GLYC(O)- + -INE.]

ă pat/ā pay/âr care/ä father/b bib/ch church/d deed/ĕ pet/ē be/f fife/g gag/h hat/hw which/ĭ pit/ī pie/îr pier/j judge/k kick/l lid, needle/m mum/n no, sudden/ng thing/ŏ pot/ō toe/ô paw, for/oi noise/ou out/ŏŏ took/ōō boot/p pop/r roar/s sauce/sh ship, dish/

17

Word Study
Stems and Affixes

Using context clues is one way to discover the meaning of an unfamiliar word. Another way is word analysis, that is, looking at the meanings of parts of words. Many English words have been formed by combining parts of older English, Greek, and Latin words. If you know the meanings of some of these word parts, you can often guess the meaning of an unfamiliar English word, particularly in context.

For example, *report* is formed from *re-*, which means "back," and *-port*, which means "carry." *Scientist* is derived from *sci-*, which means "know," and *-ist*, which means "one who." *Port* and *sci* are called **stems.** A stem is the basic part on which groups of related words are built. *Re* and *ist* are called **affixes,** that is, word parts that are attached to stems. Affixes like *re*, which are attached to the beginnings of stems, are called **prefixes.** Affixes attached to the end, like *ist*, are called **suffixes.** Generally, prefixes change the meaning of a word, and suffixes change its part of speech. Here is an example.

Stem	Prefix	Suffix
pay (verb)	*re*pay (verb)	repay*ment* (noun)
honest (adjective)	*dis*honest (adjective)	dishonest*ly* (adverb)

Word analysis is not enough to give you the precise definition of a word you encounter in a reading passage, but often along with context it will help you to understand the general meaning of the word so that you can continue reading without stopping to use a dictionary.

Below is a list of some commonly occurring stems and affixes. Study their meanings. Your teacher may ask you to give examples of other words you know that are derived from these stems and affixes. Then do the exercises that follow.

Prefixes		
com-, con-, col-, cor-, co-	together, with	*cooperate, connect*
in-, im-, il-, ir-	in, into, on	*invade, insert*
in-, im-, il, ir-	not	*impolite, illegal*
micro-	small	*microscope, microcomputer*
pre-	before	*prepare, prehistoric*
re-, retro-	back, again	*return, retrorocket*

Stems		
-audi-, -audit-	hear	*auditorium, auditor*
-chron-	time	*chronology, chronological*
-dic-, -dict-	say, speak	*dictator, dictation*
-graph-, -gram-	write, writing	*telegraph, telegram*
-log-, -logy	speech, word, study	*biological*
-phon-	sound	*telephone*

-scrib-, -script-	write	*describe, script*
-spect-	look at	*inspect, spectator*
-vid-, -vis-	see	*video, vision*

Suffixes		
-er, -or	one who	*worker, spectator*
-ist	one who	*typist, biologist*
-tion, -ation	condition, the act of	*action, celebration*

EXERCISE 1

1. For each item, select the best definition of the italicized word.

    a. He lost his *spectacles.*

        _____ 1. glasses   _____ 3. pants

        _____ 2. gloves   _____ 4. shoes

    b. He drew *concentric* circles.

        _____ 1. ◯◯   _____ 3. ◯◯

        _____ 2. ◉   _____ 4. ⬭

    c. He *inspected* their work.

        _____ 1. spoke highly of   _____ 3. examined closely

        _____ 2. did not examine   _____ 4. did not like

2. Circle the words where *in-* means *not.* Watch out; there are false negatives in this list.

    inject   inside   insane   inspect

    invaluable   inflammable   inactive   invisible

3. In current usage, the prefix *co-* is frequently used to form new words (for example, *co-* + *editors* becomes *coeditors*). Give another example of a word that uses *co-* in this way.

    _____

4. The prefix *re-* (meaning *again*) often combines with simple verbs to create new verbs (for example, *re-* + *do* becomes *redo*). List three words familiar to you that use *re-* in this way.

    _____

EXERCISE 2

Word analysis can help you to guess the meanings of unfamiliar words. Using context clues and what you know about word parts, write a synonym, description, or definition of the italicized word or phrase.

1. _____ The doctor asked Martin to *inhale* deeply and hold his breath for 10 seconds.

2. _____ Many countries *import* most of the oil they use.

3. _____ Three newspaper reporters *collaborated* in writing this series of articles.

4. _____ Calling my professor by her first name seems too *informal* to me.

5. _____ It is Lee's *prediction* that by the year 2050 most automobiles will be solar powered.

6. _____ Historians use the *inscriptions* on the walls of ancient temples to guide them in their studies.

7. _____ You cannot sign up for a class the first day it meets in September; you must *preregister* in August.

8. _____ After his long illness, he didn't recognize his own *reflection* in the mirror.

9. _____ I *dictated* the letter to my assistant over the phone.

10. _____ I'm sending a sample of my handwriting to a *graphologist* who says he can use it to analyze my personality.

11. _____ The university has a very good *microbiology* department.

12. _____ *Phonograph recordings* of early jazz musicians are very valuable now.

13. _____ At the drugstore, the pharmacist refused to give me my medicine because she could not read the doctor's *prescription*.

14. _____ He should see a doctor about his *chronic* cough.

15. _____ Maureen was not admitted to graduate school this year, but she *reapplied* and was admitted for next year.

16. _____ I recognize his face, but I can't *recall* his name.

17. _____ Ten years ago, I decided not to complete high school; *in retrospect*, I believe that was a bad decision.

18. _____ She uses *audiovisual* aids to make her speeches more interesting.

19. _____ Some people believe it is *immoral* to fight in any war.

20. _____ Babies are born healthier when their mothers have good *prenatal* care.

EXERCISE 3

Following is a list of words containing some of the stems and affixes introduced in this unit. Definitions of these words appear on the right. Put the letter of the appropriate definition next to each word.

1. _____ microbe

2. _____ phonology

3. _____ audience

4. _____ chronicler

5. _____ chronology

6. _____ irregular

7. _____ microphone

8. _____ invisible

a. an instrument used to make soft sounds louder

b. not able to be seen

c. a group of listeners

d. the study of speech sounds

e. not normal

f. a historian; one who records events in the order in which they occur

g. an organism too small to be seen with the naked eye

h. a listing of events arranged in order of their occurrence

Paragraph Reading
Main Idea

In this exercise, you will practice finding the main idea of a short text. Being able to determine the main idea of a passage is one of the most useful reading skills you can develop. It is a skill you can apply to any kind of reading. For example, when you read for enjoyment or to obtain general information, it is probably not important to remember all the details of a selection. Instead, you want to quickly discover the general message—the main idea of the passage. For other kinds of reading, such as reading textbooks or articles in your own field, you need both to determine the main ideas and to understand the way in which these are developed.

The main idea of a passage is the thought that is present from the beginning to the end. In a well-written paragraph, most of the sentences support, describe, or explain the main idea. It is sometimes stated in the first or last sentence of the paragraph. Sometimes the main idea is only implied.

In order to determine the main idea of a piece of writing, you should ask yourself what idea is common to most of the text. What is the idea that relates the parts to the whole? What opinion do all the parts support? What idea do they all explain or describe?

When reading short passages, you need to be able to both recognize the main idea and sometimes to express the main idea in your own words. Read the following short texts to discover the main idea. After each of the first five passages, select the statement that best expresses the main idea. For Passages 6 and 7, you will write a sentence that expresses the main idea. Finally, for Passage 8, which is several paragraphs long, you will move to doing this task on a larger scale; you will be asked to both identify the main idea and create a summary of the entire text.

When you have finished, your teacher may want to divide the class into small groups for discussion. Study the example carefully before you begin.

Example

By the time the first European travelers on the American continent began to record some of their observations about Native Americans, the Cherokee people had developed an advanced culture that probably was exceeded only by the civilized tribes of the Southwest: Mayan and Aztec groups. The social structures of the Cherokee people consisted of a form of clan kinship in which there were seven recognized clans. All members of a clan were considered blood brothers and sisters and were bound by honor to defend any member of that clan from wrong. Each clan, the Bird, Paint, Deer, Wolf, Blue, Long Hair, and Wild Potato, was represented in the civil council by a councillor or councillors. The chief of the tribe was selected from one of these clans and did not inherit his office from his kinsmen. Actually there were two chiefs, a Peace chief and a War chief. The Peace chief served when the tribe was at peace, but the minute war was declared, the War chief was in command.

Select the statement that best expresses the main idea of the passage.

_____ a. The Cherokee chief was different in wartime than in peacetime.

___✓___ b. Before the arrival of the Europeans, the Cherokees had developed a well-organized society.

_____ c. The Mayans and the Aztecs were part of the Cherokee tribe.

_____ d. Several Native American cultures had developed advanced civilizations before Europeans arrived.

Explanation

_____ a. This is not the main idea. Rather, it is one of the several examples the author uses to support his statement that the Cherokee people had developed an advanced culture.

__✓__ b. This statement expresses the main idea of the paragraph. All other sentences in the paragraph are examples supporting the idea that the Cherokees had developed an advanced culture by the time Europeans arrived on the continent.

_____ c. This statement is false, so it cannot be the main idea.

_____ d. This statement is too general. The paragraph describes the social structure of the Cherokee people only. Although the author names other advanced Native American cultures, he does this only to strengthen his argument that the Cherokees had developed an advanced culture.

Passage 1

A remarkable feature of Australian English is its comparative uniformity. Australia, a continent roughly the size of Europe, has almost no regional variation of accent. A citizen of Perth can sound much like a citizen of Adelaide or Sydney, or like a station hand in Alice Springs or Broken Hill. In Britain or the United States, by contrast, even the outsider can probably decide from the local accent whether he or she is in Scotland or Dorset, New England or Louisiana.

Select the statement that best expresses the main idea of the passage.

_____ a. Regional accents are remarkably useful in deciding where someone is from.

_____ b. In Britain or the United States, there are different accents in different regions.

_____ c. English spoken across Australia is not very different from that spoken in Britain and in the United States.

__✓__ d. There are surprisingly few regional differences in Australian English.

Passage 2

At the University of Kansas art museum, investigators tested the effects of different colored walls on two groups of visitors to an exhibit of paintings. For the first group the room was painted white; for the second, dark brown. Movement of each group was followed by an electrical system under the carpet. The experiment revealed that those who entered the dark brown room walked more quickly, covered more area, and spent less time in the room than the people in the white environment. Dark brown stimulated more activity, but the activity ended sooner. Not only the choice of colors but also the general appearance of a room communicates and influences those inside. Another experiment presented subjects with photographs of faces that were to be rated in terms of energy and well-being. Three groups of subjects were used; each was shown the same photos, but each group was in a different kind of room. One group was in an "ugly" room that resembled a messy storeroom. Another group was in an average room—a nice office. The third group was in a tastefully designed living room with carpeting and drapes. Results showed that the subjects in the beautiful room tended to give higher ratings to the faces than did those in the ugly room. Other studies suggest that students do better on tests taken in comfortable, attractive rooms than they do in ordinary-looking or ugly rooms.

Select the statement that best expresses the main idea of the passage.

_____ a. People in beautiful rooms tend to give higher ratings to photographs of faces than do people in ugly rooms.

✓ b. The color and general appearance of a room influence the behavior and attitudes of the people in it.

_____ c. The University of Kansas has studied the effects of the color of a room on people's behavior.

_____ d. Beautifully decorated, light-colored rooms make people more comfortable than ugly, dark rooms.

Passage 3

Teaching is supposed to be a professional activity requiring long and complicated training as well as official certification. The act of teaching is looked upon as a flow of knowledge from a higher source to an empty container. The student's role is one of receiving information; the teacher's role is one of sending it. There is a clear distinction assumed between one who is supposed to know (and therefore not capable of being wrong) and another, usually younger person, who is supposed not to know. However, teaching need not be the province of a special group of people nor need it be looked upon as a technical skill. Teaching can be more like guiding and assisting than forcing information into a supposedly empty head. If you have a certain skill you should be able to share it with someone. You do not have to get certified to convey what you know to others or to help them in their attempt to teach themselves. All of us, from the very youngest children to the oldest members of our cultures, should come to realize our own potential as teachers. We can share what we know, however little it might be, with someone who has need of that knowledge or skill.

Select the statement that best expresses the main idea of the passage.

_____ a. The author believes that it is not difficult to be a good teacher.

✓ b. The author believes that every person has the potential to be a teacher.

✗ c. The author believes that teaching is a professional activity requiring special training.

_____ d. The author believes that teaching is the flow of knowledge from a higher source to an empty container.

Passage 4

"The artist," Alberto Giacometti once told his boarding school classmates, "must portray things as he sees them, not as others show them." He was just 16, but those words would define and haunt him for the rest of his life. Giacometti became one of the titans of twentieth century sculpture and painting, an artist who gave Picasso advice on sculpting and was picked to draw Matisse's portrait for a medallion honoring the painter's career. Yet to his last days, Giacometti was still trying to live up to those boyhood words, and claiming that he'd failed.

Select the statement that best expresses the main idea of the passage.

_____ a. Giacometti believed he had failed to give Picasso good advice.

_____ b. Giacometti was a major artist of the twentieth century.

_____ c. Giacometti was a better sculptor than Picasso.

_____ d. Throughout his life, Giacometti was not convinced he was a true artist.

Passage 5

Some tribes in Africa speak to each other with a vocabulary that includes sharp clicking sounds. Genetic comparison of two such tribes suggests that the click languages, known as Khoisan languages, could resemble the ancestral tongue of all human kind. These tongues are most prevalent in southwestern Africa where many tribes, including the San and !Kung tribes (the ! represents a click sound) speak them. The Hadzabe people and several other tribes in the East African country of Tanzania also talk with clicks. The geographical and genetic diversity of Khoisan speakers and Africa's apparent role as the birthplace of humanity have led some scientists to propose that all living humans descended from speakers of a click language.

Select the statement that best expresses the main idea of the passage.

_____ a. Several different African tribes speak languages with clicks.

_____ b. Africa is the place where humans probably originated.

_____ c. The earliest humans may have spoken a click language.

_____ d. Click languages appear to be Khoisan languages.

Passage 6

There is widespread fear among policymakers and the public today that the family is disintegrating. Much of that anxiety stems from a basic misunderstanding of the nature of the family in the past and a lack of appreciation for its resiliency in response to broad social and economic changes. The general view of the family is that it has been a stable and relatively unchanging institution through history and is only now undergoing changes; in fact, change has always been characteristic of it.

Write a sentence that expresses the main idea of the passage. changes in the family have always been there through the history

Passage 7

Enough is known about the ancient Maya—those sophisticated artists and architects, astronomers and calendar keepers of South America—to realize that much remains to be learned before all the mysteries can be unraveled. Once considered peaceful stargazers, they are now suspected of being bloodthirsty and warlike. Dogged and brilliant scholars have wrestled with the problems for a century and a half. There has been a steady revision of ideas, regular expansion of the boundaries of knowledge, and there is certain to be more.

Write a sentence that expresses the main idea of the passage. *People should learn about ancient Maya and realize that there's much remain to be learned.*

Passage 8: Main Idea and Prose Summary

Read the passage to identify the most important ideas.

Scientists believe they have found the answer to a question that has been puzzling bird lovers and scientists alike. Typically, the common English robin is one of the earliest birds to begin singing at the dawn of each day and the last to stop singing at nightfall. Singing is the way male robins attract a mate. Around some cities, however, it is now not unusual to hear robins singing at night. This phenomenon has been the subject of study of researchers at the University of Sheffield, in the U.K., who are interested in the effects of urbanization on biodiversity.

Until recently, urban light pollution was offered as the explanation for why some robins sing at night. The theory was that light from street lamps, large office buildings, and automobiles fooled robins into thinking it was still daylight. According to Richard Fuller, a scientist at the University of Sheffield, there was inadequate research to support this claim. He and his colleagues suspected something else was at play.

In a two-year study, Fuller's research team visited 121 sites in and around the city of Sheffield. At 67 of the sites, they heard robins singing during the day, and at 18 sites, nocturnally. At each site where they heard birds, they measured nighttime light and daytime noise. The nighttime light levels at the sites did have a small effect, but the daytime noise levels were much more strongly related to nighttime singing. They found that in areas where robins sang at night, the noise levels during the day were on average twice as loud as at the other sites, loud enough to make it difficult for the birds' songs to be heard.

That birds' singing is affected by urban noise is supported by several other studies. European researchers showed that birds living in areas with a lot of traffic sing at a higher pitch than similar birds in quieter areas, to be heard over the low-frequency sound of traffic. Another study suggested that nightingales in Germany sing louder in noisy areas. Further studies will be conducted to investigate the effects of nighttime singing on birds. It is possible that the adaptation is harmless; however, it could also tire birds out and take time away from feeding, which could threaten their survival.

1. What was the main finding of Fuller's research?

   a. Nighttime singing appears to be dangerous for robins.

   b. A loud level of noise in the day appears to cause robins to sing at night.

   c. Nighttime singing by robins appears not to be as common as was once thought.

   d. English robins do not appear to sing as loud as German nightingales.

   e. Urban light pollution does not appear to affect robins' singing.

2. Imagine you are part of a study group in an ecology class. You have agreed to read this passage and write a one-paragraph summary of Fuller's research for your study group. You will begin your summary with this topic sentence:

   Richard Fuller and his colleagues investigated why some robins living near urban areas sing at night.

Now, choose three more sentences from the choices below to complete your summary. Put a check (✓) next to the three sentences that express the most important ideas about the study. Do not check the sentences that express ideas not found in the passage or ones that are less important ideas for summarizing the research study.

_____ a. They theorized that the main cause was light pollution.

_____ b. They studied places where robins sing at night and places where they do not.

_____ c. They found that most robins sing during the day.

_____ d. They measured light and noise levels at 121 sites.

_____ e. They discovered it was noisier in places where robins sang at night.

_____ f. They found that robins sing louder at night than during the day.

_____ g. They discovered that light pollution had less effect than people had theorized.

_____ h. They proved that nighttime singing threatens robins' survival.

Reading Selections 1A–1B
Language Policy

—— **Selection 1A United Nations Report** ——

Before You Begin

1. How many languages do you speak?

2. What do you consider to be your native language(s)?

3. Do you think it would be a good thing or a bad thing if everyone in the world studied English in school?

4. What would you expect to read about in an article entitled "Can English Be Dethroned?"?

What better place to think about the role of English than in an English class! "Can English Be Dethroned?" (taken from a United Nations publication) raises issues concerning the spread of English. Read the article, and see what you think. Your teacher may want you to do Vocabulary from Context Exercise 1 on pages 33–34 before you begin reading.

Can English be dethroned?

Ronald J.-L. Breton
Geolinguist and emeritus professor at the University of Paris

Major languages other than English are spoken by over half the people on the planet. What can be done to give them more clout in international bodies?

(1) Back in 1919, U.S. President Woodrow Wilson managed to have the Treaty of Versailles, which ended the First World War between Germany and the Allies, written in English as well as French. Since then, English has taken root in diplomacy and gradually economic relations and the media. The language now seems set to have a monopoly as the worldwide medium of communication.

(2) In the beginning of the 21st century, faster economic globalization is going hand in hand with the growing use of English. More and more people are being encouraged to use or send messages in English rather than in their own language. Many do not mind. They see this as part of the unavoidable trend towards worldwide uniformity and a means whereby a growing number of people can communicate directly with each other.

(3) From this point of view, the spread of English may be seen as a positive development which saves resources and makes cultural exchanges easier. After all, it might be said, the advance of English is not aimed at killing off local languages but is simply a means of reaching a wider audience.

(4) Perhaps. But accepting that as the last word ignores the deep-rooted ties between individual freedom and political power, between the linguistic, social and economic mechanisms which in every society underpin relations between people and groups and between culture and communities. A person makes a mark through his or her ability to use the most useful language or languages. And over several generations, the most useful languages eliminate the others.

(5) Cultural imperialism is much more subtle than economic imperialism, which is itself less tangible than political and military imperialism, whose excesses are obvious and easy to denounce. It would be wrong to say that the world domination of English is something deliberately organized and supported by Anglo-Saxon powers, hand in glove with political initiatives or the penetration of the world economy by their transnational firms. The "language war" has very seldom been regarded as a war and has never, anywhere, been declared.

(6) The military, diplomatic, political and economic strategies of the major powers can be studied and criticized, but linguistic strategies seem to be inconspicuous and tacit, even innocent or nonexistent. Will countries stand up to domination by a single language?

(7) Many years after the founding in 1945 of the Arab League, whose current 22 member states have 250 million people, the countries which share a French linguistic heritage broke new ground by circulating a joint policy. In order to promote linguistic, economic and political cooperation, they set up the International Organization of French-Speaking Countries, which (like the British Commonwealth) embraces more than 50 countries with over 500 million inhabitants.

(8) Since 1991, there have been conferences of Dutch speakers from eight or more communities representing some 40 million people, as well as Ibero-American summits, which every two years bring together more than 20 Spanish-speaking countries (350 million inhabitants). Turkish-speaking summits have been held biennially since 1992, with delegates from six independent countries (120 million people) of Europe, Central Asia and small ethnic communities elsewhere. Since 1996, the Association of Portuguese-speaking countries has brought together people from seven countries (200 million people).

Pockets of Resistance

(9) Will uncoordinated resistance by the world's most widely-used languages be enough to cope with the threat of cultural uniformity? Perhaps not, since each language has its own geographical sphere in which it is used with varying degrees of competence. If you add up the number of speakers of the world's dozen most-used languages, you come up with a figure of more than three billion–half of humanity–which easily surpasses the two billion for whom English is more or less the official language (the Commonwealth and the United States). Backed by a concerted strategy, these major languages would surely make headway in international institutions.

(10) It is not just the future of the world's major languages that is at stake. Further down the scale are 100 or so tongues officially recognized by governments or sub-national regions, such as the constitutional languages of India and the languages of the Russian nationalities. These languages have their place and a right to defend it. At the bottom of the scale are thousands of sometimes struggling languages variously called native, minority, communal or ethnic tongues. Most are in danger of disappearing. They are spoken by some 300 million people.

(11) Will minor languages die out, as some predict? Yes, because the best way to kill off a language is to teach another one. The monopoly that about 100 national languages have on education makes it inevitable that languages not taught in schools will be confined to the home and to folklore and eventually be pushed out of nurturing cultural environments.

(12) Language murder or "linguicide," whether it is carried out intentionally or not, is one of the basic tools of ethnocide, of the deculturation of peoples which has always been perpetuated by colonization and is still the semi-official aim of governments which do not recognize the rights of their native ethnic minorities. As local languages are increasingly excluded from education systems, "linguicide" is speeding up.

(13) The language issue in the 21st century raises two questions. How can widely-used national languages resist the encroachment of English? And how can minority languages in danger of extinction be saved and gain access to development?

Comprehension

Answer the following questions based on your understanding of the author's point of view. True/False items are indicated by a T / F preceding the statement.

1. T / F The growing use of English makes cultural and economic exchanges easier.

2. T / F Over time the most useful language eliminates other languages.

3. T / F Whether or not a language is taught in school has no impact on its use in the community.

4. T / F The growing importance of English is part of a plan by English-speaking nations for global economic domination.

5. T / F Economic policies are more obvious than language policies.

6. T / F The creation of language-based organizations such as the International Organization of French-Speaking Countries has solved the problem of the spread of English.

7. T / F Deculturation is a result of linguicide.

8. T / F The spread of English and other world languages is a threat to minority languages.

9. T / F Minority languages can be helped by using the same strategies used by speakers of major languages.

10. In what sense do you think the author uses the terms *major* and *minor* languages? The author of another article in this series uses the term *small* instead of *minority* languages. Which term do you prefer, or can you suggest an alternative? _____

_____

_____

Critical Reading

1. a. How are minority languages endangered by the spread of English and other "world languages"?

   b. How would you answer the author's final question, "How can minority languages in danger of extinction be saved?" Below is a list of actions that speakers of "minority" languages might take. Check (✓) those that you think might be effective in protecting endangered languages. You may want to work with your classmates or compare your answers after you are finished.

   _____ Write down oral languages

   _____ Have linguists learn and teach the languages to other nonnative speakers

   _____ Make tapes of native speakers

   _____ Teach minority languages in school

   _____ Teach schools in minority languages

   _____ Pass laws requiring the use of minority languages in government and business

_____ Require public signs to be in minority languages

_____ Take steps to increase the use of minority languages on the World Wide Web

_____ Encourage writers to publish in minority languages

_____ Translate classic books into minority languages

_____ Translate popular writing into minority languages

_____ Have TV programs in minority languages

_____ Use subtitles or "dub" international movies in minority languages

_____ Translate all instructions for imported appliances into minority languages ☺

_____ Other? _____

2. In Paragraphs 3–4, the author says that to accept the idea that English is "simply a means of reaching a wider audience . . . ignores the deep-rooted ties between individual freedom and political power, between the linguistic, social and economic mechanisms which in every society underpin relations between people and groups and between culture and communities." What are the "ties" (connections) the author is talking about? According to the author, how does understanding these connections make the use of English seem to be a problem? Work on this question with other classmates.

3. For this international publication, the author wrote in English about the dangers of English. Do you think he would have been more or less effective if he'd written in another language?

Discussion/Composition

1. Some people argue that English is no longer associated with British or American culture or with its colonial past. Instead, they argue that English has become a culturally neutral medium of communication. As evidence they point out that most people studying English today have as their goal communicating with _non_native speakers. And many different varieties of "World Englishes" are spoken as native languages today—for example, in India and Africa. Do you think English has become culturally neutral for second language speakers? What are arguments for and against this point of view?

2. a. Below is a list of reasons why someone might study English. How would the author of "Can English Be Dethroned?" see each of these in terms of cultural imperialism? This question allows you to explore how the author might think about these things. There is no single correct answer; do not be concerned if you have trouble coming up with an answer for each item. As an example, we've given our thinking for the first one.

   • To publish scientific papers

   The need to publish in English shows the breakdown of local research communities. It also gives an unfair advantage to English-speaking researchers.

- To read scientific papers
- To get a job in the tourist industry in your country
- To talk to nonnative-speaking businesspeople
- To do business in the United States or Britain
- To get a job in a multinational corporation
- To study in an English-speaking country
- To get a job teaching English
- To marry an English-speaking person
- To immigrate to an English-speaking country
- Other? _____

b. On the basis of your answers, do you see the use of English more as a convenience or as contributing to cultural imperialism?

c. Write a position paper that begins "English is/is not an instrument of cultural imperialism." Support your position with your own knowledge as well as information from "Can English Be Dethroned?"

3. Worldwide, governments make "language policies." These policies can include what languages are used in government, schools, and courts and even what language workers may use among themselves. In general terms, nations have two very different positions available to them: They can encourage uniformity or they may encourage diversity. Which approach do you think is best for your country? Support your position orally or in writing by presenting reasons and examples.

4. Over the next 10 years, do you think the use of major languages other than English will increase or decrease on the Internet? Support your position orally or in writing by presenting reasons and examples.

Vocabulary from Context

EXERCISE 1

Use the context provided to determine the meanings of the italicized words. Write a definition, synonym, or description of each of the italicized vocabulary items in the space provided.

English has become the dominant language for worldwide communication and business. For many people this is a convenience. Increased use of English is seen as a *trend* that simply developed gradually over time. Others see the use of English quite differently. For them, it is a form of economic, social, and political domination and control. It is, they argue, a form of cultural *imperialism*. This is the point of view the author of "Can English Be Dethroned?" examines.

1. _The most popular_

2. _Domination._

3. _Countries comunication_ If English were used only for *diplomacy,* he argues, probably few would complain. But it is used for more than international relations. Because the use of English and other world languages is

4. _Defeat_

5. _Deny_

6. _unclear_

7. _effective_

8. _~~cost~~ secure - secret_

9. _ability_

10. _mean policy_

11. _effort_

12. _Join_

13. _unexplicit_

14. _struggling_

15. _peak_

16. _improve_

17. _catch up with_

18. _Dominant_

19. _Missed_

20. _missed_

so widespread, especially in schools, the worry is that languages with fewer speakers will die out. Over several generations, the most useful language *eliminates* the others.

It's difficult to criticize cultural imperialism, such as the use of English on the Internet. How do you *denounce* something whose negative effects are so hard to see? They are, indeed, quite *inconspicuous* compared to other, more obvious forms of imperialism. Economic imperialism is more *tangible;* people can touch and see the results. And certainly political and military imperialism are not at all *subtle*. Their extreme actions are quite obvious. And their *excesses* are easy to denounce.

And it's not that English-speaking governments have had a conscious, explicit plan to support the growing importance of English, says the author. It has not been a *deliberate policy* on their parts. There have not been *intentional initiatives* to spread English as their corporations have entered the world economy, *penetrating* world markets. Linguistic strategies are not explicit. Rather they are *tacit* and unspoken.

Are there ways for speakers of other languages, particularly "minor" languages, to oppose the domination of "major" world languages if they so choose? One kind of *resistance* is to work with others to see that local languages are taught in schools. Perhaps there can be meetings of speakers in the same way that there have been *summits* for major languages such as Arabic, French, Spanish, and Dutch. In order to *promote* linguistic, economic, and political cooperation, the French-speaking countries set up an international organization, much like the British Commonwealth. These are all ways to deal with a perceived threat of cultural uniformity. Groups *cope with* this threat by working together.

However, the difficulties faced by minority languages are quite different from those faced by languages such as French. French is a major language that is losing speakers, but minority languages are in danger of disappearing completely. Linguicide, some people argue, is the equivalent of ethnocide, the death of a culture, and that has typically been a tool of *colonization*. The loss of a minority language can make a community feel like it's been taken over by others. The dangers to minor languages do not come from English alone. Around the world minority languages are endangered by both local and international events.

EXERCISE 2

This exercise is designed to give you additional clues to determine the meanings of unfamiliar vocabulary items in context. In the paragraph of "Can English Be Dethroned?" indicated by the number in parentheses, find the word or phrase that best fits the meaning given. Your teacher may want to read these aloud as you quickly scan* the paragraph to find the answer.

1. (2) What phrase means *don't care; aren't bothered by this?* _do not mint_

2. (9) Which word means *circle?* _concerted_

3. (11) Which word means *unavoidable; certain; definite?* _inevitable_

4. (11) Which word means *traditional customs?* _FolKlore_

5. (13) Which word means *spread; intrusion; advance beyond the usual limits?* _raises_

6. (13) Which word means *disappearance; death; loss?* _extinction_

EXERCISE 3

This exercise should be done after you have finished reading "Can English Be Dethroned?" The exercise is designed to give you practice using context clues to guess the meaning of unfamiliar vocabulary in the article. Give a definition, synonym, or description of each of the words below. The number in parentheses indicates the paragraph in which the word can be found. Your teacher may want you to do these orally or in writing.

1. (4) mechanisms _system, the way it works._

2. (7) embraces _take over_

3. (9) surpasses _extrem_

4. (10) tongues _languages_

Figurative Language and Idioms

In the paragraph indicated by the number in parentheses, find the phrase that best fits the meaning given. Your teacher may want to read these aloud as you quickly scan the paragraph to find the answer.

1. (1) What phrase means *has become established?* _has taken root_

2. (4) What phrase means *the truth; the final judgment; all there is to say on a subject?* _word ignore_

3. (4) What phrase means *firmly established; strong?* _deep-rooted_

4. (4) What phrase means *has influence; creates an impression?* _eliminate_

5. (5) What phrase means *together with?* (You can find a synonymous phrase in Paragraph 2.)

   orginaized or supporbet

6. (7) What phrase means *did something new?* _set up_

---

*For an introduction to scanning, see Unit 1.

7. (9) What phrase means *an action taken together; a joint action; an organized approach or plan?*

concerted strategy

8. (9) What phrase means *make progress?* _headway_

9. (10) What phrase means *at issue; at risk; in danger?* _stake_

Stems and Affixes

The sentences below are adapted from "Can English Be Dethroned?" Use your knowledge of stems and affixes* and the context to guess the meanings of the italicized terms in the sentences below. Your teacher may want you to do this orally or in writing.

1. English now seems *to have a monopoly* as the worldwide medium of communication.

dominant

2. In the beginning of the twenty-first century, faster economic *globalization* is going hand in hand with the growing use of English.

international

3. Many people see the use of English as part of the *unavoidable* trend toward worldwide uniformity.

cannot be avoided

4. To see the spread of English as being innocent is to ignore the relations between linguistic, social, and economic mechanisms that *underpin* relations between culture and communication.

support

5. It would be wrong to say that the world domination of English is deliberately organized by the Anglo-Saxon powers to help the penetration into other countries by their *transnational* firms.

manage to spread

6. Turkish-speaking summits have been held *biennially* since 1992, with delegates from six independent countries.

every while

7. Further down the scale are 100 or so tongues officially recognized by governments or *subnational* regions, such as the constitutional languages of India and the languages of the Russian nationalities.

local areas

8. Language murder, or *linguicide,* whether it is carried out intentionally or not, is one of the basic tools of *ethnocide,* of the *deculturation* of peoples which has always been perpetrated by colonization and is still the *semi-official* aim of governments which do not recognize the rights of their native ethnic minorities.

linguicide: _language killer_

ethnocide: _two langages_

deculturation: _destroying the culture_

semi-official: _not so formal_

*For a list of all stems and affixes taught in *Reader's Choice,* see the Appendix.

The previous article is concerned about the dominance of English worldwide. The next reading reports a somewhat different perspective.

Before You Begin It is often possible to get a fairly accurate idea of an article's point of view by quickly skimming* key parts. Look at the article's title, the title of the graph, and the inset quote. Read the first two paragraphs. What is the major argument of this article?

Now read the passage to understand the full argument and answer the questions that follow.

English Seen as Co-Star among Global Languages

By Randolph E. Schmid, *The Associated Press*

(1) WASHINGTON—The world faces a future of people speaking more than one language, with English no longer seen as likely to become dominant, a British language expert says in a new analysis. "English is likely to remain one of the world's most important languages for the foreseeable future, but its future is more problematic—and complex—than most people appreciate," language researcher David Graddol said. He sees English as likely to become the "first among equals" rather than having the global field to itself. "Monolingual speakers of any variety of English—American or British— will experience increasing difficulty in employment and political life, and are likely to become bewildered by many aspects of the society and culture around them," Graddol said.

(2) The share of the world's population that speaks English as a native language is decreasing, Graddol reported in Friday's issue of the journal *Science*. The idea of English becoming the world language to the exclusion of others "is past its sell-by date," Graddol said. Instead, he said, its major contribution will be in creating generations of bilingual and multilingual speakers.

(3) A multilingual population already is the case in much of the world and is becoming

> *"Monolingual speakers of any variety of English—American or British—will experience increasing difficulty in employment and political life, and are likely to become bewildered by many aspects of society and culture around them."*
>
> David Graddol, Language researcher

more common in the United States. Indeed, the Census Bureau reported last year that nearly one American in five speaks a language other than English at home, with Spanish leading, and Chinese growing rapidly. That linguistic diversity, in turn, has helped spark calls to make English the nation's official language.

(4) Yale linguist Stephen Anderson noted that multilingualism is "more or less the natural state. In most of the world multilingualism is the normal condition of people." "The notion that English shouldn't, needn't and probably won't displace local languages seems natural to me," he said. While it is important to learn English, he added, politicians and educators need to realize that doesn't mean abandoning the native language.

(5) Graddol, of the British consulting and publishing business The English Company, said he anticipates a world in which the share of people who are native English speakers slips from 9 percent in the mid-20th century to 5 percent in 2050. As of 1995, he reported, English was the second most common native tongue in the world, trailing only Chinese. By 2050, he said, Chinese will continue its predominance, with Hindi-Urdu of India and Arabic climbing past English among 15- to 24-year-olds, and Spanish

*For an introduction to skimming, see Unit 1.

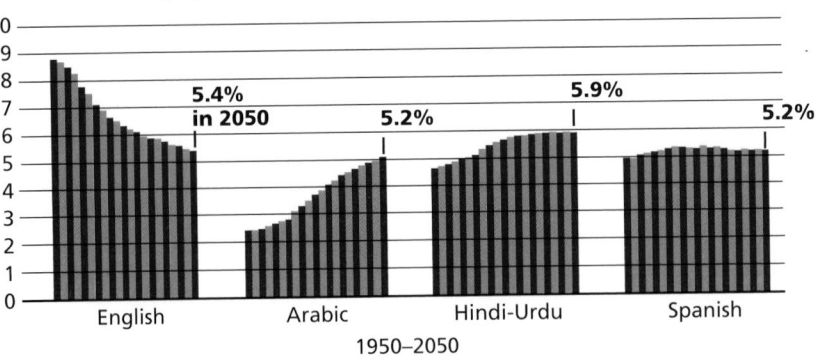

English as a native language declining

The share of people in the world who are native English speakers has been declining since 1950. Hindi-Urdu and Arabic are projected to surpass English among 15- to 24-year-olds by 2050.

Percent of total population speaking native language

5.4% in 2050 — English
5.2% — Arabic
5.9% — Hindi-Urdu
5.2% — Spanish

1950–2050

Note: For each language, a bar represents five years.

Source: The English Company

THE ASSOCIATED PRESS

nearly equal to it. Graddol said he focused on the 15- to 24-year-old group in 2050 to give an indication of the future past that point.

(6) Swarthmore College linguist K. David Harrison noted, however, that "the global share of English is much larger if you count second-language speakers, and will continue to rise, even as the proportion of native speakers declines." Even as English grows as a second language, it still may not ever be the most widely spoken language in the world, according to Graddol, since so many people are native Chinese speakers and many more are learning it as a second language.

(7) English has become the dominant language of science, with an estimated 80 percent to 90 percent of papers in scientific journals written in English, Scott Montgomery noted in a separate paper in the same issue of *Science*. That's up from about 60 percent in the 1980s, he observed. "There is a distinct consciousness in many countries, both developed and developing, about this dominance of English," Montgomery, a Seattle-based geologist and energy consultant, said. "There is some evidence of resistance to it, a desire to change it." For example, he said, sites in English dominated in the early years of the Internet. In recent years, however, there has been a proliferation of non-English sites. Nonetheless, English is strong as a second language, and teaching it has become a growth industry, Montgomery said.

(8) Graddol noted, though, that employers in parts of Asia already are looking beyond English. "In the next decade the new 'must-learn' language is likely to be Mandarin." "The world's language system, having evolved over centuries, has reached a point of crisis and is rapidly restructuring," Graddol said. As many as 90 percent of the 6,000 or so languages spoken around the world may be doomed to extinction, he estimated.

(9) Graddol does have words of consolation for those who struggle to master the intricacies of other languages. "The expectation that someone should always aspire to native-speaker competence when learning a foreign language is under challenge," he said.

Comprehension

Answer the following questions based on the perspectives reported in the article. True/False items are indicated by a T / F preceding the statement.

1. (T)/ F English is likely to remain one of the world's most important languages.

2. T /(F) English is becoming a world language to the exclusion of other languages.

3. T /(F) Currently, English is the most common native language spoken in the world.

4. T /(F) Including second language speakers, by 2050, English will be the most widely spoken language in the world.

5. (T)/ F While multilingualism is the norm in the rest of the world, it is less common in the United States.

6. (T)/ F The graph predicts that the number of English speakers will decline by 2050.

7. Why did Graddol focus on the 15- to 24-year-old group for his predictions for 2050? _____

   To show the future past of it

8. (T)/ F Graddol predicts that in the next decade, employers in the U.S. will be looking for Chinese speakers.

Critical Reading

1. Compare the following sentence from the description of the graph to the information provided in the graph itself: *Hindi-Urdu and Arabic are projected to surpass English among 15- to 24-year-olds by 2050.* Are they consistent? If not, do you have any idea(s) why this might be the case?

2. The article states that the future contribution of English will be to create generations of bilingual and multilingual speakers. Explain what this means.

3. Why is Scott Montgomery, described as a "Seattle-based geologist and energy consultant," quoted in this article about language?

Discussion/Composition

1. Graddol believes that English will become "the first among equals." What does this mean? Do you think it is possible to have both "a first" and "equals"? Why or why not?

2. In what ways does "English Seen as Co-Star . . ." support arguments made in the first article in this section, "Can English Be Dethroned?" In what ways does it present a contrasting point of view? Using data from both articles, compare and contrast their perspectives on the future of English, of other widely used languages, and of minority languages. Which article do you find more persuasive? Why?

   To compare and contrast complex arguments, it is often helpful to begin by classifying the information. In order to clarify your own thinking, make brief notes about the content of each reading in the table on the next page.

	English	Widely Used Languages	Minority Languages
"Can English Be Dethroned?"			
"English Seen as Co-Star among Global Languages"			

Vocabulary from Context

This exercise should be done after you have finished reading "English Seen as Co-Star among Global Languages." The exercise is designed to give you practice using context clues and, where appropriate, stems and affixes to guess the meaning of unfamiliar vocabulary. Give a definition, synonym, or description of each of the words below. The number in parentheses indicates the paragraph in which the word can be found. Your teacher may want you to do these orally or in writing.

1. (1) foreseeable _the farest poit_
2. (1) appreciate _understand_
3. (3) spark _make, create_
4. (5) trailing _follow_
5. (9) consolation _comfortable_
6. (9) aspire _goal._

Figurative Language and Idioms

In the paragraph indicated by the number in parentheses, find the phrase that best fits the meaning given. Your teacher may want to read these aloud as you quickly scan* the paragraph to find the answer.

1. (1) What phrase means *having no competition?* _having the global_ ~~no longer seen as likly to become do~~
2. (2) What phrase means *is no longer current; is no longer a fresh idea?* _is past its sell-by date_

*For an introduction to scanning, see Unit 1.

Reading Selection 2
Essay (Memoir)

Recent world events can make travelers nervous—nervous because of how strangers seem to them, nervous about how they may appear to strangers. The essay "Gate 4-A" captures a contemporary travel moment. It is a **memoir** (an account of a personal experience).

Before You Begin

1. Poet Naomi Nye was in an airport when she heard an announcement that anyone who spoke her father's language should come to Gate 4-A immediately. What emotions do you think you would feel if this happened to you? Check all those you might feel.

____ Curious
____ Glad you could help
____ Nervous (about what?)
____ Worried (about what?)
____ Other _____

2. In what ways might your reaction to such an announcement depend on the language you were being asked to speak? Read on to discover how Nye's world changed.

Gate 4-A

by Naomi Shihab Nye

WANDERING AROUND THE ALBUQUERQUE AIRPORT TERMINAL, after (1) learning my flight had been detained for four hours, I heard an announce- (2) ment: "If anyone in the vicinity of Gate 4-A understands any Arabic, (3) please come to the gate immediately!" Well—one pauses these days. Gate (4) 4-A was my own gate. I went there. An older woman in full traditional (5) Palestinian embroidered dress, just like my grandma wore, was crumpled to the floor, wail- (6) ing loudly. "Help," said the Flight Service Person. "Talk to her. What is her problem? We (7) told her the flight was going to be late and she did this." I stooped to put my arm around (8) the woman and spoke to her haltingly. "Shu do-a, Shu-bid-uck Habibti, Stani schway, Min (9) fadlick, Shu-bit-se-wee?" The minute she heard any words she knew, however poorly used, (10) she stopped crying. She thought our flight had been cancelled entirely. She needed to be in (11) El Paso for a major medical treatment the next day. (12)

I said, "No, no, we're fine. You'll get there, just late. Who is (13) picking you up? Let's call him." (14)

We called her son and I spoke with him in English. I told (15) him I would stay with his mother until we got on the plane and (16) would ride next to her. She talked to him. Then we called her (17) other sons just for the fun of it. Then we called my dad and he (18) and she spoke for a while in Arabic and found out, of course, (19) they had ten shared friends. Then I thought, just for the heck (20) of it, why not call some Palestinian poets I know and let them (21) chat with her? This all took up about two hours. She was (22) laughing a lot by then, telling about her life, patting my knee, (23) answering questions. She had pulled a sack of homemade (24) mamool cookies—little powdered sugar crumbly mounds (25) stuffed with dates and nuts—out of her bag and was offering (26) them to all the women at the gate. To my amazement, not a sin- (27) gle woman declined one. It was like a sacrament. The traveler (28) from Argentina, the mom from California, the lovely woman (29) from Laredo—we were all covered with the same powdered sugar. And smiling. There is (30) no better cookie. And then the airline broke out the free beverages from the huge cool- (31) ers and two little girls from our flight ran around serving us all apple juices and they (32) were covered in powdered sugar too. And I noticed my new best friend—by now we (33) were holding hands—had a potted plant poking out of her bag, some medicinal thing, (34) with green furry leaves. Such an old country traveling tradition. Always carry a plant. (35) Always stay rooted to somewhere. And I looked around that gate of late and weary ones (36) and thought, "This is the world I want to live in. The shared world." Not a single per- (37) son in this gate—once the crying of confusion stopped—seemed apprehensive about any (38) other person. They took the cookies. I wanted to hug all those other women too. This (39) can still happen anywhere. Not everything is lost. (40)

Naomi Shihab Nye lives in San Antonio, Texas. Her books include *19 Varieties of Gazelle, Sitti's Secrets,* and *Habibi* (a novel for teens).

Reading for Details

EXERCISE 1

Part of the power of this essay lies in the carefully chosen details that convey a great deal of information, often indirectly. If one has understood the details, one has understood the tale. Below are excerpts taken from "Gate 4-A" with particular details italicized. Indicate why you think the author chose to include these details and what information they convey. Line numbers are in parentheses.

1. [She was] an older woman in full Palestinian embroidered dress, *just like my grandma wore.* . . . (5–6)

   _____

2. I stooped to put my arm around the woman and spoke to her *haltingly.* (8–9)

   _____

3. She was laughing a lot by then, telling about her life, *patting my knee,* answering questions. (22–24)

   _____

4. The *traveler from Argentina, the mom from California, the lovely woman from Laredo*—we were all covered with the same powdered sugar. (28–30)

   _____

5. *And smiling.* (30)

   _____

6. . . . two little girls . . . *were covered with powdered sugar too.* (32–33)

   _____

7. —by now *we were holding hands*—(33–34)

   _____

8. And I noticed . . . [she] *had a potted plant.* . . . (33–34)

   _____

EXERCISE 2

Naomi Shihab Nye also takes great care to use just the right word. Each of the two sentences below, from "Gate 4-A" is followed by a list of definitions. Circle the number of the definition(s) that best match the meaning of the italicized word in each sentence. Line numbers from the reading passage are in parentheses.

1. (4) Well—one *pauses* these days.

| **pause** (pôz) |
| v. **paused, paus·ing, paus·es** |
v. *intr.*
1. To cease or suspend an action temporarily.
2. To linger; tarry: *paused for a while under the huge oak tree.*
3. To hesitate: *He paused before replying.*

2. (28) It was like a *sacrament.*

| **sac·ra·ment** [sak-r*uh*-m*uh*nt] |
—noun
1. a sacred religious rite; the term in Christianity can refer to a ritual involving bread as a symbol of divine/sacred connection.
2. something regarded as possessing a sacred character or mysterious significance.
3. a sign, token, or symbol.
4. an oath; solemn pledge.

EXERCISE 3

At the center of this memoir is the issue of language. The significance of events comes from the language people are using. In each of the conversations listed below, indicate which language(s) the speaker was using. There is not necessarily a single correct response for each situation; be prepared to defend your choices.

1. Naomi Shihab Nye speaking to the older woman _____

2. The older woman speaking to her sons _____

3. Nye speaking with the sons _____

4. Nye speaking to the Palestinian poets _____

5. The older woman speaking to the Palestinian poets _____

6. Nye speaking to her father _____

7. The older woman speaking to Nye's father _____

Discussion/Composition

One could argue that the main idea of the essay is captured in the last sentence, "Not everything is lost." What does Nye mean? Your teacher may want you to discuss this with your classmates or write a short essay. Use examples from the Nye's memoir and from what you know of the contemporary world to explain your point of view.

Reading Selections 3A–3C
Globalization

Before You Begin

Have you been a tourist? Where did you go? How did you choose your destination(s)?

The article that follows, from a United Nations publication, reports predictions made at the turn of the twenty-first century about the globalization of tourism. See if you can predict some of the findings in this article.

1. Which country do you predict received the most visitors at the beginning of the 21st century? Which were the top 10 destinations?

2. Which country do you predict will receive the most visitors in 2020? Which do you predict will be among the top 10 tourist destinations in 2020?

3. Where do you think most tourists will come from in 2020?

Comprehension

Read "The Globalization of Tourism" quickly to see if your predictions are confirmed, and then answer the questions that follow. True/False items are indicated by a T / F preceding the statement.

1. T / F The purpose of the pair of bar graphs at the top of page 47 is to compare spending on tourism in different years.

2. T / F The purpose of the bar graphs at the bottom of page 47 is to show changes in where tourists will be traveling to in the future.

3. T / F Tourism was the world's leading industry when this article was written.

4. What does the author say is an effect of the Internet on tourism? _____

_____

5. According to the bar graphs, in what did the United States lead the world in 1998? _____

6. T / F The number of travelers to Europe is predicted to decline 45 percent by 2020.

7. Which continent both spends the most on tourism and earns the most from tourism?

_____

8. T / F Germany spends more on tourism than it earns from tourism.

9. T / F The United States is predicted to be the most popular tourist destination in 2020.

The globalization of tourism

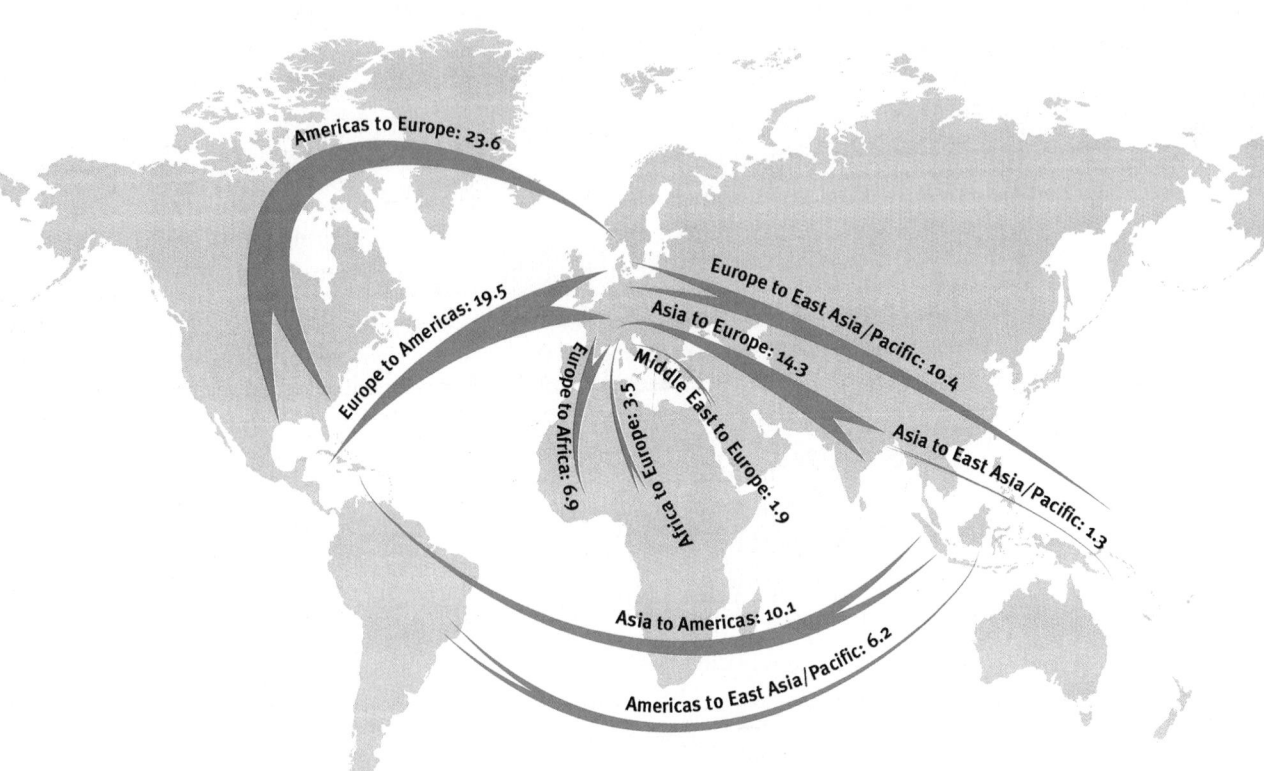

Americas to Europe: 23.6

Europe to Americas: 19.5

Europe to East Asia/Pacific: 10.4

Asia to Europe: 14.3

Europe to Africa: 6.9

Middle East to Europe: 3.5

Africa to Europe: 1.9

Asia to East Asia/Pacific: 1.3

Asia to Americas: 10.1

Americas to East Asia/Pacific: 6.2

Major intercontinental tourism flows (millions)

1997

2020

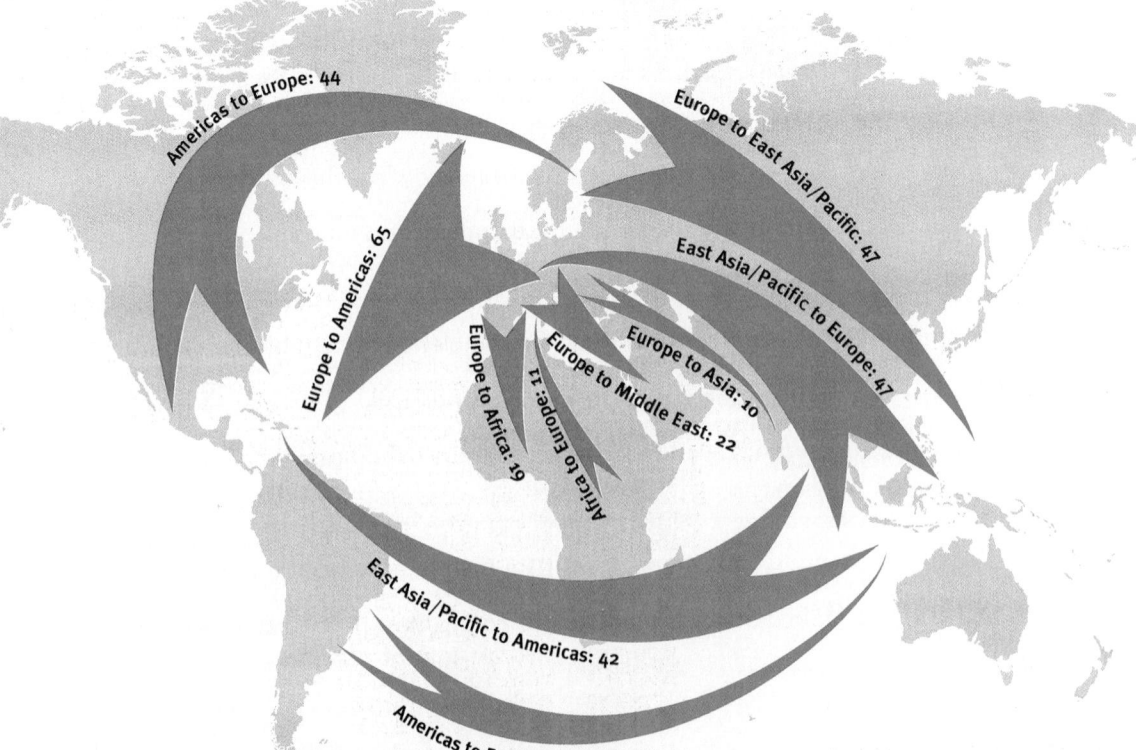

Americas to Europe: 44

Europe to East Asia/Pacific: 47

Europe to Americas: 65

East Asia/Pacific to Europe: 47

Europe to Asia: 10

Europe to Middle East: 22

Europe to Africa: 19

Africa to Europe: 11

East Asia/Pacific to Americas: 42

Americas to East Asia/Pacific: 20

Source: World Tourism Organiza

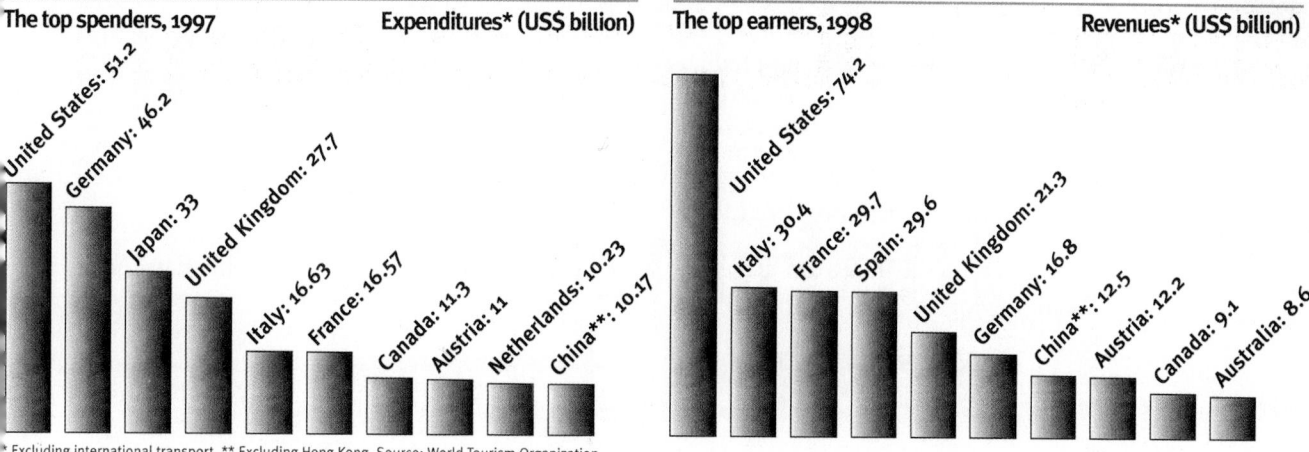

The top spenders, 1997 — Expenditures* (US$ billion)

United States: 51.2
Germany: 46.2
Japan: 33
United Kingdom: 27.7
Italy: 16.63
France: 16.57
Canada: 11.3
Austria: 11
Netherlands: 10.23
China**: 10.17

The top earners, 1998 — Revenues* (US$ billion)

United States: 74.2
Italy: 30.4
France: 29.7
Spain: 29.6
United Kingdom: 21.3
Germany: 16.8
China**: 12.5
Austria: 12.2
Canada: 9.1
Australia: 8.6

* Excluding international transport. ** Excluding Hong Kong. Source: World Tourism Organization

If the World Tourism Organization's forecasts are on target, international tourist arrivals will climb from the present 625 million a year to 1.6 billion in 2020. By this date, travellers will spend over US$2 trillion, (against US$44.5 billion in 1999), making tourism the world's leading industry.

(2) Electronic technology is facilitating this growth by offering access to fare and hotel information and online reservation services. Despite a modest annual growth rate (3.1%), Europe will remain, by far, the most popular destination (it can expect 717 million international arrivals in 2020, double the 1998 figure), though its market share will decline from 59 to 45%. Growth on the continent will be led by Central and Eastern European countries, where arrivals are expected to increase by 4.8% per year. At the same time, almost half the world's tourists will be coming from Europe. Given this dominance, it is not surprising to find that six European countries count among the top ten tourism earners and spenders. The United States holds first place in both categories.

(3) With a 7% per annum growth in international arrivals, the East Asia/Pacific region will overtake the Americas as the second most popular destination, holding a 27% market share in 2020 against 18% by the Americas. But the industry will also be doing its utmost to court the Asian traveller, since East Asia/Pacific is forecast to become the world's second most important generator of tourists, with a 7% annual growth rate, pushing the Americas into third position. China is expected to become the fourth largest source of tourists on the world market, while it was not even among the first twenty in 1999. Both arrivals to and departures from Africa (and especially Southern Africa), the Middle East and South Asia are expected to grow by about 5% per year.

(4) While France held its place as the top destination throughout the 1990s, it will be dethroned in the next decades, with China (excluding Hong Kong) expected to top the list by 2020 even though it was not even featured on it in 1998. Also making an entry into the top ten are the Russian Federation, Hong Kong, and the Czech Republic.

(5) Despite this growth forecast, tourism is and will remain the privilege of a few: WTO forecasts that only 7% of the world population will travel abroad by 2020.

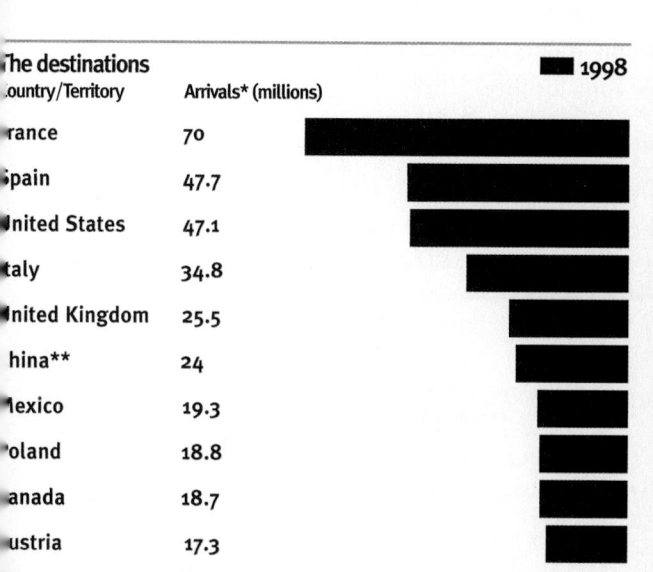

The destinations

Country/Territory	Arrivals* (millions) 1998
France	70
Spain	47.7
United States	47.1
Italy	34.8
United Kingdom	25.5
China**	24
Mexico	19.3
Poland	18.8
Canada	18.7
Austria	17.3

Country/Territory	Arrivals* (millions) 2020
China*	137.1
United States	102.4
France	93.3
Spain	71
Hong Kong, China**	59.3
Italy	52.9
United Kingdom	52.8
Mexico	48.9
Russian Fed.	47.1
Czech Rep.	44

*International, excluding same-day visitors. **Excluding Hong Kong.
Source: World Tourism Organization

*Excluding Hong Kong.**Hong Kong has been a Special Administrative Region of China since 1997.
Source: World Tourism Organization

10. What changes related to tourism are predicted for China by 2020? _____

_____

11. T / F   The arrows on the maps on page 46 show all international tourism in 1997 and all international tourism predicted for 2020.

12. T / F   According to the maps on page 46, fewer tourists from Asia will visit the East Asia/Pacific region in 2020 than visited in 1997.

Critical Reading

1. In what ways do world events (for example, economic cycles, international meetings, political unrest, or terrorist attacks) affect tourism? Are there predictions made in this article that you believe no longer hold true because of recent world events?

2. a. It is sometimes the case that the text and the graphics in technical reports aren't completely consistent. Below are two claims made in the text of "The Globalization of Tourism." Does the information in the bar graphs support these statements?

   • (Paragraph 3): "the East Asia/Pacific region will overtake the Americas as the second most popular destination."

   • (Paragraph 4): China was "expected to top the list [of tourist destinations] by 2020 even though it was not even featured on it in 1998."

   b. When you do research, if you are faced with a discrepancy (difference) in information between the text and graphics in an article, you will probably need to do further study. How might you find additional information that would make you more confident of the claims made in "The Globalization of Tourism"?

Discussion/Composition

1. From which areas do most tourists come to your home country or region? If you were developing an advertising brochure designed to encourage tourists to visit your home country or region, what kinds of information would you include? What physical and cultural sights should tourists be sure to see? What cultural and historical information would they need? Are there common things that you would want to explain to tourists? Would you mention these in your brochure? After discussing these issues, write a brochure to advertise your locality.

2. If tourism to your home country or region were to double in the next 20 years, would this be a good thing or a bad thing? Write a letter that could appear in a blog arguing your point of view.

The previous article, "The Globalization of Tourism," predicts that the number of people traveling the globe will increase dramatically. In fact, tourism is predicted to become the world's leading industry. The author of the next article, "The Politics of Travel," argues that this is a mixed blessing since tourism brings problems as well as profits.

Before You Begin

1. What are advantages to regions that become popular tourist attractions?

2. What are problems brought on by tourism?

3. Why do people become tourists? What are the attractions of travel?

Read "The Politics of Travel" to discover the author's perspective, and then answer the questions that follow. Do not be concerned if you don't know the meaning of every word. Your teacher may want you to do Vocabulary from Context Exercise 1 on pages 52–53 before you begin reading.

Comprehension

Indicate if each statement below is true (T) or false (F) according to your understanding of the author's point of view.

1. T / F   Tourism threatens the environment.

2. T / F   Taking a shower in the Himalayas can lead to global warming.

3. T / F   Taking an airplane contributes to climate change.

4. T / F   The "golf wars" took place between Iraq and Kuwait.

5. T / F   There is no good side to tourism.

6. T / F   If you kill a lion in Kenya, you can sell it for $7,000.

7. T / F   The author is disappointed that whale watching is now a bigger business than whaling.

8. T / F   The author believes that tourism can strengthen local culture.

9. T / F   Tourism changes tradition.

10. T / F   The author believes that by writing articles such as this he can persuade people to stop taking vacations.

11. T / F   Working holidays will not help the environment.

12. T / F   A major concern of the author is the environment.

Critical Reading

1. Why do you think the author talks about "consumers" instead of "tourists" in Paragraph 1?

2. Why do you think this article is titled "The Politics of Travel"? How is travel political?

Excerpt from THE POLITICS OF TRAVEL
by David Nicholson-Lord

(1) Tourism has seriously damaged fragile ecosytems like the Alps—the winter skiing playground of Europe—and the trekking areas of the Himalayas. Worldwide, it poses a serious threat to coastal habitats like dunes, mangrove forests and coral reefs. It fuels a booming and usually illegal trade in the products of threatened wildlife, from tortoiseshell and coral to ivory. Its "consumers" inevitably bring their habits and expectations with them—whether it's hot showers and flush toilets or well-watered greens for golfers. In the Himalayas, showers for trekkers often mean firewood, which means deforestation. In Hawaii and Barbados, it was found that each tourist used between six and ten times as much water and electricity as a local. In Goa, villagers forced to walk to wells for their water had to watch as a pipeline to a new luxury hotel was built through their land. Over the past decade golf, because of its appetite for land, water and herbicides, has emerged as one of the biggest culprits, so much so that "golf wars" have broken out in parts of Southeast Asia; campaigners in Japan, one of the chief exponents of golf tourism, have launched an annual World No Golf Day.

(2) This is not to say tourism can't do some good—but the cost-benefit equation is complex. Historic monuments, houses and gardens thrive on visitors. Throughout much of the world, but notably in southern and eastern Africa, tourism underpins the survival of wildlife. Why else would small farmers put up with elephants trampling their crops? Whale watching is now a bigger business than whaling. In the uplands of Rwanda, known to millions through the film *Gorillas in the Mist,* the mountain gorilla's salvation lies partly in the income and interest generated by tourists visiting in small groups. In Kenya a lion's worth is estimated at $7,000 a year in tourist income—for an elephant herd the figure is $610,000. And if large animals, with large ranges, are protected, then so are their habitats—the national parks.

(3) Yet none of these gains is unqualified. To get to see your whales and your gorillas, for example, you have to travel, by car, coach or plane. Each time you do so you're effectively setting fire to a small reservoir of gasoline—and releasing several roomfuls of carbon dioxide into the atmosphere. Transport is the world's fastest growing source of carbon dioxide emissions; leisure travel accounts for half of all transport. The cumulative result of such activity is one of the biggest disruptions in the Earth's history—global warming, climate change and rising seas.

(4) Some observers now argue that tourism can strengthen local cultures by encouraging an awareness of tradition and the ceremonies and festivals that go with it. But what's the value of tradition if it's kept alive self-consciously, for profit, and bears little relation to real life—which, today, across the world, grows ever more uniform? The pressures of tourism breed a phenomenon often referred to as "Disneyfication," in which culture and history are transformed, the authentic giving way to Disney-like replicas. What's undeniable is that tourism, in one way or another, changes tradition.

(5) In truth, there are no easy answers to the dilemmas posed by mass tourism. Awareness, certainly, is a step forward—the knowledge of what it means to be a tourist. With that comes the ability to make better choices, where and how and even whether to travel. An increasing number of nonprofit organizations offer working holidays, in which the economic and social asymmetries that lie at the heart of the holiday industry are somewhat redressed: The tourist takes but also gives. Among the best-known is the research organization Earthwatch.

 To read more about working holidays, see "Learning Holidays: A Thumbnail Guide," pages 57–58.

(6) Such initiatives are undoubtedly one of the ways forward for tourism. The world, clearly, is not going to stop taking holidays—but equally clearly we can no longer afford to ignore the consequences. And if one of the major culprits has been the industrialization of travel, a genuinely postindustrial tourism, with the emphasis on people and places rather than product and profits, could turn out to be significantly more planet-friendly.

David Nicholson-Lord, who lives in England, is former environment editor of The Independent on Sunday *and author of* The Greening of the Cities *(Routledge).*

Discussion/Composition

1. **Simulation.** You and your classmates are government officials in a nation that very much needs tourist money. However, the beautiful natural and cultural sights that bring tourists will also be threatened if too many people visit. You will have to develop a reasonable tourist policy.

   a. **Groups.** Form groups representing various government groups.
      - Ministry of the Treasury
        - This is the group that must worry about the financial state of the government.
      - Ministry of the Interior
        - This group protects natural and cultural sites.
      - Ministry of Education
        - This group needs money from tourism but also worries about the effects on the younger generation of so many visitors from other cultures.
      - Ministry of Transportation
        - On the one hand, this group hopes that tourist money will help fund new roads, but its members are worried that they can't build roads fast enough to accommodate large numbers of tourists.
      - Ministry of Health
        - This group, too, needs tourist money, but its members also worry that they don't have the resources to take care of tourist health needs.

   Your teacher may decide to have fewer groups, but you must have the final one:

      - Ministry of Tourism
        - This is the group that will be deciding on a final tourist policy for your country.

   b. **Statements.** In groups, prepare statements. First, brainstorm (additional) concerns and desires of your ministry. What do you want to see in the tourism policy? What do you want to avoid happening? Now work on preparing a two- to three-minute presentation to representatives from the Ministry of Tourism arguing for a specific tourist policy. You may use your time however you wish; you may have one speaker or more. The following are examples of issues you might want to address.

      - Why should/shouldn't your country encourage tourism?
      - Should there be unlimited tourism into your country? If not, how many tourists should you aim for?
      - Should there be a high cost for a tourist visa? Should there be no tourist visas required?
      - Should you focus your tourist advertising on certain countries?
      - Should some sites be closed to visitors all the time or during some periods of the year?
      - Should some sites limit the number of visitors?
      - Should you increase the cost of admission to cultural sites?
      - How will you protect your environment?
      - How should your tourist dollars be spent?

   During this time, the Ministry of Tourism will be meeting to decide what criteria it will be using to make decisions and to see if there are specific questions it would like to ask of the other ministries.

c. **Government hearings.** Sometimes when governments make policy, they hold public "hearings," at which groups make presentations and provide information in an effort to influence government policy. Each group will make its presentation to the Ministry of Tourism.

d. **Rebuttals.** Groups may have one minute to rebut (argue against) statements made by other ministries. Groups may then have one minute to respond to the rebuttals.

e. **Government policy.** The Ministry of Tourism will meet and deliver its policy.

f. **Written statements.** Your teacher may ask each group for a written statement. The Ministry of Tourism would present a tourism policy. The other ministries would present written statements arguing their positions.

2. In the Before You Begin section, you considered why people travel. The author addresses this question, too, in a longer version of this article. He argues that people travel to escape their lives. He quotes a Swiss academic, Jost Krippendorf, who believes that people travel because "they no longer feel happy where they are—where they work, where they live. They feel the monotony of the daily routine." The author says that "we need the unknown, what historians of religion call 'otherness,' to lend our lives significance." Do you think this is why people travel? Support your position orally or in writing by presenting reasons and examples.

3. Should you feel guilty when you travel? By and large, is travel a positive or a negative thing for travelers and the places they visit? After reading this article, will you make any different travel decisions?

Vocabulary from Context

EXERCISE 1

Both the ideas and the vocabulary in the following exercise are taken from "The Politics of Travel." Use the context provided to determine the meanings of the italicized words or phrases. Write a definition, synonym, or description of each of the italicized vocabulary items in the space provided.

1. _____

2. _____

3. _____

4. _____

5. _____

6. _____

To attract tourism to one's country was once thought of as an *unqualified* success; there seemed to be no negative aspects to it. However, today we are coming to realize that tourism is a mixed blessing: it has advantages and disadvantages. On the one hand, it can bring money to parts of the world that very much need it. People can earn a great deal through tourism. And this *income* can help to preserve the environment. Anything that helps to protect the *ecosystem,* the interrelated community of plants and animals that makes up the Earth, is, of course, positive.

A recent worry, however, is the fact that tourists can cause serious damage to the *fragile* environments they love to visit. Ecosystems are delicate and easily damaged. Around the world, areas are endangered by the large numbers of tourists who visit them. On every continent, tourism *threatens* the environment. Even *trekkers* who take difficult journeys on foot can cause damage.

7. _____

8. _____

9. _____

10. _____

11. _____

12. _____

13. _____

14. _____

15. _____

16. _____

17. _____

18. _____

19. _____

There are, then, serious dangers that come with the promise of tourism. Every advantage brings with it real disadvantages and vice versa. This *dilemma* makes planning difficult for nations trying to decide what to do. Countries can make a good deal more money from the tourist industry than they need to put into attracting tourists. This financial *profit* can help nations protect *habitats* where endangered animals (and plants) live.

These efforts can assure the *survival* of wildlife that otherwise would not continue to exist. It also may be that tourism can help strengthen local cultures by encouraging awareness of traditions and ceremonies. Historic buildings *thrive on* tourism. These cultural locations enjoy great success with the money and attention and respect brought by tourism.

But there is a downside to all this. Because cultural sites are becoming too crowded, Disneyland-like reproductions are being created. These are not *authentic* cultural sites but copies of something that may or may not have ever really existed. The author says, "what's the value of tradition if it's kept alive for profit, and bears little relation to real life?"

Taken together, the negative effects of tourism grow larger over time. The *cumulative* effects of tourism are great because every time we use cars or planes to travel we contribute to one of the greatest *disruptions* in the history of the planet: global warming and climate change are interrupting what has been the normal climate pattern for centuries.

As people understand the problems of tourism, some are beginning to organize against it through planned actions with particular goals. *Campaigns* in Japan have been *launched* against the sport of golf. Japan is one of the chief *exponents* of golf tourism. Because golf uses so much land and water, campaigners have introduced an annual World No Golf Day.

New approaches to the problem are also being developed. One *initiative* has been the development of tourist opportunities in which the tourists both give and receive through working and studying vacations. This kind of personal, small-scale tourism is meant to be a positive response to the kind of *industrialization* of tourism that has become typical with its large-scale organizing. Working tourism may not be for everyone, but the hope is that some kinds of travel can become more planet friendly.

EXERCISE 2

This exercise should be done after you have finished reading "The Politics of Travel." The exercise is designed to give you practice using context clues to guess the meaning of unfamiliar vocabulary. Give a definition, synonym, or description of each of the words below. The number in parentheses indicates the paragraph in which the word can be found. Your teacher may want you to do these orally or in writing.

1. (1) local _____

2. (1) culprits _____

3. (2) monuments _____

4. (2) notably _____

5. (2) trampling _____

6. (4) replicas _____

7. (4) awareness _____

8. (5) redressed _____

9. (6) postindustrial _____

Figurative Language and Idioms

In the paragraph indicated by the number in parentheses, find the word or phrase that best fits the meaning given. Your teacher may want to read these aloud as you quickly scan* the paragraph to find the answer.

1. (1) What phrase means *creates a significant danger?* _____

2. (1) What phrase means *hunger for; need for?* _____

3. (2) What phrase means *relation of advantages to disadvantages, of costs to benefits?* _____

4. (2) What phrase means *rescue/recovery/saving/survival depends on?* _____

5. (4) Which word means *create?* _____

---

*For an introduction to scanning, see Unit 1.

Stems and Affixes

The sentences below were adapted from "The Politics of Travel." Use your knowledge of stems and affixes*
and the context to guess the meanings of the italicized terms in the sentences below. Your teacher may want
you to do this orally or in writing.

1. In the Himalayas, showers for tourists often mean cutting down firewood to make warm water,
   which leads to *deforestation.* _____

2. Because of golf's appetite for land, water, and *herbicides,* people worried about the ecosystem have
   launched an annual World No Golf Day. _____

3. Because tourism brings in money, in southern and eastern Africa, tourism *underpins* the survival of
   wildlife. _____

   _____

4. Each time we travel by car, bus, or train, we're effectively setting fire to a small *reservoir* of gasoline.

   _____

5. Through the Disneyfication of culture, what we think of as "tradition" around the world can come
   to look more and more *uniform.* _____

6. Through Disneyfication, authentic culture and history are *transformed* into Disney-like replicas.

   _____

7. To give people better travel choices, *nonprofit* organizations offer working holidays that address the
   economic and social *asymmetries* that are characteristic of many tourist experiences.

   _____

   _____

---

*For a list of all stems and affixes taught in *Reader's Choice,* see the Appendix.

Dictionary Study

Many words have more than one meaning. When you use a dictionary to discover the meaning of an unfamiliar word or phrase, you need to use the context to determine which definition is appropriate. Use the portions of the dictionary provided to select the best definition for each of the italicized words below. Write the number of the definition in the space provided.

_____ 1. Tourism *fuels* a *booming* trade in buying and selling products made from threatened

_____ 2. wildlife, such as the illegal sale of ivory from elephants' tusks.

_____ 3. If large animals, with large *ranges,* are protected, then so are their habitats—the national parks.

fu·el (fyōō′əl) *n.* **1.** Something consumed to produce energy, esp.: **a.** A material such as coal, gas, or oil burned to produce heat or power. **b.** Fissionable material used in a nuclear reactor. **c.** Nutritive material metabolized by a living organism; food. **2.** Something that maintains or stimulates an activity or emotion. — *v.* **-eled, -el·ing, -els** also **-elled, -el·ling, -els.** — *tr.* **1.** To provide with fuel. **2.** To support or stimulate the activity or existence of. — *intr.* To take in fuel. [ME *feuel* < OFr. *feuaile* < VLat. **focália,* neut. pl. of **focális,* of the hearth < Lat. *focus,* hearth.] — **fu′el·er** *n.*

boom¹ (bōom) *v.* **boomed, boom·ing, booms.** — *intr.* **1.** To make a deep resonant sound. **2.** To grow or develop rapidly; flourish. — *tr.* **1.** To utter or give forth a boom. **2.** To cause to boom; boost. — *n.* **1.** A deep resonant sound, as of an explosion. **2.** A time of economic prosperity. **3.** A sudden increase. [ME *bomben,* imit. of a loud noise.]
boom² (bōom) *n.* **1.** *Naut.* A spar extending from a mast to hold or extend the foot of a sail. **2.** A long pole extending upward from the mast of a derrick to support or guide objects being lifted or suspended. **3.a.** A barrier composed of a chain of floating logs enclosing other free-floating logs. **b.** A floating barrier serving to contain an oil spill. **4.** A long movable arm used to support a microphone. **5.** A spar connecting the tail surfaces and the main structure of an airplane. [Du., tree, pole < MDu. See **bheuə-*.**]

range (rānj) *n.* **1.a.** Extent of perception, knowledge, experience, or ability. **b.** The area or sphere in which an activity takes place. **c.** The full extent covered: *the range of possibilities.* **2.a.** An amount or extent of variation. **b.** *Mus.* The gamut of tones that a voice or an instrument is capable of producing. **3.a.** The maximum extent or distance limiting operation, action, or effectiveness, as of an aircraft or a sound. **b.** The maximum distance that can be covered by a vehicle with a specified payload before its fuel supply is exhausted. **c.** The distance between a projectile weapon and its target. **4.** A place equipped for practice in shooting at targets. **5.** *Aerospace.* A testing area for rockets and missiles. **6.** An extensive area of open land for livestock. **7.** The geographic region in which a plant or an animal normally lives or grows. **8.** The act of wandering or roaming over a large area. **9.** *Math.* The set of all values a given function may take on. **10.** *Statistics.* The difference or interval between the smallest and largest values in a frequency distribution. **11.** A class, a rank, or an order. **12.** An extended group or series, esp. a row or chain of mountains. **13.** One of a series of double-faced bookcases in a library stack room. **14.** A north-south strip of townships, each six miles square, numbered east and west from a specified meridian in a U.S. public land survey. **15.** A stove with spaces for cooking a number of things at the same time. — *v.* **ranged, rang·ing, rang·es.** — *tr.* **1.** To arrange or dispose in a particular order, esp. in rows or lines. **2.** To assign to a particular category; classify. **3.** To align (a gun, for example) with a target. **4.a.** To determine the distance of (a target). **b.** To be capable of reaching (a maximum distance). **5.** To pass over or through (an area or a region). **6.** To turn (livestock) onto an extensive area of open land for grazing. **7.** *Naut.* To uncoil (a line or rode) along the deck so that it will pay out smoothly. — *intr.* **1.** To vary within specified limits. **2.** To extend in a particular direction. **3.** To extend or lie in the same direction. **4.** To pass over or through an area or a region in or as if in exploration. See Syns at **wander. 5.** To wander freely; roam. **6.** To live or grow within a particular region. [ME, row, rank < OFr. < *rangier,* to put in a row < *rang, reng,* line, of Gmc. orig. See **sker-²*.**]

In the previous selection, "The Politics of Travel," the author suggests that working holidays are more planet friendly than typical tourism. If you were trying to locate such trips, you might try guides such as the one below and on page 58. "Learning Holidays: A Thumbnail Guide" includes a variety of options. Skim* the guide first to get a general sense of its contents. Then do the Comprehension exercise that follows.

Learning holidays: a thumbnail guide

Garry Marchant

People wanting to spend their vacations in pursuit of culture have a fairly wide choice of options that go beyond mere sightseeing. Numerous companies organize tours for lovers of architecture or art. Those who don't mind roughing it can do volunteer project work, join archaeological digs or help with cultural studies. Though not an endorsement of any tour organization or programme, the following sample includes just a few of the many options available.

ART AND ARCHITECTURE

• Instituto per l'Arte e il Restauro Palazzo Spinelli offers throughout the summer two- to four-week courses on Italian art including fresco, painting, ceramics, stone, archaeological, paper, glass, carpet, textile and wood restoration; study of the antique trade; drawing and painting; graphic design; computer graphics; interior design; garden design and planning; and Italian language. **www.spinelli.It**

• The Instituto Allende in San Miguel de Allende, Mexico, has short-term courses in painting, silver work, drawing, lithography and etching, silk screening, ceramics, multi-media sculpture, traditional Mexican weaving, Mexican art history, Spanish language classes and iron sculpture. **www.instituto-allende.edu**

• Wisconsin, USA-based Living Adventure brings together Mayan, Mexican, and American artists to teach painting, batik making, ceramics, and photography from their respective cultures. Week-long courses take place on Mexico's Caribbean coast and the Yucatan Peninsula, homeland of the ancient Maya. **www.livingadventure.com**

• Sua Bali offers two-week and longer courses in batik painting, local music,

cookery, herbal medicine and the Indonesian language. Classes take place at a mini-resort of seven traditional guest houses in a rural setting south of the village of Ubud, renowned for its painting. **http://suabali.com**

ARCHAEOLOGICAL SITE WORK

• There are numerous opportunities to take part in archaeological digs. For example, every spring, *Current Archaeology* magazine publishes the Directory of British Archaeology, listing more than 700 societies, universities, and professional units. A small number of these open their archaeological fieldwork to outsiders on weekends, or for several weeks in the summer. **www.archaeology.co.uk**

• In the Sonoran Desert in Arizona, USA, adventure travelers spend ten days in an archaeological immersion program. It combines hands-on field archaeology with lectures on archaeological and historical topics related to the native peoples of the region. **www.archaeologicaladventures.com**

• In Peru, volunteers help excavate Cotocotuyoc, an ancient settlement of the Wari (540–900 ACE). For two weeks, they work with professional staff to excavate, screen, wash, and sort arti-

facts of this pre-Hispanic civilization in the Andes. **(See Earthwatch entry under Further Information.)**

• Amateur archaeologists learn about native cultures of the southwest USA while helping to preserve these ancient lands. Small groups of participants, led by a professional archaeologist, assist in mapping land and in identifying and recording artifacts. **www.archaeologicaladventures.com**

CULTURE

• Educational programmes relating to a specific culture can often be found through a country's official tourism board. (**www.towd.com** has the address of every tourist board in the world, along with all of their branches.)

LANGUAGE

• A language stay of two or three weeks arranged through Eurocentres combines a summer holiday with serious language learning, for adults, ages 16 and over. Students stay with a host family and participate in sports, culture, and other entertainment. They can learn Japanese in Kanazawa, on Honshu, Japan's main island, French in Paris, Amboise, La Rochelle and Lausanne, Russian at the Moscow Linguistic University, and Italian

*For an introduction to skimming, see Unit 1.

in the Scuola Leonardo da Vinci, Siena. English schools in North America are in Washington, DC; New York; East Lansing, Michigan; San Diego, California; Toronto, Ontario; and Vancouver, British Columbia. **www.eurocentres.com**

LIVING IN

• Asian Overland Services operates a five-day tropical adventure tour in various parts of Malaysia. Students live with local tribes to learn how indigenous people hunt, trap, fish and gather edible plants and medicinal herbs. Aborigines give practical lessons on how to build shelters and make traps. **www.asiaoverland.com.my**
• Wind, Sand & Stars, a British tour company, runs eight-day camel treks through the Sinai desert in which tourists travel and live with local Bedouin. Also eight-day Biblical tours. **www.windsandstars.co.uk**

MUSIC

• Senior citizens who love to sing spend five days in a lake-side Wisconsin resort community learning and practicing a variety of Broadway musical show tunes. A performance for a live audience caps off this musical holiday. **www.elderhostel.org**

FURTHER INFORMATION

• US-based Earthwatch Institute funds scientific research by charging members of the public, aged 16-85, to help on some 130 projects worldwide. Many projects are based on cultural themes, including, for example, documenting Africa's musical traditions and excavating Mayan ruins. Teams are small and no previous research skills are required. Participants pay their air fare to the site, room and board and a fee to join the project. **www.earthwatch.org**
• The Specialty Travel Guide lists tour operators around the world offering a variety of commercial special interest tours and courses–although these can be expensive. **www.infohub.com**
• Tourism Concern, a London, UK-based NGO which campaigns for responsible tourism, lists travel agents around the world offering home stays and opportunities of "real human exchange." **www.tourismconcern.org.uk**

Comprehension

Answer the following questions. Your teacher may want you to answer the questions orally, in writing, or by underlining parts of the text. True/False items are indicated by a T / F preceding the statement. Some questions may have more than one right answer.

1. T / F This magazine recommends these particular tours and programs.

2. T / F You can get college credit for taking courses offered in these learning holidays.

3. If you wanted to take courses on your vacation to learn Italian, which two holidays listed might interest you? _____

4. T / F If you wanted to spend your vacation relaxing in a warm, faraway location, you would probably like the "Living In" tours.

5. How would you describe the types of holidays that are listed under the heading "Living In"? Would you enjoy them? _____

6. T / F If you wanted to watch a musical on Broadway, you could do that on the Music tour.

7. If you were interested in the culture of the native tribes of the Americas, name two holidays that might interest you. _____

8. If you wanted to live with local people instead of just with other tourists, which holidays listed might interest you? _____

9. T / F You should be an experienced archaeologist to sign up for one of the archaeology holidays.

10. In which section would you look to find out about other learning holidays and special interest tours that are not described in this article? _____

11. Which of these trips is most interesting to you? Why? Which one would be your least favorite? Why? _____

Nonprose Reading
Newspaper Advertisements

Classified advertisements, or "want ads," like the ones on pages 60–61 appear in most print newspapers and on their websites.

Before You Begin

1. Have you ever tried to use this kind of advertisement? For what purpose(s)?

2. In what ways does the writing differ from normal prose writing?*

The ads on pages 60–61 come from a university newspaper called *The Daily*. If you were living in this community, you might use the ads in this newspaper to find a job or to rent an apartment.

Overview

Skim the classified ads on pages 60–61 to get a general layout of the pages. Then scan for the answers to the following questions.** Your teacher may want to read these aloud as you scan for the answers.

1. If you needed to earn money, under which section(s) would you look?

2. If you were looking for an apartment, under which sections(s) would you look?

3. If you were looking for someone to share housing with, under which section(s) would you look?

   _____

4. If you were willing to pay to have a parking place close to campus, under which section would you

   look? _____

5. Where would you look for jobs that prepare you for professional positions? _____

   _____

*For an explanation of nonprose reading, see Unit 1.
**For an introduction to skimming and scanning, see Unit 1.

CLASSIFIED ADS

Help Wanted

PART-TIME PIZZA DELIVERY driver, base pay + tips. Our vehicle. Must be over 26 for insurance purposes. Dellino's Pizzeria, University Village, 555-3466.

PART-TIME RECEPTIONIST. PRESTIGIOUS real estate firm seeks customer service oriented receptionist for 20-30 hours per week and occasional weekends. FAX resume to (206)555-0368 or call Lisa at (206)555-5462.

PART-TIME WORK = FULL-TIME PAY
The Seattle Times newspaper is currently hiring people to sell subscriptions door-to-door. No experience is necessary; top-notch training is provided. Qualified applicants must be enthusiastic, outgoing, and at least 16 years of age. College students encouraged. Call the office nearest you today.
Lynnwood: (425)555-7822
Seattle area: (206)555-6247
Eastside: (425)555-3411
$$$$$$$$$$$$$$$$$

RESTAURANT–SUMMER JOB in Alaska! Experienced, presentable waitresses and cooks needed for busy restaurant in Valdez, Alaska. Fax resume/application to 907-555-2877, att: Mike.

SAT TUTORS NEEDED! SCORE! Prep is currently hiring for positions starting in June, August and September. Make your own schedule, reliable transportation required. Graduate students preferred. $15-$25/hour. Call 800-555-7182 for more information.

SECURITY OFFICERS
WANTED
-IMMEDIATE OPENINGS-
Full-time/Part-time
Seattle and Bellevue Sites
$10.50/Hour Minimum
Plus Benefits &
Tuition Reimbursement Plan
$12.00/Hour
in 6 months
Check the Competition
Then See us
We Value our Employees!
Guaranteed Interviews
8am-4pm Monday-Friday
Other Times By Appointment
Uniforms and Training Provided
We promote from within!
NORTHWEST SECURITY SERVICES
555-8142

SMART, ENERGETIC, CREATIVE help needed for daycare. Part-time/full-time positions available, $10/hour. Paid vacations. 206-555-1767.

SUMMER JOB IN Seattle! $10-$14/hour. Work outside & get a tan! Hard work = good pay. Jon 555-0432.

SUMMER JOBS
FOOD PROCESSING:
DARK SWEET CHERRIES. SEASON APPROXIMATELY JUNE 22ND TO AUGUST 5TH FULL-TIME POSITIONS. DAY AND NIGHT SHIFT. PAY SCALE $7 TO $10 per hour, plus Season bonus.
Call Penny Wykes (206)555-1730
Georgetown area of Seattle
Tree Fruit Packers, Inc.

TEACHER AND ASSISTANT positions open in early childhood program. Downtown and UW locations. Beautiful environments. Great staff. Ed Psych or Sociology students or graduates preferred. For interview call (206)555-6878 or (206)555-9850.

TEACHER/TUTORS. ESL Secondary English/ Math part-time, summer full-time. 425-555-0120.

TELEMARKETER/APPOINTMENT SETTER. $12/hour, part-time. No experience necessary. 800-555-5198.

TREKLEADER
Lead small groups of world travelers on adventure camping tours during the summer in the USA, Canada, Alaska, Mexico, Belize, and Hawaii. Must be available until mid-September. Please call 800-555-8735.

WANTED! PART-TIME TELEMARKETER. Make up to $14/hour setting up appointments. Monday-Thursday evenings. Call from office or home. Call 253-555-1200.

WASHINGTON ATHLETIC CLUB, a private hotel and athletic club in downtown Seattle, has openings for part-time lifeguards and swim instructors. Please call Stuart at 206-555-3067.

Help Wanted Over 21

EVENING CASHIER OVER 21. Part-time, good pay, some benefits. Apply Northlake Tavern and Pizza House, 660 NE Northlake Way between 2:00-4:00 pm, Monday-Thursday.

FOOD SERVER FULL- OR PART-TIME. OVER 21. EXPERIENCE PREFERRED, BUT NOT NECESSARY. APPLY NORTHLAKE PIZZA, 660 NE NORTHLAKE WAY BETWEEN 2-4 PM, MONDAY-THURSDAY.

VALET PARKING POSITION. Perfect student part-time job. Evenings and weekends. Good driving record. Must be 21 or older. Excellent pay. Call (206)555-3754, leave message.

Business Opportunities

The Daily makes every effort to ensure you are responding to a reputable and legitimate job opportunity. REMEMBER: Legitimate employers do not ask for money as part of the application process. Do not send money, especially out of state, or give any credit card information. The majority of our Business Opportunities are at least in part commission-based, as well as multi-level marketing and self-employment opportunities. A small investment MAY be required, and you may be asked to work from your home. If you have responded to an ad that seems deceptive, please call the Daily at 555-2390.

#1 HOME-BASED BUSINESS
Famous Millionaire Maker Reveals
How to Earn Multiple Streams of $$$.
For Info + Free Tape Call
877-555-8948

EARN NEW COMPUTER and make money at the same time. $2800 in your first two weeks with unlimited income potential. This offer is going fast. Call and get the facts. 800-555-9758.

US GOVERNMENT JOBS hiring now all levels. Paid training, benefits. $14-$35/hour. Call free, 800-555-1680, ext. 801.

Internships

STUDENT INTERN - Summer intern position in DNA Sequencing department for Eastside biotech. Responsibilities include various duties in sequencing lab. Requires undergrad molecular biology experience and experience using micropipetor. $10-$12/hr DOE. For more info call Holly at 425-555-8140.

VOLUNTEER INTERNSHIP IN CRIMINAL DEFENSE INVESTIGATION with King County Public Defender. Training and supervision provided. 20 hour per week commitment required. June 9th deadline for applications. Training begins June 21st. Call 555-3900, ext. 692 for application packet.

Child Care

BABYSITTER WANTED: CARING and responsible babysitter for adorable good natured 21 month old boy. 15 hours/week. Days/times negotiable. Experience preferred. 555-1293

CHILD CARE NEEDED during summer in Wallingford for three great children: 6, 10, 13. 25-30 hours/ week, Monday, Wednesday, Friday. $10/hour. Begins 6/28. Own car/references required. (206) 555-2375.

LAURELHURST FAMILY SEEKS Nanny/ Mother's Helper approximately 25 hours/ week in non-smoking home. Great opportunity for student taking time off, 1 or 2 classes, or recent grad. Some flexibility with days/times. Must be fun, loving, energetic, reliable, and swimmer with references. Competitive wages and fun travel opportunities. Need reliable car and WSDL. No full-time students or bring-along children. Approximate start date: 8/1. Please call 555-7355.

NANNY/ MOTHER'S HELPER needed immediately for Eastside family. Full time/live-out. 2 boys. Experience and references necessary. Must have own car. One year commitment. Benefits, vacation negotiable. Great pay, great family.

SEATTLE ATHLETIC CLUB/Northgate Childcare is looking for a part-time helper. Monday-Friday, and occasional Saturdays. Fun atmosphere with membership benefits. Salary DOE. Call (206)555-7664 for information.

Volunteers

INTERESTED IN A HEALTH CARE CAREER, BUT DON'T KNOW WHERE TO START? TRY VOLUNTEERING! VOLUNTEER OPPORTUNITIES AVAILABLE ON CAMPUS AT UNIVERSITY OF WASHINGTON MEDICAL CENTER. CALL 555-4218.

Tutoring

HIGH-SCHOOL FRESHMAN NEEDS math tutoring in advanced trigonometry/algebra. Math major and teaching experience required. 555-1471 (evenings).

Rooms

$600, NEW BUILDING. Studio room with private full bath, fridge, intercom and built-ins. Quiet building. No smoking, no musical instruments or pets. (206)555-6608.

1-1/2 BLOCKS TO UW—Clean, quiet, non-smoking room, private refrigerator. Month to month agreement. $500 includes all utilities. Also, daylight basement room, $450.
555-2488

1/2 BLOCK TO UW
HUSKY COURT
Newer Building
Rooms with private bath
555-5544

BRAND NEW BUILDING close to UW. Furnished rooms with private baths and deck. Starting at $600. 5608 15th Ave. NE (206)555-1435.

CLEAN SPACIOUS 2 bed/1 bath house, large deck, w/d in Ballard. $600/month + utilities (about $50) deposit needed. Nice neighborhood near Golden Gardens. Roommate is male 20 yr. Student/waiter/outdoors person.
Call 555-8346

FROM $300 - $350. Rooms, 1-1/2 blocks north of UW. Clean and quiet, studious residence. No smoking, no musical instruments. (206) 555-6608.

LARGE BEDROOM, FURNISHED, phone. Shared kitchen, etc. Nice family home, safe neighborhood, two miles to campus, near bus. Seeking mature female student, non-smoking. $400 plus utilities. (206) 555-9754.

TWO BEDROOMS AVAILABLE in ten bedroom house. June 10th - August 31st. Free laundry, cool roommates. 52nd/16th. Call for details! 555-8065.

Furnished Apartments

STUDIO APARTMENTS AVAILABLE starting June 10th-20th, walking distance to campus, washer/dryer on site. $700/month. Call Monika (425)-555-8330, ext. 434.

WALK TO UW. Attractive, fully furnished apartment. Kitchenware, linens. All utilities. Studio $900. 1 bedroom $1200. 2 bedroom $1300. 1 month minimum possible. Call 555-9009, cell 555-2544.

Unfurnished Houses

2 HOUSES: 4 rooms, 1 bath or 5 rooms, 1 bath. Both with washer, dryer. Walk to UW. $1600 or $1800. 425-555-3788, 6-9 pm.

Duplex - Newly Remodeled for FALL!!
2 BLOCKS FROM CAMPUS!!
Available September 9th

7 bedrooms, 2 bath, large, $3000/month

3 bedrooms, 1 bath, large, $1500/month

OPEN HOUSE- 4728 18th Avenue NE, Sunday, May 23rd, 1:30-3:30 pm. (206)555-0358.

HEY DORMIES! Get a real house, one left– 9+ Bedrooms, near UW. (206)555-5306.

Parking

COVERED PARKING. CLOSE TO UW, Secure garage, $80 per month, 5608 15th AVE. NE, 206-555-1435.

PARKING NEAR UW. 3 locations, $75/ month. Secured Garage, $100/month. (206) 555-2944.

Shared Housing

FEMALE ROOMMATE WANTED for coed housing. Large room on bus route. Ravenna $600. 555-5411.

FEMALE ROOMMATE WANTED to share 3 bedroom U-District house with two females for summer, $450, utilities included. 555-7293.

SHARE 3 BEDROOM apartment with easygoing guy, 6/15 (negotiable) through 8/31. $500/ month. 555-8661.

Unfurnished Apartments

**SUMMER RENTALS
ONE STOP SHOPPING!**

Locations on 8th
1 Bedroom 1 bath $650
1 Bedroom w/den $750
2 Bedroom 1 bath $775
3 Bedroom 1 bath $900
4 Bedroom 1 bath $1100
Call managers at
555-8885, 555-6899 and 555-4824.

Locations on 12th
1 Bedroom w/den $780
2 Bedroom 1 bath $825
2 Bedroom 2 bath $875
3 Bedroom 1 bath $1050
4 Bedroom 2 bath $1150

Call managers at
555-1320, 555-0832, and 555-0424.

Guaranteed lowest prices or we'll match. Newer units, well-managed, secured entrances, parking, decks, skylights, microwaves and dishwashers. No smoking and no pets. Apartments available mid June.
Customer Service Line 555-0424

0 BLOCKS TO UW
OPEN HOUSE, 1:00-5:00 pm every day, 2-bedroom, $950-$1100; 3-bedroom, $1200-$1500; Washington Square Apartments, 4504 16th NE, A101-Office. Also showing Brooklyn Plaza Apartments, 4106 Brooklyn, by appointment only after May 10, 1:00-5:00pm. (206)555-2829, 555-9988.

APARTMENTS FOR RENT fall and sublease this summer. 1, 3, 5 and 6 bedroom units located at 4233 7th Ave NE. Mondays and Wednesdays 2-6pm and Saturdays 1-4pm. Phone 555-5240 or 555-7613. Leave message if no answer.

LAKE CITY, HIGH-end apartment. Washer/dryer, New, security. 2-bedroom, 2-bath: $900. 2-bedroom, 1-bath: $1000. Studio: $600. 11038 Lake City Way NE. 555-6495.

ONE AND TWO bedroom apartments. Walk to campus. Very spacious, lots of light. Very quiet. 555-0810.

WALK TO UW. 2-bedroom, $1000; 5-bedroom/ 2-bath, $2000. Intercom, modern kitchen, laundry, on-site manager, rooftop deck. Garage parking available. (206)555-2974.

Comprehension

Now that you have a general sense of the layout of the ads, scan for the answers to the following questions. True/False items are indicated by a T / F preceding the statement. <u>Note</u>: Because there are so many ads, just put the number of the question that you are answering next to appropriate ads.

1. If you were looking for a job and liked to teach adolescents and adults, find three job ads you could answer.

2. If you wanted to work with young children but didn't want to work in someone's home, find three ads you could answer.

3. If you were looking for a job only for the summer, which ad(s) would you answer? We found six ads. Which three look interesting to you?

4. Which ad(s) could you answer if you had good telephone skills?

5. Do you have the qualifications necessary to apply for the valet job? Do you have to be a perfect student? _____

6. T / F   *The Daily* ensures that the companies who advertise in the Business Opportunities section are lawful and trustworthy businesses.

7. If you were interested in a health care career and needed to earn money this summer, would you answer the ad for health care volunteers?

8. T / F   The student intern position in DNA is a volunteer position.

9. T / F   If you are a smoker, you probably shouldn't apply for the Laurelhurst nanny job.

10. If you're looking for a place to live and are allergic to cigarette smoke, circle two ads you would answer.

11. If you like a quiet environment, would you answer the Two Bedrooms Available ad? _____

12. Which apartment is closest to UW?

13. Your sister is moving to town and wants to share housing for less than $400 per month. Which ads would you tell her about?

14. If you have access to the Internet, can you read *Daily* ads online? _____

Critical Reading

1. If you needed a new computer, would you answer Earn New Computer in the Business Opportunities section? Why or why not?

2. Under Business Opportunities what do you think is the opportunity offered by the famous millionaire maker? Would you answer this ad? Why or why not?

3. If you are familiar with Mexico but have no camping experience, would you answer the Trekleader ad?

4. Are there any job ads that you would want to answer?

Web Work

If you have access to the Internet, you can also check classified ads online. On page 64 you will find an index for the online classified ads for *The Daily*. (Note: If an online classified ad page is updated daily, the index will also change daily.)

1. Which numbers would you click on to look for apartments?

2. Which number would you click on to find someone to type your school papers?

3. What kinds of ads are found under the "personals"? Why might you need to be cautious about meeting someone this way?

4. You want to submit an ad for the Online *Daily*.

   a. How much will it cost to run a 10-word ad for three days?

   b. Can you get a refund if you don't want to run the ad for the full three days?

   c. What day will your ad appear if you submit it electronically at 2:00 PM on Thursday?

5. You need a roommate to share your apartment close to campus. Write a 10-word ad in the box labeled Enter Your Ad.

Classifieds updated daily

Submit a Classified Ad

- RATE: 20¢ per word, $4.00 minimum. Pay for four days, get the fifth day free.
- DEADLINE: 2:00 pm the weekday before publication. 12:00 noon the day before publication for ads sent via e-mail.
- NO REFUNDS for cancellation once ad has begun.
- NO CHANGES in ad text once ad has begun.
- The Daily must be notified of errors before 2:00 pm on the first day of publication. The Daily is not responsible for errors past the first day.
- Before your ad appears in the Daily you must arrange payment. Please CONTACT:

The Daily Classified Advertising
144 Communications
PO Box 353720
Seattle, WA 98195
(206) 543-2335
E-mail: dailycls@u.washington.edu

Enter your Ad:

Classified Ads

040 Announcements
050 Special Notices
080 Adoptions
090 Personals
100 Automobiles For Sale
110 Motorcycles
150 Automotive Repair
270 Entertainment
360 Typing/Word Processing
400 Work-Study
410 Help Wanted
420 Help Wanted Over 18
440 Business Opportunities
450 Volunteers
460 Internships
530 Child Care
620 Music
630 Tutoring
720 Garage/Yard Sales
770 Sporting Goods/Supplies
800 Miscellaneous For Sale
810 Rooms
835 Furnished Apartments
840 Unfurnished Houses
845 Unfurnished Apartments
850 Parking
900 Shared Housing
910 Housesitting
920 Homes For Sale

Articles
Front Page
Arts/Entertainment
Newsroom Specials
Features
News
Opinion
Sports

Web Features
Campus Calendar
Classifieds
Comics
Online Articles
Intramural Sports
Slate.com
Soundboard / Radio

Services
Advertising
Business Directory
Career Directory
Contact Us
Archives

Recent Issues:

Word Study
Stems and Affixes

Below is a list of some commonly occurring stems and affixes.* Study their meanings and then do the exercises that follow. Your teacher may ask you to give examples of other words you know that are derived from these stems and affixes.

Prefixes

ante-	before	*anterior, ante meridiem (AM)*
circum-	around	*circumference*
contra-, anti-	against	*anti-war, contrast*
inter-	between	*international, intervene*
intro-, intra-	within	*introduce, intravenous*
post-,	after	*post-game, post-graduate*
sub-, suc-, suf-, sug-, sup-, sus-	under	*subway, support*
super-	above, greater, better	*superior, supermarket*
trans-	across	*trans-Atlantic, transportation*

Stems

-ced-	go, move, yield	*precede*
-duc-	lead	*introduce*
-flect-	bend	*reflect, flexible*
-mit-, -miss-	send	*remit, missionary*
-pon-, -pos-	put, place	*postpone, position*
-port-	carry	*portable*
-sequ-, -secut-	follow	*consequence, consecutive*
-spir-	breathe	*inspiration, conspiracy*
-tele-	far	*telegraph, telephone*
-ven-, -vene-	come	*convene, convention*
-voc-, -vok-	call	*vocal, revoke*

Suffixes

-able-, ible-, -ble	capable of, fit for	*trainable, defensible*
-ous, -ious, -ose	full of, having the qualities of	*poisonous, anxious, verbose*

---

*For a list of all stems and affixes taught in *Reader's Choice*, see the Appendix.

EXERCISE 1

For each item, select the best definition of the italicized word or phrase or answer the question.

1. The first thing Jim did when he arrived at the airport was look for a *porter.*

   _____ a. person who sells tickets   __✓__ c. person who carries luggage

   _____ b. taxi cab   _____ d. door to the luggage room

2. No matter what Fred said, Noam *contradicted him.*

   __✓__ a. said the opposite   _____ c. laughed at him

   _____ b. yelled at him   _____ d. didn't listen to him

3. The doctor is a specialist in the human *respiratory* system. She is an expert on _____.

   _____ a. bones.   _____ c. nerves.

   __✓__ b. lungs.   _____ d. the stomach.

4. He *circumvented* the problem.

   _____ a. described   __✓__ c. went around, avoided

   _____ b. solved   _____ d. wrote down, copied

5. Which is a postscript?

   _____ a.

   _____ b.

   __✓__ c.

   _____ d.

   Dear J,
   ─ ─ ─ ─
   ─ ─ ─ ─
   Sincerely,
   P.
   P.S. ─ ─ ─ ─

   Mr. John Smith
   ─ ─ ─ ─
   ─ ─ ─
   ─ ·─

6. Use what you know about stems and affixes to explain how the following words were derived.

   a. telephone __it comes from far away sound__

   b. telegram __it came from far away text message__

   c. television __it comes from far away picture__

7. When would a photographer use a telephoto lens for her camera? __when the photograph want to take far away picture__

8. Use word analysis to explain what *support* means. __Sup means under, and port means carry__

9. What is the difference between interstate commerce and intrastate commerce? _____
   The first one means business between diffrent states, while the second one only one state

10. At one time, many European towns depended on the system of aqueducts built by the Romans
    for their water supply. What is an aqueduct? *Something built to transfer water from one point to the another point*

11. If a person has a *receding* hairline, what does he look like? *he is going balt*

    _____

12. The abbreviation *AM* (as in 10:30 AM) stands for *ante meridiem*. What do you think *PM* (as in
    10:30 PM) stands for? *post meridiem*

    _____

13. Consider these sentences.

    a. She *subscribes* to *Time* magazine.

    b. She *subscribes* to the theory that the moon is made of green cheese.

    Explain how these meanings of *subscribe* developed from the meanings of *sub* and *scribe*.
    Sub means under, scribe means write.

    _____

    _____

    _____

    _____

EXERCISE 2

Word analysis can help you to guess the meanings of unfamiliar words. Using context clues and what you know about word parts, write a synonym, description, or definition of the italicized word or phrase.

1. _against_ — Despite evidence *to the contrary*, Mark really believes that he can pass an exam without studying.

2. _dely_ — I haven't finished the report you asked for yet; let's *postpone* our meeting until next Tuesday.

3. _boss_ — Ask your *supervisor* if you can take your vacation next month.

4. _resend_ — Please *remit* your payment in the enclosed envelope.

5. _over letters_ — Something must be wrong with this machine. It doesn't always type *superscripts* correctly: $\overset{2}{x}$ $x2$ $\underset{2}{x}$ x^2

6. _somp_ — *Antibiotics,* such as penicillin, help the body fight bacterial but not viral infections.

7. _carry_ — Nowadays, very little mail is *transported* by train.

8. _too bad_ — Don't invite Frank again; his behavior tonight was *inexcusable*.

9. _actions between_ many people — Scientists study the *interaction* between parents and their babies to better understand how infants learn.

10. _sent_ — After the plane crash, the pilot had to fix his radio before he could *transmit* his location.

11. _remeet_ — The committee decided to stop working at noon and to *reconvene* at 1:30.

12. _recall_ — The state of Texas *revoked* his driver's license because he had had too many accidents.

13. _able to bend_ — This material is very useful because it is strong yet *flexible*.

14. _not heavy_ — Barbara wanted to buy a *portable* DVD player.

15. _sail around_ — The Portuguese sailor Magellan set out to *circumnavigate* the world.

16. _placed upon_ — The king *imposed* a heavy tax on his people to pay for his foreign wars.

EXERCISE 3

Following is a list of words containing some of the stems and affixes introduced in this unit and the previous one. Definitions of these words appear on the right. Put the letter of the appropriate definition next to each word.

1. __b__ *anteroom*

2. __d__ *antecedent*

3. __a__ *vociferous*

4. __c__ *vocation*

5. __e__ *subsequent*

6. __h__ *subscript*

7. __i__ *superscript*

8. __k__ *intervene*

9. __f__ *introspection*

10. __j__ *convene*

11. __l__ *consequence*

a. characterized by a noisy outcry or shouting

b. a room forming an entrance to another one

c. the career one believes oneself called to; one's occupation or profession

d. something that happened or existed before another thing

e. following in time, order, or place

f. the observation or examination of one's own thought processes

g. a letter or symbol written immediately below and to the right of another symbol

h. a logical result or conclusion; the relation of effect to cause

i. a letter or symbol written immediately above and to the right of another symbol

j. to come between people or points in time

k. to come together as a group

Word Study
Dictionary Use

EXERCISE 1

In Unit 1, you were introduced to the types of information that a dictionary can provide. In this exercise, you will again scan* for information from a dictionary page, but here you will concentrate only on the definition of words. Read the questions, and then scan the dictionary page (page 72) or the dictionary entries on the website **www.dictionary.com** to find the answers.

1. In the following sentences, first determine the part of speech of the italicized word, and then use the dictionary page to find a synonym for the word.

    a. Because of her all-night study sessions, Sandy is *run-down.*

        1. noun, verb, adjective, adverb

        2. synonym: _____

    b. José's telephone call to Peter caused a *rupture* in their four-year friendship.

        1. noun, verb, adjective, adverb

        2. synonym: _____

2. Find a synonym for *running* as it is used in the following sentence.

    We have won the contest four years *running.* _____

3. Check all the following words that are synonyms of *rural.*

    _____ a. rustic   _____ b. rubric   _____ c. pastoral

4. What would you look up to find synonyms of *run-of-the-mill*?

    _____ a. mill   _____ b. average   _____ c. run   _____ d. run-of-the-mill

5. What words must you look up to find a description of a running knot?

    _____ a. slipknot   _____ b. running   _____ c. knot   _____ d. running knot

6. A running mate can be either _____

    _____ a. a horse or a person.

    _____ b. a horse or a machine.

    _____ c. a person or a machine.

_____

*For an introduction to scanning, see Unit 1.

7. Which word must you look up to find the definition of *rung* as used in the following sentence?

I would have rung you earlier but I didn't have time.

_____ a. ring

_____ b. rang

_____ c. rung

8. From the dictionary definitions give the number of the appropriate definition for each of the italicized words in the following sentences.

a. We put a *runner* in the hall from the front door to the kitchen. _____

b. The singer walked onto the *runway* in order to get closer to the audience. _____

c. There were 24 *runes* in the Germanic alphabet. _____

9. Which of the following runes is a modern *m*?

_____ a. ᛉ

_____ b. ᛗ

_____ c. ᛗ

10. What is the meaning of the italicized word in the following sentence?

John complained that *Ruse* was dangerous.

_____ a. a misleading action

_____ b. a city

_____ c. an artifice

11. Complete the following sentence with the appropriate form of the word *rural*.

Because of his anti-urban feelings Kenworthy Piker is known as the leading _____ of his time.

12. Choose the word that correctly completes the following sentence.

Let me give you a brief _____ of what we talked about before you arrived.

a. run-off
b. rundown

runcinate
Runcinate leaf of dandelion

rune

f u th a r k
g w h n i j e
p z s t b e
m l ng o d

basic Germanic runic alphabet

ð ʒ
edh yogh

two later runes used in English

run·a·gate (rŭn′ə-gāt′) *n. Archaic.* **1.** A renegade or deserter. **2.** A vagabond. [Variant of RENEGADE (influenced by RUN).]
run-a-round (rŭn′ə-round′) *n.* Also **run·round** (rŭn′round′). **1.** Deception, usually in the form of evasive excuses. **2.** *Printing.* Type set in a column narrower than the body of the text, as on either side of a picture.
run·a·way (rŭn′ə-wā′) *n.* **1.** One that runs away. **2.** An act of running away. **3.** *Informal.* An easy victory. —*adj.* **1.** Escaping or having escaped from captivity or control. **2.** Of or done by running away. **3.** Easily won, as a race. **4.** Of or pertaining to a rapid price rise.
run·back (rŭn′băk′) *n.* **1.** The act of returning a kickoff, punt, or intercepted forward pass. **2.** The distance so covered.
run·ci·ble spoon (rŭn′sə-bəl). A three-pronged fork, as a pickle fork, curved like a spoon and having a cutting edge. [*Runcible,* a nonsense word coined by Edward Lear.]
run·ci·nate (rŭn′sə-nāt′, -nĭt) *adj. Botany.* Having saw-toothed divisions directed backward: *runcinate leaves.* [Latin *runcinātus,* past participle of *runcināre,* to plane, from *runcina,* carpenter's plane (formerly taken also to mean a saw), from Greek *rhukanē*†.]
run down. 1. a. To slow down and stop, as a machine. **b.** To exhaust or wear out. **c.** To lessen in value. **2.** To pursue and capture. **3.** To hit with a moving vehicle. **4.** To disparage; decry. **5.** To give a brief or summary account of. **6.** *Baseball.* To put out a runner after trapping him between two bases.
run-down (rŭn′doun′) *n.* **1.** A summary or résumé. **2.** *Baseball.* A play in which a runner is put out when he is trapped between bases. —*adj.* **1.** In poor physical condition; weak or exhausted. **2.** Unwound and not running.
rune (ro͞on) *n.* **1.** One of the letters of an alphabet used by ancient Germanic peoples, especially by the Scandinavians and Anglo-Saxons. **2.** Any poem, riddle, or the like written in runic characters. **3.** Any occult characters. **4.** A Finnish poem or canto. [In sense 4, from Finnish *runo.* In other senses, Middle English *roun, rune,* secret writing, rune, from Old Norse *rūn* (unattested). See **rūno-** in Appendix.*] —**run′ic** *adj.*
rung¹ (rŭng) *n.* **1.** A rod or bar forming a step of a ladder. **2.** A crosspiece supporting the legs or back of a chair. **3.** The spoke in a wheel. **4.** *Nautical.* One of the spokes or handles on a ship's steering wheel. [Middle English *rung, rong,* Old English *hrung,* akin to Old High German *runga,* Gothic *hruggat*.]
rung². Past tense and past participle of **ring.** See Usage note at **ring.**
run in. 1. To insert or include as something extra. **2.** *Printing.* To make a solid body of text without a paragraph or other break. **3.** *Slang.* To take into legal custody.
run-in (rŭn′ĭn′) *n.* **1.** A quarrel; an argument; a fight. **2.** *Printing.* Matter added to a text. —*adj.* Added or inserted in text.
run·let (rŭn′lĭt) *n.* A rivulet. [Diminutive of RUN (stream).]
run·nel (rŭn′əl) *n.* **1.** A rivulet; a brook. **2.** A narrow channel or course, as for water. [Middle English *rynel,* Old English *rynel,* from *rinnan,* to run, flow. See **er-¹** in Appendix.*]
run·ner (rŭn′ər) *n.* **1.** One who or that which runs, as: **a.** One that competes in a race. **b.** A fugitive. **c.** A messenger or errand boy. **2.** An agent or collector, as for a bank or brokerage house. **3.** One who solicits business, as for a hotel or store. **4.** A smuggler. **5.** A vessel engaged in smuggling. **6.** One who operates or manages something. **7.** A device in or on which a mechanism slides or moves, as: **a.** The blade of a skate. **b.** The supports on which a drawer slides. **8.** A long narrow carpet. **9.** A long narrow tablecloth. **10.** A roller towel. **11.** *Metallurgy.* A channel along which molten metal is poured into a mold; gate. **12.** *Botany.* **a.** A slender, creeping stem that puts forth roots from nodes spaced at intervals along its length. **b.** A plant, such as the strawberry, having such a stem. **c.** A twining vine, such as the **scarlet runner** *(see).* **13.** Any of several marine fishes of the family Carangidae, such as the blue runner, *Caranx crysos,* of temperate waters of the American Atlantic coast.
run·ner-up (rŭn′ər-ŭp′) *n.* One that takes second place.
run·ning (rŭn′ĭng) *n.* **1.** The act of one that runs. **2.** The power or ability to run. **3.** Competition: *in the running.* **4.** An operating: *the running of a machine.* **5. a.** That which runs or flows. **b.** The amount that runs. —*adj.* Continuous: *a running commentary.* —*adv.* Consecutively: *four years running.*
running board. A narrow footboard extending under and beside the doors of some automobiles and other conveyances.
running gear. 1. The working parts of an automobile, locomotive, or other vehicle. **2.** **Running rigging** *(see).*
running hand. Writing done rapidly without lifting the pen from the paper.
running head. *Printing.* A title printed at the top of every page or every other page. Also called "running title."
running knot. A **slipknot** *(see).*
running light. 1. One of several lights on a boat or ship kept lighted between dusk and dawn. **2.** One of several similar lights on an aircraft; a navigation light.
running mate. 1. A horse used to set the pace in a race for another horse. **2.** The candidate or nominee for the lesser of two closely associated political offices.
running rigging. The part of a ship's rigging that comprises the ropes with which sails are raised, lowered, or trimmed, booms and gaffs are operated, etc. Also called "running gear."
running stitch. One of a series of small, even stitches.
run·ny (rŭn′ē) *adj.* **-nier, -niest.** Inclined to run or flow.
Run·ny·mede (rŭn′ĭ-mēd). A meadow on the Thames, 19 miles west of London, where King John is thought to have signed the Magna Carta in 1215. [Middle English *Runimede,* "meadow on the council island" : Old English *Rūnīeg,* council island : *rūn,* secret, secret council (see **rūno-** in Appendix*) + *īeg, īg,* island (see **akwā-** in Appendix*) + *mede,* MEAD (meadow).]
run off. 1. To print, duplicate, or copy. **2.** To run away; elope. **3.** To spill over; to overflow. **4.** To decide a contest or competition by a run-off.
run-off (rŭn′ôf′, -ŏf′) *n.* **1. a.** The overflow of a fluid from a container. **b.** Rainfall that is not absorbed by the soil. **2.** Eliminated waste products from manufacturing processes. **3.** An extra competition held to break a tie.
run-of-the-mill (rŭn′əv-*th*ə-mĭl′) *adj.* Ordinary; not special; average. See Synonyms at **average.** [From *run of (the) mill,* products of a mill that are not graded for quality.]
run on. 1. To continue on and on. **2.** *Printing.* To continue a text without a formal break.
run-on (rŭn′ŏn′, -ôn′) *n. Printing.* Matter that is appended or added without a formal break. —*adj.* Being run on.
run·round. Variant of **run-around.**
runt (rŭnt) *n.* **1.** An undersized animal; especially, the smallest animal of a litter. **2.** A person of small stature. Often used disparagingly. [Possibly from Dutch *rund,* small ox. See **ker-¹** in Appendix.*] —**runt′i·ness** *n.* —**runt·y** *adj.*
run through. 1. To pierce. **2.** To use up (money, for example) quickly. **3.** To examine or rehearse quickly.
run-through (rŭn′thro͞o′) *n.* A complete but rapid review or rehearsal of something, such as a theatrical work.
run·way (rŭn′wā′) *n.* **1.** A path, channel, or track over which something runs. **2.** The bed of a water course. **3.** A chute down which logs are skidded. **4.** *Bowling.* A narrow track on which balls are returned after they are bowled. **5.** A smooth ramp for wheeled vehicles. **6.** A narrow walkway extending from a stage into an auditorium. **7.** A strip of level ground, usually paved, on which aircraft take off and land.
Run·yon (rŭn′yən), **(Alfred) Damon.** 1884–1946. American journalist and author of short stories.
ru·pee (ro͞o-pē′, ro͞o′pē) *n. Abbr.* **Re., r., R. 1. a.** The basic monetary unit of Ceylon and Mauritius, equal to 100 cents. **b.** The basic monetary unit of India, equal to 100 paise. **c.** The basic monetary unit of Nepal, equal to 100 pice. **d.** The basic monetary unit of Pakistan, equal to 100 paisas. See table of exchange rates at **currency. 2.** A coin worth one rupee. [Hindi *rupaiyā,* from Sanskrit *rūpya,* wrought silver, from *rūpa*†, shape, image.]
Ru·pert (ro͞o′pərt). A river of Quebec, Canada, flowing 380 miles westward from Mistassini Lake to James Bay.
Ru·pert (ro͞o′pərt), **Prince.** 1619–1682. German-born English military, naval, and political leader; supporter of Charles I; inventor.
Ru·pert's Land (ro͞o′pərts). The Canadian territory granted the Hudson's Bay Company in 1670, most of which was incorporated in The Northwest Territories after its purchase by Canada in 1870.
ru·pi·ah (ro͞o-pē′ä) *n., pl.* **rupiah** or **-ahs. 1.** The basic monetary unit of Indonesia, equal to 100 sen. See table of exchange rates at **currency. 2.** A note worth one rupiah. [Hindi *rupaiyā,* RUPEE.]
rup·ture (rŭp′chər) *n.* **1. a.** The act of breaking open or bursting. **b.** The state of being broken open or burst. **2.** A break in friendly relations between individuals or nations. **3.** *Pathology.* **a.** A **hernia** *(see),* especially of the groin or intestines. **b.** A tear in bodily tissue. —*v.* **ruptured, -turing, -tures.** —*tr.* To break open; burst. —*intr.* To undergo or suffer a rupture. —See Synonyms at **break.** [Middle English *ruptur,* from Old French *rupture,* from Latin *ruptūra,* from *rumpere* (past participle *ruptus*), to break. See **reup-** in Appendix.*] —**rup′tur·a·ble** *adj.*
ru·ral (ro͝or′əl) *adj.* **1.** Of or pertaining to the country as opposed to the city; rustic. **2.** Of or pertaining to people who live in the country. **3.** Of or relating to farming; agricultural. Compare **urban.** [Middle English, from Old French, from Latin *rūrālis,* from *rūs* (stem *rūr-*), country. See **rewe-** in Appendix.*] —**ru′ral·ism′** *n.* —**ru′ral·ist** *n.* —**ru′ral·ly** *adv.*
Synonyms: *rural, arcadian, bucolic, rustic, pastoral, sylvan.* These adjectives are all descriptive of existence or environment which is close to nature; those with a literary flavor are often used facetiously. *Rural* applies to sparsely settled or agricultural country, as distinct from settled communities. *Arcadian* implies ideal or simple country living. *Bucolic* is often used derisively of country people or manners. *Rustic,* sometimes uncomplimentary, applies to country people who seem unsophisticated, but may also apply favorably to living conditions or to natural environments which are pleasingly primitive. *Pastoral* implies the supposed peace of rural living and the shepherd's life, with a suggestion of artificiality. *Sylvan* refers to wooded as opposed to cultivated country, and carries the sense of unspoiled beauty.
rural free delivery. *Abbr.* **R.F.D., RFD** Free government delivery of mail in rural areas.
ru·ral·i·ty (ro͞o-răl′ə-tē) *n., pl.* **-ties. 1.** The state or quality of being rural. **2.** A rural trait or characteristic.
ru·ral·ize (ro͝or′əl-īz′) *v.* **-ized, -izing, -izes.** —*tr.* To make rural. —*intr.* To live or visit in the country. —**ru′ral·i·za′tion** *n.*
rural route. *Abbr.* **R.R.** A rural mail route.
Ru·rik (ro͞o′rĭk). Died A.D. 879. Scandinavian warrior; founder of the dynasty that ruled Russia until 1598.
Rus. Russia; Russian.
Ru·se (ro͞o′sā). *Turkish* **Rus·chuk** (ro͞os′cho͝ok). A Danubian port in northeastern Bulgaria. Population, 118,000.
ruse (ro͞oz) *n.* An action or device meant to confuse or mislead. See Synonyms at **artifice.** [Middle English, detour of a hunted animal, from Old French, from *ruser,* to repulse, detour. See **rush** (to dash off).]

72

ă pat/ā pay/âr care/ä father/b bib/ch church/d deed/ĕ pet/ē be/f fife/g gag/h hat/hw which/ĭ pit/ī pie/îr pier/j judge/k kick/l lid, needle/m mum/n no, sudden/ng thing/ŏ pot/ō toe/ô paw, for/oi noise/ou out/o͝o took/o͞o boot/p pop/r roar/s sauce/sh ship, dish/

EXERCISE 2

Online resources like the website **www.dictionary.com** allow users to access different kinds of information. More than just definitions, **dictionary.com** provides links to and information about a variety of language-related issues. Quickly skim* the website homepage below to see what kind of information the site provides, and then answer the questions.

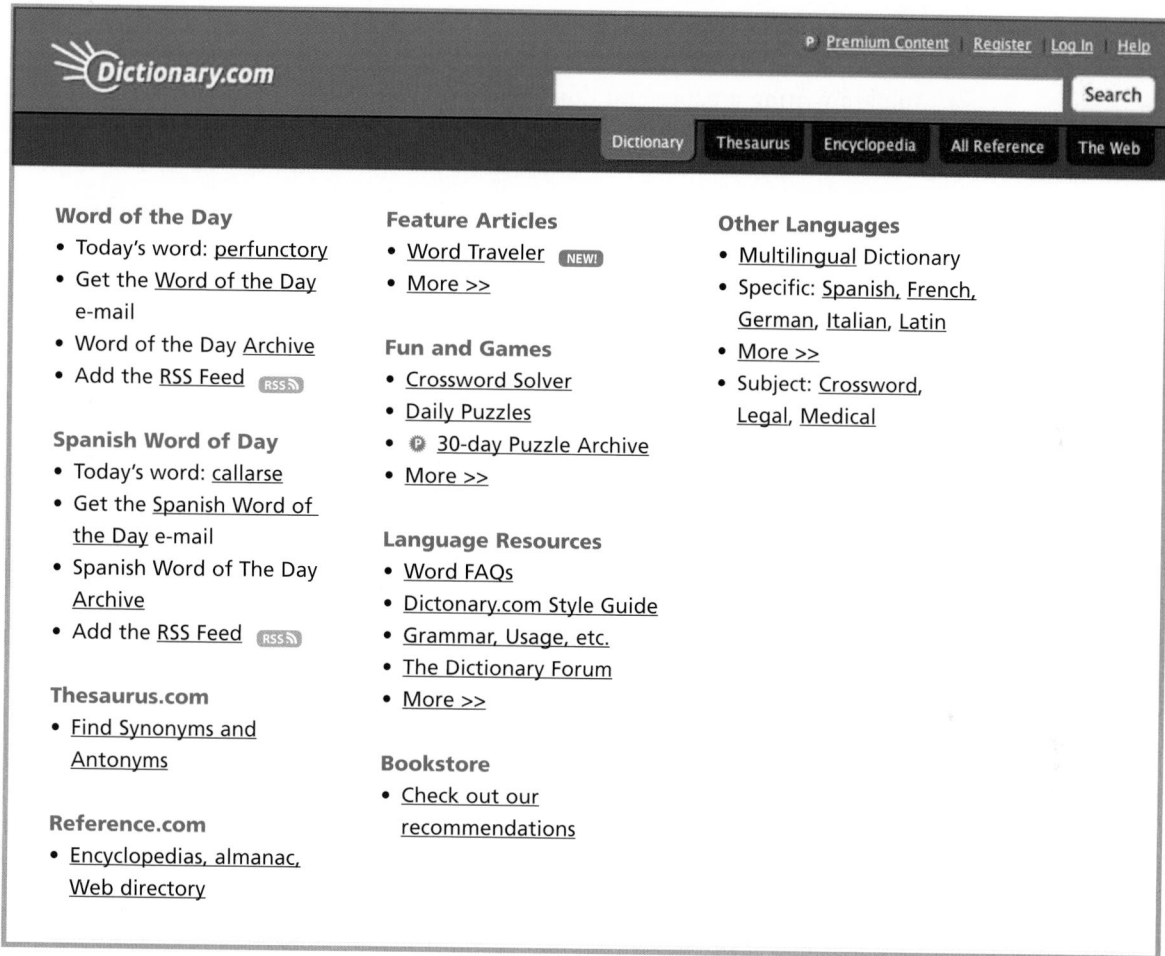

---

*For an introduction to skimming, see page 1.

1. Below is a list of situations that might send you to a dictionary or other reference tool. Using the **dictionary.com** homepage on page 73, decide whether you would use this website in each situation. If you would, put a check (✔) next to the letter and, on the line following, write what you would click on.

> Example   I ✓ You'd like to learn a new word each day by receiving a daily e-mail message.
>
>   *Get the Word of the Day e-mail*

_____ a. You are writing a paper and don't want to keep using the same word. You need to find another term that means approximately the same thing. If yes, what would you click on?

_____

_____ b. You've written a paragraph and you're not sure that several of the sentences are grammatical or are linked together properly. If yes, what would you click on?

_____

_____ c. You're looking for the word list used to create the TOEFL®. If yes, what would you click on?

_____

_____ d. You need a print dictionary and want a recommendation for a good one to buy.

_____

_____ e. You're looking for the definition of a word in Latin.

_____

_____ f. You're having trouble understanding specialized medical terminology.

_____

2. Indicate if the statements below are probably true (T) or probably false (F). Be prepared to defend your answers.

a. T / F This website could help you get a translation of a Spanish paragraph into English.

b. T / F This is a good website for people who like word puzzles.

c. T / F This website only provides links to information about words.

d. T / F This website cannot link you to a Russian dictionary.

e. T / F FAQ probably means Facts About Quizzes.

Sentence Study
Introduction

The exercises in this book provide you with practice in using a number of reading skills and strategies to understand a reading passage. Context Clues, Stems and Affixes, and Dictionary Use exercises provide you with practice in quickly finding specific pieces of information in a passage. Skimming, introduced in Unit 1, focuses on reading a passage quickly for a general idea of its meaning.

When you have difficulty understanding a passage, just reading further will often make the passage clearer. Sometimes, however, comprehension of an entire passage depends on your being able to understand a single sentence. Sentences that are very long and sentences that contain difficult vocabulary or difficult grammatical patterns often cause comprehension problems for readers. The sentence study exercise that follows as well as similar ones in later units gives you the opportunity to develop strategies for understanding complicated sentences.

Although there is no easy formula that will help you to arrive at an understanding of a difficult sentence, you should keep the following points in mind.

1. Try to determine what makes the sentence difficult:

   a. If the sentence contains a lot of difficult vocabulary, it may be that the sentence can be understood without knowing the meaning of every word. Try crossing out unfamiliar items.

      > The West had sent armies to ~~capture and~~ hold Jerusalem; instead they themselves fell ~~victim~~ to ~~a host of~~ new ideas and ~~subtle~~ influences which left their mark on the development of European literature, ~~chivalry,~~ warfare, ~~sanitation,~~ commerce, political institutions, medicine, ~~and the papacy itself.~~

   b. If the sentence is very long, try to break it up into smaller parts:

      > The West had sent armies to capture and hold Jerusalem. The West fell victim to a host of new ideas and subtle influences. These ideas and influences left their mark on the development of European literature, chivalry, warfare, sanitation, commerce, political institutions, medicine, and the papacy.

   c. Also, if the sentence is very long, try to determine which parts of the sentence express specific details supporting the main idea. Often clauses that are set off by commas, or introduced by words such as *which, who,* and *that,* are used to introduce extra information or to provide supporting details. Try crossing out the supporting details in order to determine the main idea:

      > These ideas, ~~which left their mark on the development of European literature, chivalry, warfare, sanitation, commerce, political institutions, medicine, and the papacy,~~ greatly changed Western culture.

Be careful! A good reader reads quickly but accurately!

2. Learn to recognize the important grammatical and punctuation clues that can change the meaning of a sentence:

   a. Look for single words and affixes* that can change the entire meaning of a sentence.

> Summery weather is *not un*common.
> The *average* daytime *high* temperature is *approximately* 56°.

   b. Look for punctuation clues:

> Wally ⓐsingsⓑ at all of his friends' parties.
> Barry said, "George has been elected presidentⓒ"

Note that all of the italicized words or affixes and the circled punctuation above are essential to the meaning of the sentences; if any of these are omitted, the meaning of the sentences changes significantly.

   c. Look for key words that tell you of relationships within a sentence:

> The school has grown *from* a small building holding 200 students *to* a large institute that educates 4,000 students a year.

>   *From . . . to* indicates the beginning and end points of a period of change.

> Many critics have proclaimed Doris Lessing as *not only* the best writer of the postwar generation, *but also* a penetrating analyst of human affairs.

>   *Not only . . . but also* indicates that both parts of the sentence are of equal importance.

> *In order to* graduate on time, you will need to take five courses each semester.

>   *In order to* is like *if;* it indicates that some event must occur before another event can take place.

> The West had sent armies to capture and hold Jerusalem; *instead* they themselves fell victim to new ideas and subtle influences.

>   *Instead* indicates that something happened contrary to expectations.

> *As a result of* three books, a television documentary, and a special exposition at the Library of Congress, the mystery has aroused considerable public interest.

>   *As a result of* indicates a cause and effect relationship. The clause that follows *as a result of* is the cause of some event. The three books, television program, and exposition are the *cause;* the arousal of public interest is the *effect.*

> *Because of* the impact of these ideas, *which* had been introduced originally to Europe by soldiers returning from the East, the West was greatly changed.

>   *Because of* indicates a cause and effect relationship. The West was changed as a result of these ideas. The information between the word *which* and the final comma (,) refers to *these ideas.*

---

*For a list of all stems and affixes taught in *Reader's Choice,* see the Appendix.

Sentence Study
Comprehension

Read the following sentences carefully. The questions that follow are designed to test your comprehension of complex grammatical structures. Select the *best* answer.

Example   The student revolt is not only a thorn in the side of the president's newly established government, but it has international implications as well.

Whom or what does the revolt affect?

_____ a. the students

_____ b. the side of the president's body

_____ c. only the national government

_____ d. national and international affairs

Explanation

_____ a. According to the sentence, the students are the cause of certain events, not among those affected.

_____ b. Although you may not have been familiar with the idiom *a thorn in someone's side*, context clues should have told you that this phrase means *a problem* and does not actually refer to the side of the president's body.

_____ c. National government is an incomplete answer. The construction *not only . . . but . . . as well* should tell you that more than one element is involved. The president's newly established government (the national government) is not the only area affected by the revolt.

_✓_ d. The revolt affects both national and international affairs.

1. I disagreed then as now with many of John Smith's judgments but always respected him, and this book is a welcome reminder of his big, honest, friendly, stubborn personality.

How does the author of this sentence feel about John Smith?

_____ a. He dislikes him but agrees with his ideas.

_____ b. He considers him to be a disagreeable person.

_✓_ c. He disagrees with his ideas but respects him.

_____ d. He disagreed with him then but agrees with him now.

2. Concepts like *passivity*, *dependence*, and *aggression* may need further research if they are to continue to be useful ways of thinking about human personalities.

What might require more research?

_____ a. human thought processes

_✓_ b. certain concepts

_____ c. human personalities

_____ d. useful ways of thinking

3. In order for you to follow the schedule set by the publisher, your paper must be looked over over the weekend, revised, and handed in in its final form on Monday.

What must you do on Saturday and Sunday?

_____ a. meet the publisher

_____ b. examine your paper

_____ c. hand in a paper

__✓__ d. look over the weekend

4. The real reason why prices were, and still are, too high is complicated, and no short discussion can satisfactorily explain this problem.

What word or phrase best describes prices?

_____ a. complicated

_____ b. adequately explained

_____ c. too high in the past, but low now

__✓__ d. too high in the past and in the present

5. This is not just a sad-but-true story; the boy's experience is horrible and damaging, yet a sense of love shines through every word.

How does the author of this sentence feel about the story?

__✓__ a. It transmits a sense of love.

__✓__ b. It is just sad

_____ c. It is not true

_____ d. It is horrible and damaging.

6. In the past five years the movement has grown from unorganized groups of poorly armed individuals to a comparatively well-armed, well-trained army of anywhere from 10,000 to 16,000 members.

What is the present condition of this movement?

_____ a. The members are poorly armed.

_____ b. There are only a few poor individuals.

_____ c. There are over 16,000 members.

__✓__ d. The members are organized and well armed.

7. The financial situation isn't bad yet, but we believe that we have some vital information and, if it is correct, unemployment will soon become a serious problem.

What do we know about the financial situation?

_____ a. It won't change.

_____ b. It will become a serious problem.

__✓__ c. It is not bad now.

_____ d. It will improve.

8. The general then added, "The only reasonable solution to the sort of problems caused by the current unstable political situation is one of diplomacy and economic measures and not the use of military force."

What type of solution does the general support?

__✓__ a. economic and diplomatic action

_____ b. diplomatic and economic action if military force fails

_____ c. only diplomatic action

_____ d. military actions in response to political problems

9. Because the supply of natural gas was plentiful in comparison to other choices like coal and fuel oil, and because it burns cleaner, many people changed their heating systems to natural gas, thereby creating shortages.

Why did people prefer natural gas?

_____ a. It was natural.

_____ ✓ c. The other fuels were dirtier and less plentiful.

_____ b. There were no other choices.

_____ ✗ d. There is, even today, a plentiful supply of it.

Paragraph Reading
Main Idea

This exercise is similar to one in Unit 1. Read the following passages. Concentrate on discovering the main idea.

After each of the first five passages, select the statement that best expresses the main idea. After Passages 6, 7, and 8, write a sentence that expresses the main idea in your own words. For Passage 9 you will be asked to read several paragraphs, identify the main idea, and create a summary. When you have finished, your teacher may want to divide the class into small groups for discussion.

Passage 1

John Cabot was the first Englishman to land in North America. However, this man who legitimized England's claim to everything from Labrador to Florida left no sea journal, no diary or log, not even a portrait or a signature. Until 1956 most learned encyclopedias and histories indicated that Cabot's first landfall in America was Cape Breton, Nova Scotia. Then a letter was discovered in the Spanish archives, making it almost certain that he had touched first at the northernmost tip of Newfoundland, within five miles of the site of Leif Ericsson's ill-fated settlement at L'Anse-aux-Meadows. Researchers studying the voyages of Columbus, Cartier, Frobisher, and other early explorers had a wealth of firsthand material with which to work. Those who seek to recreate the life and routes used by Cabot must make do with thirdhand accounts, the disloyal and untruthful boasts of his son, Sebastian, and a few hard dates in the maritime records of Bristol, England.

Select the statement that best expresses the main idea of the passage.

_____ a. John Cabot claimed all the land from Labrador to Florida for England.

_____ b. Much of what is known about Cabot is based on the words of his son, Sebastian, and on records in Bristol, England.

_____ ✓ c. The lack of firsthand accounts of Cabot's voyage has left historians confused about his voyages to North America.

_____ d. Historians interested in the life and routes used by Cabot recently discovered an error they made in describing his discovery of North America.

Passage 2

The Bible, while mainly a theological document, is secondarily a book of history and geography. Selected historical materials were included in the text for the purpose of illustrating and underlining the religious teaching of the Bible. Historians and archaeologists have learned to rely upon the amazing accuracy of historical memory in the Bible. The smallest references to persons and places and events contained in the accounts of the Exodus, for instance, or the biographies of such Biblical heroes as Abraham and Moses and David, can lead, if properly considered and pursued, to extremely important historical discoveries. The archaeologists' efforts are not directed at "proving" the correctness of the Bible, which is neither necessary nor possible, any more than belief in God can be scientifically demonstrated. It is quite the opposite, in fact. The historical clues in the Bible can lead the archaeologist to a knowledge of the civilizations of the ancient world in which the Bible developed and with whose religious concepts and practices the Bible so radically differed. It can be considered as an almost unfailing indicator, revealing to the experts the locations and characteristics of lost cities and civilizations.

Select the statement that best expresses the main idea of the passage.

_____ a. The Bible can provide valuable geographical information.

_____ b. The Bible is primarily a religious document.

_____ c. The Bible was intended by its authors to be a record of the history of the ancient world.

__✓__ d. The Bible, though primarily a religious text, is a valuable tool for people interested in history.

Passage 3

At one time it was the most important city in the region—a bustling commercial center known for its massive monuments, its crowded streets and commercial districts, and its cultural and religious institutions. Then, suddenly, it was abandoned. Within a generation most of its population departed and the once magnificent city became a ghost town. This is the history of a pre-Columbian city called Teotihuacán (the Aztec Indians' word for "the place the gods call home"), once a metropolis of as many as 200,000 inhabitants 33 miles northeast of present-day Mexico City and the focus of a far-flung empire that stretched from the arid plains of central Mexico to the mountains of Guatemala. Why did this city die? Researchers have found no signs of epidemic disease or destructive invasions. But they have found signs that suggest the Teotihuacanos themselves burned their temples and  some of their other buildings. Excavations revealed that piles of wood had been placed around these structures and set afire. Some speculate that Teotihuacán's inhabitants may have abandoned the city because it had become "a clumsy giant . . . too unwieldy to change with the times." But other archaeologists think that the ancient urbanites may have destroyed their temples and abandoned their city in rage against their gods for permitting a long famine.

Select the statement that best expresses the main idea of the passage.

_____ a. Teotihuacán, once the home of 200,000 people, was the center of a large empire.

_____ b. Many archaeologists are fascinated by the ruins of a pre-Columbian city called Teotihuacán.

_____ c. Teotihuacán, once a major metropolitan area, was destroyed by an invasion.

__✓__ d. A still unsolved mystery is why the people of Teotihuacán suddenly abandoned their city.

Passage 4

In any archaeological study that includes a dig, the procedures are basically the same: (1) selecting a site (2) hiring local workers (3) surveying the site and dividing it into sections (4) digging trenches to locate levels and places to excavate (5) mapping architectural features (6) developing a coding system that shows the exact spot where an object is found (7) and recording, tagging, cleaning and storing excavated materials. Neilson C. Debevoise, writing on an expedition to Iraq in the early 1930s, described the typical "route" of excavated pottery. Workers reported an object to staff members before removing it from the ground. The date, level, location and other important information were written on a piece of paper and placed with the object. At noon the objects were brought in from the field to the registry room where they were given a preliminary cleaning. Registry numbers were written with waterproof India ink on a portion of the object previously painted with shellac. The shellac prevented the ink from soaking into the object, furnished a good writing surface, and made it possible to remove the number in a moment. From the registry room objects were sent to the drafting department. If a clay pot, for example, was of a new type, a scale drawing was made on graph paper. Measurements of the top, greatest diameter, base, height, color of the glaze, if any, the quality and texture of the body, and the quality of the workmanship were recorded on paper with the drawing. When the drafting department had completed its work, the materials were placed on the storage shelves, grouped according to type for division with the Iraq government, and eventually shipped to museums. Today, the steps of a dig remain basically the same, although specific techniques vary.

Select the statement that best expresses the main idea of the passage.

_____ a. For a number of years, archaeologists have used basically the same procedure when conducting a dig.

_____ b. Neilson C. Debevoise developed the commonly accepted procedure for organizing a dig.

_____ c. Archaeologists take great care to assure that all excavated objects are properly identified.

__✓__ d. A great deal of important historical and archaeological information can be provided by a dig.

Passage 5

The unprecedented expansion of Modern architecture throughout the world must be considered one of the great events in the history of art. Within the space of a single generation, the contemporary movement became the dominant style of serious building not only in the United States and Europe, where pioneers had been at work since the late nineteenth century, but also in nations such as Brazil and India, where almost no Modern architecture existed until much later. Only the Gothic perhaps, among all styles of the past, gained popular acceptance with anything like the speed of the Modern. And like the Gothic—which required a full seventy-five years of experimentation before it produced the cathedral of Chartres—the Modern continually improved its structural techniques, gained in scale, and revised its aesthetics as it attempted to meet the full range of people's civilized needs.

Select the statement that best expresses the main idea of the passage.

_____ a. Gothic architecture gained popular acceptance faster than Modern architecture did.

_____ b. Modern architecture has not changed fast enough to meet the needs of civilization.

_✓_ c. The rapid growth and development of Modern architecture (as an art form) is nearly unequaled in the history of art.

_____ d. If architectural styles are to endure, they must develop and improve in an attempt to meet society's needs.

Passage 6

A summit is not any old meeting between two heads of state. Potentates have been visiting each other since the beginning of time. The Queen of Sheba came to visit King Solomon and exchanged riddles with him. Mark Antony came to visit Cleopatra and stayed on. Royalty, presidents and prime ministers of allied nations have sometimes gotten together after a victorious war to divide the spoils, as they did at the Congress of Vienna in 1814 and then at Paris after World War I. But a summit, in the sense in which Winston Churchill introduced the word into the language when he called for one in 1950, is something quite different and quite specific: it is a meeting between the leaders of two or more rival enemy Great Powers trying to satisfy their mutual demands and head off future conflict.

Write a sentence that expresses the main idea of the passage.

_____

Passage 7

Through most of the time we are growing from infancy to adulthood, we are told that we have to do certain things: "You have to go to school," "You have to go to bed now." Most people seem to spend the rest of their lives thinking that they "have to" do the things that they do: "I have to go to work," "I have to go to the dentist." Initially, it may seem like mere rhetoric, but you don't *have* to do anything. Next time you find yourself on the verge of saying "I have to . . . ," try replacing it by "I choose to . . . ," "I want to . . . ," "I've decided to . . . ." It's incredibly liberating! Reminding your-self that you do things by choice gives you the sense that you are in control of your life.

Write a sentence that expresses the main idea of the passage.

_____

Passage 8

The Man in Bogota

The police and emergency service people fail to make a dent. The voice of the pleading spouse does not have the hoped-for effect. The woman remains on the ledge—though not, she threatens, for long.

I imagine that I am the one who must talk the woman down. I see it, and it happens like this.

I tell the woman about a man in Bogota. He was a wealthy man, an industrialist who was kidnapped and held for ransom. It was not a TV drama; his wife could not call the bank and, in twenty-four hours, have one million dollars. It took months. The man had a heart condition, and the kidnappers had to keep the man alive.

Listen to this, I tell the woman on the ledge. His captors made him quit smoking. They changed his diet and made him exercise every day. They held him that way for three months.

When the ransom was paid and the man was released, his doctor looked him over. He found the man to be in excellent health. I tell the woman what the doctor said then—that the kidnap was the best thing to happen to that man.

~

Maybe this is not a come-down-from-the-ledge story. But I tell it with the thought that the woman on the ledge will ask herself a question, the question that occurred to that man in Bogota. He wondered how we know that what happens to us isn't good.

"The Man in Bogota" is a parable, a short story designed to illustrate or teach a lesson about life. This lesson is the main idea of the parable. Write a sentence that expresses the main idea of "The Man in Bogota."

_____

If you are having trouble identifying the main idea, try answering these comprehension questions about the story.

1. T / F The woman on the ledge thinks her life is going badly.

2. T / F People think that being kidnapped is a bad thing to happen to someone.

3. T / F Being kidnapped was bad for the man in Bogota.

Read the passage below to identify the most important ideas.

Passage 9: Main Idea and Prose Summary

Recent research led by Andrew Whiten, a scientist at St. Andrew University in Scotland who studies primate behavior, provides evidence suggesting that chimpanzees, like humans, desire to conform to the behavior of others in their social group. Whiten, with British and American colleagues, studied three groups of captive chimpanzees at the Yerkes National Primate Research Centre in Atlanta, Georgia, U.S.A. They investigated the ways in which the chimpanzees learned to use a tool to get food trapped behind a blockage in a network of pipes called "pan-pipes."

The scientists presented the same problem to two high-ranking females from two different groups of chimpanzees. Food they wanted was placed just out of reach, behind a blockage, within pan-pipes. The females were each taught a different way to solve the problem. Erika was taught to use a stick to lift the blockage so the food would fall towards her. Georgia was taught to use a stick to poke the blockage until it pushed the food backwards, rolled down another pipe and out into her hand.

When they had mastered their lessons, Erika and Georgia rejoined their own groups of chimpanzees, which were kept separate from each other. Each of the two females demonstrated what she had learned to the other chimpanzees in her group, who gathered around her to observe what she was doing. Most chimpanzees in each of these groups soon began using the particular technique they had been shown, either lifting or poking.

Unexpectedly, some of the members of the first two groups did independently learn how to extract the food using the technique used by the other group. That is, some in Erika's group taught themselves the poking technique and some in Georgia's, the lifting technique. However, according to Whiten, when the pan-pipes were taken away for two months and then re-introduced to the two groups of chimps, all the chimps in each group reverted to their group's normal way of doing things. They conformed to tradition. This was true even for the animals in the lifting group, some of whom gave up the poking technique, which is actually a more natural movement for chimpanzees than is lifting.

The researchers are intrigued by this evidence of members of a non-human species conforming to a group norm, even when they are capable of using an alternative technique that is typical for another group. They believe this suggests that the tendency of humans to conform to others in their social group, which is the hallmark of culture, may have ancient origins and that further research into primate culture could provide insights into why people prefer to do one thing rather than another simply because their colleagues are doing it.

1. Imagine you are part of a study group in a psychology class. You have agreed to read this passage and write a one-paragraph summary of it for your study group. You will begin your summary paragraph with a sentence that is the main idea of the entire passage that you have read. Circle the letter next to the sentence below that expresses the main idea.

   a. Recent research shows that female chimpanzees play an important role in teaching members of their social group.

   b. Findings of an international team of primatologists provide evidence that some groups of chimpanzees are more intelligent than others.

   c. Primate researchers have found that it is difficult to teach chimpanzees new methods to solve problems when they already have a method that works.

   d. A recent study suggests that chimpanzees, like humans, want to behave like others in their social group.

2. Now, you will continue your summary. First, however, check your answer to Question 1 with your classmates. Use the answer to Question 1 as the first sentence of your paragraph. Choose six more sentences from the choices below to complete your summary. Put a check (✔) next to the six sentences that express the most important ideas from the passage. Do not check sentences that express ideas not found in the passage or ones that present minor ideas.

   _____ a. Two chimpanzees, Erica and Georgia, were taught two different methods to solve a single problem.

   _____ b. Chimpanzees cannot learn different ways to get food that is trapped in pipes.

   _____ c. Chimpanzees like using tools.

   _____ d. Erica and Georgia taught the others in their social groups how to get the trapped food.

   _____ e. Most chimpanzees in each group used the method they had learned from their female leader.

   _____ f. Some chimpanzees in each group taught themselves the method used by the other group.

   _____ g. After some time passed, however, all chimps in Erica's group used her method and all chimps in Georgia's group used her method.

   _____ h. Erica's lifting method is not a natural motion for chimpanzees.

   _____ i. Research shows that chimpanzees are intelligent and can use tools.

   _____ j. This study suggests that humans' interest in conformity may have ancient origins.

Discourse Focus
Reading for Different Goals—Web Work

Effective readers use all the clues available to make decisions about what they read and how they read. Web surfing is particularly demanding in this regard because of the amount and variety of information that compete for your attention. In order to find the information you want, you must skim to discover if you are at an appropriate website, scan to discover what information is relevant, and read thoroughly and critically to decide if the information is accurate and trustworthy.*

This exercise is designed to give you practice in web-based research. We provide the following web pages to serve as examples in conducting an Internet search. If you are online, your teacher may want you to use the *Reader's Choice* website to work on the exercises in this section: **www.press.umich.edu/esl/readerschoice/**.

~

You have heard many interesting things about San Diego, California. There are beautiful beaches where surfers gather to catch waves, and whale-watching tour boats can be seen cruising on the horizon. You are attracted by reports of warm temperatures, gorgeous flowers, and friendly people. You've been told that professional sports compete with cultural attractions such as world-class museums, art exhibits, and classical and popular concerts. You decide to check it out for yourself. You find the description of San Diego shown on page 87.

Getting Oriented

EXERCISE 1

Just to make sure that you know what San Diego has to offer, answer the following questions according to the travel information on page 87. True/False items are indicated by at T / F preceding the statement.

1. T / F   San Diego is a pretty place.

2. List the three most important sources of income for San Diego.

   a. _____

   b. _____

   c. _____

3. Circle the most important industry listed in Question 2.

4. T / F   San Diegans are not happy with their smog, traffic, and fast-paced life.

5. T / F   San Diego is known for its friendliness.

6. T / F   San Diego is over-shadowed by Los Angeles.

---

*For an introduction to reading for different goals, see Unit 1.

Tourism remains San Diego's third-biggest industry (behind manufacturing and the military), driven by a convention-friendly downtown. Each year, 26 million visitors come to the city, generating $5.2 billion for the local economy. What tourists come for is still largely focused on the beach, the zoo, and the weather, but what many discover is that there's more than meets the eye here. This is a city blessed with a picturesque location and glorious climate, and San Diegans are beginning to find graceful ways to define their home beyond being "not like Los Angeles." They're happy not to have the L.A. smog, crowded freeways, and fast-paced life. Long-time residents are fighting to slow growth, but they're also delighted to be nurturing some of the cultural attractions previously taken for granted. So the city is emerging from the shadow of L.A. It may not have a postcard picture as recognizable as San Francisco's Golden Gate Bridge, or an industry as glamorous as movie-making in L.A.'s Hollywood, but its personality continues to be defined with a broad smile and an inviting welcome.

EXERCISE 2

You're convinced that San Diego is a great city to visit, and you begin planning your trip. You want to combine historical and recreational activities and stay in a picturesque and comfortable historic hotel or bed and breakfast. You decide to get more information about San Diego on the Internet. You use a search engine such as Google™, and the following options pop up on your screen. Skim these quickly.

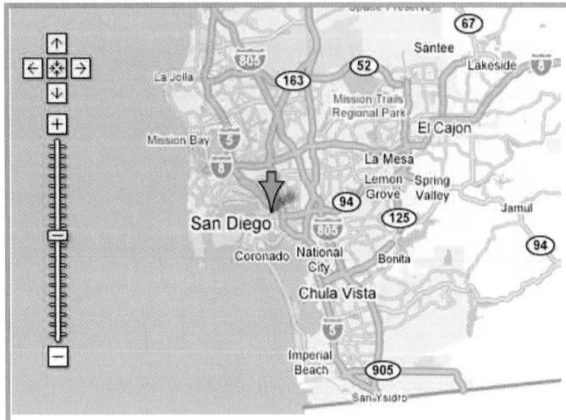

Map of San Diego, CA
maps.google.com

San Diego <u>Convention & Visitors Bureau</u>
Providing information for visitors, meeting planners and travel agents including events calendar, restaurant listings and other news.
www.**sandiego**.org/ - 42k - Mar 7, 2007 -
<u>Cached</u> - <u>Similar pages</u>

<u>City of **San Diego** Official Website</u>
The City of **San Diego's** Official website offers information and online services for departments,business assistance, job opportunities, attractions, . . .
www.**sandiego**.gov/ - 62k - <u>Cached</u> - <u>Similar pages</u>

<u>University of California, **San Diego**</u>
Home Page of the University of California, **San Diego.**
www.ucsd.edu/ - Mar 7, 2007 - <u>Similar pages</u>

<u>**San Diego,** California - Wikipedia, the free encyclopedia</u>
San Diego is a coastal Southern California city located in the southwestern corner . . .
The Centre City Development Corporation (CCDC), **San Diego's** downtown . . .
en.wikipedia.org/wiki/**San_Diego,**_California - 202k - Mar 7, 2007 - <u>Cached</u> - <u>Similar pages</u>

<u>**San Diego's** sandiego.com: Local News, Culture, Hotels, Coupons ...</u>
San Diego local information including news, sports, music, arts, consumer, history, hotel reservations, dining reservations, restaurant reviews, . . .
www.**sandiego**.com/ - <u>Similar pages</u>

<u>SignOnSanDiego.com > Breaking news from The **San Diego** Union ...</u>
Daily newspaper covering **San Diego** County. Local and international news.
www.signon**sandiego**.com/ - 70k - <u>Cached</u> - <u>Similar pages</u>

<u>**San Diego** Zoo</u>
Buy tickets online and use our calendar of events to plan your visit to the **San Diego** Zoo and **San Diego** Zoo's Wild Animal Park.
www.**sandiego**zoo.org/ - Mar 7, 2007 - <u>Similar pages</u>

Refine results for san diego:

<u>Dining guides</u>	<u>Attractions</u>	<u>Suggested itineraries</u>
<u>Lodging guides</u>	<u>Shopping</u>	<u>Tours & day trips</u>

Web surfing always yields far more information than you can use. The following items are designed to help you narrow your choices. Some items may have more than one correct response. Be prepared to defend your choices.

1. Circle the links you would click on to continue your search.

2. Two choices look very similar. What do you think is the difference between the San Diego Convention & Visitors Bureau and the City of San Diego Official Website? _____

   _____

3. Would you personally consider visiting the University of California, San Diego? What sort of tourist attractions might you find there?

   _____

4. One of the entries on page 88 comes from **http://wikipedia.org**. Below is a description of *Wikipedia*.

Wikipedia (IPA: /□wiki□piːdi.ə/ or /□wɪki□piːdi.ə/) name coined by Larry Sanger) is a multilingual, Web-based, free content encyclopedia project. Wikipedia is written collaboratively by volunteers; its articles can be edited by anyone with access to the website. The name is a BLEND of the words *wiki* (a type of collaborative website) and *encyclopedia*. Its primary servers are in Tampa, Florida, with additional servers in Amsterdam and Seoul.

---

a. T/F   The authors who contribute to *Wikipedia* are acknowledged experts in their fields.

b. Would you click on the *Wikipedia* entry on page 88? Why or why not? _____

   _____

EXERCISE 3

The web page for the San Diego Convention & Visitors Bureau is shown on page 91. Skim and scan the page quickly, and answer the questions. Some items may have more than one answer.

1. Where might you click for information on flights to San Diego? What do you think you would find if you clicked on *San Diego Travel News?* _____

    _____

2. What do you think you will get if you click on the Vacation Packages tab? _____

    _____

3. What number would you call if you wanted to talk to a person rather than buy a ticket online?

    _____

4. Where would you click if you wanted to search this website in your native language? _____

    _____

5. How many hotels list prices on this web page? _____

    a. What is the cheapest hotel price listed on this page? _____

    b. What would you click if you wanted to find a cheaper one? _____

6. Where is the Hotel del Coronado? _____

San Diego ®

CONVENTION & VISITORS BUREAU

- Visitor Information
- Where to Stay
- Dining & Nightlife
- What to Do
- Event Calendar
- Getting Around
- Resources

BUSINESS SERVICES

Visitors
Meeting Professionals
Media
Travel Professionals
Members

SAN DIEGO TRAVEL NEWS ✉

Sign up now and discover the best travel deals!

Enter E-Mail Address

Why Sign Up? | GO ▶

Welcome to San Diego, California's second largest city. Where blue skies keep watch on 70 miles of beaches and a gentle Mediterranean climate begs for a day of everything and nothing. Bordered by Mexico, the Pacific Ocean, the Anza-Borrego Desert and the Laguna Mountains, San Diego county's 4,200 square miles offer immense options for business and pleasure.

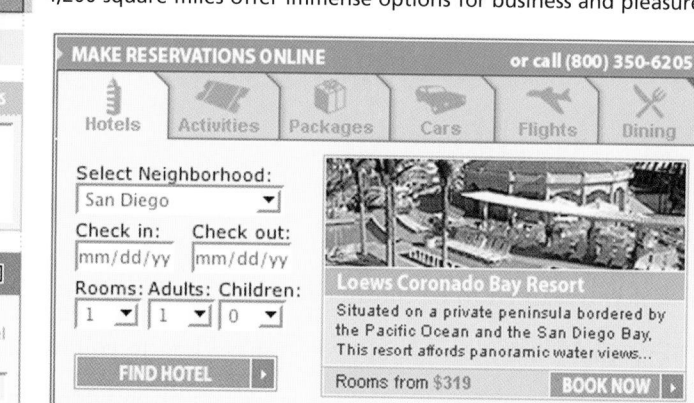

MAKE RESERVATIONS ONLINE   or call (800) 350-6205

| Hotels | Activities | Packages | Cars | Flights | Dining |

Select Neighborhood:
San Diego ▾

Check in: Check out:
mm/dd/yy mm/dd/yy

Rooms: Adults: Children:
1 ▾ 1 ▾ 0 ▾

FIND HOTEL ▶

Loews Coronado Bay Resort
Situated on a private peninsula bordered by the Pacific Ocean and the San Diego Bay. This resort affords panoramic water views...
Rooms from $319   **BOOK NOW** ▶

STREET SCENE

> **09/22 – 09/23** – California's largest urban music festival, Street Scene, is the ultimate San Diego end-of-summer celebration. Come out and enjoy two days of non-stop music and entertainment. Born in 1984, . . .

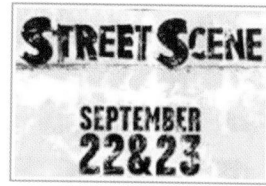

STREET SCENE
SEPTEMBER 22&23

> **PLAN AHEAD:**   Aug | Sep | Oct | ALL

> **10/12 – 10/15** – Marine Corps Air Station Miramar Air Show

> **09/22 – 09/23** – Street Scene

> **7/18 – 09/05** – Racing Season at the Del Mar Racetrack

> **09/27 – 09/30** – 6th Annual San Diego Film Festival

> **FEATURES:**   More...

> **Cruise-Friendly Hotels in San Diego** Hotels Near the San Diego Cruise Port Best Western Island Palms Surrounded by the San . . .

Getting There

EXERCISE 1

You go to **www.Expedia.com** to look for a plane ticket. Skim and scan the web page on page 93 quickly, and answer the following questions. Some items may have more than one correct answer. True/False items are indicated by a T / F preceding the statement.

1. Circle links you might click on to find cheap air fares.

2. T / F   "Shop for deals" is available only if you want to travel to Las Vegas, New York, or Orlando.

3. You notice the little red box RSS in the lower right corner. When you check the meaning of this acronym on the Internet, you find the following choices. Which one do you think it means?

   a. Rich Site Summary

   b. Royal Statistical Society

   c. Rail Security Systems

   d. Radar Signal Simulator

4. Where would you click if you wanted to be informed of special offers by email? _____

5. Are you a member of Expedia? If not, how would you join? What do you think the benefits of membership would be? _____

   _____

6. T / F   You can get guaranteed low fares through this web page.

EXERCISE 2

You are making arrangements for your friend in New York to join you in San Diego. Using any online travel website, search for fares from New York to San Diego. Answer the questions below based on what you find. Your teacher may want you to discuss your fndings in groups.

1. What is the cheapest round-trip fare from New York to San Diego available on the website you used?_____

2. How many airlines can you choose from? _____

3. If you want to leave after noon, how many flights are available? _____

4. What is the earliest time you could arrive in San Diego? _____

5. Are any non-stop flights shown? _____

Hotel Accommodations

Using any online travel website, find information about hotels. Using that website, answer the questions below. Your teacher may want you to discuss your fndings in groups.

1. On this website, how would you find the cheapest lodging? _____

2. What would you click on if you wanted to stay at a Holiday Inn? _____

3. Which is the cheapest of the hotels listed on the website? _____

4. Does this website give information on bed & breakfast options? _____

5. Where do you click to get a map to the hotel? _____

6. If you want to search for a hotel near the zoo, what would you click? _____

Activities

You decide to spend a day in Balboa Park, and you visit the web page shown below. The following questions are designed to help you plan your visit. True/False items are indicated by a T / F preceding the statement. Some items may have more than one correct answer.

1. How many museums are there in Balboa Park? _____

2. Where would you click to find out what is happening during the time you are in San Diego?

    _____

3. T / F   You'll need to pack a lunch before entering the park.

4. T / F   You should click on Impressionist Giverny if you want to visit an artist colony.

5. T / F   You need your passport to visit the Park.

6. T / F   The San Diego Zoo is in the Park.

Reading Selections 1A–1C
Educational Policy

In our modern world an education is rapidly becoming a necessity if one hopes to earn a good living. The readings in this section provide you with the opportunity to examine your ideas about education. Your teacher may want you to talk over some of the issues in small groups before discussing answers with the class as a whole.

Before You Begin

The following questions are intended to focus your thoughts on education. The questions have no absolute right or wrong answer; each society has different opinions on the importance and structure of education. Indicate if you believe each statement is True (T) or False (F). Be prepared to give reasons and examples to support your answers.

1. _____ An education is a basic human right—every child is entitled to an education.

2. _____ Society must take responsibility for the education of all individuals.

3. _____ It is the responsibility of the family to provide an education for children.

4. _____ All children must attend school.

5. _____ School is not necessary for all children.

6. _____ A good education includes music, art, sports, social activities, etc.

7. _____ Schools should focus only on the "basics": reading, writing, and arithmetic.

8. _____ Education policy should be made at the national level, and all schools should follow a uniform plan.

9. _____ Schools should be controlled by the community in which they are located.

10. _____ Children are natural learners; education should nurture their interests and skills.

11. _____ Learning occurs primarily and most effectively in a carefully organized environment.

12. _____ The role of school is to help children learn how to function in the business world.

13. ____ Children must learn to follow the rules of society.

14. ____ Competition is essential for effective learning.

15. ____ If children are left on their own they will waste time.

16. ____ If children are encouraged to explore their interests, they will eventually learn everything that is important.

Selection 1A   Reference Book

Before You Begin Take a few minutes to think about the following questions before you read the selection on pages 97–99.

1. Can you describe the conditions under which you do your best work?

2. What are your favorite memories of school? Your least favorite memories?

3. How would you organize schools to encourage creativity and learning?

Beginning on page 97 is an excerpt from a book written for the layperson (the nonprofessional, such as a parent, a grandparent, or an everyday citizen) who is interested in teaching and learning. Read it and answer the questions that follow. Your teacher may want you to do the Vocabulary from Context exercise on pages 101–2 before you begin reading.

Comprehension

Answer the following questions according to your understanding of the authors' point of view. True/False items are indicated by a T / F preceding the statement.

1. What are the "creativity killers" the authors discuss? _____

_____

2. T / F   It is difficult to be creative when you are being observed.

3. T / F   Telling learners that they are doing a good job may hinder their creativity.

4. T / F   You should never reward a student for his or her accomplishments.

5. Do you think competition helps or hinders creativity? Give examples from your own experience.

_____

_____

6. T / F   Creativity requires freedom.

7. T / F   Teachers who want to encourage creativity should limit student choice.

8. T / F   Unreasonably high expectations can reduce creativity.

9. T / F   It is difficult to be creative on someone else's schedule.

The Creative Spirit

by Dan Goleman, Paul Kaufman, and Michael Ray

IF CREATIVITY is a child's natural state, what happens on the way to adulthood? Many of us will recognize ourselves in the sad tale of little Teresa Amabile, now a specialist in creativity.

"I was in kindergarten and my beloved teacher, Mrs. Bollier, had come to our home for an end-of-the-year conference with my mother. And, of course, I was eavesdropping on this conference from the next room."

Teresa was thrilled to hear Mrs. Bollier tell her mother, "I think Teresa shows a lot of potential for artistic creativity, and I hope that's something she really develops over the years."

"I didn't know what 'creativity' was," she recalls, "but it sure sounded like a good thing to have.

"When I was in kindergarten," she went on, "I remember rushing in every day, very excited about getting to the easel and playing with all these bright colors and these big paintbrushes we had. And there was a clay table set up where we had free access to all these art materials. I remember going home every day after kindergarten and telling my mother I wanted to play with crayons, I wanted to draw, I wanted to paint."

But kindergarten was to be the high point of Teresa's artistic career. The next year she entered a strict, traditional school, and things began to change. As she tells it, "Instead of having free access to art materials every day, art became just another subject, something that you had for an hour and a half every Friday afternoon."

Week after week, all through elementary school, it was the same art class. And a very restricted, even demoralizing one at that. "We would be given small reprints of one of the masterworks in painting, a different one every week. So, for example, I remember one week in second grade, we all got a small copy of da Vinci's *Adoration of the Magi*.

"This was meant for art appreciation, but that's not how our teacher used it. Instead we were told to take out our materials and copy it. Second-graders being asked to copy da Vinci—with their loose-leaf paper and their Crayola crayons. An exercise in frustration!

"You don't have the skill development at that age to even make all those horses and angels fit on the page, let alone make them look like anything. It was very demoralizing. You could see yourself that what you were doing was very bad.

"We weren't given any help developing skills. Worse, we were graded on these monstrosities that we produced, so we felt a heavy evaluation pressure. I was really aware at the time that my motivation for doing artwork was being completely wiped out. I no longer wanted to go home at the end of the day and take out my art materials and draw or paint."

THE CREATIVITY KILLERS

THE PSYCHOLOGICAL PRESSURES that inhibit a child's creativity occur early in life. Most children in preschool, kindergarten—even in first grade—love being in school. They are excited about exploring and learning. But by the time they are in the third or fourth grade, many don't like school, let alone have any sense of pleasure in their own creativity.

Dr. Amabile's research has identified the main creativity killers:

• **Surveillance:** hovering over kids, making them feel that they're constantly being watched while they're working. When a child is under constant observation, the risk-taking, creative urge goes underground and hides.

• **Evaluation:** making kids worry about how others judge what they're doing. Kids should be concerned primarily with how satisfied they are with their accomplishments, rather than focusing on how they are being evaluated or graded, or what their peers will think.

• **Rewards:** excessive use of prizes, such as gold stars, money, or toys. If overused, rewards deprive a child of the intrinsic pleasure of creative activity.

• **Competition:** putting kids in a desperate win-lose situation, where only one person can come out on top. Children should be allowed to progress at their own rate. (There can, however, be healthy competition that fosters team or group spirit.)

• **Over-control:** telling kids exactly how to do things—their schoolwork, their chores, even their play. Parents and teachers often confuse this kind of micromanagement with their duty to instruct. This leaves children feeling that any originality is a mistake and any exploration a waste of time.

• **Restricting Choice:** telling children which activities they should engage in instead of letting them follow where their curiosity and passion lead. Better to let a child choose what is of interest, and support that inclination.

• **Pressure:** establishing grandiose expectations for a child's performance. For example, those "hothouse" training regimes that force toddlers to learn the alphabet or math before they have any real interest can easily backfire and end up instilling an aversion for the subject being taught.

One of the greatest creativity killers, however, is more subtle and so deeply rooted in our culture that it is hardly noticed. It has to do with time.

If intrinsic motivation is one key to a child's creativity, the crucial element in cultivating it is time: open-ended time for the child to savor and explore a particular activity or material to make it his or her own. Perhaps one of the greatest crimes adults commit against a child's creativity is robbing the child of such time.

Children more naturally than adults enter that ultimate state of creativity called *flow*, in which total absorption can engender peak pleasure and creativity. In flow, time does not matter; there is only the timeless moment at hand. It is a state that is more comfortable for children than adults, who are more conscious of the passage of time.

"One ingredient of creativity is open-ended time," says Ann Lewin, Director of the Capital Children's Museum in Washington, D.C. The children's museum is an arena designed to draw children into the flow state. But, as Lewin sees there every day, there is a marked difference between the rhythms of the children who come there and the adults who bring them.

"Children have the capacity to get lost in whatever they're doing in a way that is much harder for an adult," she says. "Children need the opportunity to follow their natural inclinations, their own particular talents, to go wherever their proclivities lead them."

Unfortunately, children are interrupted, torn out of deep concentration; their desire to work something through is frustrated. Lewin explains: "Adults have the compulsion to march through and see everything. But there are hundreds of things that can deeply engross a child here, things they can spend hours with. And you see the adults pulling them away, tugging at them and telling them, 'Enough, stop it, let's go.'

"It's a terribly frustrating thing to be stopped when you're in the middle of the process. But we live in such a hurry-up way. So again and again children are stopped in the middle of things they love to do. They are scheduled. There isn't the time for children to relax into their own rhythm."

Critical Reading

The following questions are designed to give you an opportunity to explore ideas presented in "The Creative Spirit." Answer each question according to your understanding of the passage and your own experience. Some questions may have more than one correct answer. True/False items are indicated by a T / F preceding the statement.

1. T / F   If we do not evaluate students, they will not learn how to do things correctly.

2. T / F   Goals are necessary for learning.

3. At what point does a goal become unreasonable for a learner? Who sets goals for learning?

_____

_____

4. The authors assert that children arrive at school full of energy and curiosity but that by the third or fourth year, they have lost the sense of pleasure in their own learning. Do you agree or disagree? Why? _____

_____

5. T / F   Children must learn to complete tasks on time.

Discussion/Composition

1. Each of the "creativity killers" is listed below, paired with a word that expresses a similar or related idea. For each pair,
   a. define the difference between the two terms;
   b. discuss an experience in school when your creativity was encouraged or "killed." (You are not allowed to give this exercise as an example. ☺)

surveillance	observation
evaluation	self-assessment
rewards	recognition
competition	personal achievement
control	support
restricting choice	guidance
pressure	goal setting

2. What is the relationship between structured, organized activity and individual creativity? Is it the responsibility of schools to encourage creativity in individual children or to promote cooperation and conformity to society's values? Can both be accomplished in the same school?

3. What is the relationship between learning and creativity? Is all learning creative? Can you think of situations where important learning occurs in spite of controls by school?

4. What is "flow" (described near the end of the article)? When was the last time you experienced flow? What were the circumstances? What can an individual learner do to create this experience for him- or herself? How should schools be organized to promote flow?

Vocabulary from Context

Both the ideas and the vocabulary in the following exercise are taken from "The Creativity Killers." Use the context provided to determine the meanings of the italicized words. Write a definition, synonym, or description of each of the italicized vocabulary items in the space provided.

A continuing debate in education concerns the tension between the need for children to be given freedom to explore and learn and the responsibility of school to organize their experience and structure their environment so that they learn attitudes and skills that are important for society. It is clear that children are naturally creative, curious, and original in their approach to learning.

1. _____

2. _____

3. _____

This *creativity* needs to be encouraged. As children begin to walk, usually between the ages of 12 months and 2 years, they begin to explore their surroundings. *Toddlers* are naturally curious; they want to explore, and they are not afraid to take risks, to try out new things. This is good; *risk taking* is a natural part of learning.

4. _____

5. _____

6. _____

7. _____

But parents and teachers have a responsibility to make sure children are safe, and we also want children to learn the skills and attitudes considered appropriate by society. Schools need to create environments in which children learn what is expected of them when they grow up. The difficulty is structuring activities that help children learn without limiting them. When we *inhibit* them, we reduce the chances that they will develop their creativity. We want activities that provide guidance without overly *restricting* their choices. We want children to *savor* new experiences. Intense enjoyment of experiences is a natural state for youngsters, an *intrinsic* part of their natures.

8. _____

9. _____

10. _____

11. _____

12. _____

13. _____

14. _____

15. _____

16. _____

17. _____

18. _____

19. _____

An important aspect of this issue is related to the nature of learning and the institutional structures that encourage learning. For learning to occur, children have to find school motivating—it has to provide interesting and energizing activities that appeal to their interests, their loves, their passions. Whether they are playing alone or with *peers,* they have the ability to become so totally involved in their activity that they appear to become lost in time. This state of being totally *engrossed* in an activity is often referred to as *flow*—when learning is so involving that time doesn't matter. The *rhythm* of the activity is similar to the rhythm of the learner; like dancers who move together on the dance floor, the learner and the activity are working together. When the child's inner rhythm and the school's schedule are not the same, children's creativity suffers. And this is often a problem, because schools are organized by adults, who often follow the clock rather than their creativity. It is almost as if they are governed by clock *compulsions;* they seem to be driven or forced, unable to do anything without time limits.

The difficulty is in developing programs that support learning without inhibiting creativity. How do we provide structure without holding back creativity? How do you observe children, for example, without making them feel as if they are under *surveillance*? How do you stay close to them as they play without appearing to *hover*? At what point does some amount of concern for their well-being become too much, with this *excessive* attention limiting learning and creativity? We want children to have a healthy self-confidence in their abilities, and there are times when it is appropriate for them to attempt to do better than others. However, we do not want *competition* to become so important that they lose sight of the joy of learning. We don't want children to have too great a desire for success; a *desperate* desire to win actually makes learning more difficult. It is also true that when overly complex programs are imposed on children, the result is often *aversion* rather than attraction to learning activities. Programs such as preschool reading programs, or programs intended to boost children's intelligence through intense competition, are likely to have the opposite effect. School programs need to support children's *proclivities.* When activities support their natural inclinations, they will learn, naturally and easily.

Figurative Language and Idioms

1. In the section "Surveillance," the authors say that constant observation causes the creative urge to "go underground and hide." What is meant by this? _____

2. In the final section, the authors comment that children have the ability to "get lost in" an activity. Do they see this as a good thing? Why or why not? _____

Below is an exerpt from an American textbook for schoolchildren. Read the selection, and answer the questions that follow.

American Values in Education

Our school system has developed as it has because the American people value education highly. Some of the traditional values which have developed over the years are:

1. Public education should be *free*. There should be no hidden charges to prevent any citizen from receiving a good education at public expense.

2. Schooling should be *equal* and open to all. No one should be discriminated against because of race, religion, or financial status.

3. The public schools should be *free of any creed or religion*. The schools of the United States are open to all Americans regardless of their religious beliefs. The Supreme Court has held that no special prayer or Bible reading shall be required. However, religious schools (sometimes called parochial schools) are permitted outside of the public school system.

4. Public schools are *controlled by the state and local governments* within which they are located. Local school boards run the public schools under laws passed by the state legislature. The State Board of Education assists the local schools, but does not give orders to the district board. The United States Department of Education also assists with advice and information, but the actual control is located in the local school district, where the people know the local situation.

5. Attendance at school is *compulsory*. Parents cannot decide to keep their children out of school. Each state compels the attendance of young people, usually between the ages of 7 and 16.

6. Schooling should be *enriched* and not just confined to the fundamentals. Most Americans believe that schools should be places where young people can grow in body, mind, and spirit. Athletics, clubs, social events, and creative arts are a part of each person's education. Schools should be lively places where individuals are encouraged to develop to their greatest potential.

Critical Reading

Using the six "traditional values" of American education described above, summarize the educational philosophy of another country with which you are familiar. Where do you find similarities? What are the differences?

Discussion/Composition

1. Who should make decisions about the schools—parents? professional educators? elected officials? religious leaders? specially appointed experts? the children themselves? Read the statements below and discuss the pros and cons of each. With whom do you agree?

   a. Parents: "They are our kids. We know what is best for them. We should decide what they learn and how they are taught."

   b. Teachers: "What do parents know? We are the ones with the special training. We should make the decisions."

   c. Government officials: "We have the best view of the issues. We know the budget, and we understand the laws and how they apply. Only we can make the best decisions."

   d. Religious authorities: "Schools that teach facts but no values weaken the moral strength of the country. We can provide the wisdom and insight on which all teaching should be based."

   e. University experts: "We have studied the problems and done the research. We should be consulted before any decisions are made."

   f. Children: "It is our lives and education that are at stake. No decisions should be made without our advice and agreement."

2. Does the United States live up to the philosophical ideals listed above? Do you think other countries fulfill their educational goals? To what extent can a country live up to its educational ideals? Give examples to support your opinions.

The previous articles in this section discuss how schools best educate children and outline "traditional values" of education in the United States. The balance between public values and personal beliefs can be a challenging one for any school system. The article that follows discusses these issues in the context of a recent legal case in Great Britain.

Before You Begin

1. Do you believe students should be able to wear whatever they want to school? If not, what kinds of rules would you recommend?

2. The term *human rights* refers to the basic rights and freedoms that should belong to all human beings. What would you list as basic human rights?

Read the article to discover what a British court considers a human right. During your initial reading, do not worry about unfamiliar vocabulary. Read for a general understanding; you can always return to the article if you need to, to answer specific comprehension questions.

School Violated Student's Rights, British Court Rules
Muslim Girl Sent Home for Wearing Jilbab

Jill Lawless. Associated Press.

(1) LONDON — A school violated a student's human rights by banning her from wearing a traditional Muslim gown to class, a British court ruled yesterday, ending a more than two-year legal battle.

(2) Assimilating Muslim students is a sensitive political issue in Europe, especially in France, which last year banned "conspicuous religious symbols" such as head scarves from state schools. Britain allows each school to decide what form of dress is appropriate.

(3) Shabina Begum, now 16, was sent home from school in Luton, north of London, in September 2002 for wearing the jilbab, a long, flowing gown covering all her body except her hands and face.

(4) She first went to the High Court, arguing that the ban breached her right to religious freedom under the European Convention on Human Rights. The court rejected that argument in June. But yesterday a panel of three Court of Appeal judges ruled that Begum had been illegally excluded from the school, which "unlawfully denied her the right to manifest her religion." The teenager was repre-

sented in her appeal by Cherie Booth, wife of [former] Prime Minister Tony Blair.

(5) Muslim leaders welcomed the ruling that Denbigh High School had breached Begum's right to freedom of religion. The school said it was trying to respect the views of all its students—and balance competing views of what is "appropriate" Muslim attire.

(6) Begum, who now attends a school that allows her to wear the jilbab, said the ruling was "a victory for all Muslims who wish to preserve their identity and values despite prejudice and bigotry. It is amazing that in the so-called free world I have to fight to wear this attire," she said.

(7) Four-fifths of Denbigh High's students are Muslims, and the school said its ban on the jilbab had the support of many students and parents, who looked to the school to protect children from the influence of religious extremists.

(8) The school argued that the jilbab posed a health and safety risk, and might cause divisions among pupils, with those who wore traditional dress being seen as "better Muslims" than others. Pupils are allowed to wear trousers, skirts or a

traditional shalwar kameez, consisting of trousers and a tunic, and female pupils may wear head scarves.

(9) Yasin Rehman of the Luton Council of Mosques said the school's existing dress code was "very satisfactory" and worried the court's ruling could complicate matters. "There is no prescribed Islamic dress code," he said. "People of Islam, like other religions, say that you should dress modestly. The question is How do you define that? This will create a lot of complications. Where is the end to this?"

Comprehension

Answer the following questions. True/False questions are indicated by a T / F preceding an item. Instead of writing out a response to the open-ended questions, underline the answer in the text.

2 1. T /(F) Shabina Begum was not allowed to wear a headscarf to school.

4 2. (T)/ F According to a British court, refusing to allow a student to wear traditional Muslim dress to school violated her human rights.

5 3. (T)/ F At the time the article was written Shabina attended Denbigh High School.

6 4. T /(F) All Muslims considered the court's decision a victory against prejudice and bigotry.

7 5. According to the article, why did many parents support banning the jilbab? *to Prevent the in* *of religion*

8 6. What two reasons did the school give for banning the jilbab? *it cause health and safety risk, cause divis*

9 7. T /(F) Islam is the only religion that says that people should dress modestly.

3 8. The article describes two kinds of traditional attire. What is a *jilbab?* What is a *shalwar kameez?* *it's a long flowing gown covering all her body except hand, face. Trousers and a tunic.*

Critical Reading

1. Do you think it helped Shabina's case that her lawyer was the wife of the former Prime Minister?

2. Do you think the court decision reported in the article will affect all of Britain's state schools? What makes you think one way or the other?

3. The article describes different reactions to the court's decision.

   • Why do you think some Muslim leaders "welcomed the ruling"?

   • Why do you think Yasin Rehman of the Luton Council of Mosques feels that the school's existing dress code is "very satisfactory"? What do you think he meant when he asked, "Where is the end to this?"

Discussion/Composition

1. Many societies face the complex issue of how to welcome minority students into the larger culture, while still respecting and maintaining the home culture. What steps do you think schools should take to respect students' home cultures and beliefs? Support your point of view with examples.

2. Do you believe the court made the right decision? Do you believe that wearing religious clothing is a "human right"? Why or why not?

3. Returning to a question you considered before you began reading: Beyond religious clothing, do you believe that there are limits to what students should be able to wear in school? Why or why not?

Vocabulary from Context

This exercise is designed to give you additional clues to determine the meanings of unfamiliar vocabulary items in context. In the paragraph of "School Violated Student's Rights" indicated by the number in parentheses, find the word that best fits the meaning given. Your teacher may want to read these aloud as you quickly scan* the paragraph to find the answer.

1. (1) Which word means *took away; went against; disrespected?* ___violated___

2. (1) Which word means *disallowing; refusing to allow; prohibiting; forbidding?* ___banned___

3. (4) Which word means *violated; went against; failed to maintain?* ___arguing reached___

4. (4) Which word means *decided; declared?* ___ruled___

5. (4) Which word means *to show; to make clear?* ___said___

6. (5) Which word means *clothing?* ___attire___

7. (6) Which word means *to keep; to maintain?* ___preserve___

8. (6) Which word means *prejudice; racism; narrow-mindedness; intolerance?* ___bigotry___

9. (9) Which word means *moderately; carefully; not overly sexual; not drawing attention to oneself?*
   ___modestly___

Stems and Affixes

Both the ideas and the italicized words in the sentences below are taken from "School Violated Student's Rights." Beneath the sentences is a list of synonyms and definitions. Use your knowledge of stems and affixes* and the context to match each italicized word with its definition by placing the appropriate letter on the line before each sentence.

V __d__ 1. Efforts *to assimilate* Muslim students are a sensitive political issue in Europe.

adj __b__ 2. Last year, France banned "*conspicuous* religious symbols."

V __c__ 3. Because she wore traditional Muslim attire, Shabina Begum was *excluded* from school.

N __f__ 4. Shabina felt that the ban on traditional attire was the result of *prejudice*.

V __e__ 5. The first court *rejected* the argument that wearing a jilbab is a human right.

adj __a__ 6. Some people argued that Shabina did not have to wear the jilbab, that there is no *prescribed* Islamic dress code.

a. required; set down in writing or otherwise

b. easily seen; obvious

c. kept out; prevented from entering

d. to make similar; to absorb into society

e. threw out; refused to accept

f. prejudging the situation before one has the facts; bigotry; preconceived ideas

---

* For list of all stems and affixes taught in *Reader's Choice*, see the Appendix.

Dictionary Study

Many words have more than one meaning. When you use the dictionary to discover the meaning of an unfamiliar word or phrase, you need to use the context to determine which definition is appropriate. Use the dictionary entries provided to select the best definition(s) for each of the italicized words below. Write the number of the definition in the space provided.

_____ 1. Muslim leaders welcomed the *ruling*.

_____ 2. The teenager was represented in her *appeal* by Cherie Booth, wife of the former Prime Minister Tony Blair.

YourDictionary.com

rul·ing [rōō'lĭng]

–adjective
1. Exercising control or authority: *the ruling junta; ruling circles of the government.*
2. Widespread, predominant: *the ruling principle.*

–noun
1. The act of governing or controlling.
2. The act of drawing straight lines with a ruler.
3. An authoritative or official decision: *a court ruling.*

Dictionary.com Unabridged (v 1.1)

ap·peal [uh-**peel**]

–noun
1. an earnest request for aid, support, sympathy, mercy, etc.; entreaty; petition; plea.
2. a request or reference to some person or authority for a decision, corroboration, judgment, etc.
3. *Law.*
   a. an application or proceeding for review by a higher tribunal.
   b. (in a legislative body or assembly) a formal question as to the correctness of a ruling by a presiding officer.
   c. Obsolete. a formal charge or accusation.
4. the power or ability to attract, interest, amuse, or stimulate the mind or emotions: *The game has lost its appeal.*
5. *Obsolete.* a summons or challenge.

–verb (used without object)
6. to ask for aid, support, mercy, sympathy, or the like; make an earnest entreaty: *The college appealed to its alumni for funds.*
7. *Law.* to apply for review of a case or particular issue to a higher tribunal.
8. to have need of or ask for proof, a decision, corroboration, etc.
9. to be especially attractive, pleasing, interesting, or enjoyable: *The red hat appeals to me.*

–verb (used with object)
10. *Law.*
   a. to apply for review of (a case) to a higher tribunal.
   b. *Obsolete.* to charge with a crime before a tribunal.

Vocabulary Review

Two of the words in each line below are similar in meaning. Circle the word that does not belong.

1. prejudice	bigotry	assimilation
2. unlawful	ruling	illegal
3. violated	breached	banned
4. dress	appeal	attire

The following story is an excerpt from the novel *How the Garcia Girls Lost Their Accents* by Julia Alvarez. In the novel, the four García sisters, born in the Dominican Republic, come with their parents to the United States as young girls. They find themselves in a fast-moving and confusing new culture with all of its choices and challenges. Somehow, they have to balance the differences between their new life and the values and traditions of their native culture as represented by their parents. The excerpt provides an example of the sort of challenges Yolanda, the third daughter, faces as she attempts to establish herself as a poet in a society whose values are very different from the one that shaped her mother's expectations of her daughters.

Before You Begin Part of becoming an adult is establishing one's own identity, independent of the expectations of one's parents.

1. Have you ever given a public presentation with your mother in the audience?

2. Do you have friends whose views of you are very different from the views your parents have of you?

3. Have you ever been in a situation where you were nervous because your parents were going to learn something about you that you thought they might not like?

As you read the story, try to imagine yourself in Yolanda's place. Do not worry about unfamiliar words; keep reading to appreciate the humor and discomfort of the situation.

Yolanda

(1) Yolanda, the third of the four girls, became a schoolteacher but not on purpose. For years after graduate school, she wrote down poet under profession on questionnaires and income tax forms, and later amended it to *writer*-slash-*teacher*. Finally, acknowledging that she had not written much of anything in years, she announced to her family that she was not a poet anymore.

(2) Secretly, the mother was disappointed because she had always meant for her Yo to be the famous one. The story she told about her third daughter no longer had the charm of a prophetic ending: "And, of course, she became a poet." But the mother tried to convince her daughter that it was better to be a happy nobody than a sad somebody. Yolanda, who was still as clever as when the mother had tried to persuade her that white was a better color than pink, was not convinced.

(3) The mother used to go to all the poetry readings her daughter gave in town and sit in the front row applauding each poem and giving standing ovations. Yolanda was so

embarrassed that she tried to keep her readings a secret from her mother, but somehow the mother always found out about them and appeared, first row, center. Even when she behaved herself, the mother threw her daughter off just by her presence. Yolanda even read poems addressed to lovers, sonnets set in bedrooms, but she knew her mother did not believe in sex for girls. But the mother seemed not to notice the subject of her poems, or if she did, to ascribe the love scenes to her Yoyo's great imagination.

(4) "That one has always had a great imagination," the mother confided to whoever sat next to her. At a recent reading the daughter gave after her long silence, the mother's neighbor was the daughter's lover. The mother did not know that the handsome, graying professor at her side knew her daughter at all; she thought he was just someone interested in poetry. "Of all the four girls," the mother told the lover, "that Yo has always loved poetry."

(5) "That's her nickname, Yo, Yoyo," the mother explained. "She complains she wants her name, but you have to take shortcuts when there's four of them. Four girls, imagine!"

(6) "Really?" the lover said, although Yolanda had already filled him in on her family and her bastardized name—Yo, Joe, Yoyo. He knew better than to take shortcuts. Jo-laahn-dah, she had drilled him. Supposedly, the parents were heavy-duty Old World, but the four daughters sounded pretty wild for all that. There had been several divorces among them, including Yolanda's. The oldest, a child psychologist, had married the analyst she'd been seeing when her first marriage broke up, something of the sort. The second one was doing a lot of drugs to keep her weight down. The youngest one had just gone off with a German man when they discovered she was pregnant.

(7) "But that Yo," the mother continued, pointing to her daughter where she sat with the other readers waiting for the sound system to work properly so the program could begin, "that Yo has always had a great imagination." The buzz of talk was punctuated now and then by a crackling, amplified "testing" spoken too close to the microphone. Yolanda watched the absorbed conversation of her mother and lover with growing uneasiness.

(8) "Yes, Yoyo has always loved poetry. Why, I remember the time we went on a trip to New York. She couldn't have been more than three." The mother was warming to her story. The lover noticed that the mother's eyes were those that looked at him softly at night from the daughter's face.

(9) "Testing," a voice exploded into the room.

(10) The mother looked up, thinking the poetry reading had begun. The lover waved the voice away. He wanted to hear the story.

(11) "We went up to New York, Lolo and I. He had a convention there, and we decided to make a vacation of it. We hadn't had a vacation since the first baby was born. We were very poor." The mother lowered her voice. "Words can't describe how poor we were. But we were starting to see better days."

(12) "Really?" the lover said. He had fixed on that word as one that gave the appropriate amount of encouragement but did not interrupt the flow of the mother's story.

(13) "We left the girls back home, but that one"—the mother pointed again to the daughter, who widened her eyes at her lover—"that one was losing all her hair. We took her with us so she could see a specialist. Turned out to be just nerves."

(14) The lover knew Yolanda would not have wanted him to know about this indelicacy of her body. She did not even like to pluck her eyebrows in his presence. An immediate bathrobe after her bath. Lights out when they made love. Other times, she carried on about the Great Mother and the holiness of the body and sexual energy being eternal delight. Sometimes, he complained he felt caught between a women's libber and the Catholic senorita. "You sound like my ex," she accused him.

(15) "We got on this crowded bus one afternoon." The mother shook her head remembering how crowded the bus had been. "I couldn't begin to tell you how crowded it was. It was more sardines in a can than you could shake sticks at."

(16) "Really?"

(17) "You don't believe me?" the mother accused him. The lover nodded his head to show he was convinced. "But let me tell you, that bus was so crowded, Lolo and I got our wires totally mixed up. I was sure Lolo had her, and Lolo was sure she was with me. Anyhow, to make it a short story, we got off at our stop, and we looked at each other. Where's Yo? we asked at the same time. Meanwhile, that bus was roaring away from us."

(18) "Well, I'll tell you, we broke into a run like two crazy people! It was rush hour. Everyone was turning around to look at us like we were running from the police or something." The mother's voice was breathless remembering that run. The lover waited for her to catch up with the bus in her memory.

(19) "Testing?" a garbled voice asked without much conviction.

(20) "After about two blocks, we flagged the driver down and climbed aboard. And you won't believe what we found?"

(21) The lover knew better than to take a guess.

(22) "We found that one surrounded by a crowd like Jesus and the elders."

(23) "Really?" The lover smiled, admiring the daughter from a distance. Yolanda was one of the more popular instructors at the college where he chaired the Comp Lit Department.

(24) "She hadn't even realized we were gone. She had a circle of people around her, listening to her reciting a poem! As a matter of fact, it was a poem I'd taught her. Maybe you've heard of it? It's by that guy who wrote that poem about the blackbird."

(25) "Stevens?" the lover guessed.

(26) The mother cocked her head. "I'm not sure. Anyhow," she continued, "imagine! Three years old and already drawing crowds. Of course, she became a poet."

(27) "You don't mean Poe, do you? Edgar Allan Poe?"

(28) "Yes, that's him! That's him!" the mother cried out. "The poem was about a princess who lived by the sea or something. Let's see." She began to recite:

> Many many years ago, something. . . . something,
> In a . . . . . something by the sea . . . . .
> A princess there lived whom you may remember
> By the name of Annabel Lee . . .

(29) The mother looked up and realized that the hushed audience was staring at her. She blushed. The lover chuckled and squeezed her arm. At the podium, the poet had been introduced and was waiting for the white-haired woman in the first row to finish talking. "For Clive," Yolanda said, introducing her first poem, "'Bedroom Sestina.'" Clive smiled sheepishly at the mother, who smiled proudly at her daughter.

Comprehension

EXERCISE 1

This exercise is intended to help you check your comprehension of the basic story. Indicate if each of the statements below is true (T) or false (F) according to your understanding of the story. Your teacher may want you and your classmates to discuss your answers to these questions before going on to Exercise 2.

1. _____ Yolanda is getting ready to teach a class.

2. _____ Yolanda wants her mother to hear her speak.

3. _____ Yolanda sees her mother in the audience.

4. _____ Yolanda wants her mother to know all about her life.

5. _____ Yolanda's poems are sometimes about sexual situations.

6. _____ Yolanda's mother thinks that Yolanda writes about personal experiences.

7. _____ Yolanda's mother knows the man she is sitting next to.

8. _____ Yolanda is happy that her mother is talking to someone in the audience.

9. _____ Clive knows Yolanda.

10. _____ Clive is Yolanda's boss.

11. _____ Yolanda's mother is more traditional than Yolanda.

12. _____ Yolanda's mother is ashamed of Yolanda.

13. _____ Yolanda's mother is nervous watching Yolanda on stage.

14. _____ Yolanda has liked poetry for most of her life.

15. _____ Yolanda's mother recited a poem written by her daughter.

16. _____ Yolanda's poem is about the man sitting next to her mother.

17. _____ Yolanda's mother thinks Yolanda's poem is about the man sitting next to her.

EXERCISE 2

People's identities are an important part of this story. Below are words from the story that refer to particular people. The paragraph where each word or phrase is located is given in parentheses. Next to each item, write S if the words all refer to the same person and D if the words refer to different people.

1. ____ (4) Yo (6) Yoyo (6) Jo-laahn-dah

2. ____ (4) mother's neighbor (4) daughter's lover (4) graying professor

3. ____ (14) Yolanda (14) woman's libber (14) Catholic señorita

4. ____ (17) Yo (17) Lolo (17) Lover

5. ____ (23) lover (23) popular instructor

6. ____ (23) lover (23) chair of the Comp Lit Department

7. ____ (29) mother (29) poet (29) white-haired woman

8. ____ (29) mother (29) she (29) woman in the first row

9. ____ (4) mother's neighbor (29) lover (29) Clive

Critical Reading

1. Humor is created in this story when the reader knows something that a character does not know. Can you find examples of this in the story?

2. In the first paragraph of the story, Yolanda announces that she is no longer a poet. But in the fourth paragraph, the author refers to a "recent reading the daughter gave after her long silence." Do you think that this means that Yolanda once again considers herself a poet? Why or why not?

3. In this short narrative, the author manages to tell us a great deal about the three main characters. Below is a list of descriptors. Indicate which ones you think describe Yolanda (Y), her mother (M), and Clive (C). Each word may describe more than one character, and there may be more than one correct answer. Be prepared to defend your choices.

____ poet   ____ confident

____ older   ____ storyteller

____ conservative   ____ proud

____ embarrassed   ____ outgoing

____ lover

Discussion/Composition

1. In what ways is this a story about love? Use examples from the text to support your point of view.

2. "Yolanda" comes from a book entitled *How the Garcia Girls Lost Their Accents*. The book contains stories about the adjustments an immigrant family makes to build a life in a new country. Think of the term *accent* in the broadest sense, as a metaphor. What can it mean to "lose an accent" when moving to a new country? In what ways has Yolanda "lost her accent"?

3. In what ways has Yolanda turned out as her mother hoped and expected she would? In what ways is her life different?

Vocabulary from Context

EXERCISE 1

Use the context provided to determine the meaning of the italicized words. Write a definition, synonym, or description of each of the italicized vocabulary items in the space provided.

1. _____

2. _____

Many people are not comfortable giving a speech when their family is in the audience watching them. As Yolanda stood on stage preparing to speak, it was easy to see she was embarrassed because she *blushed* bright red. Her mother, Yolanda's greatest supporter, didn't seem to notice, though. Perhaps she *ascribed* Yolanda's red face to the hot lights of the stage.

Later, Yolanda was afraid that everyone would laugh at her mother, but she heard only soft laughter from someone sitting in the front row. As she looked down, she saw it was the man sitting

3. _____ next to her mother who was *chuckling*.

EXERCISE 2

This exercise is designed to give you additional clues to determine the meanings of unfamiliar vocabulary items in context. In the paragraph of "Yolanda" indicated by the number in parentheses, find the word or phrase that best fits the meaning given. Your teacher may want to read these aloud as you quickly scan* the paragraph to find the answer.

1. (6) Which word means *not officially or legally or formally correct; not genuine?*

2. (12) Which two-word phrase means *decided on; selected?*

3. (14) Which word means *something that is personal, private, and a bit unpleasant?*

_____

* For an introduction to scanning, see Unit 1.

EXERCISE 3

This exercise should be done after you have finished reading "Yolanda." The exercise is designed to give you practice using context clues and your knowledge of stems and affixes to guess the meaning of unfamiliar vocabulary. Give a definition, synonym, or description of each of the words or phrases below. The number in parentheses indicates the paragraph in which the word or phrase can be found. Your teacher may want you to do these orally or in writing.

1. (1) amended _____

2. (1) acknowledging _____

3. (4) confided _____

4. (6) heavy-duty _____

5. (7) uneasiness _____

6. (26) cocked _____

7. (26) drawing _____

8. (29) podium _____

Figurative Language and Idioms

In the paragraph indicated by the number in parentheses, find the phrase that best fits the meaning given. Your teacher may want to read these aloud as you quickly scan the paragraph to find the answer.

1. (3) What phrase means *made her daughter feel nervous?* _____

2. (5) What phrase means *do things to save time or energy?* _____

3. (6) What phrase means *old fashioned; traditional?* _____

4. (8) What phrase means *becoming excited about; becoming enthusiastic about?* _____

5. (10) What phrase means *ignored the speaker?* _____

6. (14) What phrase is an informal term for a *person who believes in equal rights for women?* _____

_____

Dictionary Study

Many words have more than one meaning. When you use a dictionary to discover the meaning of an unfamiliar word or phrase, you need to use the context to determine which definition is appropriate. Use the dictionary entries provided to select the best definition(s) for each of the italicized words below. Write the number of the definition in the space provided.

_____ 1. Yolanda's mother and lover were *absorbed* in conversation.

_____ 2. He *chaired* the Comparative Literature Department at the college.

_____ 3. "You sound like my *ex*," Yolanda accused him.

_____ 4. Clive smiled *sheepishly* at the mother, who smiled proudly at her daughter.

Dictionary.com Unabridged (v 1.1)
ab·sorb [ab-sawrb]

–verb (used with object)
1. to suck up or drink in (a liquid); soak up: *A sponge absorbs water.*
2. to swallow up the identity or individuality of; incorporate: *The empire absorbed many small nations.*
3. to involve the full attention of; to engross or engage wholly: *so absorbed in a book that he did not hear the bell.*
4. to occupy or fill: *This job absorbs all of my time.*
5. to take up or receive by chemical or molecular action: *Carbonic acid is formed when water absorbs carbon dioxide.*
6. to take in without echo, recoil, or reflection: *to absorb sound and light; to absorb shock.*
7. to take in and utilize: *The market absorbed all the computers we could build. Can your brain absorb all this information?*
8. to pay for (costs, taxes, etc.): *The company will absorb all the research costs.*
9. *Archaic.* To swallow up.

[Origin:1480–90; < L *absorbére*, equiv. to ab- AB- + *sorbére* to suck in, swallow]

---

chair [châr]

–noun
1. A piece of furniture consisting of a seat, legs, back, and often arms, designed to accommodate one person.
2. A seat of office, authority, or dignity, such as that of a bishop.
3. a. An office or position of authority, such as a professorship.
   b. A person who holds an office or a position of authority, such as one who presides over a meeting or administers a department of instruction at a college; a chairperson.
4. The position of a player in an orchestra.
5. *Slang.* The electric chair.
6. A seat carried about on poles; a sedan chair.
7. Any of several devices that serve to support or secure, such as a metal block that supports and holds railroad track in position.

tr.v. **chaired, chair·ing, chairs**
1. To install in a position of authority, especially as a presiding officer.
2. To preside over as chairperson: *chair a meeting.*

[Middle English *chaiere*, from Old French, from Latin *cathedra*; see **cathedra.**]

---

ex¹ [ĕks]

–preposition
1. Not including; without: *a stock price ex dividend.*
2. Abbr. x. Business Free of any transport or handling charges incurred before removal from a given location: *bought the goods ex warehouse.*
3. From, but not having graduated with, the class of: *a Columbia alumnus, ex '70.*

[Latin; see *eghs* in Indo-European roots.]

ex² [ĕks]

–noun

The letter *X, x.*

tr.v. **exed, ex·ing, ex·es**
To delete or cross out: *He exed each item off the to-do list.*

ex³ [ĕks]

–noun Slang

A former spouse or partner. [From ex-.]

---

sheep·ish [shee-pish]

–adjective
1. embarrassed or bashful, as by having done something wrong or foolish.
2. like sheep, as in meekness, docility, etc.

[Origin: 1150–1200; ME *shepisshe,* See SHEEP, -ISH¹]

—Related forms
sheep·ish·ly, *adverb*
sheep·ish·ness, *noun*

Before You Begin

1. What are stereotypes? Can you give an example of stereotypes you have about other nations? Can you give an example of a mistaken stereotype that others have about your country/culture?

2. Are stereotypes good or bad?

Do stereotypes represent incorrect prejudices, or do they function as useful first steps in cross-cultural contact? Read "The Stereotype of Stereotypes" to see what you think. First, read the article quickly to get an overall sense of the arguments presented. Then do Comprehension Exercise 1. Your teacher may want you to do Vocabulary from Context Exercise 1 on page 121 before you begin reading.

The Stereotype of Stereotypes

Bruce Bower

(1) Psychologist Yueh-Ting Lee received an electronic mail message several years ago that included some barbed observations about the quality of life in several countries. "Heaven is a place with an American house, Chinese food, British police, a German car, and French art." Lee's correspondent wrote, "Hell is a place with a Japanese house, Chinese police, British food, German art, and a French car."

(2) While these national stereotypes fall short of absolute truths, asserts Lee of Westfield (Mass.) State College, they are accurate enough to give the aphorism its humorous punch. Houses in the United States indeed boast more space, on average, than Japanese dwellings. A Chinese inn probably holds greater culinary potential than a British pub.

(3) In this respect, stereotypes, rather than representing unjustified prejudices, typically function as thought-efficient starting points for understanding other cultures and social groups, as well as the individuals who belong to them, Lee holds.

(4) "Stereotypes are probabilistic beliefs we use to categorize people, objects, and events," Lee proposes. "We have to have stereotypes to deal with so much information in a world with which we are often uncertain and unfamiliar."

(5) Many psychologists find this opinion about as welcome as a cut in their research grants. They view stereotyping as a breeding ground for errant generalizations about others that easily lead to racism, sexism, and other forms of bigotry.

(6) In the realm of stereotypes, intelligence gives way to misjudgment, maintains Charles Stangor of the University of Maryland at College Park. People employ stereotypes mainly to simplify how they think about others and to enhance their views of themselves and the groups to which they belong, Stangor holds. In the hands of politically powerful folks, stereotypes abet efforts to stigmatize and exploit selected groups, he adds.

(7) Stangor's argument fails to give stereotypes their due as often helpful, if not absolutely precise, probes of the social world, Lee responds. He contends that a growing body of research suggests that in many real-life situations, stereotypes accurately capture cultural or group differences.

(8) For more than 60 years, scientists have treated stereotypes as by definition erroneous, illogical, and inflexible. This view was voiced in journalist Walter Lippman's 1922 book *Public Opinion,* in which he argued that stereotypes of social groups invariably prove incomplete and biased.

(9) In the 1950s, psychologist Gordon W. Allport characterized stereotypes as invalid beliefs about all members of a group. Allport treated the opinion "all Germans are efficient" as a stereotype, but not "Germans, on average, are more efficient than people in other countries." Debate arose at that time over whether some stereotypes encase a "kernel of truth."

(10) Lippman's fear that stereotypes cause social harm gained particular favor after 1970, as psychologists rushed to expose errors and biases in social judgments.

Recently, however, psychologists have shown more interest in delineating the extent to which decision making proves accurate in specific contexts.

(11) Lee's approach to stereotypes falls squarely within the focus on accuracy of judgment. His interest in how people comprehend ethnic and cultural differences intensified after he emigrated from China to the United States in 1986 to attend graduate school. At that point, he began to suspect that a keener scientific understanding of stereotypes might have valuable applications. For instance, Lee asserts, efforts at conflict resolution between ethnic groups or nations may work best if both sides receive help in confronting real cultural differences that trigger mutual animosities.

(12) "Group differences, not prejudice, are the root cause of tension and conflict between various cultural and racial groups," he contends. "The most effective way to improve intergroup relations is to admit and to discuss frankly the existing differences at the same time explaining that there is nothing wrong with being different."

(13) Bridge-building efforts of this kind counteract the natural tendency to emphasize negative features in stereotypes, argues Reuben M. Baron of the University of Connecticut in Storrs. Humans evolved in groups that negotiated a dangerous world, he states. Our ancestors must have relied on stereotypes to marshal quick responses to potential threats, such as distinguishing predators from prey, friends from enemies, and fellow group members from outsiders, Baron asserts.

(14) The ability to categorize individuals into "types" may also have been crucial for communicating with others as groups grew in size and complexity, Baron proposes. In large communities, stereotypes capitalized on people's propensity to fill social roles that match their own personal qualities. Warriors in an ancient society, for instance, might reasonably have been stereotyped as aggressive and unemotional, while storytellers and musicians were accurately tagged as expressive and friendly.

(15) Despite their handiness, even accurate stereotypes can result in mistaken beliefs about others, according to Baron.

(16) Consider the misunderstandings over punctuality that develop between Mexican and U.S. businesspeople. Lee says that north of the border, Mexicans get stereotyped as "the mañana people" because of their tendency to show up for meetings considerably after prearranged times and to miss deadlines for completing assigned tasks. U.S. officials may see this trait as unforgivable deal breaking, whereas their Mexican counterparts—who do not dispute their own tardiness—deride Americans as "robots" who rigidly reach conclusions by specified dates before gathering all relevant data and fully grasping the issues.

(17) Businesspeople from each culture perceptively categorize the behavior of those in the other group but misunderstand the cultural roots of their different time perspectives, Lee says.

(18) Such subtleties of stereotyping have gone largely unexplored, remarks David C. Funder, a psychologist at the University of California, Riverside. Most research of the past 25 years has tried to catalog the ways in which expectations about social categories distort a person's judgment, usually by placing the individual in laboratory situations intended to elicit racial or sexual stereotypes.

(19) This approach neglects to ask whether people in a wide array of real-life situations incorporate accurate information into their stereotypes, Funder holds.

(20) "We desperately need to know which of the judgments we make of each other and of ourselves are right, which are wrong, and when," Funder contends. ■

Comprehension

EXERCISE 1

The following questions check your understanding of the main ideas in "The Stereotype of Stereotypes." Indicate if each of the statements below is true (T) or false (F) according to the article.

1. T / F   According to Yueh-Ting Lee, national stereotypes represent unjustified prejudices.

2. T / F   Some researchers believe that we need stereotypes to deal with a large and dangerous world.

3. T / F   Charles Stangor believes that stereotypes accurately reflect cultural or group differences.

4. T / F   Charles Stangor believes that stereotypes can be used by the powerful to harm the less powerful.

5. _T_ / F   For much of the last century, psychologists and writers believed that stereotypes were invalid.

6. _T_ / F   Our ancestors may have used stereotypes to survive in a complex and dangerous world.

7. _T_ / F   Lee believes that understanding stereotypes can be helpful in understanding others.

8. T / _F_   Lee and Baron see no dangers in stereotypes.

9. T / _F_   The article demonstrates why further research is not necessary.

EXERCISE 2

Look back at the article to complete the following task. "The Stereotype of Stereotypes" presents a variety of points of view and research on stereotypes. Below is a list of researchers and writers cited in the article. Put a P next to the names of those who see positive effects of stereotypes. Put an N next to those who are reported to have negative opinions of stereotypes.

1. __P__ Yueh-Ting Lee

2. __N__ Charles Stangor

3. __N__ Walter Lippman

4. __N__ Gordon W. Allport

5. __P__ Reuben M. Baron

6. __P__ David C. Funder

Critical Reading

1. What does the title "The Stereotype of Stereotypes" mean? Do you think that we have stereotypes about stereotypes?

2. In Paragraphs 6 and 7, the author contrasts the views of Stangor and Lee concerning the effects of stereotypes. With whom do you agree? When does a useful generalization about other people become a harmful stereotype?

3. Yueh-Ting Lee (Paragraph 11) believes that people can use stereotypes to help with conflict resolution. Can you give an example from your own experience? Do you agree or disagree with Lee?

4. a. Did you enjoy the joke that began this article? Why or why not? When they work, what makes such jokes funny? When are they not funny?

   b. The following question is meant in fun. Every culture has stereotypes and generalizations about other groups. If you or those in your home culture were writing the email message, what would be good and bad characteristics of different countries? Fill in the chart in the spirit of fun; be careful to respect the feelings of your classmates.

	Good	**Bad**
Food		
Car		
Art		
House		
Toilet Paper		

   c. Give examples of ways by which you might discover that your stereotypes are inaccurate.

Discussion/Composition

1. By and large, do you believe stereotypes are positive or negative? You will be debating this issue. In preparation, go through "The Stereotype of Stereotypes" and put a P next to any arguments that would support a positive view of stereotypes. Put an N next to negative arguments. Work with your classmates to develop a debate. (Do you believe that using a debate format to clarify your thoughts is a stereotypically North American way to proceed?)

2. If you were going to develop a high school curriculum on stereotypes, what would you teach? Work with your classmates to develop a list of ideas and a list of possible activities.

3. In Paragraph 5 the author says that many psychologists find Lee's opinions "about as welcome as a cut in their research grants." What does this mean? What does it tell us about scientists and their research grants? Can you make up other expressions using this phrasing, for example, "about as welcome as running out of gas in the desert"?

4. Below is a statement by Yueh-Ting Lee, quoted in the article (Paragraph 12).

   Group differences, not prejudice, are the root cause of tension and conflict between various cultural and racial groups.

   What does this mean? Do you agree or disagree? Which do you think is the major cause of cultural conflict: real differences between groups or prejudice? Support your position orally or in writing by presenting reasons and examples.

Vocabulary from Context

EXERCISE 1

Both the ideas and the vocabulary in the following exercise are taken from "The Stereotype of Stereotypes." Use the context provided to determine the meanings of the italicized words. Write a definition, synonym, or description of each of the italicized vocabulary items in the space provided.

1. _negative opinion with- out any fact_

2. _deal_

3. _stereo_

4. _biased against_

5. _treat them unfairly_

6. _no reason of fact to do bad thing_

7. _unfair_

8. _common belief_

9. _tendency_

10. _stop + prevent_

11. _collect_

12. _deeds_

13. _____

14. _____

Are stereotypes always bad? Many people believe that stereotypes are the equivalent of *prejudices:* negative opinions without any basis in fact. If people decide that they don't like anyone with brown hair, for example, they are simply *biased* against brown-haired folks. Racism and sexism are other forms of *bigotry.* Many worry that stereotypes are always dangerous. They can be used to *stigmatize* groups, to mark them as shameful and dishonored. Stereotypes can be used by people in power to *exploit* other people, as an excuse to treat them unfairly and take advantage of them. The problem with stereotypes is that they are most often without any basis in fact—they tend to be *unjustified* and *erroneous.* Although not all stereotypes are completely false, this *tendency* of stereotypes to be negative and erroneous is what worries many. This *propensity* of humans to believe good things about themselves and bad things about others is what makes many people mistrust all stereotypes.

Others feel that stereotypes reflect a bit of truth, that they reflect real differences between people. In this sense, stereotypes help people make sense of the world, keep them safe, and therefore cannot be overlooked. Stereotypes might even *abet* efforts to make peace. It may be that the only way to make true peace in the world is to face the differences that cause strong dislikes between different cultures. The theory is that if people *confront* the causes of their *animosities,* they can begin to solve intercultural misunderstandings. It may be that people can come to understand the source of cultural characteristics and not find these *traits* so frustrating.

Clearly stereotyping requires more study. It's a complex issue that requires delicate reasoning, making fine distinctions, and looking for the less obvious. The new researchers on stereotypes hope to bring this *subtlety* to their investigations.

EXERCISE 2

This exercise is designed to give you additional clues to determine the meanings of unfamiliar vocabulary items in context. In the paragraph of "The Stereotype of Stereotypes" indicated by the number in parentheses, find the word or phrase that best fits the meaning given. Your teacher may want to read these aloud as you quickly scan* the paragraph to find the answer.

1. (6) Which word means *improve; make more attractive?* _____

2. (7) Which word means *analyses; studies; assessments; examinations?* _____

3. (10) Which word means *outlining; defining; describing?* _____

4. (11) Which word means *sharper; more precise or accurate?* _____

5. (13) Which word means *organize; manage; come up with?* _____

6. (16) Which word means *being on time?* _____

7. (16) Which word means *time limits; cut-off dates; target dates?* _____

8. (19) What phrase means *doesn't ask; fails to deal with?* _____

9. (19) What phrase means *a large number; a broad range?* _____

EXERCISE 3

This exercise should be done after you have finished reading "The Stereotype of Stereotypes." The exercise is designed to give you practice using context clues to guess the meaning of unfamiliar vocabulary. Give a definition, synonym, or description of each of the words below. The number in parentheses indicates the paragraph in which the word can be found. Your teacher may want you to do these orally or in writing.

1. (2) dwellings _apartment_
2. (6) realm _area_
3. (6) employ _hire for use_
4. (9) invalid _not to be used_
5. (9) encase _in any event_
6. (13) counteract _against_
7. (14) crucial _important - fateful_
8. (14) tagged _marked_
9. (16) tardiness _late late_
10. (18) distort _hide the truth_

*For an introduction to scanning, see Unit 1.

Figurative Language and Idioms

In the paragraph indicated by the number in parentheses, find the phrase that best fits the meaning given. Your teacher may want to read these aloud as you quickly scan* the paragraph to find the answer.

1. (2) What phrase means *are not; are less than?* _____

2. (7) What phrase means *to give credit; to give what is deserved; to be fair?* _____

3. (10) What phrase means *became popular; developed support?* _____

4. (11) What phrase means *peacemaking; solving disagreements?* _____

5. (13) What phrase means *peacemaking; creating relationships across groups?* _____

Dictionary Study

Many words have more than one meaning. When you use a dictionary to discover the meaning of an unfamiliar word or phrase, you need to use the context to determine which definition is appropriate. Use the dictionary entries on page 124 to select the best definition(s) for each of the italicized words below. Write the number(s) of the definition in the space provided.

_____ 1. While these national stereotypes don't represent absolute truths, they are accurate enough to give the joke its humorous *punch.*

_____ 2. Houses in the United States may indeed *boast* more space, on average, than Japanese dwellings.

_____ 3. A growing body of research suggests that in many real-life situations, stereotypes accurately *capture* cultural or group differences.

_____ 4. Humans evolved in groups that *negotiated* a dangerous world.

_____ 5. In large communities, stereotypes *capitalized* on people's tendency to fill social roles that matched their own personal qualities.

---

*For an introduction to scanning, see Unit 1.

punch¹ (pŭnch) *n.* **1.** A tool for circular or other piercing. **2.** A tool for forcing a pin, bolt, or rivet in or out of a hole. **3.** A tool for stamping a design on a surface. **4.** A tool for making a countersink. — *intr. & tr.v.* **punched, punch·ing, punch·es.** To use a punch or use a punch on. [ME *pounce, punche* < OFr. *poinçon, ponchon.* See PUNCHEON¹. V. < ME *pouncen, punchen,* to prick < OFr. *poinçoner, ponchoner,* to emboss with a punch. See PUNCH².]

punch² (pŭnch) *tr.v.* **punched, punch·ing, punch·es. 1.** To hit with a sharp blow of the fist. **2.a.** To poke or prod with a stick. **b.** *Western U.S.* To herd (cattle). **3.** To depress (a key or button, for example) in order to activate a device or perform an operation. — *n.* **1.** A blow with the fist. **2.** Vigor or drive. — *phrasal verbs.* **punch in.** To check in formally at a job upon arrival. **punch out. 1.** To check out formally at a job upon departure. **2.** *Slang.* To eject from a military aircraft. — *idiom.* **beat to the punch.** To make the first decisive move. [ME *punchen,* to thrust, prod, prick < OFr. *poinçonner, ponchonner,* to emboss with a punch < *poinçon, ponchon,* pointed tool. See PUNCHEON¹.] — **punch′less** *adj.*

punch³ (pŭnch) *n.* A beverage of fruit juices and sometimes carbonated water, often spiced and mixed with wine or liquor. [Perh. < Hindi *pañc-,* five- < Skt. *pañca,* (< the hypothesis that it was originally prepared from five ingredients). See **penkʷe***.]

boast¹ (bōst) *v.* **boast·ed, boast·ing, boasts.** — *intr.* To glorify oneself in speech; talk in a self-admiring way. — *tr.* **1.** To speak of with excessive pride. **2.** To possess or own (a desirable feature). **3.** To contain; have. — *n.* **1.** The act or an instance of bragging. **2.** A source of pride. [ME *bosten* < *bost,* a brag.] — **boast′er** *n.* — **boast′ful** *adj.* — **boast′ful·ly** *adv.* — **boast′ful·ness** *n.*

boast² (bōst) *tr.v.* **boast·ed, boast·ing, boasts.** To shape or form (stone) roughly with a broad chisel.

cap·ture (kăp′chər) *tr.v.* **-tured, -tur·ing, -tures. 1.** To take captive, as by force or craft; seize. **2.** To gain possession or control of, as in a game or contest. **3.** To attract and hold: *capture the imagination.* **4.** To succeed in preserving in lasting form: *capture a likeness.* — *n.* **1.** The act of catching, taking, or winning, as by force or skill. **2.** One that has been seized, caught, or won. **3.** *Phys.* The phenomenon in which an atom or a nucleus absorbs a subatomic particle. [< Fr., capture < OFr. < Lat. *captūra* < *captus,* p.part. of *capere,* to seize. See **kap-***.]

ne·go·ti·ate (nĭ-gō′shē-āt′) *v.* **-at·ed, -at·ing, -ates.** — *intr.* To confer with another or others in order to come to terms or reach an agreement. — *tr.* **1.** To arrange or settle by discussion and mutual agreement. **2.a.** To transfer title to or ownership of (a promissory note, for example) to another party by delivery or by delivery and endorsement in return for value received. **b.** To sell or discount (securities, for example). **3.a.** To succeed in going over or coping with. **b.** To succeed in accomplishing or managing. [Lat. *negōtiārī, negōtiāt-,* to transact business < *negōtium,* business : *neg-,* not; see ne* + *ōtium,* leisure.] — **ne·go′ti·a′tor** *n.* — **ne·go′tia·to′ry** (-shə-tôr′ē, -tōr′ē, -shē-ə-) *adj.*

cap·i·tal·ize (kăp′ĭ-tl-īz′) *v.* **-ized, -iz·ing, -iz·es.** — *tr.* **1.** To use as or convert into capital. **2.** To supply with capital or investment funds. **3.** To authorize the issue of a certain amount of capital stock of. **4.** To convert (debt) into capital stock or shares. **5.** To calculate the current value of (a future stream of earnings or cash flows). **6.** To include (expenditures) in business accounts as assets instead of expenses. **7.a.** To write or print in capital letters. **b.** To begin a word with a capital letter. — *intr.* To turn something to one's advantage; benefit. — **cap′i·tal·iz′a·ble** *adj.*

Vocabulary Review

Three of the words in each line below are similar or related in meaning. Circle the word that does not belong.

1. prejudice   bias   accuracy   bigotry

2. justified   erroneous   illogical   invalid

3. tendency   animosity   propensity   inclination

4. stereotype   generalization   oversimplification   trait

5. qualities   characteristics   deadlines   traits

5

Nonprose Reading
Questionnaire

Before You Begin

Before completing the questionnaire on page 126, take a few minutes to think about the following.

1. What activities are you good at? What do you enjoy doing?

2. What do you struggle with? What are the things that you do not enjoy doing?

3. How intelligent are you?

4. Have you ever considered that the answer to Question 3 is related to the answers to Questions 1 and 2? How could this be?

Scholars agree that intelligence is far more complex than commonly thought. Howard Gardner, of Harvard University, has determined that there are multiple intelligences and that people vary in the ways they think and solve problems.*

> For more information about multiple intelligences, check out this site about Gardner: **www.howardgardner.com/MI/mi.html**.

The questionnaire on page 126 is designed to help you understand how Gardner's theory of multiple intelligences might relate to the ways that you study languages. Respond to each statement, indicating the extent to which you think it represents your way of thinking and problem solving, and then continue with the activities in Exercise 1 (pages 127–28) and Exercise 2 (pages 129–30).

---

*For an explanation of nonprose reading, see Unit 1.

	Strongly Disagree			Strongly Agree	
	1	2	3	4	5	1. I enjoy collecting and organizing things.

1 2 3 4 5   2. I see words in my mind before I write them down.

1 2 3 4 5   3. I am interested in new developments in science.

1 2 3 4 5   4. I can generally find my way around unfamiliar territory.

1 2 3 4 5   5. I find it difficult to sit still for long periods of time.

1 2 3 4 5   6. I am good at remembering names and characteristics of things such as animals, rocks, and minerals.

1 2 3 4 5   7. I know the tunes of many songs.

1 2 3 4 5   8. I prefer to use a dictionary when I encounter a word I do not know.

1 2 3 4 5   9. I listen to music all the time, even when studying.

1 2 3 4 5   10. I am considered a leader by others.

1 2 3 4 5   11. I prefer outdoor activities such as hiking, gardening, and observing nature.

1 2 3 4 5   12. I remember the lyrics to songs after hearing them once or twice.

1 2 3 4 5   13. I use symbols and charts to solve problems.

1 2 3 4 5   14. I like books. Reading is a favorite pastime.

1 2 3 4 5   15. I like to physically practice a new skill rather than just study it.

1 2 3 4 5   16. On a rainy day I would choose to go to a natural history museum rather than a movie.

1 2 3 4 5   17. I have ideas and opinions that set me apart from the majority of my peers.

1 2 3 4 5   18. I like to play word games.

1 2 3 4 5   19. I have set goals for my life, and I work to achieve those goals.

1 2 3 4 5   20. I engage in sports and physical activity regularly.

1 2 3 4 5   21. I enjoy using microscopes and binoculars to study nature.

1 2 3 4 5   22. I can easily compute mathematical problems in my head.

1 2 3 4 5   23. I have vivid dreams at night.

1 2 3 4 5   24. I search for patterns, regularities, or logical sequences in everyday events.

1 2 3 4 5   25. I prefer group activities rather than doing things alone.

1 2 3 4 5   26. I like to sing.

1 2 3 4 5   27. I am able to learn and remember things better when I see them written down.

1 2 3 4 5   28. My best ideas come to me when I am jogging or exercising.

1 2 3 4 5   29. I prefer illustrated textbooks.

1 2 3 4 5   30. I prefer to measure, categorize, and analyze when problem solving.

1 2 3 4 5   31. I feel comfortable in a crowd.

1 2 3 4 5   32. I have at least three close friends.

1 2 3 4 5   33. I am well coordinated.

1 2 3 4 5   34. I consider myself to be strong willed and independent.

1 2 3 4 5   35. I enjoy working with others on problem-solving tasks.

1 2 3 4 5   36. I regularly spend time alone meditating or reflecting on important matters.

1 2 3 4 5   37. I am sensitive to color.

1 2 3 4 5   38. I often draw or doodle while thinking, talking, or problem solving.

1 2 3 4 5   39. I often choose to spend time alone rather than seek out friends for company.

1 2 3 4 5   40. I sometimes catch myself singing a song from a TV program or a movie I recently saw.

EXERCISE 1

Scoring Your Responses

The questionnaire was developed to help you explore your intelligences. It is based on the research of Howard Gardner, a psychologist at Harvard University, who believes that people have multiple intelligences. Gardner developed the theory of multiple intelligences in his 1983 book, *Frames of Mind,* and he has continued to conduct research since that time. He argued that most intelligence tests measure primarily verbal, logical-mathematical, and spatial intelligence. He believed that there are many other kinds of intelligence including visual-spatial, bodily-kinesthetic, musical, interpersonal, and intrapersonal intelligences. More recently, he added naturalist intelligence to this list and suggested that there may be other possibilities including spiritual and existential intelligences. Brief descriptions of each of the intelligences are below and on page 128. Each of the items in the questionnaire you just completed corresponds to one of the intelligences.

Read the description of each intelligence and total your scores to discover your preferred ways of learning.

1. **Linguistic Intelligence** concerns words, spoken or written. People who possess this intelligence are good at learning languages, word games, and playing with meanings. They typically enjoy reading, telling stories, debates, and activities involving learning new words. They tend to become writers, politicians, and teachers.

   Total your scores for this category: Items 2, 8, 14, 18, 27 _____

2. **Logical-Mathematical Intelligence** concerns logic, patterns, and numbers. People who possess this intelligence excel in mathematics, chess, computer programming, and other logical or scientific activities. Careers that attract people with logical-mathematical intelligence include scientists, mathematicians, lawyers, doctors, and philosophers.

   Total your scores for this category: Items 3, 13, 22, 24, 30 _____

3. **Visual-Spatial Intelligence** has to do with vision and spatial judgment. People with strong visual-spatial intelligence are typically very good at visualizing and mentally manipulating objects. They have a strong visual memory and are often artistically inclined. They also generally have a very good sense of direction and may also have good hand-eye coordination. Individuals with spatial intelligence include artists, engineers, and architects.

   Total your scores for this category: Items 4, 23, 29, 37, 38 _____

4. **Bodily-Kinesthetic Intelligence** concerns movement and activity. In this category, people are generally adept at physical activities such as sports and dance and often prefer activities that require movement. They learn well by physically doing something, rather than reading or hearing about it. Those with strong bodily-kinesthetic intelligence seem to use what might be termed muscle memory; they remember things through their body. Careers that suit those with this intelligence include athlete, dancer, actor, comedian, builder, and artisan.

   Total your scores for this category: Items 5, 15, 20, 28, 33 _____

5. **Musical Intelligence** involves music and hearing. Those who have a high level of musical-rhythmic intelligence display sensitivity to sounds, rhythms, tones, and music. They like to sing, play musical instruments, and compose music. Since there is a strong aural component to this intelligence, those who are strongest in it may learn well through listening. In addition, they will often use songs or rhythms to learn and memorize information and may work well with music playing. People with musical intelligence tend to become musicians, singers, conductors, and composers.

Total your scores for this category: Items 7, 9, 12, 26, 40 _____

6. **Interpersonal Intelligence** involves interacting with others. People in this category are usually sensitive to others people's feelings and needs. They are skilled at cooperating and enjoy working in groups. They communicate effectively and sympathize easily with others and may be either leaders or followers. They typically learn well by working with others and often enjoy discussion and debate. Careers that suit those with this intelligence include politician, manager, social worker, and diplomat.

Total your scores for this category: Items 10, 25, 31, 32, 35 _____

7. **Intrapersonal Intelligence,** in contrast to interpersonal intelligence, has to do with oneself. Those who are strongest in this intelligence typically prefer to work alone. They are usually extremely sensitive and understand their own emotions, goals, and motivations. They often prefer activities that require reasoning, such as philosophy. They learn well when allowed to concentrate on the subject by themselves. There is often a high level of perfectionism associated with this intelligence. Careers that suit those with this intelligence include philosopher, psychologist, theologian, and writer.

Total your scores for this category: Items 17, 19, 34, 36, 39 _____

8. **Naturalistic Intelligence** has to do with nature and classification. Those with it are said to have greater sensitivity to nature and their place within it, the ability to grow things, and greater ease in caring for and interacting with animals. They are also good at recognizing and classifying different species. Careers which suit those with this intelligence include scientist, naturalist, conservationist, gardener, and farmer.

Total your scores for this category: Items 1, 6, 11, 16, 21 _____

EXERCISE 2

Identifying Your Preferred Learning Activities

a. Gardner's theory of multiple intelligences should be able to help you identify or construct learning activities that match your strengths. Below are 24 activities that might be used to improve your language proficiency. Check (✓) the five activities that you would most prefer as a learner. Put an X next to the five activities that you would find the most unpleasant or unproductive.

_____ 1. Going on a nature study with native speakers of the language.

_____ 2. Doing workbook exercises or end-of-chapter assignments.

_____ 3. Learning new vocabulary through painting or drawing.

_____ 4. Learning songs.

_____ 5. Playing on a sports team with native speakers of the language.

_____ 6. Attending a lecture on plants and animals.

_____ 7. Keeping a journal in the target language that helps you reflect on your language learning experiences.

_____ 8. Volunteering at a community center to help children or the elderly.

_____ 9. Making charts to help you remember details of the grammar of the language.

_____ 10. Teaching a subject or skill that you know to native speakers of the target language.

_____ 11. Working for a landscaping business.

_____ 12. Learning songs in the new language.

_____ 13. Closing your eyes and imagining a town that you populate with people, events, and services to help you remember new vocabulary.

_____ 14. Getting a job.

_____ 15. Acting out new concepts in order to practice vocabulary and grammar.

_____ 16. Painting or drawing to remember concepts and practice the language.

_____ 17. Writing a story to practice idioms.

_____ 18. Getting away from people in order to concentrate.

_____ 19. Doing mathematical calculations in your head using the target language.

_____ 20. Working by yourself to solve riddles and language problems.

_____ 21. Playing language games on your computer.

_____ 22. Bouncing a ball with friends as you memorize a dialogue.

_____ 23. Using songs or chants to memorize dialogues.

_____ 24. Playing word games.

b. Can you categorize your five favorite activities using Gardner's intelligences? Here's a way to find out. Each of the intelligences is listed in the table below. In the left-hand column, put the numbers of your favorite activities (the ones you checked on page 129) next to the appropriate intelligence. In order to decide how to categorize each activity, use the intelligence descriptions on pages 127–28. In the right-hand column, put the numbers of the activities you found most unpleasant or unproductive (the ones you put an X next to on page 129) next to the appropriate intelligence.

Activities You Like	Intelligences	Activities You Don't Like
	Linguistic	
	Logical-Mathematical	
	Visual-Spatial	
	Bodily-Kinesthetic	
	Musical	
	Interpersonal	
	Intrapersonal	
	Naturalistic	

c. Now, compare your scores from Exercise 1 on pages 127–28 with what you entered in the table. What did you discover?

- Do your favorite activities correspond to the intelligences on which you received the highest score?

- What about the least favorite activities? Do they correspond to the intelligences on which you received the lowest score?

d. How well does Gardner's theory work for you? To help evaluate the theory, circle the appropriate number for each statement.

Strongly Disagree				Strongly Agree	
1	2	3	4	5	Gardner's multiple intelligences accurately capture my strengths and weaknesses as a learner.
1	2	3	4	5	The different categories of intelligence are clear-cut and useful.
1	2	3	4	5	This information will affect how I choose courses in the future.
1	2	3	4	5	Knowing my intelligence profile will change the way I study.

e. Considering how you answered these questions, what is your opinion of Gardner's theory of multiple intelligences? Do you agree with him or not?

Word Study
Context Clues

EXERCISE 1

In the following exercise, do NOT try to learn the italicized words. Concentrate on developing your ability to guess the meanings of unfamiliar words using context clues.* Read each sentence carefully and write a definition, synonym, or description of the italicized word on the line provided.

1. _confusing_ — The major points of your plan are clear to me, but the details are still *hazy*.

2. _guessing_ — By *anticipating* the thief's next move, the police were able to arrive at the bank before the robbery occurred.

3. _(large)_ — All of the palace's laundry, when gathered for washing, formed a *massive* bundle that required the combined efforts of all the servants to carry.

4. _general deep_ — "Give me specific suggestions when you criticize my work," said the employee. "*Vague* comments do not help me improve."

5. _filled_ — The apple *appeased* my hunger temporarily, but I could still eat a big dinner.

6. _anger_ — After the workers walked off the job, a committee met to try to discover what could have *provoked* such action.

7. _showed jollis_ — The audience *manifested* its pleasure with hearty laughter.

8. _number - percent_ — The nation's highway death *toll* has increased every year since the invention of the automobile.

9. _poor - helpless_ — The worker's lives were *wretched*; they worked from morning to night in all kinds of weather, earning only enough money to buy their simple food and cheap clothes.

10. _No huge_ — In a series of bold moves, government attorneys attacked the *mammoth* computer company, saying that the size of the business endangered the financial freedom of the individual buyer.

---

*For an introduction to using context clues, see Unit 1.

EXERCISE 2

This exercise is designed to give you practice using context clues from a passage. Use your general knowledge along with information from the entire text below to write a definition, synonym, or description of the italicized word on the line provided. Read through the entire passage before making a decision. Note that some of the words appear more than once; by the end of the passage you should have a good idea of their meaning. Do not worry if your definition is not exact; a general idea of the meaning will often allow you to understand the meaning of a written text.

Hummingbirds: A Portrait of the Animal World

The hummingbird is truly extraordinary. It is, of course, most famous for its *diminutive* size; even the largest of these little birds weighs barely half an ounce; the tiniest, at barely two inches long, is the smallest of all warm-blooded creatures. But the hummingbird is *notable* for many other reasons. Its ability to *hover*, seemingly motionless, in midair and even to fly upside down is amazing. Its vividly hued iridescent plumage gives it a remarkable appearance. And its specialized feeding habits, its extraordinary migration patterns, and its unusual courtship and mating rituals make it *unique* in the realm of *ornithology*.

diminutive: _tiny - small_

notable: _noted_

hover: _explore_

unique: _rare_

ornithology: _sience of birds_

Word Study
Stems and Affixes

Below is a list of some commonly occurring stems and affixes.* Study their meanings, and then do the exercises that follow. Your teacher may ask you to give examples of other words you know that are derived from these stems and affixes.

Prefixes

a-, an-	without, lacking, not	*atypical, apolitical*
bene-	good	*benefit, benefactor*
bi-	two	*bicycle, binary*
mis-	wrong	*misspell, mistake*
mono-	one, alone	*monarch, monopoly*
poly-	many	*polynomial, polytechnic*
syn-, sym-, syl-	with, together	*symphony, sympathy*

Stems

-anthro-, -anthropo-	human	*anthropology*
-arch-	first, chief, leader	*patriarch, monarch, archbishop*
-fact-, -fect-	make, do	*affect, benefactor, factory*
-gam-	marriage	*monogamy, polygamous*
-hetero-	different, other	*heterosexual, heterogeneous*
-homo-	same	*homogenized milk*
-man-, -manu-	hand	*manually, manage*
-morph-	form, structure	*polymorphous*
-onym-, -nomen-	name	*synonym, nomenclature*
-pathy-	feeling, disease	*sympathy, telepathy, pathological*
-theo-, -the-	god	*theology, polytheism*

Suffixes

-ic, -al	relating to, having the nature of	*comic, musical*
-ism	action or practice, theory or doctrine	*Buddhism, communism*
-oid	like, resembling	*humanoid*

---

*For a list of all stems and affixes taught in *Reader's Choice*, see the Appendix.

EXERCISE 1

For each item, select the best definition of the italicized word, or answer the question.

1. The small country was ruled by a *monarch* for 500 years.

   _____ a. king or queen   _____ c. group of the oldest citizens

   _____ b. single family   _____ d. group of the richest citizens

2. He was interested in *anthropology.*

   _____ a. the study of apes   _____ c. the study of royalty

   _____ b. the study of insects   _____ d. the study of humans

3. Some citizens say the election of William Blazer will lead to *anarchy.*

   _____ a. a strong central government

   _____ b. a government controlled by one person

   _____ c. the absence of a controlling government

   _____ d. an old-fashioned, outdated government

4. If a man is a *bigamist,* he

   _____ a. is married to two women.   _____ c. has two children.

   _____ b. is divorced.   _____ d. will never marry.

5. Which of the following pairs of words are *homonyms?*

   _____ a. good   bad   _____ c. lie   die

   _____ b. Paul   Peter   _____ d. two   too

6. Which of the following pairs of words are *antonyms?*

   _____ a. sea   see   _____ c. read   read

   _____ b. wet   dry   _____ d. Jim   Susan

7. The reviewer criticized the poet's *amorphous* style.

   _____ a. unimaginative   _____ c. stiff, too ordered

   _____ b. unusual   _____ d. lacking in organization and form

8. Dan says he is an *atheist*.

   _____ a. one who believes in one god

   _____ <u>b.</u> one who believes there is no god

   _____ c. one who believes in many gods

   _____ d. one who is not sure if there is a god

9. There was a great *antipathy* between the brothers.

   _____ a. love   _____ c. dislike

   _____ b. difference   _____ d. resemblance

10. Which circle is *bisected*?

    a.   b.   c.   d.

11. This design is symmetric: ○ □ ▯ □ ○

    Which of the following designs is *asymmetric*?

    a. □ ▯ □   b. □ ▯ ▮ □ □   c. ○ ∘ ○   d. □ ▯ ▯

12. Consider these sentences:

    Many automobiles are *manufactured* in Detroit.
    The authors must give the publisher a *manuscript* of their new book.

    How are the meanings of *manufacture* and *manuscript* different from the meanings of the stems
    from which they are derived? _____

    _____

EXERCISE 2

Word analysis can help you to guess the meanings of unfamiliar words. Using context clues and what you know about word parts, write a synonym, description, or definition of the italicized word.

1. ____good____ Doctors say that getting regular exercise is *beneficial* to your health.

2. ____forget____ He's always *mislaying* his car keys, so he keeps an extra set in the garage.

3. __speak two lang__ Because some of our patients speak Spanish and some speak English, we need a nurse who is *bilingual*.

4. __wrong a behavior__ My parents always told me not to *misbehave* at my grandparents' house.

5. ____no name____ Some people prefer to remain *anonymous* when they call the police to report a crime.

EXERCISE 3

Following is a list of words containing some of the stems and affixes introduced in this unit and the previous one. Definitions of these words appear on the right. Put the letter of the appropriate definition next to each word.

1. __e__ *archenemy*   a. care of the hands and fingernails

2. __f__ *archetype*   b. the saying of a blessing

3. __c__ *anthropoid*   c. resembling humans

4. __b__ *benediction*   d. one who performs good deeds

5. __d__ *benefactor*   e. a chief opponent

6. __a__ *manicure*   f. the original model or form after which a thing is made

7. __h__ *monotheism*   g. made up of similar parts

8. __l__ *polytheism*   h. belief in one god

9. __j__ *polygamy*   i. the practice of having one marriage partner

10. __i__ *monogamy*   j. the practice of having several marriage partners

11. __k__ *heterogeneous*   k. consisting of different types; made up of different types

12. __g__ *homogeneous*   l. belief in more than one god

Sentence Study
Comprehension

Read each sentence carefully.* The questions that follow are designed to test your comprehension of complex grammatical structures. Select the *best* answer.

1. My discovery of Tillie Olsen was a gift from a friend; years ago she gave me her copy of *Tell Me a Riddle* because she liked the stories and wanted to share the experience.

   What do we know about Tillie Olsen?

   _____ a. She is a friend.

   _____ b. She likes stories.

   _____ c. She gives gifts.

   _____ (d.) She is an author.

2. A few government officials even estimate that the flood has created more than half a million refugees who need immediate food, clothing, and shelter.

   Exactly how many refugees are there?

   _____ a. half a million

   _____ b. over half a million

   _____ (c.) We don't know exactly.

   _____ d. Only a few government officials know the exact figure.

3. The Green Tiger Press believes that the relatively unknown works of great children's illustrators are sources of vast beauty and power and is attempting to make these treasures more easily available.

   What is the goal of this printing company?

   _____ a. to publish more children's books

   _____ b. to develop powerful stories

   _____ (c.) to make children's illustrations more easily available

   _____ d. to encourage artists to become children's illustrators

---

*For an introduction to sentence study, see Unit 3.

4. Although he calls the $1,000 donation "a very generous amount, especially in these times," the president expresses hope that the project will attract additional funds from companies and other sources so that it can continue beyond this first year.

What does the president know about the project?

_____ a. It will cost only $1,000.

_____ (b) It is very special.

_____ c. Special sources will support it.

_____ d. It cannot continue without additional funding.

5. Any thought that this new custom will remain unchanged—or in Europe will remain uniquely English—is ridiculous.

What does the author believe about the new custom?

_____ a. It will remain limited.

_____ b. The custom will change.

_____ c. Acceptance of the custom is ridiculous.

_____ (d) The custom will remain in Europe.

6. Robust and persistent sailors gathered from all the sea-faring nations set out on voyages that laid foundations for great empires with no other power than sail and oar.

Why were these voyages important?

_____ (a) Sailors came from many countries.

_____ b. The voyages laid the foundations for sea-faring nations.

_____ c. The foundations for empires were established.

_____ d. Sea-faring nations lost their power.

7. Young people need to develop the values, attitudes, and problem-solving skills essential to their participation in a political system that was designed, and is still based, on the assumption that all citizens would be so prepared.

What is the basic assumption of this political system?

_____ (a) All people will be capable of participation.

_____ b. All people participate in the system.

_____ c. All people should have the same values and attitudes.

_____ d. Most people cannot develop the skills to participate in the system.

8. While we may be interested in the possibilities of social harmony and individual fulfillment to be achieved through nontraditional education, one cannot help being cautious about accepting any sort of one-sided educational program as a cure for the world's ills.

How does the author feel about nontraditional education?

_____ a. He believes that it has no possibility of success.

_____ (b) He doubts that it can cure the world's ills.

_____ c. He feels that it is a cure for the world's ills.

_____ d. He believes that it will bring social harmony.

9. The complexity of the human situation and the injustice of the social order demand far more fundamental changes in the basic structure of society itself than some politicians are willing to admit in their speeches.

What is necessary to correct the problems of society?

_____ (a) basic changes in its structure

_____ b. fewer political speeches

_____ c. honest politicians

_____ d. basic changes in political methods

Paragraph Reading
Restatement and Inference

Each passage is followed by five statements. The statements are of four types.

1. Some of the statements are restatements of ideas in the original passage. They give the same information in a different way.

2. Some of the statements are inferences (conclusions) that can be drawn from the information given in the passage.

3. Some of the statements are false based on the information given.

4. Some of the statements cannot be judged true or false based on the information given in the original passage.

Put a check (✓) next to all restatements and inferences (types 1 and 2). <u>Note</u>: Do not check a statement that is true of itself but cannot be inferred from the passage.

Example

Often people who hold higher positions in a given group overestimate their performance, while people in the lowest levels of the group underestimate theirs. While this may not always be true, it does indicate that often the actual position in the group has much to do with the feeling of personal confidence a person may have. Thus, members who hold higher positions in a group or feel that they have an important part to play in the group will probably have more confidence in their own performance.

_____ a. If people have confidence in their own performance, they will achieve high positions in a group.

_____ b. If we let people know they are an important part of a group, they will probably become more self-confident.

_____ c. People who hold low positions in a group often overestimate their performance.

_____ d. People in positions of power in a group may feel they do better work than they really do.

_____ e. People with higher positions in a group do better work than other group members.

Explanation

_____ a. This cannot be inferred from the paragraph. We know that people who hold high positions have more self-confidence than those who don't. However, we don't know that people with more confidence will achieve higher status. Confidence may come only *after* one achieves a higher position.

✓ b. This is an inference that can be drawn from the last sentence in the paragraph. We know that if people feel they have an important part to play in a group, they will probably have more self-confidence. We can infer that if we let people know (and therefore make them feel) that they have an important part to play, they will probably become more self-confident.

_____ c. This is false. The first sentence states that the people in the lowest levels of a group underestimate, not overestimate, their performance.

✓ d. This is a restatement of the first sentence. People who hold higher positions tend to overestimate their performance: they may feel they do better work than they really do.

_____ e. We do not know this from the paragraph. We know that people who hold higher positions often *think* they do better work than others in a group. (They "overestimate their performance.") We do not know that they actually do better work.

Passage 1

Like any theory of importance, that of social or cultural anthropology was the work of many minds and took on many forms. Some, the best known of its proponents, worked on broad areas and attempted to describe and account for the development of human civilization in its totality. Others restricted their efforts to specific aspects of the culture, taking up the evolution of art, or the state, or religion.

_____ a. Social anthropology concerns itself with broad areas while cultural anthropology concerns itself with specific aspects of culture.

✓ b. Cultural anthropologists, also known as social anthropologists, may work in either broad or restricted areas.

_____ c. Cultural anthropology is a new field of study.

✓ d. Any important area of study requires the work of many minds and is therefore likely to have different approaches.

✓ e. The best-known people in cultural anthropology attempted to describe the development of human civilization.

I saw by the clock of the city jail that it was past eleven, so I decided to go to the newspaper immediately. Outside the editor's door I stopped to make sure my pages were in the right order; I smoothed them out carefully, stuck them back in my pocket, and knocked. I could hear my heart thumping as I walked in.

_____ a. The teller of this story has just left the city jail.

__✓__ b. He has been carrying his papers in his pocket.

_____ c. We know that the storyteller is a newspaper writer by profession.

__✓__ d. We might infer that the storyteller is going to show his papers to the editor.

__✓__ e. The meeting is important for the storyteller.

Passage 3

First Light tells the story of astronomers at the Palomar Observatory in the San Gabriel Mountains of California who peer through the amazing Hale Telescope at the farthest edges of space, attempting to solve the riddle of the beginning of time. "Science is a lot weirder and more human than most people realize," Preston writes in his foreword to this revised and updated edition of his first book, and he skillfully weaves together stories of the eccentricities of his characters and the technical wonders of their work to create a riveting narrative about what scientists do and why they do it. The telescope itself is the main character. It is huge, seven stories tall, the heaviest working telescope on earth, with a mirror that is two hundred inches wide and took fourteen years to cast and polish. Although there are now larger telescopes and telescopes in space, the Hale telescope is still used by astronomers on almost every clear night. Preston's rendering of their obsessions and adventures is a witty and illuminating portrait of scientists in action and a luminous story of what modern astronomy is all about.

__✓__ a. *First Light* is the title of a book.

_____ b. This paragraph was written by the author of *First Light*.

_____ c. The purpose of *First Light* is to detail the eccentricities of scientists.

__✓__ d. *First Light* tells the story of the astronomers who use the Hale Telescope.

__✓__ e. The author of the paragraph likes *First Light*.

Passage 4

The Incas had never acquired the art of writing, but they had developed a complicated system of knotted cords called *quipus*. These were made of the wool of the alpaca or llama, dyed in various colors, the significance of which was known to the officials. The cords were knotted in such a way as to represent the decimal system. Thus an important message relating to the progress of crops, the amount of taxes collected, or the advance of an enemy could be speedily sent by trained runners along the post roads.

_____ a. Because they could not write, the Incas are considered a simplistic, poorly developed society.

___√__ b. Through a system of knotted cords, the Incas sent important messages from one community to another.

_____ c. Because runners were sent with cords, we can safely assume that the Incas did not have domesticated animals.

___√__ d. Both the color of the cords and the way they were knotted formed part of the message of the *quipus*.

___√__ e. The *quipus* were used for important messages.

Passage 5

There was a time when scholars held that early humans lived in a kind of beneficent anarchy, in which people were granted their rights by their fellows and there was no governing or being governed. Various early writers looked back to this Golden Age but the point of view that humans were originally *children of nature* is best known to us in the writings of Rousseau, Locke, and Hobbes. These men described the concept of *social contract*, which they said had put an end to the *state of nature* in which the earliest humans were supposed to have lived.

___√__ a. For Rousseau, Locke, and Hobbes, the concept of *social contract* put an end to the time of beneficent anarchy in which early humans lived.

___√__ b. According to the author, scholars today do not hold that early humans lived in a state of anarchy.

_____ c. Only Rousseau, Locke, and Hobbes wrote about early humans as *children of nature*.

_____ d. The early writers referred to in this passage lived through the Golden Age of early humans.

___√__ e. We can infer that the author of this passage feels that concepts of government have always been present in human history.

Discourse Focus
Careful Reading / Drawing Inferences

Mystery stories, like most other texts, require readers to note important facts and draw inferences based on these. To solve the following mysteries, you must become a detective, drawing inferences from the clues provided. Each mystery below has been solved by the fictional Professor Fordney, a master detective—the expert the police call for their most puzzling cases. Your job is to match wits with the great professor. Your teacher may want you to work with your classmates to answer the question following each mystery. Be prepared to defend your solution with details from the passage.

Mystery 1: Class Day

"I shall tell you," Fordney said to his class some years ago, of an exploit of the famed scientist, Sir Joshua Beckwith, Professor of Egyptology in London.

"He had uncovered an ancient tomb in Egypt and, through his undisputed knowledge and ability to read hieroglyphics, had definitely established the date of the birth and the reign of a great Pharaoh whose mummy he had discovered. A man of volatile temper, and emphatic scientific views which he did not hesitate to express in exposing charlatanism, he had many enemies.

"The British Museum soon received a message, signed by Sir Joshua Beckwith, which in part read as follows: 'Have discovered the tomb of an important Pharaoh who reigned from 1410 to 1428 B.C.E. and who died at the age of 42 years, leaving two sons and two daughters. Great wealth found in sarcophagus. One of his sons died shortly after his reign began, etc. . . . '

"The museum officials at first were astonished," continued Fordney, "but examination of the communication quickly told them it was either a very stupid fake or an attempt at a 'practical joke'!

"They were right in their belief that the message did not come from Sir Joshua Beckwith. He did make a most important discovery—but how did the Museum authorities know the communication was not authentic?"

How did they know? _____

_____

Mystery 2: Ruth's Birthday

A multitude of small accidents had delayed Ruth Mundy. The battery in her car had gone dead and she had to call a cab; she had mislaid the key to the strong box! Just as the taxi pulled up she located it. Hastily snatching from the dresser drawer two twenty-dollar bills, one old and crumpled, one crisp and new, she thrust them loosely into her bag. In her hurry, the perfume bottle on the dresser upset, spilling perfume on her lovely moire purse! If this kept up she'd be late for her birthday party! Now, where was that book she was to return? She was sure she had just put it on the dresser! Finally locating it under her coat on the bed, she grabbed it and ran.

Once in the taxi she opened her bag and fumbled for her vanity case. Its clasp opened and she stuck her finger in the paste rouge. Another casualty! Well, it didn't get on anything else, that was one break. Removing all traces of the rouge with her handkerchief, she threw it away.

Arriving at the Mayflower Hotel she handed the driver a bill. While she waited for her change Professor Fordney alighted from his car and greeted her with a "Hello Ruth."

Acknowledging the greeting she turned to the driver. "You've made a mistake. This is change for five. I gave you a twenty."

"Oh no, lady! You gave me five dollars!"

Fordney listened amused while Ruth excitedly proved she'd given the driver a twenty-dollar bill.

"How's that, Professor?" she laughed.

How did Ruth prove her story? _____

_____

Mystery 3: The Ex-Wife Murder

"Who shot her?" cried Rogers as he rushed into the hospital three minutes after his ex-wife died from a bullet through her head.

"Just a minute," Professor Fordney said. "I'd like to ask you a few questions . . . routine, you know. Although divorced for the past six months, you have been living in the same house with your ex-wife, have you not?"

"That's right."

"Had any trouble recently?"

"Well . . . yesterday when I told her I was going on a business trip, she threatened suicide. In fact, I grabbed a bottle of iodine from her as she was about to drink it. When I left last evening at seven, however, telling her I was spending the night with friends in Sewickley, she made no objections. Returning to town this afternoon," he continued, "I called my home and the maid answered."

"Just what did she say?"

"'Oh, Mr. Rogers, they took poor mistress to St. Anne's hospital 'bout half an hour ago. Please hurry to her!' She was crying so I couldn't get anything else out of her; then I hurried here. Where is she?"

"The nurse here will direct you," responded the Professor. "A queer case this, Joe," said Inspector Kelley, who had been listening to the conversation. "These moderns are a little too much for me! A man and woman living together after being divorced six months!"

"A queer case, indeed, Jim," sighed Fordney. "You'd better detain Rogers. If he didn't shoot her himself, I'm confident he knows who did."

Why did the Professor advise the Inspector to detain Rogers? _____

_____

Mystery 4: Case #463

At 8:10 PM, July 4, 1945, Miss Ruby Marshall left her apartment on the fifth floor of the Hotel Oakwood. As she walked toward the elevator she passed Jane McGuire. The fourteen-year-old child had her Scottish terrier on a long leash and as they came opposite each other the dog growled and leaped at Miss Marshall. The woman screamed and ran back to her apartment.

Thirty minutes later Mrs. McGuire had a call from police headquarters informing her that Miss Marshall had received first aid at Mercy Hospital for a wound on the knee where the McGuire dog had bitten her. Invalided for the past two years, Mrs. McGuire was unable to look into the situation herself. She immediately called her friend, Professor Fordney, informing him of the above and asking him to look into the matter.

He found Miss Marshall sitting on a chair in the emergency ward, about to leave the hospital. Receiving permission to examine the wound from the doctor who had just taken care of her, Fordney raised Miss Marshall's immaculate evening dress, noticed her hose were rolled below her knees, removed the bandage and found cauterized marks on the right knee cap. Turning to the physician he inquired, "Are you sure those are teeth marks?"

"Why . . . they look like it to me!"

Lowering the woman's dress, the Professor told her, "You certainly didn't show much intelligence in trying to frame this charge against Mrs. McGuire, toward whom you hold a personal grudge. Her dog did not bite you!"

How did he know? _____

_____

Reading Selection 1
Economics

The article that follows from *Science News* summarizes research by a team of economists and physicists. The research provides a new way to answer an old question: Why do some countries stay poor?

Before You Begin The research paper* on which this article is based begins by asking the question in a way that economists think about it, "Does the type of product a country exports matter for subsequent economic performance?" Another way to say this might be: Can we predict how economically successful a country will be in the future based on what it exports today?

1. What do you think? To develop your opinion, begin by filling in the following chart with information that you already know.

Countries	Exports
Already economically successful countries 1. 2. 3.	
Rapidly developing countries 1. 2. 3.	
Poor countries 1. 2. 3.	

Based on the chart do you think that you can predict the economic success of various countries in the future? How?

---

*Hildago, C.A., R.B. Klinger, A.-L. Barabasi, and R. Hausmann. "The Product Space Conditions the Development of Nations," *Science 317* (27 July 2007): 482–87.

2. Here is an abstract of the original research report. Write a two- to three-sentence summary of this abstract.

Economies grow by improving the type of products they produce and export. The technology, capital, institutions and skills needed to make such new products are more easily adapted from some products than others. The researchers study the network of relatedness between products, or "product space," finding that the most profitable products are closely associated with each other. They create "maps" that show these relationships. The distances on these maps are not geographical; rather, they reveal the degree of relationship between products. The research shows that countries tend to develop products that are related (or "close") to ones they already produce. Nations whose products are more similar to other highly valued products are able to move to new, wealth-producing products faster. Poor countries may not already produce exports that are related to other highly valued products. This may help explain why poor countries have trouble developing more competitive exports, failing to converge toward the income levels of rich countries.

_____

_____

_____

_____

Now that you have a general sense of what the research is about, read the *Science News* discussion of it titled "The Wealth of Nations." Your teacher may want you to read it through once quickly and then reread carefully to answer the comprehension questions; or your teacher may want you to read the article section by section, answering the related questions before moving on. True/False items are indicated by a T / F preceding the statement.

The Wealth of Nations

A country's competitive edge can spread industry to industry, like a disease

DAVID CASTELVECCHI

(1) The economies of poor and developing countries often depend almost exclusively on a single product—perhaps timber or coffee—or on a handful of products at most. That's hardly a startling observation, but what's puzzled economists over the years is why it's been so difficult for these countries to start up new activities in the hope of spurring economic growth and lifting themselves out of poverty.

(2) While there have been a few success stories, such efforts have often ended up consuming heaps of money to little lasting effect.

(3) A team of economists and physicists is now proposing a new way to look at development. The researchers have shown that a country's competitive edge can spread from one kind of product to another along a well-defined network of links, much as disease epidemics tend to spread among people who are socially connected.

(4) The newly charted map of products could help countries design good policies by indicating the most promising paths to creating new industries. The network's structure also presages the hurdles that many developing countries will face along that path.

(5) Traditionally, economists have tried to link a country's commercial expansion to "factors of production," such as reliable transportation infrastructure or the availability of skilled and unskilled labor, explains Ricardo Hausmann, an economist at Harvard University. For example, says Hausmann's colleague and graduate student Bailey Klinger, conventional economic theory predicts that a country with the capacity for making computer chips should also be competitive in other industries that require skilled labor, such as vehicle manufacturing.

(6) But when the two economists looked at actual data, such correlations often failed to show up. Many countries that export computer chips don't export cars, and vice versa. Building and shipping cars requires very different skills and infrastructure than making computer chips does, the researchers point out.

(7) Instead, the two found correlations that standard economic reasoning didn't predict. For example, fish exporters are often successful at exporting fresh produce as well. That's because both activities require similar infrastructures—good roads, ports with refrigerated storage facilities, and bureaucracies able to monitor food safety—Hausmann and Klinger suggest. A country that has developed the means to generate and export one product can easily branch into the other.

Path to success

(8) To refine their perspective on economic linkages, Hausmann and Klinger developed a new notion of closeness between products. By analyzing global export data on numerous categories of goods, the two economists calculated, for each pair of categories, the probability that if a country is good at exporting one type of product, it will also be good at exporting the other. When that probability is high, those two products have a short "distance" between them. When the probability is low, the products are far apart.

(9) The researchers focused on export data because they are good indicators of high-quality production, and because they are the best global data available. While many countries don't compile reliable data on domestic production and consumption, exports are carefully recorded worldwide.

(10) Hausmann and Klinger created a table listing the distance between each pair among 775 types of goods. To make sense of this mountain of data, Hausmann sought the help of Albert-László Barabási, a physicist at the University of Notre Dame in Indiana. Barabási specializes in applying the abstract theory of networks to real-life situations, such as the structure of the Internet or the degrees of separation between people.

(11) Cesar Hidalgo, a graduate student working with Barabási, translated the distance data into a network. He represented each category of goods as a node and drew links between nodes only when they were close according to Hausmann's metric. Nodes that were strongly connected to many other nodes formed clusters, whereas those that had only a few connections straggled out toward the edge of the diagram. Hidalgo chose an arrangement of the nodes to spread out the network on a page as clearly as possible.

(12) The resulting network, which the four researchers call the product space, maps out world exports. But it represents a kind of cartography that has nothing to do with the geography of the countries involved. Instead, the map shows how industries gather in clusters according to how likely it is that those industries thrive in the same countries. The team's findings appear in the July 27 *Science*.

(13) In the middle of the product space lies a large "continent" of products tightly connected to each other. These include the vast majority of industrial products, from machinery and steel to chemicals. Garments, textiles, and electronics form their own, smaller, clusters.

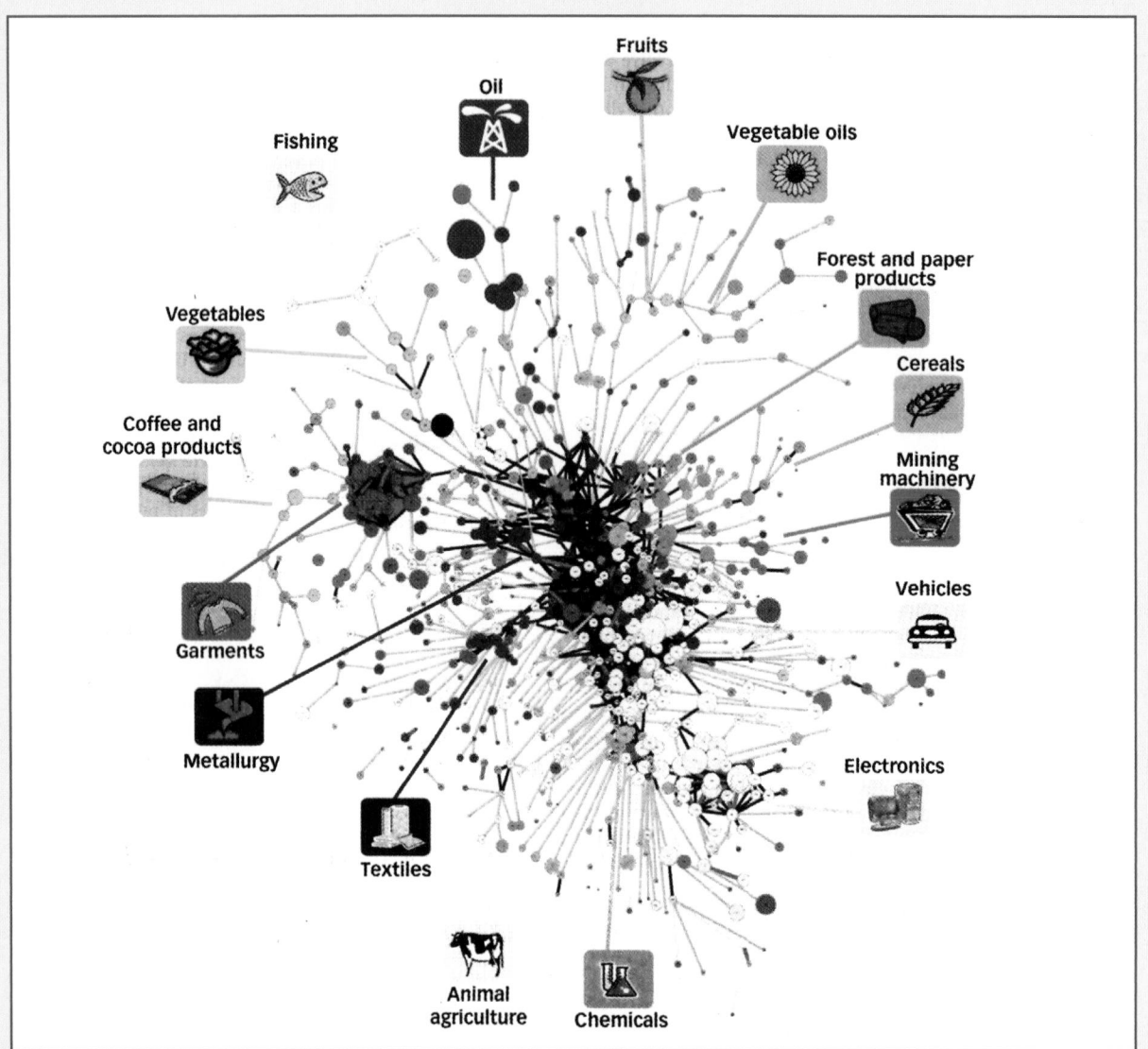

Fruits

Oil

Fishing

Vegetable oils

Forest and paper products

Vegetables

Cereals

Coffee and cocoa products

Mining machinery

Vehicles

Garments

Metallurgy

Electronics

Textiles

Animal agriculture

Chemicals

HIDDEN LINKS. In the product space network above, nodes represent products. The more closely products are linked, the more likely they are to be produced and exported by the same countries. Each node's size represents the total world trade in that product, and the nodes' colors follow an older classification of products.

(14) Farther out, almost in isolation at the network's periphery, are products such as oil, minerals, cereals, and coffee.

(15) The rich countries of the industrialized world tend to have broad portfolios of industries, and accordingly occupy large areas of the product space, usually including much of the network's core. Fast-growing developing countries such as China, Thailand, and Hungary are strong in some of those central, well-connected regions. The poorest countries, especially those in sub-Saharan Africa, tend to specialize in a few of the peripheral products—such as oil for Nigeria and copper for Zambia.

(16) The product space is a snapshot of the status quo in the global trade of goods. It represents empirical data, not an interpretation of the causes of the status quo or of its consequences. However, the researchers

also argue that the network can help explain why some economies have grown, while others have not.

(17) By crunching two decades' worth of data, the team showed that countries that have expanded into new industries have usually done so by stepping from one node to another one directly linked to it. The process is reminiscent of how information or diseases spread across a social network.

(18) For example, the team looked at Malaysia's and Colombia's exports during the 1980s and 1990s. In those decades, both countries were successful at branching out into new industries close to those in which they were already competitive. Colombia widened its production of garments to include lingerie, while Malaysia expanded into cameras from other electronics products.

(19) On the other hand, economic activities toward the periphery of the product space have fewer links.

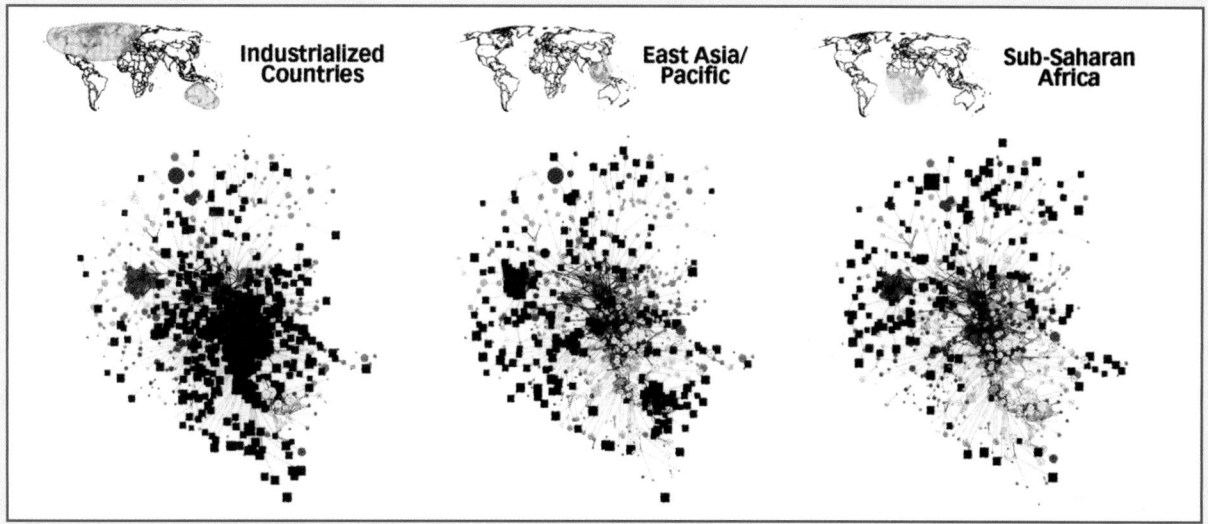

REGIONAL DIFFERENCES. In these illustrations, black squares mark products successfully exported. The industrialized countries' products (left) occupy the highly connected core of world trade. Goods from Southeast Asia and the Pacific region (center) cluster in the garment industry and in electronics, while sub-Saharan Africa's products (right) are mostly peripheral.

These tend to be industries, such as mining or the growing of certain crops, that require infrastructure or skills with few alternative uses. Historically, countries that rely on them have had a hard time branching out into new industries. The network's structure is a stark reminder of the difficulties that these countries face, and the four authors admit that it doesn't point to an easy solution. "Nevertheless," Barabási says, "it's important to understand what are the causes and the consequences of where these countries are."

Treasure hunting

(20) Hausmann and his collaborators say that their new approach might help governments and aid organizations orient themselves when deciding how to invest money, though it won't point to specific policies. "It's kind of like having a map that allows countries to move around from product to product," Hausmann says. "But the map doesn't tell you where to go."

(21) To emphasize the contrast between their model and standard economic theories, the researchers color coded the network's nodes using an existing classification that groups products according to the similarity of the factors of production they require. Nodes of the same color often ended up far apart, meaning that in practice, countries have rarely been able to move directly between them. "It's telling you that these factors of production are not [the factors] that matter" to predict how diversification can succeed, Hidalgo says.

(22) "This is a highly original approach," says physicist Eugene Stanley of Boston University. "What makes it unique is that the network is not a network of countries, but of products."

(23) "The analysis is pretty revealing," says Luis Amaral, a physicist at Northwestern University in Evanston, Illinois. "If you just had the data on a table, it would be impossible to see these patterns at all." Amaral says that the team's methods might help economists understand the growth of companies as well as of countries.

(24) Columbia University's Joseph Stiglitz, a recipient of the 2001 Nobel Prize in Economics, says that the team has come up with "a very interesting and appealing idea." He says that he emphasized the importance of product-specific skills over factors of production as early as 1969. That was before network theory and computers enabled economists to tackle extreme complexity.

(25) For Hausmann, the ultimate question is, "Will the world converge, or will it continue to be a world of poor and rich countries?" In the past few months, he has been traveling around the world, invited by officials of developing countries and international organizations to brief them on his team's approach. At least two countries—South Africa and Colombia—have begun reviewing possible policy changes based on the new ideas. His team's research has highlighted how countries' potentials differ. Perhaps it will someday help countries figure out how best to exploit their potentials. ■

References:

Atkinson, A.B., and J.E. Stiglitz. 1969. A new view of technological change. *Economic Journal 79*:573–578.

Hildago, C., B. Klinger, A.-L. Barabási, and R. Hausmann. 2007. The product space conditions the development of nations. *Science 317*(July 27):482–487. Abstract available at **www.sciencemag.org/cgi/content/abstract/317/5837/482.**

Further Readings:

Supplemental information about the Product Space and the Wealth of Nations is available online at: **http://www.nd.edu/~networks/productspace/index. htm.**

Comprehension

Answer the following questions. True/False questions are indicated by a T / F preceding an item.

Paragraphs 1–7

In this section of the article, the author introduces the economic development problem that interests these researchers. He summarizes how Hausmann and Klinger's approach is different from earlier approaches to understanding the problem, and he suggests how the researchers' work might be helpful.

1. Underline the author's statement of the economic development problem discussed in this article.

2. T / F Traditionally, economists have thought that "factors of production" are important in explaining why and how a country's economy expands.

3. Which of the following is NOT an example of a "factor of production"?

   (a) computer chips

   b. skilled labor force

   c. transportation infrastructure

4. Why did Hausmann and Klinger decide to study this problem in a new way? _____
   To show that new researches may be more helpful than the earlier one

5. What does the author say is one way the research might be helpful to countries who want to expand their economies? _the diversity of products_
   _____

Paragraphs 8–11

Hausmann and Klinger decided to try to find a more accurate way to predict how countries' economies become more diverse, how they develop new products for export. Their new theory looked at "distance" between products. They asked, "If a country is good at exporting one particular product, how likely is it to be good at exporting another particular product?" If the chances were high, the products were said to have a short distance between them. If the chances were low, the two products had a long distance between them. Hausmann and Klinger did these calculations for many types of products and for many countries. These data were used to make a map illustrating the distance between products.

   For this section, questions about the maps can be answered by looking at the text alone.

6. Why did researchers choose to use export data as opposed to other kinds of data about goods (such as production rates or consumption rates)? _Because each country has_
   its own exports and products are relying at each other
   & by their type

7. How did the physicists help in this economic study? _They translated the data into a areal map for describe the reality._

8. In the network the researcher made, what does a node represent?

   a. a country

   (b.) a category of goods

   c. a link between countries

   d. a single product

9. When were links drawn between nodes?

   a. when each node represented a single product

   b. when each node represented a category of products

   c. when the nodes were "far" from each other

   (d) when the nodes were "close" to each other

10. How were "clusters" formed on the map? _by the close to each other nodes_

11. What are the nodes at the edge of the space map? _nodes that has less connect. to each other_

Paragraphs 12–15

For this section also, questions about the maps can be answered by looking at the text alone.

12. T / (F) The product space map that the researchers made is a geographical map.

13. What does the map of the product space do? _Show the exports of countries and their relation_

14. According to the article, what does the dark cluster of dots in the middle of the product space map represent? _the diversity of industrial products._

15. T / (F) Garments and textiles are closely linked to each other in the network.

16. Match each category of country with the types of products it exports. Put the abbreviation of the exports next to the appropriate group of countries.

   MCP a. developed countries   (PP)   peripheral products

   SCP b. fast-developing countries   (MCP) many core products

   _PP_ c. poorer developing countries   (SCP) some core products

Paragraphs 16–19

In this section, the author points out both the limits of the product space map and its possibilities. Questions about the maps can be answered by looking at the text alone.

17. (T)/ F The product space map is a picture of what global trade looked like at the time the research was conducted.

18. T /(F) According to the author, the product space map proves what caused these relationships among products.

19. (T)/ F The researchers are interested in considering what the product space map may suggest about why some economies have grown while others have not.

20. (T)/ F The researchers' data shows that countries that have added new industries have added ones that are "close" to industries in which they already are involved.

21. In Paragraph 18, what is Malaysia an example of?

    a. a country having difficulty expanding its economy to new products

    b. a country that is an economic competitor of Colombia

    (c.) a country that developed a new industry close to an industry it was already successful in

    d. a country that has been successful in moving from garment production to electronics production

Paragraphs 20–25

The article concludes with a discussion of further implications of the research.

22. How does the research team think that their work might be helpful to economic planners?

    It helps governments to know the way of improving their economy.

23. (T) / F Other academics have said positive things about the work of Hausmann and his colleagues.

24. T /(F) Some countries have already set new economic policies based on the work of Hausmann and his colleagues.

The Maps

Look at the map on page 150. It shows products' relationships to each other.

25. T /(F) Tourists would find this map helpful.

26. T /(F) This is a map of the North American continent.

27. (T) /(F) The circles on the map represent cities.

28. Can you infer why some of the lines between the circles are longer than others? _They depend on the distace between cities_

29. T / F The map includes information explaining why the lines are shown in different colors.

Now look at the maps on page 151. The small maps show three different groups of countries. The maps below them show how the products exported by those three groups of countries are related to world exports in general and how closely connected they are to the core of world trade.

30. (T)/(F) The black squares on the maps represent products.

31. What differences do you notice among the maps for the industrialized countries, East Asia/Pacific countries, and the countries of sub-Saharan Africa? _rich countries have diversity in products_

32. (T)/ F The industrialized countries shown on the map export more products than the countries shown in either of the other maps.

33. T /(F) Most of the products exported from Sub-Saharan African countries are closely related to each other.

34. (T)/ F The products of industrialized countries are more closely connected to each other than the products of either of the other two groups of countries.

35. The map of East Asia/Pacific countries shows two areas where there are clusters of related products. What types of products do these two clusters represent? _Garment and electronics_

36. T / F The maps on this page are helpful in explaining this research.

Critical Reading

The article argues that a country increases its wealth by producing more products. Consider the following questions.

a. Why is it important for a country to produce more than one product?

b. If wealth depends on having many different products to export, how can we explain rich countries whose wealth depends primarily on one product?

How would the researchers answer these questions? Would your answers be the same? Do answers conflicting with those of the researchers weaken their theory?

Discussion/Composition

1. The article states (Paragraph 25) that South Africa and Colombia have begun reviewing this research for possible changes in economic policy. Think of a country you are familiar with. What recommendations would you provide to that country based on your understanding of this article? What products does that country export? What new products should they focus on?

2. Do you think the product distribution maps on pages 150–51 display the cause of wealth or the results? This has been a controversial issue. Below are comments made by a blogger (lloyd667) to the online magazine *Slate* [**www.slate.com/id/2171898** (captured Nov. 11, 2007)].

> It may not be surprising that rich countries produce stuff that is at the center of the network. After all, rich countries produce most of the stuff that is produced: depending on how you measure it, the US alone produces about a third of the world's stuff, and OECD countries produce half of it. Do they [the rich countries] not therefore define the center of the network, and therefore are at its center by definition? In other words, do the authors have the direction of causality reversed? (Being rich means being at the center, not the other way around.)

   a. What word in the paragraph does the blogger use to refer to exports or products? _____

   b. T / F The blogger doubts that the researchers have discovered the cause of the wealth of nations.

   c. T / F You must be an expert to post opinions to *Slate* magazine.

   What is your opinion? Do you agree with the researchers or the blogger? Support your position with information from the article and/or your own knowledge.

3. What features of a country that were not discussed in this article might contribute to the wealth of a nation? List as many as you can, and then compare your list with your classmates'. Discuss how the factors you identified affect a nation's economy, either positively or negatively. Your teacher may want you to write an essay in which you identify which three features you believe are most important to a country's economic health. Explain why you believe these particular features are so important.

Vocabulary from Context

This exercise is designed to give you additional clues to determine the meanings of unfamiliar vocabulary items in context. In the paragraph of "The Wealth of Nations" indicated by the number in parentheses, find the word or phrase that best fits the meaning given. Your teacher may want to read these aloud as you quickly scan* the paragraph to find the answer.

1. (1) Which word means *increasing the speed of; making [something] happen more quickly?*

   _____ *spurring* _____

2. (3) Which word means *advantage?* _____ *edge* _____

3. (3) Which word means *connections?* _____ ~~well defined~~ *links* _____

4. (5) Which word means *traditional; customary; standard; ordinary; typical?* *conventional*

5. (6) Which two-word Latin phrase means *the reverse; conversely?* *vice versa*

6. (11) Which word means *groups of similar things occurring close to each other; bunches?* ~~nests~~ *clusters*

7. (14) Which word means *edge; outer limit?* ~~Prephery~~ *Periphery*

8. (16) Which word means *picture; summary?* *snapshot*

9. (16) Which two-word Latin phrase means *the existing state of affairs; the present situation; the way things are now?* *status quo*

10. (18) What two-word phrase means *spreading out; expanding; extending; growing outward?*

    _____ *branching out* _____

11. (25) Which word means *possibilities for growth and development?* *potentials*

Stems and Affixes

Both the ideas and the italicized words in the sentences below are taken from "The Wealth of Nations." On page 158 is a list of synonyms and definitions. Use your knowledge of stems and affixes** and the context to match each italicized word with its definition by placing the appropriate letter on the line before each sentence.

__e__ 1. The work of these researchers is a different kind of *cartography;* their maps are not geographical ones.

__b__ 2. The researchers believe their map *presages* difficulties that a country will face as it tries to expand its economy.

__d__ 3. It is difficult for a country to export products if it does not have a good transportation *infrastructure.*

__a__ 4. In general, the more products a country exports, the wealthier it is; however the *correlation* is not perfect.

__c__ 5. Most countries *compile* reliable records of the value of their exported products.

---

* For an introduction to scanning, see Unit 1.
**For a list of all stems and affixes taught in *Reader's Choice,* see the Appendix.

_→g_ 6. Hausmann says that an important question to consider is whether the world will *converge* or whether it will continue to be a world of rich and poor countries.

_f_ 7. This study *highlights* how different the economies of poor countries are from the economies of rich, industrialized countries.

a. relationship between two things

b. foretells; predicts; gives advance warning of

c. put together; gather; collect

d. underlying base or foundation; basic facilities and equipment to support a system or operation

e. map-making

f. makes it easy to see; shows; emphasizes

g. come together; meet

Dictionary Study

Many words have more than one meaning. When you use a dictionary to discover the meaning of an unfamiliar word or phrase, you need to use the context to determine which definition is appropriate. Use the dictionary entries provided (page 159) to select the best definition(s) for each of the italicized words below. Write the number of the definition in the space provided.

_2 a_ 1. Hausmann and Klinger developed a new *notion* of closeness between products as a way to explain economic development patterns.

_8_ 2. Network theory and computers are tools that have helped economists *tackle* extremely complicated information.

_2_ 3. Rich countries occupy large areas of the product space, including the network's *core*.

_1_ 4. Officials of developing countries have invited Hausmann to *brief* them on his research findings.

_1_ 5. Countries need to *exploit* their strengths in order to grow economically.

YourDictionary.com

no·tion [nō 'shən]

–noun

1. a. a mental image; general idea
   b. a vague thought
2. a belief; opinion; view
3. a desire; inclination; whim
4. a plan or intention
5. small, useful articles, as needles, thread, etc., sold in a store

[Etymology: Fr < L *notio* < *notus*]

Dictionary.com Unabridged (v 1.1)

tack·le [**tak**-uhl] or, for 2–4, [**tey**-kuhl]

–noun

1. equipment, apparatus, or gear, esp. for fishing: *fishing tackle.*
2. a mechanism or apparatus, as a rope and block or a combination of ropes and blocks, for hoisting, lowering, and shifting objects or materials; purchase.
3. any system of leverage using several pulleys.
4. *Nautical.* the gear and running rigging for handling a ship or performing some task on a ship.
5. an act of tackling, as in football; a seizing, grasping, or bringing down.
6. *Football.*
   a. either of the linemen stationed between a guard and an end.
   b. the position played by this lineman.
7. (formerly) TACK¹ (def. 8).

–verb (used with object)

8. to undertake to handle, master, solve, etc.: *to tackle a difficult problem.*
9. to deal with (a person) on some problem, issue, etc.
10. to harness (a horse).
11. *Football.* to seize, stop, or throw down (a ball-carrier).
12. *Soccer, Field Hockey.* to block or impede the movement or progress of (an opponent having the ball) with the result of depriving the opponent of the ball.
13. to seize suddenly, esp. in order to stop.

–verb (used without object)

14. *Football.* to tackle an opponent having the ball.

[Origin: 1200–50; ME *takel* gear, apparatus < MLG; akin to TAKE]

Dictionary.com Unabridged (v 1.1)

core [kawr, kohr] *noun, verb,* **cored, cor·ing.**

–noun

1. the central part of a fleshy fruit, containing the seeds.
2. the central, innermost, or most essential part of anything.
3. Also called magnetic core. *Electricity.* the piece of iron, bundle of iron wires, or other ferrous material forming the central or inner portion in an electromagnet, induction coil, transformer, or the like.
4. (in mining, geology, etc.) a cylindrical sample of earth, mineral, or rock extracted from the ground by means of a corer so that the strata are undisturbed in the sample.
5. the inside wood of a tree.
6. *Anthropology.* a lump of stone, as flint, from which prehistoric humans struck flakes in order to make tools. Compare FLAKE TOOL.
7. *Carpentry.*
   a. a thickness of wood forming a base for a veneer.
   b. a wooden construction, as in a door, forming a backing for veneers.

–verb (used with object)

8. to remove the core of (fruit).
9. to cut from the central part.
10. to remove (a cylindrical sample) from the interior, as of the earth or a tree trunk: to core the ocean bottom.
11. to form a cavity in (a molded object) by placing a core, as of sand, in the mold before pouring.

[Origin: 1275–1325; 1945–50 for def. 11; ME; orig.uncert.;perh.<of *cors* body < L *corpus*]

YourDictionary.com

brief [brēf]

–adjective

1. Short in time or duration.
2. Short in length or extent.
3. Condensed in expression; succinct.
4. Curt; abrupt.

–noun

1. A summary or abstract
2. *Abbr.* **br.** *Law.*
   a. An abstract of all the documents affecting the title of real property.
   b. A document containing all facts and points of law pertinent to a specific case, filed by an attorney before arguing the case in court.

–tr.v.

1. To make a summary of
2. To supply with necessary instructions or information

YourDictionary.com

exploit [eks 'ploit']

–noun

An act remarkable for brilliance or daring; a bold deed

–tr.v.

1. to make use of; turn to account; utilize productively
2. to make unethical use of for one's own advantage or profit
3. to promote

Amy Tan was born in 1952 to immigrant parents from China. Her parents wanted her to become a famous neurosurgeon and concert pianist. At one point she was a doctoral student in the UC–Berkeley Linguistics Department, and she is a member of a garage rock band, The Rockbottom Remainders. But at the age of 24, she experienced a difficult year of personal loss and self-discovery, and she became a writer. She is the author of *The Joy Luck Club, The Kitchen God's Wife, The Hundred Secret Senses, The Bonesetter's Daughter,* and *Saving Fish from Drowning,* all *New York Times* best sellers. She has received many literary awards, and she was the co-producer and co-screenwriter for the film adaptation of *The Joy Luck Club.* To learn more about her, go to **www.amytan.net.**

Before You Begin

1. Why are you learning English? What role do you expect it to play in your future?

2. How important is it to speak grammatically correct, unaccented English?

3. Do you believe people treat nonnative English speakers differently depending on their command of English? Have you ever been in situations where you believe you were treated disrespectfully or dismissed because of your use of English?

4. Do you think it is the same with other languages? Are people treated differently depending on their proficiency with other languages you speak?

In this essay Amy Tan examines her understanding of English as a tool of communication for her as a writer and for her mother as an immigrant. She raises important questions for teachers and learners of English to consider.

Read the essay to get a general understanding of Tan's analysis, and then do the exercises that follow. Your teacher may want you to do Vocabulary from Context Exercise 1 on page 165 before you begin.

Mother Tongue

(1) I am not a scholar of English or literature. I cannot give you much more than personal opinions on the English language and its variations in this country or others.

(2) I am a writer. And by that definition, I am someone who has always loved language. I am fascinated by language in daily life. I spend a great deal of my time thinking about the power of language—the way it can evoke an emotion, a visual image, a complex idea, or a simple truth. Language is the tool of my trade. And I use them all—all the Englishes I grew up with.

(3) Recently, I was made keenly aware of the different Englishes I do use. I was giving a talk to a large group of people, the same talk I had already given to half a dozen other groups. The talk was about my writing, my life, and my book *The Joy Luck Club,* and it was going along well enough, until I remembered one major difference that made the whole talk sound wrong. My mother was in the room. And it was perhaps the first time she had heard me give a lengthy speech, using the kind of English I have never used with her. I was saying

things like "the intersection of memory and imagination" and "There is an aspect of my fiction that relates to thus-and-thus"—a speech filled with carefully wrought grammatical phrases, burdened, it suddenly seemed to me, with nominalized forms, past perfect tenses, conditional phrases, forms of standard English that I had learned in school and through books, the forms of English I did not use at home with my mother.

(4) Just last week, as I was walking down the street with her, I again found myself conscious of the English I was using, the English I do use with her. We were talking about the price of new and used furniture, and I heard myself saying this: "Not waste money that way." My husband was with us as well, and he didn't notice any such switch in English. And then I realized why. It's because over the twenty years we've been together I've often used the same kind of English with him, and sometimes he even uses it with me. It has become our language of intimacy, a different sort of English that relates to family talk, the language I grew up with.

(5) So that you'll have some idea of what this family talk sounds like, I'll quote what my mother said during a conversation that I videotaped and then transcribed. During this conversation, she was talking about a political gangster in Shanghai who had the same last name as her family's, Du, and how in his early years the gangster wanted to be adopted by her family, who were rich by comparison. Later, the gangster became more powerful, far richer than my mother's family, and he showed up at my mother's wedding to pay his respects. Here's what she said in part:

(6) "Du Yusong having business like fruit stand. Like off-the-street kind. He is Du like Du Zong—but not Tsung-ming Island people. The local people call *putong*. The river east side, he belong to that side local people. That man want to ask Du Zong father take him in like become own family. Du Zong father wasn't look down on him, but didn't take seriously, until that man big like become a mafia. Now important person, very hard to inviting him. Chinese way, came only to show respect, don't stay for dinner. Respect for making big celebration, he shows up. Mean gives lots of respect. Chinese custom. Chinese social life that way. If too important won't have to stay too long. He come to my wedding. I didn't see, I heard it. I gone to boy's side, they have YMCA dinner. Chinese age I was nineteen."

(7) You should know that my mother's expressive command of English belies how much she actually understands. She reads the *Forbes* report, listens to *Wall Street Week*, converses daily with her stockbroker, reads Shirley MacLaine's books with ease—all kinds of things I can't begin to understand. Yet some of my friends tell me they understand fifty percent of what my mother says. Some say they understand eighty to ninety percent. Some say they understand none of it, as if she were speaking pure Chinese. But to me, my mother's English is perfectly clear, perfectly natural. It's my mother tongue. Her language, as I hear it, is vivid, direct, full of observation and imagery. That was the language that helped shape the way I saw things, expressed things, made sense of the world.

(8) Lately I've been giving more thought to the kind of English my mother speaks. Like others, I have described it to people as "broken" or "fractured" English. But I wince when I say that. It has always bothered me that I can think of no way to describe it other than "broken," as if it were damaged and needed to be fixed, as if it lacked a certain wholeness and soundness. I've heard other terms used, "limited English," for example. But they seem just as bad, as if everything is limited, including people's perceptions of the limited-English speaker.

(9) I know this for a fact, because when I was growing up, my mother's "limited" English limited my perception of her. I was ashamed of her English. I believed that her English reflected the quality of what she had to say. That is, because she expressed them imperfectly, her thoughts were imperfect. And I had plenty of empirical evidence to support me: the fact that people in department stores, at banks, and in restaurants did not take her seriously, did not give her good service, pretended not to understand her, or even acted as if they did not hear her.

(10) My mother has long realized the limitations of her English as well. When I was a teenager, she used to have me call people on the phone and pretend I was she. In this guise, I was forced to ask for information or

even to complain and yell at people who had been rude to her. One time it was to call her stockbroker in New York. She had cashed out her small portfolio, and it just so happened we were going to New York the next week, our first trip outside California. I had to get on the phone and say in an adolescent voice that was not very convincing, "This is Mrs. Tan."

(11) My mother was standing in the back whispering loudly, "Why he don't send me check, already two weeks late. So mad he lie to me, losing me money."

(12) And then I said in perfect English on the phone, "Yes, I'm getting rather concerned. You had agreed to send the check two weeks ago, but it hasn't arrived."

(13) Then she began to talk more loudly. "What he want, I come to New York tell him front of his boss, you cheating me?" And I was trying to calm her down, make her be quiet, while telling the stockbroker, "I can't tolerate any more excuses. If I don't receive the check immediately, I am going to have to speak to your manager when I'm in New York next week." And sure enough, the following week, there we were in front of this astonished stockbroker, and I was sitting there red-faced and quiet, and my mother, the real Mrs. Tan, was shouting at his boss in her impeccable broken English.

(14) We used a similar routine more recently, for a situation that was far less humorous. My mother had gone to the hospital for an appointment to find out about a CAT scan she had had a month earlier. She said she had spoken very good English, her best English, no mistakes. Still, she said, the hospital staff did not apologize when they informed her they had lost the CAT scan and she had come for nothing. She said they did not seem to have any sympathy when she told them she was anxious to know the exact diagnosis, since both her husband and her son had died of brain tumors. She said they would not give her any more information until the next time and she would have to make another appointment for that. So she said she would not leave until the doctor called her daughter. She wouldn't budge. And when the doctor finally called her daughter, me, who spoke in perfect English—lo and behold—we had assurances the CAT scan would be found, promises that a conference call on Monday would be held, and apologies for any suffering my mother had gone through for a most regrettable mistake.

(15) I think my mother's English almost had an effect on limiting my possibilities in life as well. Sociologists and linguists probably will tell you that a person's developing language skills are more influenced by peers than by family. But I do think that the language spoken in the family, especially in immigrant families which are more insular, plays a large role in shaping the language of the child. And I believe that it affected my results on achievement tests, IQ tests, and the SAT*. While my English skills were never judged poor, compared with math, English could not be considered my strong suit. In grade school I did moderately well, getting perhaps B's, sometimes B-pluses, in English and scoring perhaps in the sixtieth or seventieth percentile on achievement tests. But those scores were not good enough to override the opinion that my true abilities lay in math and science, because in those areas I achieved A's and scored in the ninetieth percentile or higher.

(16) This was understandable. Math is precise; there is only one correct answer. Whereas, for me at least, the answers on English tests were always a judgment call, a matter of opinion and personal experience. Those tests were constructed around items like fill-in-the-blank sentence completion, such as "Even though Tom was _____ Mary thought he was _____." And the correct answer always seem to be the most bland combinations, for example, "Even though Tom was shy, Mary thought he was charming," with the grammatical structure "Even though" limiting the correct answer to some sort of semantic opposites, so you wouldn't get answers like "Even though Tom was foolish, Mary thought he was ridiculous." Well, according to my mother, there

---

* **IQ tests and the SAT:** Two standardized tests taken by many children in the United States. The first tests general intelligence (*IQ* stands for Intelligence Quotient). The SAT is the Scholastic Aptitude Test, taken by students applying to U.S. colleges and universities.

were very few limitations as to what Tom could have been and what Mary might have thought of him. So I never did well on tests like that.

(17) The same was true with word analogies, pairs of words for which you were supposed to find some logical semantic relationship, for instance, "Sunset is to nightfall as _____ is to _____." And here you would be presented with a list of four possible pairs, one of which showed the same kind of relationship: *red* is to *stoplight, bus* is to *arrival, chills* is to *fever, yawn* is to *boring*. Well, I could never think that way. I knew what the tests were asking, but I could not block out of my mind the images already created by the first pair, *sunset* is to *nightfall*—and I would see a burst of colors against a darkening sky, the moon rising, the lowering of a curtain of stars. And all the other pairs of words—*red, bus, stoplight, boring*—just threw up a mass of confusing images, making it impossible for me to see that saying "A sunset precedes nightfall" was as logical as saying "A chill precedes a fever." The only way I would have gotten that answer right was to imagine an associative situation, such as my being disobedient and staying out past sunset, catching a chill at night, which turned into feverish pneumonia as punishment—which indeed did happen to me.

(18) I have been thinking about all this lately, about my mother's English, about achievement tests. Because lately I've been asked, as a writer, why there are not more Asian-Americans represented in American literature. Why are there few Asian-Americans enrolled in creative writing programs? Why do so many Chinese students go into engineering? Well, these are broad sociological questions I can't begin to answer. But I have noticed in surveys—in fact, just last week—that Asian-American students, as a whole, do significantly better on math achievement tests than on English tests. And this makes me think that there are other Asian-American students whose English spoken in the home might also be described as "broken" or "limited." And perhaps they also have teachers who are steering them away from writing and into math and science, which is what happened to me.

(19) Fortunately, I happen to be rebellious and enjoy the challenge of disproving assumptions made about me. I became an English major my first year in college, after being enrolled as pre-med. I started writing nonfiction as a freelancer the week after I was told by my boss at the time that writing was my worst skill and I should hone my talents toward account management.

(20) But it wasn't until 1985 that I began to write fiction. At first I wrote what I thought to be wittily crafted sentences, sentences that would finally prove I had mastery over the English language. Here's an example from the first draft of a story that later made its way into *The Joy Luck Club*, but without this line: "That was my mental quandary in its nascent state." A terrible line, which I can barely pronounce.

(21) Fortunately, for reasons I won't get into here, I later decided I should envision a reader for the stories I would write. And the reader I decided on was my mother, because these were stories about mothers. So with this reader in mind—and in fact she did read my early drafts—I began to write stories using all the Englishes I grew up with: the English I spoke to my mother, which for lack of a better term might be described as "simple"; the English she used with me, which for lack of a better term might be described as "broken"; my translation of her Chinese, which could certainly be described as "watered down"; and what I imagined to be her translation of her Chinese if she could speak in perfect English, her internal language, and for that I sought to preserve the essence, but neither an English nor a Chinese structure. I wanted to capture what language ability tests could never reveal: her intent, her passion, her imagery, the rhythms of her speech and the nature of her thoughts.

(22) Apart from what any critic had to say about my writing, I knew I had succeeded where it counted when my mother finished reading my book and gave me her verdict: "So easy to read."

Comprehension

Answer the following questions. Your teacher may want you to answer the questions orally, in writing, or by underlining appropriate portions of the text. True/False questions are indicated by a T / F preceding the statement. For some items, there is not a single correct answer. Be prepared to defend your choices.

1. What is the meaning of the title of the essay, "Mother Tongue"? _____

   _____

2. T / F Tan speaks different kinds of English depending on her audience.

3. T / F Tan often uses the same English with her husband as she does with her mother.

4. T / F Tan tells the story of the Shanghai gangster to illustrate her mother's English.

5. Below are words and phrases that describe language. Check (✔) all those that characterize Tan's opinion of her mother's English.

   a. ____ perfectly clear

   b. ____ vivid

   c. ____ direct

   d. ____ full of observation and imagery

   e. ____ broken

   f. ____ fractured

   g. ____ limited

6. T / F Tan is embarrassed by her mother's English.

7. In which classes did Tan excel when she was in school? _____

8. T / F Tan enjoyed taking English tests when she was in school.

9. T / F Tan believes that children of immigrants should study math and science.

10. Who is Tan's primary audience when she writes? _____

11. T / F Tan's mother enjoyed her daughter's stories.

Critical Reading

T / F Tan's mother is limited by her imperfect English. Defend your answer with evidence from the text.

Discussion/Composition

Tan decided to write using all the Englishes she grew up with, which she describes as:

a. Simple: the English she spoke to her mother.

b. Broken: the English her mother spoke to her.

c. Watered down: the English she used to translate her mother's Chinese.

d. Her mother's internal language: the powerful language with which her mother understood the world.

What experience do you have using different varieties of the same language? What factors make you decide which type of language to use?

Vocabulary from Context

EXERCISE 1

Use the context provided to determine the meaning of the italicized words. Write a definition, synonym, or description of each of the italicized vocabulary items in the space provided.

1. _____

2. _____

3. _____

4. _____

5. _____

6. _____

7. _____

8. _____

9. _____

10. _____

11. _____

12. _____

Many teenagers are *rebellious*, fighting against everything, especially what their parents want them to do. However when Amy Tan was an *adolescent*, she was often cooperative and helpful to her mother. For example, once Tan's mother needed help talking to the man who sold her stocks and other financial investments. Tan phoned her mother's *stockbroker*, pretending to be her mother. Later when they went to see him in his New York office, they could see he was surprised when he met them. He was *astonished* when he realized that the person he had been talking with on the phone was just a young girl. He thought he had been talking with a grown woman, but his *perception* had been wrong. Tan's mature way of talking *belied* her young age.

Tan also helped her mother talk with doctors. Once she went with her mother to hear her doctor's *diagnosis* of a medical problem she had. When the doctor told her she had a brain tumor, she was frightened. However the doctor said he could guarantee that the tumor was not cancerous but *benign*. He *assured* her that she would be all right.

As a nonnative speaker, Tan's mother spoke her own variety of English. Even though her grammar was not *impeccable*, her *intent* was clear to most people. They could usually understand what she meant in spite of her grammatical mistakes. Her language was delightful to listen to. It was never *bland*; indeed, far from being ordinary and dull, it was a colorful version of English.

EXERCISE 2

This exercise should be done after you have finished reading "Mother Tongue." The exercise is designed to give you practice using context clues to guess the meaning of unfamiliar vocabulary. Give a definition, synonym, or description of each of the words or phrases below. The number in parentheses indicates the paragraph in which the word or phrase can be found. Your teacher may want you to do these orally or in writing.

1. (4) language of intimacy _____

2. (15) peers _____

3. (16) judgment call _____

4. (18) steering _____

EXERCISE 3

This exercise is designed to give you additional clues to determine the meanings of unfamiliar vocabulary items in context. In the paragraph of "Mother Tongue" indicated by the number in parentheses, find the word or phrase that best fits the meaning given. Your teacher may want to read these aloud as you quickly scan* the paragraph to find the answer.

1. (2) What phrase means *something considered necessary to carry out my occupation or profession?*

    _____

2. (5) Which word means *member of a gang; someone who belongs to an organized group of criminals?*

    _____

3. (8) Which word means *feel embarrassed, especially, to make a face showing embarrassment?*

    _____

4. (9) Which two words mean *information or proof that is based on observation or practical experience?*

    _____

5. (10) Which word means *identity; often a false identity or disguise?* _____

6. (10) What phrase means *sold her few financial investments for cash?* _____

7. (15) Which word means *isolated; separated from others as an island is from the mainland?*

    _____

8. (21) Which word means *the most important or underlying meaning of something?*

    _____

---

*For an introduction to scanning, see Unit 1.

Figurative Language and Idioms

Like the previous exercise, this one is designed to give you practice using context clues to guess the meaning of unfamiliar vocabulary, in this case, figurative language and idioms. Give a definition, synonym, or description of each of the words or phrases below. The number in parentheses indicates the paragraph in which the word or phrase can be found. Your teacher may want you to do these orally or in writing.

1. (3) Which word means *made difficult; weighted down; overloaded?* _____

2. (15) Which two words mean *greatest talent or skill?* _____

3. (17) What phrase means *ignore; forget?* _____

4. (19) What phrase means *shape or polish or improve my skills?* _____

5. (22) What phrase means *where it was important; when it mattered?* _____

Stems and Affixes

Both the ideas and the italicized words in the sentences below are taken from "Mother Tongue." Beneath the sentences is a list of synonyms and definitions. Use your knowledge of stems and affixes* and the context to match each italicized word with its definition by placing the appropriate letter on the line before each sentence.

_____ 1. Tan describes her mother's English as *vivid* and full of images.

_____ 2. Tan recorded and then *transcribed* her mother's speech so she could study her mother's language more closely.

_____ 3. Tan's telephone call to her mother's stockbroker *preceded* their visit to his office.

_____ 4. Tan's success as a writer *disproves* the claim that grades in school predict future performance.

_____ 5. When Tan writes a story, it helps her to *envision* her mother reading it.

a. shows to be not true; shows to be false or an error

b. came before; occurred earlier than

c. wrote down; made a written copy of

d. see a picture in her mind; imagine

e. lively; animated

---

*For a list of all stems and affixes taught in *Reader's Choice*, see the Appendix.

Dictionary Study

Many words have more than one meaning. When you use a dictionary to discover the meaning of an unfamiliar word or phrase, you need to use the context to determine which definition is appropriate. Use the dictionary entries provided to select the best definition(s) for each italicized word. Write the number of the definition in the space provided.

_____ 1. What was the *nature* of Tan's talk? It was an academic discussion of her writing, her life, and her book.

_____ 2. Tan speaks differently at home than when she is giving a professional talk, but she does not always notice the *switch* when she makes it.

_____ 3. Tan has a good *command* of many Englishes.

_____ 4. Tan believes her mother can give her *sound* advice about her writing.

_____ 5. After carefully reading Tan's work, her mother's *verdict* on it was positive.

YourDictionary.com

na-ture [nā'chər]

—noun
1. the essential character of a thing; quality or qualities that make something what it is; essence
2. inborn character; innate disposition; inherent tendencies of a person
3. the vital functions, forces, and activities of the organs: often used as a euphemism
4. kind; sort; *type things of that nature*
5. any or all of the instincts, desires, appetites, drives, etc. of a person or animal
6. what is regarded as normal or acceptable behavior
7. the sum total of all things in time and space; the entire physical universe
8. the power, force, principle, etc. that seems to regulate the physical universe: often personified, sometimes as **Mother Nature**
9. the primitive state of man
10. a simple way of life close to or in the outdoors
11. natural scenery, including the plants and animals that are part of it

YourDictionary.com

switch [swĭch]

—noun Abbr. **sw.**
1. a thin flexible rod, stick, twig, used for whipping
2. a shift or change from one (kind of) thing to another
3. an abrupt, sharp, lashing movement, as with a switch
4. a device that controls the flow of current in an electric circuit
5. a. a movable section of railroad track used to transfer a train from one track to another
   b. **siding** (sense)

—v. tr.
switched, switching, switches.
1. to whip with or as if with a switch
2. To jerk or swish abruptly or sharply
3. To shift, transfer, change, or divert
4. a. to operate the switch of (an electric circuit) so as to connect, disconnect, or divert
   b. to turn (an electric light or appliance) on or off in this way
5. to transfer (a railroad train or car) from one set of tracks to another by use of a switch
6. to change or exchange

Dictionary.com Unabridged (v 1.1)
command [kuh-**mand**]

–verb (used with object)

1. to direct with specific authority or prerogative; order: *The captain commanded his men to attack.*
2. to require authoritatively; demand: *She commanded silence.*
3. to have or exercise authority or control over; be master of; have at one's bidding or disposal: *The Pharaoh commanded 10,000 slaves.*
4. to deserve and receive (respect, sympathy, attention, etc.): *He commands much respect for his attitude.*
5. to dominate by reason of location; overlook: *The hill commands the sea.*
6. to have authority over and responsibility for (a military or naval unit or installation); be in charge of.

–verb (used without object)

7. to issue an order or orders.
8. to be in charge; have authority.
9. to occupy a dominating position; look down upon or over a body of water, region, etc.

–noun

10. the act of commanding or ordering.
11. an order given by one in authority: *The colonel gave the command to attack.*
12. the possession or exercise of controlling authority: *a lieutenant in command of a platoon.*
13. expertise; mastery: *He has a command of French, Russian, and German.*

Dictionary.com Unabridged (v 1.1)
sound[1] [sound]

–noun

1. the sensation produced by stimulation of the organs of hearing by vibrations transmitted through the air or other medium.
2. mechanical vibrations transmitted through an elastic medium, traveling in air at a speed of approximately 1087 ft. (331 m) per second at sea level.
3. the particular auditory effect produced by a given cause: *the sound of music.*
4. any auditory effect; any audible vibrational disturbance: *all kinds of sounds.*
5. a noise, vocal utterance, musical tone, or the like: *the sounds from the next room.*
6. a distinctive, characteristic, or recognizable musical style, as from a particular performer, orchestra, or type of arrangement: *the big-band sound.*
7. *Phonetics.*
   a. SPEECH SOUND.
   b. the audible result of an utterance or portion of an utterance: *the s-sound in "slight"; the sound of m in "mere."*

sound[2] [sound]

–er, –est, *adverb*

–adjective

1. free from injury, damage, defect, disease, etc.; in good condition; healthy; robust: *a sound heart; a sound mind.*
2. financially strong, secure, or reliable: *a sound business; sound investments.*
3. competent, sensible, or valid: *sound judgment.*
4. having no defect as to truth, justice, wisdom, or reason: *sound advice.*
5. of substantial or enduring character: *sound moral values.*
6. following in a systematic pattern without any apparent defect in logic: *sound reasoning.*
7. uninterrupted and untroubled; deep: *sound sleep.*
8. vigorous, thorough, or severe: *a sound thrashing.*
9. free from moral defect or weakness; upright, honest, or good; honorable; loyal.
10. having no legal defect: *a sound title to property.*
11. theologically correct or orthodox, as doctrines or a theologian.

–adverb

12. deeply; thoroughly: *sound asleep.*

YourDictionary.com
ver·dict [vûr'dĭkt]

–noun

1. LAW the formal finding of a judge or jury on a matter submitted to them in a trial
2. any decision or judgment

[Etymology: ME *verdit* < Anglo-Fr < ML *veredictum,* true saying, verdict < L *vere,* truly + *dictum,* a thing said: see very & dictum]

Vocabulary Review

EXERCISE 1

Select the word or phrase from the list of vocabulary items that correctly fits in each of the blanks in this paragraph. Some words will not be used.

sound	adolescents	block out	envision	steer
peers	astonish	strong suit	intent	rebellious

Being a teenager can be difficult. (1)_____ want to be accepted by their

(2)_____, and sometimes these friends can (3)_____ them into

troublesome or even dangerous situations. Sometimes parents worry too much. They can

(4)_____ the worst possible things that could happen. They may forget how

responsible their children really are. Worry may make parents (5)_____ of

their minds all the ways in which their children have shown good judgment and made

(6)_____ decisions. During these years, patience may not be the

(7)_____ of either parents or teenagers.

EXERCISE 2

For each pair of words, write S if the words as used in "Mother Tongue" have a similar meaning. Write D if the words have different meanings.

1. _____ nature   essence
2. _____ stockbroker   gangster
3. _____ disproves   belies
4. _____ vivid   bland
5. _____ talent   strong suit

Longer Reading
Short Story

Before You Begin

Since the beginning of time, people have left their families to build new lives in distant locations.

- Which things do you think people most miss from their home cultures?

- Which things are they least likely to change?

- What things help people become part of a new setting?

"The Third and Final Continent" is from Jhumpa Lahiri's Pulitzer prize–winning book, *Interpreter of Maladies.* You may be familiar with the novel that grew out of this story, *The Namesake,* or the movie by the same name. The story details a modern journey across continents. In the words of one reviewer, it deals with "the loss of the familiar." But it also deals with the creation of a new life. This is a touching story. We see the narrator move from being a young student in England to being the father of a student in the U.S. His is an arranged marriage. He moves from being able to recall nothing more than his wife's name to no longer being able to remember a time when they were strangers.

Your teacher may want you to read the story through once as quickly as you can to get a sense of the movement through a life, or your teacher may want you to read the story section by section and do the related exercises. In either case, you may want to do Vocabulary from Context Exercise 1 on pages 192–94 before you begin reading. <u>Note</u>: On the first page of the story and elsewhere, some unfamiliar vocabulary is defined in the margins next to where the words appear.

The Third and Final Continent

Jhumpa Lahiri from *Interpreter of Maladies*

Certificate in Commerce: a pre-university certificate in business economics

(1) I left India in 1964 with a certificate in commerce and the equivalent, in those days, of ten dollars to my name. For three weeks I sailed on the *SS Roma*, an Italian cargo vessel, in a third-class cabin next to the ship's engine, across the Arabian Sea, the Red Sea, the Mediterranean, and finally to England. I lived in north London, in Finsbury Park, in a house occupied entirely by penniless Bengali bachelors like myself, at least a dozen and sometimes more, all struggling to educate and establish ourselves abroad.

LSE: London School of Economics

(2) I attended lectures at LSE and worked at the university library to get by. We lived three or four to a room, shared a single, icy toilet, and took turns cooking pots of egg curry, which we ate with our hands on a table covered with newspapers. Apart from our jobs we had few responsibilities. On weekends we lounged barefoot in drawstring pajamas, drinking tea and smoking Rothmans, or set out to watch cricket at Lord's. Some weekends the house was crammed with still more Bengalis, to whom we had introduced ourselves at the greengrocer, or on the Tube, and we made yet more egg curry, and played Mukhesh on a Grundig reel-to-reel, and soaked our dirty dishes in the bathtub. Every now and then someone in the house moved out, to live with a woman whom his family back in Calcutta had determined he was to wed. In 1969, when I was thirty-six years old, my own marriage was arranged. Around the same time I was offered a full-time job in America, in the processing department of a library at MIT. The salary was generous enough to support a wife, and I was honored to be hired by a world-famous university, and so I obtained a sixth-preference green card, and prepared to travel farther still.

Lord's: Lord's Ground in London is often referred to as "The Home of Cricket"

reel-to-reel: a kind of tape recorder (particularly common in the 1960s) that uses magnetic tape which must be threaded through the equipment and onto large reels

(3) By now I had enough money to go by plane. I flew first to Calcutta, to attend my wedding, and a week later I flew to Boston, to begin my new job. During the flight I read *The Student Guide to North America*, a paperback volume that I'd bought before leaving London, for seven shillings six pence on Tottenham Court Road, for although I was no longer a student I was on a budget all the same. I learned that Americans drove on the right side of the road, not the left, and that they called a lift an elevator and an engaged phone busy. "The pace of life in North America is different from Britain as you will soon discover," the guidebook informed me. "Everybody feels he must get to the top. Don't expect an English cup of tea." As the plane began its descent over Boston Harbor, the pilot announced the weather and time, and that President Nixon had declared a national holiday: two American men had landed on the moon. Several passengers cheered. "God bless America!" one of them hollered. Across the aisle, I saw a woman praying.

YMCA: Young Men's Christian Association; the organization has very inexpensive rooms for rent in cities around the world

(4) I spent my first night at the YMCA in Central Square, Cambridge, an inexpensive accommodation recommended by my guidebook. It was walking distance from MIT, and steps from the post office and a supermarket called Purity Supreme. The room contained a cot, a desk, and a small wooden cross on one wall. A sign on the door said cooking was strictly forbidden. A bare window overlooked Massachusetts Avenue, a major thoroughfare with traffic in both directions. Car horns, shrill and prolonged, blared one after another. Flashing sirens heralded endless emergencies, and a fleet of buses rumbled past, their doors opening and closing with a powerful hiss, throughout the night. The noise was constantly distracting, at times suffocating. I felt it deep in my ribs, just as I had felt the furious drone of the engine on the *SS Roma*. But there was no ship's deck to escape to, no glittering ocean to thrill my soul, no breeze to cool

my face, no one to talk to. I was too tired to pace the gloomy corridors of the YMCA in my drawstring pajamas. Instead I sat at the desk and stared out the window, at the city hall of Cambridge and a row of small shops. In the morning I reported to my job at the Dewey Library, a beige fortlike building by Memorial Drive. I also opened a bank account, rented a post office box, and bought a plastic bowl and a spoon at Woolworth's, a store whose name I recognized from London. I went to Purity Supreme, wandering up and down the aisles, converting ounces to grams and comparing prices to things in England. In the end I bought a small carton of milk and a box of cornflakes. This was my first meal in America. I ate it at my desk. I preferred it to hamburgers or hot dogs, the only alternative I could afford in the coffee shops on Massachusetts Avenue, and, besides, at the time I had yet to consume any beef. Even the simple chore of buying milk was new to me; in London we'd had bottles delivered each morning to our door.

2.

(5) In a week I had adjusted, more or less. I ate cornflakes and milk, morning and night, and bought some bananas for variety, slicing them into the bowl with the edge of my spoon. In addition I bought tea bags and a flask, which the salesman in Woolworth's referred to as a thermos (a flask, he informed me, was used to store whiskey, another thing I had never consumed). For the price of one cup of tea at a coffee shop, I filled the flask with boiling water on my way to work each morning, and brewed the four cups I drank in the course of a day. I bought a larger carton of milk, and learned to leave it on the shaded part of the windowsill, as I had seen another resident at the YMCA do. To pass the time in the evenings I read the *Boston Globe* downstairs, in a spacious room with stained-glass windows. I read every article and advertisement, so that I would grow familiar with things, and when my eyes grew tired I slept. Only I did not sleep well. Each night I had to keep the window wide open; it was the only source of air in the stifling room, and the noise was intolerable. I would lie on the cot with my fingers pressed into my ears, but when I drifted off to sleep my hands fell away, and the noise of the traffic would wake me up again. Pigeon feathers drifted onto the window-sill, and one evening, when I poured milk over my cornflakes, I saw that it had soured. Nevertheless I resolved to stay at the YMCA for six weeks, until my wife's passport and green card were ready. Once she arrived I would have to rent a proper apartment, and from time to time I studied the classified section of the newspaper, or stopped in at the housing office at MIT during my lunch break, to see what was available in my price range. It was in this manner that I discovered a room for immediate occupancy, in a house on a quiet street, the listing said, for eight dollars per week. I copied the number into my guidebook and dialed from a pay telephone, sorting through the coins with which I was still unfamiliar, smaller and lighter than shillings, heavier and brighter than *paisas*.

(6) "Who is speaking?" a woman demanded. Her voice was bold and clamorous.

"Yes, good afternoon, madame. I am calling about the room for rent."

"Harvard or Tech?"

"I beg your pardon?"

"Are you from Harvard or Tech?"

Gathering that Tech referred to the Massachusetts Institute of Technology, I replied, "I work at Dewey Library," adding tentatively, "at Tech."

"I only rent rooms to boys from Harvard or Tech!"

"Yes, madame."

(7) I was given an address and an appointment for seven o'clock that evening. Thirty minutes before the hour I set out, my guidebook in my pocket, my breath fresh with Listerine. I turned down a street shaded with trees, perpendicular to Massachusetts Avenue. Stray blades of grass poked between the cracks of the footpath. In spite of the heat I wore a coat and a tie, regarding the event as I would any other interview; I had never lived in the home of a person who was not Indian. The house, surrounded by a chain-link fence, was off-white with dark brown trim. Unlike the stucco row house I'd lived in in London, this house, fully detached, was covered with wooden shingles, with a tangle of forsythia bushes plastered against the front and sides. When I pressed the calling bell, the woman with whom I had spoken on the phone hollered from what seemed to be just the other side of the door, "One minute, please!"

(8) Several minutes later the door was opened by a tiny, extremely old woman. A mass of snowy hair was arranged like a small sack on top of her head. As I stepped into the house she sat down on a wooden bench positioned at the bottom of a narrow carpeted staircase. Once she was settled on the bench, in a small pool of light, she peered up at me with undivided attention. She wore a long black skirt that spread like a stiff tent to the floor, and a starched white shirt edged with ruffles at the throat and cuffs. Her hands, folded together in her lap, had long pallid fingers, with swollen knuckles and tough yellow nails. Age had battered her features so that she almost resembled a man, with sharp, shrunken eyes and prominent creases on either side of her nose. Her lips, chapped and faded, had nearly disappeared, and her eyebrows were missing altogether. Nevertheless she looked fierce.

(9) "Lock up!" she commanded. She shouted even though I stood only a few feet away. "Fasten the chain and firmly press that button on the knob! This is the first thing you shall do when you enter, is that clear?"

(10) I locked the door as directed and examined the house. Next to the bench on which the woman sat was a small round table, its legs fully concealed, much like the woman's, by a skirt of lace. The table held a lamp, a transistor radio, a leather change purse with a silver clasp, and a telephone. A thick wooden cane coated with a layer of dust was propped against one side. There was a parlor to my right, lined with bookcases and filled with shabby claw-footed furniture. In the corner of the parlor I saw a grand piano with its top down, piled with papers. The piano's bench was missing; it seemed to be the one on which the woman was sitting. Somewhere in the house a clock chimed seven times.

(11) "You're punctual!" the woman proclaimed. "I expect you shall be so with the rent!"

"I have a letter, madame." In my jacket pocket was a letter confirming my employment from MIT, which I had brought along to prove that I was indeed from Tech.

(12) She stared at the letter, then handed it back to me carefully, gripping it with her fingers as if it were a dinner plate heaped with food instead of a sheet of paper. She did not wear glasses, and I wondered if she'd read a word of it. "The last boy was always late! Still owes me eight dollars! Harvard boys aren't what they used to be! Only Harvard and Tech in this house! How's Tech, boy?"

"It is very well."

"You checked the lock?"

"Yes, madame."

(13) She slapped the space beside her on the bench with one hand, and told me to sit down. For a moment she was silent. Then she intoned, as if she alone possessed this knowledge:

"There is an American flag on the moon!"

(14) "Yes, madame." Until then I had not thought very much about the moon shot. It was in the newspaper, of course, article upon article. The astronauts had landed on the shores of the Sea of Tranquility, I had read, traveling farther than anyone in the history of civilization. For a few hours they explored the moon's surface. They gathered rocks in their pockets, described their surroundings (a magnificent desolation, according to one astronaut), spoke by phone to the president, and planted a flag in lunar soil. The voyage was hailed as man's most awesome achievement. I had seen full-page photographs in the *Globe*, of the astronauts in their inflated costumes, and read about what certain people in Boston had been doing at the exact moment the astronauts landed, on a Sunday afternoon. A man said that he was operating a swan boat with a radio pressed to his ear; a woman had been baking rolls for her grandchildren.

(15) The woman bellowed, "A flag on the moon, boy! I heard it on the radio! Isn't that splendid?"

"Yes, madame."

But she was not satisfied with my reply. Instead she commanded, "Say 'splendid'!"

(16) I was both baffled and somewhat insulted by the request. It reminded me of the way I was taught multiplication tables as a child, repeating after the master, sitting cross-legged, without shoes or pencils, on the floor of my one-room Tollygunge school. It also reminded me of my wedding, when I had repeated endless Sanskrit verses after the priest, verses I barely understood, which joined me to my wife. I said nothing.

(17) "Say 'splendid'!" the woman bellowed once again.

"Splendid," I murmured. I had to repeat the word a second time at the top of my lungs, so she could hear. I am soft-spoken by nature and was especially reluctant to raise my voice to an elderly woman whom I had met only moments ago, but she did not appear to be offended. If anything the reply pleased her because her next command was:

"Go see the room!"

(18) I rose from the bench and mounted the narrow carpeted staircase. There were five doors, two on either side of an equally narrow hallway, and one at the opposite end. Only one door was partly open. The room contained a twin bed under a sloping ceiling, a brown oval rug, a basin with an exposed pipe, and a chest of drawers. One door, painted white, led to a closet, another to a toilet and a tub. The walls were covered with gray and ivory striped paper. The window was open; net curtains stirred in the breeze. I lifted them away and inspected the view: a small back yard, with a few fruit trees and an empty clothesline. I was satisfied. From the bottom of the stairs I heard the woman demand, "What is your decision?"

(19) When I returned to the foyer and told her, she picked up the leather change purse on the table, opened the clasp, fished about with her fingers, and produced a key on a thin wire hoop. She informed me that there was a kitchen at the back of the house, accessible through the parlor. I was welcome to use the stove as long as I left it as I found it. Sheets and towels were provided, but keeping them clean was my own responsibility. The rent was due Friday mornings on the ledge above the piano keys. "And no lady visitors!"

(20) "I am a married man, madame." It was the first time I had announced this fact to anyone.

But she had not heard. "No lady visitors!" she insisted. She introduced herself as Mrs. Croft.

3.

(21) My wife's name was Mala. The marriage had been arranged by my older brother and his wife. I regarded the proposition with neither objection nor enthusiasm. It was a duty expected of me, as it was expected of every man. She was the daughter of a schoolteacher in Beleghata. I was told that she could cook, knit, embroider, sketch landscapes, and recite poems by Tagore, but these talents could not make up for the fact that she did not possess a fair complexion, and so a string of men had rejected her to her face. She was twenty-seven, an age when her parents had begun to fear that she would never marry, and so they were willing to ship their only child halfway across the world in order to save her from spinsterhood.

(22) For five nights we shared a bed. Each of those nights, after applying cold cream and braiding her hair, which she tied up at the end with a black cotton string, she turned from me and wept; she missed her parents. Although I would be leaving the country in a few days, custom dictated that she was now a part of my household, and for the next six weeks she was to live with my brother and his wife, cooking, cleaning, serving tea and sweets to guests. I did nothing to console her. I lay on my own side of the bed, reading my guidebook by flashlight and anticipating my journey. At times I thought of the tiny room on the other side of the wall which had belonged to my mother. Now the room was practically empty; the wooden pallet on which she'd once slept was piled with trunks and old bedding. Nearly six years ago, before leaving for London, I had watched her die on that bed, had found her playing with her excrement in her final days. Before we cremated her I had cleaned each of her fingernails with a hairpin, and then, because my brother could not bear it, I had assumed the role of eldest son, and had touched the flame to her temple, to release her tormented soul to heaven.

4.

(23) The next morning I moved into the room in Mrs. Croft's house. When I unlocked the door I saw that she was sitting on the piano bench, on the same side as the previous evening. She wore the same black skirt, the same starched white blouse, and had her hands folded together the same way in her lap. She looked so much the same that I wondered if she'd spent the whole night on the bench. I put my suitcase upstairs, filled my flask with boiling water in the kitchen, and headed off to work. That evening when I came home from the university, she was still there.

(24) "Sit down, boy!" She slapped the space beside her.

I perched beside her on the bench. I had a bag of groceries with me—more milk, more cornflakes, and more bananas, for my inspection of the kitchen earlier in the day had revealed no spare pots, pans, or cooking utensils. There were only two saucepans in the refrigerator, both containing some orange broth, and a copper kettle on the stove.

(25) "Good evening, madame."

She asked me if I had checked the lock. I told her I had.

For a moment she was silent. Then suddenly she declared, with the equal measures of disbelief and delight as the night before, "There's an American flag on the moon, boy!"

"Yes, madame."

"A flag on the moon! Isn't that splendid?"

I nodded, dreading what I knew was coming. "Yes, madame."

"Say 'splendid'!"

(26) This time I paused, looking to either side in case anyone were there to overhear me, though I knew perfectly well that the house was empty. I felt like an idiot. But it was a small enough thing to ask. "Splendid!" I cried out.

(27) Within days it became our routine. In the mornings when I left for the library Mrs. Croft was either hidden away in her bedroom, on the other side of the staircase, or she was sitting on the bench, oblivious to my presence, listening to the news or classical music on the radio. But each evening when I returned the same thing happened: she slapped the bench, ordered me to sit down, declared that there was a flag on the moon, and declared that it was splendid. I said it was splendid, too, and then we sat in silence. As awkward as it was, and as endless as it felt to me then, the nightly encounter lasted only about ten minutes; inevitably she would drift off to sleep, her head falling abruptly toward her chest, leaving me free to retire to my room. By then, of course, there was no flag on the moon. The astronauts, I had read in the paper, had taken it down before flying back to Earth. But I did not have the heart to tell her.

5.

(28) Friday morning, when my first week's rent was due, I went to the piano in the parlor to place my money on the ledge. The piano keys were dull and discolored. When I pressed one, it made no sound at all. I had put eight one-dollar bills in an envelope and written Mrs. Croft's name on the front of it. I was not in the habit of leaving money unmarked and unattended. From where I stood I could see the profile of her tent-shaped skirt. She was sitting on the bench, listening to the radio. It seemed unnecessary to make her get up and walk all the way to the piano. I never saw her walking about, and assumed, from the cane always propped against the round table at her side, that she did so with difficulty. When I approached the bench she peered up at me and demanded:

"What is your business?"

"The rent, madame."

"On the ledge above the piano keys!"

(29) "I have it here." I extended the envelope toward her, but her fingers, folded together in her lap, did not budge. I bowed slightly and lowered the envelope, so that it hovered just above her hands. After a moment she accepted, and nodded her head.

(30) That night when I came home, she did not slap the bench, but out of habit I sat beside her as usual. She asked me if I had checked the lock, but she mentioned nothing about the flag on the moon. Instead she said:

"It was very kind of you!"

"I beg your pardon, madame?"

"Very kind of you!"

She was still holding the envelope in her hands.

6.

(31) On Sunday there was a knock on my door. An elderly woman introduced herself: she was Mrs. Croft's daughter, Helen. She walked into the room and looked at each of the walls as if for signs of change, glancing at the shirts that hung in the closet, the neckties draped over the doorknob, the box of cornflakes on the chest of drawers, the dirty bowl and spoon in the basin. She was short and thick-waisted, with cropped silver hair and bright pink lipstick. She wore a sleeveless summer dress, a row of white plastic beads, and spectacles on her chain that hung like a swing against her chest. The

backs of her legs were mapped with dark blue veins, and her upper arms sagged like the flesh of a roasted eggplant. She told me that she lived in Arlington, a town farther up Massachusetts Avenue. "I come once a week to bring Mother groceries. Has she sent you packing yet?"

(32) "It is very well, madame."

"Some of the boys run screaming. But I think she likes you. You're the first boarder she's ever referred to as a gentleman."

"Not at all, madame."

(33) She looked at me, noticing my bare feet (I still felt strange wearing shoes indoors, and always removed them before entering my room). "Are you new to Boston?"

"New to America, madame."

"From?" She raised her eyebrows.

"I am from Calcutta, India."

"Is that right? We had a Brazilian fellow, about a year ago. You'll find Cambridge a very international city."

(34) I nodded, and began to wonder how long our conversation would last. But at that moment we heard Mrs. Croft's electrifying voice rising up the stairs. When we stopped into the hallway we heard her hollering:

"You are to come downstairs immediately!"

"What is it?" Helen hollered back.

"Immediately!"

I put on my shoes at once. Helen sighed.

(35) We walked down the staircase. It was too narrow for us to descend side by side, so I followed Helen, who seemed to be in no hurry, and complained at one point that she had a bad knee. "Have you been walking without your cane?" Helen called out. "You know you're not supposed to walk without that cane." She paused, resting her hand on the banister, and looked back at me. "She slips sometimes."

(36) For the first time Mrs. Croft seemed vulnerable. I pictured her on the floor in front of the bench, flat on her back, staring at the ceiling, her feet pointing in opposite directions. But when we reached the bottom of the staircase she was sitting there as usual, her hands folded together in her lap. Two grocery bags were at her feet. When we stood before her she did not slap the bench, or ask us to sit down. She glared.

"What is it, Mother?"

"It's improper!"

"What's improper?"

"It is improper for a lady and gentleman who are not married to one another to hold a private conversation without a chaperone!"

(37) Helen said she was sixty-eight years old, old enough to be my mother, but Mrs. Croft insisted that Helen and I speak to each other downstairs, in the parlor. She added that it was also improper for a lady of Helen's station to reveal her age, and to wear a dress so high above the ankle.

"For your information, Mother, it's 1969. What would you do if you actually left the house one day and saw a girl in a miniskirt?"

(38) Mrs. Croft sniffed. "I'd have her arrested."

Helen shook her head and picked up one of the grocery bags. I picked up the other one, and followed her through the parlor and into the kitchen. The bags were filled with cans of soup, which Helen opened up one by one with a few cranks of a can opener. She tossed the old soup in the saucepans into the sink, rinsed the pans under the tap, filled them with soup from the newly opened cans, and put them back in the refrigerator. "A few years ago she could still open the cans herself," Helen said. "She hates that I do it for her now. But the piano killed her hands." She put on her spectacles, glancing at the cupboards, and spotted my tea bags. "Shall we have a cup?"

I filled the kettle on the stove. "I beg your pardon, madame. The piano?"

(39) "She used to give lessons. For forty years. It was how she raised us after my father died." Helen put her hands on her hips, staring at the open refrigerator. She reached into the back, pulled out a wrapped stick of butter, frowned, and tossed it into the garbage. "That ought to do it," she said, and put the unopened cans of soup in the cupboard. I sat at the table and watched as Helen washed the dirty dishes, tied up the garbage bag, watered a spider plant over the sink, and poured boiling water into two cups. She handed one to me without milk, the string of the tea bag trailing over the side, and sat down at the table.

(40) "Excuse me, madame, but is it enough?"

Helen took a sip of her tea. Her lipstick left a smiling pink stain on the inside rim of the cup. "Is what enough?"

"The soup in the pans. Is it enough food for Mrs. Croft?"

"She won't eat anything else. She stopped eating solids after she turned one hundred. That was, let's see, three years ago."

(41) I was mortified. I had assumed Mrs. Croft was in her eighties, perhaps as old as ninety. I had never known a person who had lived for over a century. That this person was a widow who lived alone mortified me further still. It was widowhood that had driven my own mother insane. My father, who worked as a clerk at the General Post Office of Calcutta, died of encephalitis when I was sixteen. My mother refused to adjust to life without him; instead she sank deeper into a world of darkness from which neither I, nor my brother, nor concerned relatives, nor psychiatric clinics on Rashbihari Avenue could save her. What pained me most was to see her so unguarded, to hear her burp after meals or expel gas in front of company without the slightest embarrassment. After my father's death my brother abandoned his schooling and began to work in the jute mill he would eventually manage, in order to keep the household running. And so it was my job to sit by my mother's feet and study for my exams as she counted and recounted the bracelets on her arm as if they were the beads of an abacus. We tried to keep an eye on her. Once she had wandered half naked to the tram depot before we were able to bring her inside again.

(42) "I am happy to warm Mrs. Croft's soup in the evenings," I suggested, removing the tea bag from my cup and squeezing out the liquor. "It is no trouble."

Helen looked at her watch, stood up, and poured the rest of her tea into the sink. "I wouldn't if I were you. That's the sort of thing that would kill her altogether."

7.

(43) That evening, when Helen had gone back to Arlington and Mrs. Croft and I were alone again, I began to worry. Now that I knew how very old she was, I worried that something would happen to her in the middle of the night, or when I was out during the day. As vigorous as her voice was, and imperious as she seemed, I knew that even a scratch or a cough could kill a person that old; each day she lived, I knew, was something of a miracle. Although Helen had seemed friendly enough, a small part of me worried that she might accuse me of negligence if anything were to happen. Helen didn't seem worried. She came and went, bringing soup for Mrs. Croft, one Sunday after the next.

(44) In this manner the six weeks of that summer passed. I came home each evening, after my hours at the library, and spent a few minutes on the piano bench with Mrs. Croft. I gave her a bit of my company, and assured her that I had checked the lock, and told her that the flag on the moon was splendid. Some evenings I sat beside her long after she had drifted off to sleep, still in awe of how many years she had spent on this earth. At times I tried to picture the world she had been born into, in 1866—a world, I imagined, filled with women in long black skirts, and chaste conversations in the parlor. Now, when I looked at her hands with swollen knuckles folded together in her lap, I imagined them smooth and slim, striking the piano keys. At times I came downstairs before going to sleep, to make sure she was sitting upright on the bench, or was safe in her bedroom. On Fridays I made sure to put the rent in her hands. There was nothing I could do for her beyond these simple gestures. I was not her son, and apart from those eight dollars, I owed her nothing.

8.

(45) At the end of August, Mala's passport and green card were ready. I received a telegram with her flight information; my brother's house in Calcutta had no telephone. Around that time I also received a letter from her, written only a few days after we had parted. There was no salutation; addressing me by name would have assumed an intimacy we had not yet discovered. It contained only a few lines. "I write in English in preparation for the journey. Here I am very much lonely. Is it very cold there. Is there snow. Yours, Mala."

(46) I was not touched by her words. We had spent only a handful of days in each other's company. And yet we were bound together; for six weeks she had worn an iron bangle on her wrist, and applied vermilion powder to the part in her hair, to signify to the world that she was a bride. In those six weeks I regarded her arrival as I would the arrival of a coming month, or season—something inevitable, but meaningless at the time. So little did I know her that, while details of her face sometimes rose to my memory, I could not conjure up the whole of it.

(47) A few days after receiving the letter, as I was walking to work in the morning, I saw an Indian woman on the other side of Massachusetts Avenue, wearing a sari with its free end nearly dragging on the footpath, and pushing a child in a stroller. An American woman with a small black dog on a leash was walking to one side of her. Suddenly the dog began barking. From the other side of the street I watched as the Indian woman, startled, stopped in her path, at which point the dog leapt up and seized the end of the sari between its teeth. The American woman scolded the dog, appeared to apologize, and walked quickly away, leaving the Indian woman to fix her sari in the middle of the footpath, and quiet her crying child. She did not see me standing there, and eventually she continued on her way. Such a mishap, I realized that morning, would soon be my concern. It was my duty to take care of Mala, to welcome her and protect her. I would have to buy her her first pair of snow boots, her first winter coat. I would have to tell her which streets to avoid, which way the traffic came, tell her to wear her sari so that the free end did not drag on the footpath. A five-mile separation from her parents, I recalled with some irritation, had caused her to weep.

(48) Unlike Mala, I was used to it all by then: used to cornflakes and milk, used to Helen's visits, used to sitting on the bench with Mrs. Croft. The only thing I was not used to was Mala. Nevertheless I did what I had to do. I went to the housing office at MIT and found a furnished apartment a few blocks away, with a double bed and a pri-

vate kitchen and bath, for forty dollars a week. One last Friday I handed Mrs. Croft eight one-dollar bills in an envelope, brought my suitcase downstairs, and informed her that I was moving. She put my key into her change purse. The last thing she asked me to do was hand her the cane propped against the table, so that she could walk to the door and lock it behind me. "Good-bye, then," she said, and retreated back into the house. I did not expect any display of emotion, but I was disappointed all the same. I was only a boarder, a man who paid her a bit of money and passed in and out of her home for six weeks. Compared to a century, it was no time at all.

9.

(49) At the airport I recognized Mala immediately. The free end of her sari did not drag on the floor, but was draped in a sign of bridal modesty over her head, just as it had draped my mother until the day my father died. Her thin brown arms were stacked with gold bracelets, a small red circle was painted on her forehead, and the edges of her feet were tinted with a decorative red dye. I did not embrace her, or kiss her, or take her hand. Instead I asked her, speaking Bengali for the first time in America, if she was hungry.

(50) She hesitated, then nodded yes.

I told her I had prepared some egg curry at home. "What did they give you to eat on the plane?"

"I didn't eat."

"All the way from Calcutta?"

"The menu said oxtail soup."

"But surely there were other items."

"The thought of eating an ox's tail made me lose my appetite."

(51) When we arrived home, Mala opened up one of her suitcases, and presented me with two pullover sweaters, both made with bright blue wool, which she had knitted in the course of our separation, one with a V neck, the other covered with cables. I tried them on; both were tight under the arms. She had also brought me two new pairs of drawstring pajamas, a letter from my brother, and a packet of loose Darjeeling tea. I had no present for her apart from the egg curry. We sat at a bare table, each of us staring at our plates. We ate with our hands, another thing I had not yet done in America.

(52) "The house is nice," she said. "Also the egg curry." With her left hand she held the end of her sari to her chest, so it would not slip off her head.

"I don't know many recipes."

She nodded, peeling the skin off each of her potatoes before eating them. At one point the sari slipped to her shoulders. She readjusted it at once.

"There is no need to cover your head," I said. "I don't mind. It doesn't matter here."

She kept it covered anyway.

(53) I waited to get used to her, to her presence at my side, at my table and in my bed, but a week later we were still strangers. I still was not used to coming home to an apartment that smelled of steamed rice, and finding that the basin in the bathroom was always wiped clear, our two toothbrushes lying side by side, a cake of Pears soap from India resting in the soap dish. I was not used to the fragrance of the coconut oil she rubbed every other night into her scalp, or the delicate sound her bracelets made as she moved about the apartment. In the mornings she was always awake before I was. The first morning when I came into the kitchen she had heated up the leftovers

and set a plate with a spoonful of salt on its edge on the table, assuming I would eat rice for breakfast, as most Bengali husbands did. I told her cereal would do, and the next morning when I came into the kitchen she had already poured the cornflakes into my bowl. One morning she walked with me down Massachusetts Avenue to MIT, where I gave her a short tour of the campus. On the way we stopped at a hardware store and I made a copy of the key, so that she could let herself into the apartment. The next morning before I left for work she asked me for a few dollars. I parted with them reluctantly, but I knew that this, too, was now normal. When I came home from work there was a potato peeler in the kitchen drawer, and a tablecloth on the table, and chicken curry made with fresh garlic and ginger on the stove. We did not have a television in those days. After dinner I read the newspaper, while Mala sat at the kitchen table, working on a cardigan for herself with more of the bright blue wool, or writing letters home.

(54) At the end of our first week, on Friday, I suggested going out. Mala set down her knitting and disappeared into the bathroom. When she emerged I regretted the suggestion; she had put on a clean silk sari and extra bracelets, and coiled her hair with a flattering side part on top of her head. She was prepared as if for a party, or at the very least for the cinema, but I had no such destination in mind. The evening was balmy. We walked several blocks down Massachusetts Avenue, looking into the windows of restaurants and shops. Then, without thinking, I led her down the quiet street where for so many nights I had walked alone.

(55) "This is where I lived before you came," I said, stopping at Mrs. Croft's chain-link fence.

"In such a big house?"

"I had a small room upstairs. At the back."

"Who else lives there?"

"A very old woman."

"With her family?"

"Alone."

"But who takes care of her?"

I opened the gate. "For the most part she takes care of herself."

(56) I wondered if Mrs. Croft would remember me; I wondered if she had a new boarder to sit with her on the bench each evening. When I pressed the bell I expected the same long wait at that day of our first meeting, when I did not have a key. But this time the door was opened almost immediately, by Helen. Mrs. Croft was not sitting on the bench. The bench was gone.

(57) "Hello there," Helen said, smiling with her bright pink lips at Mala. "Mother's in the parlor. Will you be visiting awhile?"

"As you wish, madame."

"Then I think I'll run to the store, if you don't mind. She had a little accident. We can't leave her alone these days, not even for a minute."

(58) I locked the door after Helen and walked into the parlor. Mrs. Croft was lying flat on her back, her head on a peach-colored cushion, a thin white quilt spread over her body. Her hands were folded together on top of her chest. When she saw me she pointed at the sofa, and told me to sit down. I took my place as directed, but Mala wandered over to the piano and sat on the bench, which was now positioned where it belonged.

(59) "I broke my hip!" Mrs. Croft announced, as if no time had passed.

"Oh dear, madame."

"I fell off the bench!"

"I am so sorry, madame."

"It was the middle of the night! Do you know what I did, boy?"

I shook my head.

(60) "I called the police!"

She stared up at the ceiling and grinned sedately, exposing a crowded row of long gray teeth. Now one was missing. "What do you say to that, boy?"

As stunned as I was, I knew what I had to say. With no hesitation at all, I cried out, "Splendid!"

(61) Mala laughed then. Her voice was full of kindness, her eyes bright with amusement. I had never heard her laugh before, and it was loud enough so that Mrs. Croft had heard, too. She turned to Mala and glared.

"Who is she, boy?"

"She is my wife, madame."

Mrs. Croft pressed her head at an angle against the cushion to get a better look. "Can you play the piano?"

"No, madame," Mala replied.

"Then stand up!"

(62) Mala rose to her feet, adjusting the end of her sari over her head and holding it to her chest, and, for the first time since her arrival, I felt sympathy. I remembered my first days in London, learning how to take the Tube to Russell Square, riding an escalator for the first time, being unable to understand that when the man cried "piper" it meant "paper," being unable to decipher, for a whole year, that the conductor said "mind the gap" as the train pulled away from each station. Like me, Mala had traveled far from home, not knowing where she was going, or what she would find, for no reason other than to be my wife. As strange as it seemed, I knew in my heart that one day her death would affect me, and stranger still, that mine would affect her. I wanted somehow to explain this to Mrs. Croft, who was still scrutinizing Mala from top to toe with what seemed to be placid disdain. I wondered if Mrs. Croft had ever seen a woman in a sari, with a dot painted on her forehead and bracelets stacked on her wrists. I wondered what she would object to. I wondered if she could see the red dye still vivid on Mala's feet, all but obscured by the bottom edge of her sari. At last Mrs. Croft declared, with the equal measures of disbelief and delight I knew well:

"She is a perfect lady!"

(63) Now it was I who laughed. I did so quietly, and Mrs. Croft did not hear me. But Mala had heard, and, for the first time, we looked at each other and smiled.

10.

(64) I like to think of that moment in Mrs. Croft's parlor as the moment when the distance between Mala and me began to lessen. Although we were not yet fully in love, I like to think of the months that followed as a honeymoon of sorts. Together we explored the city and met other Bengalis, some of whom are still friends today. We discovered that a man named Bill sold fresh fish on Prospect Street, and that a shop in Harvard Square called Cardullo's sold bay leaves and cloves. In the evenings we walked to the Charles River to watch sailboats drift across the water, or had ice cream cones in Harvard Yard. We bought an Instamatic camera with which to document our life together, and I took pictures of her posing in front of the Prudential building, so that she could send them to her parents. At night we kissed, shy at first but quickly bold, and discovered pleasure and solace in each other's arms. I told her

about my voyage on the *SS Roma*, and about Fisbury Park and the YMCA, and my evenings on the bench with Mrs. Croft. When I told her stories about my mother, she wept. It was Mala who consoled me when, reading the *Globe* one evening, I came across Mrs. Croft's obituary. I had not thought of her in several months—by then those six weeks of the summer were already a remote interlude in my past—but when I learned of her death I was stricken, so much so that when Mala looked up from her knitting she found me staring at the wall, the newspaper neglected in my lap, unable to speak. Mrs. Croft's was the first death I mourned in America, for hers was the first life I had admired; she had left this world at last, ancient and alone, never to return.

(65) As for me, I have not strayed much farther. Mala and I live in a town about twenty miles from Boston, on a tree-lined street much like Mrs. Croft's, in a house we own, with a garden that saves us from buying tomatoes in summer, and room for guests. We are American citizens now, so that we can collect social security when it is time. Though we visit Calcutta every few years, and bring back more drawstring pajamas and Darjeeling tea, we have decided to grow old here. I work in a small college library. We have a son who attends Harvard University. Mala no longer drapes the end of her sari over her head, or weeps at night for her parents, but occasionally she weeps for our son. So we drive to Cambridge to visit him, or bring him home for a weekend, so that he can eat rice with us with his hands, and speak in Bengali, things we sometimes worry he will no longer do after we die.

(66) Whenever we make that drive, I always make it a point to take Massachusetts Avenue, in spite of the traffic. I barely recognize the buildings now, but each time I am there I return instantly to those six weeks as if they were only the other day, and I slow down and point to Mrs. Croft's street, saying to my son, here was my first home in America, where I lived with a woman who was 103. "Remember?" Mala says, and smiles, amazed, as I am, that there was ever a time that we were strangers. My son always expresses his astonishment, not at Mrs. Croft's age, but at how little I paid in rent, a fact nearly as inconceivable to him as a flag on the moon was to a woman born in 1866. In my son's eyes I see the ambition that had first hurled me across the world. In a few years he will graduate and pave his way, alone and unprotected. But I remind myself that he has a father who is still living, a mother who is happy and strong. Whenever he is discouraged, I tell him that if I can survive on three continents, then there is no obstacle he cannot conquer. While the astronauts, heroes forever, spent mere hours on the moon, I have remained in this new world for nearly thirty years. I know that my achievement is quite ordinary. I am not the only man to seek his fortune far from home, and certainly I am not the first. Still, there are times I am bewildered by each mile I have traveled, each meal I have eaten, each person I have known, each room in which I have slept. As ordinary as it all appears, there are times when it is beyond my imagination.

Comprehension

In this section, the narrator moves across three continents, from India to London to Boston. The things we learn about the narrator show us the intersecting and changing worlds he lives in.

1. Below is a list of activities the author chose to mention in the first section. Which details about the narrator tell us that he is still tied to India (I), which that he is in London (L), and which that his life is moving to the United States (U.S.)? Do this exercise quickly. Some activities may suggest more than one place.

   _____ a. lounges barefoot

   _____ b. wears drawstring pajamas

   _____ c. smokes Rothman's

   _____ d. watches cricket at Lord's

   _____ e. shops at the greengrocer

   _____ f. plays Mukhesh on a reel-to-reel

   _____ g. eats egg curry with his hands

   _____ h. watches the "Tube"

   _____ i. sees a woman praying

   _____ j. shops at the supermarket

   _____ k. buys milk

   _____ l. converts ounces to pounds

2. The author gave us this range of details to create a first impression of the narrator and his journey. What are your first impressions?

In this section, the narrator meets Mrs. Croft and moves into her home. He tells us (Paragraph 7), "I had never lived in the home of a person who was not Indian."

Comprehension

1. T / F The narrator had planned to stay at the YMCA until his wife arrived.

2. Why did he move to Mrs. Croft's? _____

_____

3. a. Below is a list of adjectives from this section. Indicate which describe Mrs. Croft (C) and which describe the narrator (N).

____ bold   ____ punctual

____ soft-spoken   ____ appears fierce

____ insulted   ____ bellowing

____ baffled   ____ commanding

b. What image do these details create for each of these characters? _____

_____

Critical Reading

1. Section 2 opens with the narrator announcing that "In a week, I had adjusted more or less." In what ways had he adjusted? Why do you think he added "more or less"?

2. In Paragraph 5, the salesman explains that what the narrator calls a *flask* is called a *thermos* in the U.S. Why do you think he continues to call it a *flask?*

3. In Paragraph 7, what are the details that suggest that he is nervous as he prepares for the meeting?

4. What details in this section paint a picture of Mrs. Croft as an old woman?

This section is a "flashback"; it goes back to an earlier time. It begins with the phrase, "My wife's name was Mala," perhaps because the narrator didn't know very much more about her when they were married. But he did know a few things.

Comprehension

1. What did he know about his wife? _____

_____

2. Indicate if each of the following statements is True (T) or False (F).

_____ a. Mala and the narrator lived together for five days before he left India for the United States.

_____ b. Before the narrator left, he and his wife became close friends.

_____ c. Mala lived with her parents until she joined her husband.

_____ d. After the marriage, the narrator was very kind and sympathetic to his wife.

_____ e. The narrator was the oldest son in his family.

Section 4 (Paragraphs 23–27)

In this section, the narrator and Mrs. Croft establish a "routine."

Comprehension

What is their routine? _____

_____

Critical Reading

1. What do we learn about Mrs. Croft from the fact that she says the same thing every day?

2. What do we learn about the narrator in the last sentence, when he says that he "did not have the heart to tell her" that the astronauts had removed the flag from the moon.

Section 5 (Paragraphs 28–30)

In this section, we see the narrator and Mrs. Croft become closer to each other.

Comprehension

1. In Paragraph 30, why does the narrator sit next to Mrs. Croft on the bench? _____

_____

2. What does the narrator do that leads Mrs. Croft to say, "Very kind of you!" _____

_____

Section 6 (Paragraphs 31–42)

In this section, Helen comes to visit.

Comprehension

1. T / F   Helen is Mrs. Croft's daughter.

2. T / F   Helen comes to visit daily.

3. T / F   Helen brings food.

4. T / F   Mrs. Croft likes to eat a wide variety of things.

5. T / F   Mrs. Croft is in her 80s.

6. a. Why does Mrs. Croft own a cane? _____

   b. Does she use it? _____

7. What did Mrs. Croft think was "improper"? _____

8. How did Mrs. Croft support herself and her daughter after her husband had died?

_____

9. T / F   Helen asks the narrator to warm the soup each evening.

Section 7 (Paragraphs 43–44)

In this section, the narrator "began to worry."

Comprehension

What does the narrator worry about? _____

_____

Critical Reading

At the end of the section, the narrator says, "I was not her son, and apart from those eight dollars, I owed her nothing." How does he feel about Mrs. Croft? Be prepared to defend your point of view.

Section 8 (Paragraphs 45–48)

In this section, the narrator anticipates Mala's arrival.

Comprehension

Indicate if each of the following statements is True (T) or False (F).

_____ 1. The author was touched to receive a letter from his new bride.

_____ 2. Since the wedding, Mala had worn an iron bracelet to indicate that she was a bride.

_____ 3. The narrator was excited that his new bride was going to arrive.

_____ 4. The narrator was able to imagine his wife's face in detail.

_____ 5. The narrator has stronger feelings for Mala than for Mrs. Croft.

Critical Reading

1. How does seeing the Indian woman and child on the street (Paragraph 47) make the narrator realize that his life will soon change?

2. What "disappoints" the narrator at the end of the section?

3. We learn that the narrator has no feelings toward Mala. Does this make him a bad person? Be prepared to defend your point of view.

Things begin to change for the narrator and Mala in this section.

Comprehension

1. In many ways, this is a story about adjustments. The author often tells us what he is "used to" and "not used to." Check (✓) those things that he has become used to.

    _____ a. Cornflakes and milk

    _____ b. Coming home to the smell of rice

    _____ c. The sound of Mala's bracelets

    _____ d. Pears soap

    _____ e. Giving Mala money

    _____ f. Helen

    _____ g. Mala

2. T /F   Mrs. Croft has a new boarder.

3. T /F   Mrs. Croft has broken her hip.

4. T /F   Mrs. Croft scrutinizes Mala with placid disdain.

Critical Reading

1. The narrator begins the following section (Section 10), describing the events in this way: "I like to think of that moment in Mrs. Croft's parlor as the moment when the distance between Mala and me began to lessen." What was it in that visit that changed things?

2. Why do you think that Mrs. Croft calls Mala "a perfect lady"?

Section 10 (Paragraphs 64–66)

In this section, the narrator summarizes his life since those early days in the United States.

Comprehension

1. What has changed since the narrator and Mala left Mrs. Croft's house that day?

   _____

   _____

2. In what ways is the son similar to the father? In what ways is his life different?

   _____

   _____

Critical Reading

In what ways is the narrator like the astronauts? In the final paragraph, what is it that makes him "bewildered" and is "beyond . . . imagination"? _____

Sections 1–10

The questions that follow refer to the entire story. Work on these after you have finished reading "The Third and Final Continent."

Critical Reading

In many ways this story about the past is an explanation of the present. Speaking in the past, the narrator foretells what will come to be through phrases such as the following (numbers in parentheses indicate the paragraphs where they can be found):

- "I had not *yet*/we were not *yet*" (45, 51, 64)
- "I had *never*" (7)
- "it was the *first*/for the *first time*" (4, 20, 49, 62, 63)
- "it *would soon be*" (47)

What does each one tell us about the changes the narrator will undergo? For this activity, your teacher may want you to work in groups, with each group working on a few of these.

Discussion/Composition

1. Why do you think we never learn the narrator's name?

2. Why do you think the author chose to tell the story from the point of view of the father/husband?

3. The author, Jhumpa Lahiri, is herself the daughter of immigrant parents. In what way(s) is this a story about the immigrant parents, and in what way(s) is it about the developing understanding of its author? In considering this question, it may help to read a description written by Jhumpa Lahiri about her growing up:

   > At home I followed the customs of my parents, speaking Bengali and eating rice and dal with my fingers. These ordinary facts seemed part of a secret, utterly alien way of life, and I took pains to hide them from my American friends. For my parents, home was not our house in Rhode Island but Calcutta, where they were raised. I was aware that the things they lived for—the Nazrul songs they listened to on the reel-to-reel, the family they missed, the clothes my mother wore that were not available in any store in any mall—were at once as precious and as worthless as an outmoded currency.

4. In what way is this a story about everyone who crosses boundaries into a new life? Use examples from the story and from your own knowledge.

5. Are there ways in which moving to a new culture is different for men than for women?

Vocabulary from Context

EXERCISE 1

Both the ideas and the vocabulary in the following sentences are taken from "The Third and Final Continent." Use the context provided to determine the meanings of the italicized words. Write a definition, synonym, or description of each of the italicized vocabulary items in the space provided.

1. _____

2. _____

3. _____

"The Third and Final Continent" describes the journey of a young student moving from India, to London, England, and then to the United States. In London, he lives in a world of other Bengali students, many of them *crammed into* a small room. They maintain their Indian customs, while slowly changing to adapt to life in England. When the narrator finishes school, he gets a job in the United States, and is forced once again to *adjust to* a new place and new surroundings. But before he can travel to America, his *duty* to his family takes him back to India. Because he has finished school and has a job, he must marry. He returns home briefly. His brother has arranged a marriage for him. A week after the wedding, the narrator flies to Boston, to become a librarian at the Massachusetts Institute of Technology (MIT). His new wife will follow later.

4. _____

5. _____

6. _____

7. _____

8. _____

9. _____

10. _____

11. _____

12. _____

13. _____

14. _____

15. _____

The narrator had planned to live in a rented room for six weeks until his new wife arrives, but he finds living at the hotel absolutely *intolerable*. What makes it unbearable is the noise. He finds he is unable to think. The noise is so *distracting* he cannot remain there. When he sees an advertisement for a rented room in a home, he decides to move there until his wife arrives and he can find a larger place. The owner of the house, Mrs. Croft, is very old. She is hard of hearing and speaks in a loud voice, almost as though she were a military officer. She is so elderly that she almost looks like a man. With her *commanding* voice and her appearance, the narrator thinks she looks *fierce*, strong and wild. He is almost afraid of her. At this stage, the relationship between Mrs. Croft and the young man is uncomfortable. It is made more *awkward* because he is confused by Mrs. Croft. He is *baffled* when she makes him angry, hurts his feelings, or seems rude. But soon, instead of feeling *offended* and *insulted*, the narrator comes to respect Mrs. Croft. He *admires* her strength and her great age.

Each day, without fail, she says and does exactly the same thing. *Inevitably* she will ask him to sit on the bench beside her in the evening, until suddenly, without warning, she *abruptly* falls asleep. In the morning, she is *oblivious* to his presence, not seeming to know that he is there.

One day Mrs. Croft's daughter arrives for a visit. Even the daughter seems quite old. The narrator for the first time realizes how old Mrs. Croft really is and discovers how traditional she is as well. She becomes angry when the narrator and her daughter, a man and woman not married to each other, are alone together, without a *chaperone*. The world she remembered was pure and nonsexual, in which men and women were never alone. They sat among others having *chaste* conversations. Discovering how old Mrs. Croft is, the narrator for the first time sees her as *vulnerable*, easily hurt. Despite how *vigorous* her voice was, that strength was not in her body. Although her manner was *imperious*, she was not really a commanding person. She was simply very old.

16. _____

17. _____

18. _____

19. _____

20. _____

21. _____

22. _____

23. _____

The narrator settles in to wait for his wife, about whom he knows very little except her name: Mala. He had been told that she had many skills, but because she did not have light skin, she had been turned down in marriage by many men. Because she did not have a *fair complexion*, her parents worried that she would never marry. To save her from *spinsterhood*, her parents allowed her to be married to a man who would take their daughter far away. Not surprisingly, at first she is terribly unhappy to be away from her parents, even just to be away from her parents' house in India. She cries every night, and the narrator recalls that he does nothing to help her. In later years the couple would become able to give comfort to each other in times of great sadness. But the narrator is not yet able to *console* his new wife.

24. _____

25. _____

26. _____

When Mala writes to say that she is arriving, the narrator is not touched by her words. Her arrival is something inevitable but meaningless. But he begins to understand that his life is about to change. One day he sees a woman in traditional Indian dress, a *sari*, on the street pushing a child in a *stroller*. An American woman and a dog pass, and the dog pulls on her dress. The Indian woman is surprised and alarmed. Seeing her become *startled*, he realizes that some day such an event will be his concern.

27. _____

28. _____

29. _____

30. _____

31. _____

After Mala arrives, the narrator takes his new wife to meet Mrs. Croft. Mrs. Croft has broken her hip and is in bed, calm and undisturbed. She smiles *sedately* and *placidly*. The narrator is very surprised when she asks him the same questions she used to when he lived in her house. But, although he is *stunned*, he knows what to do and responds as he always had. He is worried, however, when Mrs. Croft asks who Mala is. She carefully examines Mala, and after *scrutinizing* her from head to foot, she seems to regard her with *disdain*. But instead of looking down upon Mala with disrespect, Mrs. Croft announces a very different judgment. (You will have to read the story to discover what it is!)

32. _____

33. _____

34. _____

Time passes and one day the narrator reads of Mrs. Croft's death in the newspaper. When he sees the *obituary*, he is *stricken*. Mala realizes that he is shocked and deeply affected by Mrs. Croft's death, and by this time, she knows how to console him. Mrs. Croft was not only the first non-Indian the narrator had lived with, but the first person in America that he had *admired*. He respected the strength with which she had lived her life.

35. _____

At the end of the story, it is the narrator who has become older as he reflects upon his life. When he looks at the *ambition* in his son's eyes he sees his own desire to achieve, a strong drive for success that sent him across the globe to build a life on the third and final continent.

EXERCISE 2

This exercise should be done after you have finished reading "The Third and Final Continent." The exercise is designed to give you practice using context clues to guess the meaning of unfamiliar vocabulary. Give a definition, synonym, or description of each of the words below. The number in parentheses indicates the paragraph in which the word can be found. Your teacher may want you to do these orally or in writing.

1. (5) stifling _____

2. (31) glancing _____

3. (31) mapped _____

4. (32) boarder _____

5. (34) electrifying _____

6. (34) hollering _____

7. (45) salutation _____

8. (48) retreated _____

EXERCISE 3: FIGURATIVE LANGUAGE AND IDIOMS

Like the previous exercise, this one is designed to give you practice using context clues to guess the meaning of unfamiliar vocabulary, in this case, figurative language and idioms. Give a definition, synonym, or description of each of the phrases below. The number in parentheses indicates the paragraph in which the phrase can be found. Your teacher may want you to do these orally or in writing.

1. (21) a string of men _____

2. (21) to her face _____

3. (31) sent you packing _____

4. (66) pave his way _____

EXERCISE 4

This exercise is designed to give you additional clues to determine the meanings of unfamiliar vocabulary items in context. In the paragraph of "The Third and Final Continent" indicated by the number in parentheses, find the word or phrase that best fits the meaning given. Your teacher may want to read these aloud as you quickly scan* the paragraph to find the answer.

1. (10) Which word means *old; worn out?* _____

2. (15) Which word means *shouted; said in a loud powerful voice?* _____

3. (41) Which word means *shocked; horrified; stunned; shaken?* _____

4. (43) What phrase means *blame him for being careless, for not doing what he should?* _____

5. (44) Which word means *wonder; admiration; respect; amazement; surprise?* _____

6. (62) What phrase means *be against; oppose; not like; find fault with?* _____

7. (62) What phrase means *almost hidden?* _____

8. (66) Which word means *problem; difficulty; something that stands in the way?* _____

---

* For an introduction to scanning, see Unit 1.

Dictionary Study

Many words have more than one meaning. When you use the dictionary to discover the meaning of an unfamiliar word or phrase, you need to use the context to determine which definition is appropriate. Use the dictionary entries provided to select the best definition(s) for each of the italicized words below.

____ 1. There was nothing I could do for Mrs. Croft beyond the simple *gestures* of making sure she was safe and putting the rent in her hands.

____ 2. The noise in the hotel was so loud and distracting, at times it was *suffocating*.

____ 3. Once Mrs. Croft fell asleep, I was free to *retire* to my room.

Dictionary.com Unabridged (v 1.1)

ges·ture [jes-cher]

–noun
1. a movement or position of the hand, arm, body, head, or face that is expressive of an idea, opinion, emotion, etc.: *the gestures of an orator; a threatening gesture.*
2. the use of such movements to express thought, emotion, etc.
3. any action, courtesy, communication, etc., intended for effect or as a formality; considered expression; demonstration: *a gesture of friendship.*

–verb (used without object)
4. to make or use a gesture or gestures.

–verb (used with object)
5. to express by a gesture or gestures.

Dictionary.com Unabridged (v 1.1)

suf·fo·cate [suhf-*uh*-keyt]

–v. tr.
1. To kill or destroy by preventing access of air or oxygen.
2. To impair the respiration of; asphyxiate.
3. To cause discomfort to by or as if by cutting off the supply of fresh air.
4. To suppress the development, imagination, or creativity of; stifle: *"The rigid formality of the place suffocated her"* (Thackeray).

–v. intr.
1. To die from lack of air or oxygen; be asphyxiated.
2. To feel discomfort from lack of fresh air.
3. To become or feel suppressed; be stifled.

Dictionary.com Unabridged (v 1.1)

re·tire [ri-**tahy**ᵘʰ**r**]

–verb, -tired, -tir·ing, noun

–verb (used without object)
1. to withdraw, or go away or apart, to a place of privacy, shelter, or seclusion: *He retired to his study.*
2. to go to bed: *He retired at midnight.*
3. to withdraw from office, business, or active life, usually because of age: *to retire at the age of sixty.*
4. to fall back or retreat in an orderly fashion and according to plan, as from battle, an untenable position, danger, etc.
5. to withdraw or remove oneself: *After announcing the guests, the butler retired.*

–verb (used with object)
6. to withdraw from circulation by taking up and paying, as bonds, bills, etc.; redeem.
7. to withdraw or lead back (troops, ships, etc.), as from battle or danger; retreat.
8. to remove from active service or the usual field of activity, as an army officer or business executive.
9. to withdraw (a machine, ship, etc.) permanently from its normal service, usually for scrapping; take out of use.
10. *Sports.* to put out (a batter, side, etc.).

Stems and Affixes

Both the ideas and the italicized words in the sentences below are taken from "The Third and Final Continent." Beneath the sentences is a list of synonyms and definitions. Use your knowledge of stems and affixes* and the context to match each italicized word with its definition by placing the appropriate letter on the line before each sentence.

_____ 1. Although I would be leaving the country in a few days custom *dictated* that she was now a part of my household.

_____ 2. Mrs. Croft said, "It is *improper* for a lady and a gentleman who are not married to one another to hold a private conversation without a chaperone!"

_____ 3. When the narrator saw the problem the mother in the sari had with the dog, he realized that such a *mishap* would soon be his concern.

_____ 4. Years later, when the narrator thought back, those six weeks seemed like a far-off *interlude* in his past.

_____ 5. Whenever the narrator's son became *discouraged,* he would tell him that if the father could survive on three continents, then there was no obstacle the son couldn't conquer.

a. a brief period between other events

b. without confidence; hope; courage

c. required; said; commanded; determined

d. unfortunate event; unlucky happening; accident

e. not appropriate; not proper; unacceptable behavior

Vocabulary Review

Two of the sentences in each group below are related in meaning. Circle the letter of the sentence that does not belong.

1. a. The room was suffocating.

   b. The room was shabby.

   c. The room was stifling.

2. a. He found the loud noise unbearable.

   b. He found the heat intolerable.

   c. He found the customs improper.

3. a. He was ambitious.

*For a list of all stems and affixes taught in *Reader's Choice,* see the Appendix.

b. He was insulting.

c. He was offensive.

4. a. He tried to forget it.

   b. He tried to get used to it.

   c. He worked to adjust to it.

5. a. The situation was awkward.

   b. The situation was inevitable.

   c. The situation was baffling.

6. a. Her voice was commanding.

   b. Her manner was imperious.

   c. She seemed oblivious.

7. a. He was stunned by her voice.

   b. He viewed her with disdain.

   c. He was startled by her manner.

8. a. She was stricken by his manner.

   b. She smiled sedately at him.

   c. She agreed placidly.

9. a. He retired to his room.

   b. He retreated to his room.

   c. He adjusted to his room.

10. a. "There's a man on the moon," she observed.

    b. "There's a man on the moon," she bellowed.

    c. "There's a man on the moon," she hollered.

Appendix

Below is a list of the stems and affixes that appear in *Reader's Choice*. The number in parentheses indicates the unit in which an item appears.

Prefixes

- (5) **a-, an-**   without, lacking, not
- (3) **ante-**   before
- (5) **bene-**   good
- (5) **bi-**   two
- (9) **by-**   aside or apart from the common, secondary
- (3) **circum-**   around
- (1) **com-, con-, col-, cor-, co-**   together, with
- (3) **contra-, anti-**   against
- (9) **de-**   down from, away
- (9) **dia-**   through, across
- (9) **epi-**   upon, over, outer
- (9) **hyper-**   above, beyond, excessive
- (9) **hypo-**   under, beneath, down
- (1) **in-, im-, il-, ir-**   in, into, on
- (1) **in-, im-, il-, ir-**   not
- (3) **inter-**   between
- (3) **intro-, intra-**   within
- (1) **micro-**   small
- (5) **mis-**   wrong
- (5) **mono-**   one, alone
- (7) **multi-**   many
- (7) **peri-**   around
- (5) **poly-**   many
- (3) **post-**   after
- (1) **pre-**   before
- (1) **re-, retro-**   back, again
- (7) **semi-**   half, partly
- (3) **sub-, suc-, suf-, sug-, sup-, sus-**   under
- (3) **super-**   above, greater, better
- (5) **syn-, sym-, syl-**   with, together
- (3) **trans-**   across
- (7) **tri-**   three
- (7) **ultra-**   beyond, excessive, extreme
- (7) **uni-**   one

Stems

- (5) **-anthro-, -anthropo-**   human
- (5) **-arch-**   first, chief, leader
- (7) **-aster-, -astro-, -stellar-**   star
- (1) **-audi-, -audit-**   hear
- (7) **-auto-**   self
- (7) **-bio-**   life
- (9) **-capit-**   head, chief
- (3) **-ced-**   go, move, yield
- (1) **-chron-**   time
- (9) **-corp-**   body
- (7) **-cycle-**   circle
- (9) **-derm-**   skin
- (1) **-dic-, -dict-**   say, speak
- (3) **-duc-**   lead
- (5) **-fact-, -fect-**   make, do
- (3) **-flect-**   bend
- (5) **-gam-**   marriage
- (9) **-geo-**   earth
- (1) **-graph-, -gram-**   write, writing
- (5) **-hetero-**   different, other
- (5) **-homo-**   same
- (9) **-hydr-, -hydro-**   water
- (1) **-log-, -ology-**   speech, word, study
- (5) **-man-, -manu-**   hand
- (7) **-mega-**   great, large
- (3) **-mit-, -miss-**   send
- (5) **-morph-**   form, structure
- (7) **-mort-**   death
- (5) **-onym-, -nomen-**   name
- (9) **-ortho-**   straight, correct
- (5) **-pathy-**   feeling, disease
- (7) **-phil-**   love
- (1) **-phon-**   sound
- (9) **-pod-, -ped-**   foot
- (3) **-pon-, -pos-**   put, place
- (7) **-polis-**   city
- (3) **-port-**   carry
- (7) **-psych-**   mind
- (1) **-scrib-, -script-**   write
- (3) **-sequ-, -secut-**   follow
- (9) **-son-**   sound
- (1) **-spect-**   look at
- (3) **-spir-**   breathe
- (7) **-soph-**   wise
- (3) **-tele-**   far
- (5) **-theo-, -the-**   god
- (9) **-therm-, -thermo-**   heat
- (3) **-ven-, -vene-**   come
- (9) **-ver-**   true
- (1) **-vid-, -vis-**   see
- (3) **-voc-, -vok-**   call

Suffixes

(3) **-able, -ible, -ble** capable of, fit for

(9) **-ate** to make

(1) **-er, -or** one who

(9) **-fy** to make

(5) **-ic, -al** relating to, having the nature of

(5) **-ism** action or practice, theory or doctrine

(1) **-ist** one who

(7) **-ity** condition, quality, state of being

(9) **-ize** to make

(7) **-ness** condition, quality, state of being

(5) **-oid** like, resembling

(3) **-ous, -ious, -ose** full of, having the qualities of

(1) **-tion, -ation** condition, the act of